SAP PRESS e-books

Print or e-book, Kindle or iPad, workplace or airplane: Choose where and how to read your SAP PRESS books! You can now get all our titles as e-books, too:

- By download and online access
- For all popular devices
- And, of course, DRM-free

Convinced? Then go to www.sap-press.com and get your e-book today.

SAP° Leonardo

SAP PRESS is a joint initiative of SAP and Rheinwerk Publishing. The know-how offered by SAP specialists combined with the expertise of Rheinwerk Publishing offers the reader expert books in the field. SAP PRESS features first-hand information and expert advice, and provides useful skills for professional decision-making.

SAP PRESS offers a variety of books on technical and business-related topics for the SAP user. For further information, please visit our website: *www.sap-press.com*.

Bardhan, Baumgartl, Choi, Dudgeon, Lahiri, Meijerink, Worsley-Tonks
SAP S/4HANA: An Introduction (3rd Edition)
2019, 647 pages, hardcover and e-book
www.sap-press.com/4782

Butsmann, Fleckenstein, Kundu
SAP S/4HANA Embedded Analytics: The Comprehensive Guide
2018, 430 pages, hardcover and e-book
www.sap-press.com/4690

Singh, Messinger-Michaels, Feurer, Vetter
SAP C/4HANA: An Introduction (2nd Edition)
2019, 383 pages, hardcover and e-book
www.sap-press.com/4852

Herzig, Heitkötter, Wozniak, Agarwal, Wust
Extending SAP S/4HANA: Side-by-Side Extension with the SAP S/4HANA Cloud SDK
2018, 618 pages, hardcover and e-book
www.sap-press.com/4655

Pierre Erasmus, Vivek Vinayak Rao, Amit Sinha, Ganesh Wadawadigi

SAP® Leonardo

An Introduction to the Intelligent Enterprise

Rheinwerk
Publishing

Editor Meagan White
Acquisitions Editor Hareem Shafi
Copyeditor Yvette Chin
Cover Design Graham Geary
Photo Credit iStockphoto.com/695965042/© Wi6995
Layout Design Vera Brauner
Production Graham Geary
Typesetting III-satz, Husby (Germany)
Printed and bound in the United States of America, on paper from sustainable sources

ISBN 978-1-4932-1784-7
© 2019 by Rheinwerk Publishing, Inc., Boston (MA)
1st edition 2019

Library of Congress Cataloging-in-Publication Data
Names: Erasmus, Pierre, author. | Sinha, Àmit, 1980- author. | Wadawadigi,
Ganesh, author. | Rao, Vivek Vinayak, author.
Title: SAP Leonardo : an introduction / Pierre Erasmus, Amit Sinha, Ganesh
Wadawadigi, Vivek Vinayak Rao.
Description: 1st edition. | Bonn ; Boston : Rheinwerk Publishing, 2019. |
Includes index.
Identifiers: LCCN 2018061151 (print) | LCCN 2018061773 (ebook) | ISBN
9781493217854 (ebook) | ISBN 9781493217847 (alk. paper)
Subjects: LCSH: Business--Data processing. | Big data. | SAP Leonardo.
Classification: LCC HD30.2 (ebook) | LCC HD30.2 .E69 2019 (print) | DDC
004.67/82--dc23
LC record available at https://lccn.loc.gov/2018061151

Contents at a Glance

Dear Reader,

Like most people, I have my areas of expertise (editing, 20th century literature, pizza-making) and areas where I'm... less than fluent. Diesel engines, for example, are something I hear a lot about in my day-to-day life, as my partner manages a fleet of them and delights in all the nitty-gritty details. A crank bearing, a starter solenoid, a flywheel, or a harmonic balancer? At first listen, I don't have any idea what they are—or how they come together to propel a truck.

Like most things, however, further explanation makes it clear. The harmonic balancer, for example, absorbs vibration that would otherwise cause part of the engine to fail. While I certainly couldn't build an engine, I feel like I'm starting to develop an understanding of how they work. I hope this book serves something of the same purpose for you. You've almost certainly been hearing a lot about SAP Leonardo and, if you've picked up this book, I'm betting you don't know exactly what parts it is made up of—or how they can help propel your business forward.

What did you think about *SAP Leonardo: An Introduction to the Intelligent Enterprise*? Your comments and suggestions are the most useful tools to help us make our books the best they can be. Please feel free to contact me and share any praise or criticism you may have.

Thank you for purchasing a book from SAP PRESS!

Meagan White
Editor, SAP PRESS

meaganw@rheinwerk-publishing.com
www.sap-press.com
Rheinwerk Publishing · Boston, MA

Contents

PART I Digital Transformation and the Intelligent Enterprise

1   Introduction   31

4   Analytics   139

5   Machine Learning   153

6   Data Intelligence   175

PART III   SAP Leonardo Business Processes

9   Products and Inventory   227

10   Manufacturing and Assets   273

11 Transportation and Warehousing

12   Finance

13   Assorted Business Processes

14　Digitization of Industries

15　Roadmap and Outlook

Appendices

Foreword by Hans Thalbauer

Business innovation is front and center for companies around the world. Same-day delivery of products and services directly to customers has become the norm and is no longer an exception. Not only is the delivery customer-centric but also the product itself is personalized in many cases. To achieve this level of flexibility, companies must understand that they need to digitally transform their entire business and increase the level of automation in all processes.

But business model innovation is not the only driver for digitization; increased uncertainty in the market can also spark innovation. From geopolitical influences, like Brexit and trade wars, to environmental challenges, such as earthquakes, hurricanes, and typhoons, etc., clearly, businesses need to create predictive supply chains and can no longer succeed with reactive, alert-driven supply chains. As a prerequisite for predictability, you'll need total visibility, which means creating a digital mirror of the real world.

In other words, not only do we need to create seamlessly integrated, end-to-end business processes, we need to make them intelligent. SAP has introduced the intelligent enterprise strategy precisely to achieve intelligent processes: building integrated, best-in-class applications that leverage SAP Leonardo to address the Internet of Things (IoT), machine learning, blockchain, big data, and analytics. All these technologies are crucial for an intelligent enterprise and exceptionally important for creating a predictive supply chain.

This book focuses on end-to-end business scenarios and SAP Leonardo's impact by discussing real-life use cases and by covering recent developments in the economy, the market, and the technology, including analytics, machine learning, IoT, artificial intelligence, and blockchain. I highly recommend this book to anyone who is working on a digital transformation strategy or project.

Hans Thalbauer
Senior Vice President, Digital Supply Chain, SAP

Foreword by Darwin Deano

Sustainable business success is highly dependent on the ability to anticipate and rapidly evolve in a world of constant, converging disruption across multiple dimensions. Whether because of industry consolidation, geopolitical events, climate change, the latest sweeping social media sentiment, or the exponential growth and ubiquity of drones and robots, businesses have never been more challenged to develop new capabilities. In a world where "network is the new scale" and "data is the new oil," innovation has become a nonnegotiable board room priority.

In this context, the longstanding premise that the pursuit of business value and competitive advantage is exclusively within the core (more specifically, within ERP) is no longer valid. The crusade of the last quarter century to unleash value from relational data based on business process models has taken great leaps forward. Does this mean that ERP is dead, as has been repeatedly claimed in recent years? The answer is an unequivocal, resounding "No!" But ERP is *no longer enough*.

ERP must be part of a broader architectural ecosystem that incorporates intelligent, edge technologies to enable next-generation business processes. This architectural ecosystem is made complete with SAP Leonardo, which allows your business to intelligently automate manual computations with machine learning. SAP Leonardo allows you to go beyond data entry and capture Internet of Things (IoT) data signals directly from machines. You'll be able to implement a private blockchain to improve visibility and accountability across a multitier supply chain. The possibilities with this architectural ecosystem enabled by SAP Leonardo are endless.

This excellent book is a great starting point for your innovation journey. Amit Sinha and Vivek Rao from Deloitte and Pierre Erasmus and Ganesh Wadawadigi from SAP are excellent thought leaders who have curated a wealth of knowledge to help you explore all those possibilities and more. They'll review the market developments that are driving the call for innovation, provide a comprehensive overview of SAP Leonardo's capabilities, and discuss end-to-end business scenarios and real-life use cases to train your innovation muscles for action.

Darwin Deano
Principal and SAP Chief Technology Officer
Deloitte Consulting LLP

Preface

We're excited to launch the first ever comprehensive book on SAP Leonardo! We wrote this book is in response to the thousands of requests from professionals and practitioners for a definitive and thorough text on SAP Leonardo focusing on how to comprehend, implement, and use SAP Leonardo technologies for fulfilling the goal of an intelligent enterprise.

As practically all industries undergo rapid change, business processes will need to constantly change and evolve with shorter feedback cycles. Operations will need to become more responsive, not just in terms of real-time reporting, but also responsive in terms of actions and outcomes. Planning and response operations needs to work simultaneously in tandem. SAP Leonardo technologies provide the fundamental building blocks to observe, listen, signal, learn, and react much more responsively. Competing with operational effectiveness and increased customer service in many cases is a matter of survival in many industries. The ability to create new solutions, products, or services while reusing existing waste (unused capacity) can be effective ways to improve both competitiveness and profitability.

This book will cover in detail the impact of the digital transformation and describe how SAP Leonardo technologies, along with associated SAP solutions and other solutions, can help you master the art of enhancing efficiency and value creation in your company. SAP Leonardo is a combination of intelligent technologies, services, and industry expertise that can help your organization optimize both processes and resources while realizing the promise of a digital intelligent enterprise. In this book, we've explored technologies that together serve as part of the SAP Leonardo family, described business processes that can be automated and made more efficient using SAP Leonardo, explained associated services, and outlined a path of adoption to achieve these goals.

We've separated fact from fiction and illustrated the basic concepts behind big data, data analytics, machine learning, the Internet of Things (IoT), and blockchain for our business and technical readers. Throughout this book, we'll deliver knowledge about end-to-end business processes now transformed by digital technologies and automation through SAP Leonardo.

This book will also provide you with extensive knowledge about SAP Cloud Platform, design thinking concepts and applications, SAP Leonardo technology elements, and applications in end-to-end business processes, including supply chains, logistics, customer service, finance, and human resources (HR).

We hope that this book can serve as a one-stop shop for understanding what SAP Leonardo is, its elements, and its technologies and for exploring cutting-edge use cases illustrating how you can use SAP Leonardo to transform end-to-end business processes, and thus your organization and maybe even the world! While this book does not require prior knowledge of SAP Leonardo or SAP technologies, we hope this book can serve as a solid reference textbook for business executives, business users, system managers, solution developers, and consultants.

Target Audience

The topics, coverage, and approach we chose for this book aim to be relevant for a wide variety of readers, ranging from business managers, to business analysts to technical help, from students to consultants, as well as anyone interested in learning more about the digital transformation, intelligent enterprises, and SAP Leonardo. We've covered end-to-end business processes in such a way that people with varied background and interests, for instance, in supply chains, finance, order processing, human resources, and technical development, will hopefully find this book relevant and useful.

This book is applicable for multiple stakeholders and users. Business executives and decision-makers will discover opportunities for automation to reduce inefficiency and to create competitive advantage using SAP Leonardo technologies. In addition, we hope this book will assist executives plotting a course to increase visibility into operations, investments, and customers, with improved insights for decision-making roles in areas like product lifecycle management, finance, and asset management.

Supply chain planners and managers can gain a better understanding of their supply networks as well as better visibility and improved execution.

Marketing, sales, and customer service managers will learn how to be more competitive in terms of improved customer experiences, for example, using tracking data to provide your customers with more collaborative experiences.

Operations can automate processes, thus reducing human-made errors. Predictive maintenance can reduce downtimes and improve asset utilization while reducing asset spend.

Technologists, consultants, and industry leaders can imagine new business models with technologies such as machine learning, the sharing economy, connected assets, or pay-per-use billing, which can change the way you create value, compete in the market, and improve customer service while creating new markets.

Digital transformation, intelligent enterprises, and automation through SAP technologies open up a wealth of exciting career opportunities with exciting work. Students and others interested in these topics can refer to this book to gain the knowledge required to becoming successful in the job market.

How This Book Is Organized

This book consists of fifteen chapters, divided into three parts, as follows:

- **Part I: Digital Transformation and the Intelligent Enterprise**
  In the first part of the book, we'll introduce you to SAP Leonardo, discussing what it is and what business value and benefit it brings through some example use case.

  - **Chapter 1: Introduction**
    In this chapter, we'll introduce you to SAP Leonardo and discuss the platform's benefits and uses. You'll learn about the digital transformation and how SAP technologies like SAP Cloud Platform and SAP Leonardo can enable your business to transform and modernize its processes. We'll briefly discuss some business use cases for SAP Leonardo in this chapter, which are then expanded upon throughout the rest of the book.

  - **Chapter 2: Digital Transformation: Ecosystem and Approach**
    A successful digital transformation requires a collaborative ecosystem of people, processes, and objects. In this chapter, we'll explore how digital innovation can be achieved by enabling intelligent connections throughout your organization.

- **Part II: Technologies**
  In the second part, you'll learn about SAP Leonardo technologies and show you how SAP Leonardo can be leveraged to enhance your business processes.

  - **Chapters 3, 4, and 5: Big Data, Analytics, and Machine Learning**
    Data is being generated at a rapid pace from a variety sources—not only within an enterprise but from business partners, customers, and customers' customers. Over the past decade, the capability to process this data has vastly improved, both technologically (i.e. fast, affordable computing power and user interfaces) and mathematically to derive multifaceted insights through sophisticated algorithms. These three chapters will cover three pillars—big data, analytics, and machine learning—enabled by the SAP Leonardo technologies introduced in Part I and describe how your company can leverage these technologies to accelerate your digital transformation journey.

- **Chapters 6, 7, and 8: Data Intelligence, Blockchain, and the Internet of Things**
  Data intelligence, blockchain, and the Internet of Things (IoT) are the basic building blocks of SAP Leonardo, which we'll explore in detail in these three chapters. The applications of these technologies for digital innovation in action is also illustrated through examples.

- **Part III: SAP Leonardo Business Processes**
  In this part, you'll learn about applications of SAP Leonardo, how it's been used in different line of business operations and, how it changes business practices.

  - **Chapter 9: Products and Inventory**
    While product development has and continues to undergo massive innovation, from products being made of mechanical and/or electrical parts, to products embedded with sensors and software, IoT has also brought about the capability to make products and assets smarter by allowing you to remotely monitor inventory levels, consumption rates, locations, storage conditions, etc., all in real time. In this chapter, we'll show you how SAP Leonardo technologies can help your company enable digital transformation by modifying current business models as well as by creating new business models to offer superior service levels to your customers while maximizing revenue-generating opportunities by optimizing your inventory and demand management processes. In this chapter, we'll use screenshots from live systems as examples of how SAP Leonardo technologies can be used in a variety of industries in the digitization of connected products.

  - **Chapter 10: Manufacturing and Assets**
    Digital manufacturing wires the world of machines with the world of business processes. In this chapter, we'll discuss the concepts behind smart manufacturing facilitated by the digital capabilities of SAP Leonardo. Usage of digital manufacturing operations aimed at manufacturing optimization will be illustrated in this chapter. Adopting digital asset management to manage your asset network improves manufacturing efficiency. Data analytics, machine learning, digitization, and additive manufacturing have transformed maintenance operations for manufacturers. We'll explore how predictive maintenance with SAP Leonardo can enhance business value through the use of digital twins.

  - **Chapter 11: Transportation and Warehousing**
    The digitization of supply chains means having the right number of products at the right time at the right place with the right service levels and price points. To achieve this goal, supply chain networks require end-to-end visibility into both your own supply chain and the extended supply chain, which includes the

supply chains of your partners. A connected fleet offers visibility into fleet vehicles and the ability to measure operational performance, such as utilization, operational costs, and other key performance indicators (KPIs) for efficiency. Connecting moving assets via IoT can also enable you to optimize your supply chain planning processes, such as the use of dynamic planning algorithms to more efficiently use assets, more accurate delivery windows, and improved customer service. The connected fleet and machine learning can ensure minimum disruption or close to zero downtime of fleet vehicles through predictive maintenance.

- **Chapter 12: Finance**
  If business leaders around the world are going to compete in the digital world, they'll need to process more information more efficiently and turn that information into deeper insights more quickly than ever. To keep pace with the rapid evolution of digital technologies in recent years, the SAP Leonardo suite of digital systems offers a variety of options to implement smarter and more intelligent business applications to fast track the digital transformation. The aim of this chapter is to explore and understand how SAP Leonardo technologies can impact core finance functions and explore what the new tools could do to your organization's revenue growth and bottom line. In this chapter, we'll also illustrate some of the financial successes achieved by early adopters of SAP Leonardo and SAP S/4HANA.

- **Chapter 13: Assorted Business Processes**
  SAP Leonardo's applications also touch on the process areas of human resource management, sourcing and procurement, and sales and marketing, as we'll describe in this chapter using examples of value creation areas. We'll also discuss SAP Leonardo's reimagined solution architecture and microservices in detail in this chapter.

- **Chapter 14: Digitization of Industries**
  Multiple leading organizations from different industries have adopted SAP Leonardo to add value to their firms, their employees, and their stakeholders. In this chapter, we'll describe example business use cases for different industry segments.

- **Chapter 15: Roadmap and Outlook**
  This chapter concludes the book by exploring the planned development and solution roadmap of SAP Leonardo.

- **Appendix A: Future Cities**
  In addition of transforming the business processes in a company, SAP Leonardo

can also optimize cities and communities, improving livability, aiding in resource management, and growing the local economy. This appendix serves as an illustration of the broader applicability of SAP Leonardo technologies.

Conclusion

We hope that reading this book will provide you the comprehensive knowledge of SAP Leonardo that you need to keep pace with fast-moving technological change. We tried to develop this book specifically to cover four broad important categories: First, our introduction to SAP Leonardo will explain what SAP Leonardo is and why it is important. Second, our overview of SAP Leonardo technologies will hopefully provide in-depth view into how these technologies can be applied along with existing processes and SAP solutions. Third, this book also describes the application of the SAP Leonardo solutions to facilitate the digital transformation in most industries. Finally, this book looks to the future on the SAP Leonardo roadmap. With these four goals in mind, we hope that this book will be your one-stop solution for creating an intelligent enterprise with SAP Leonardo.

Acknowledgments

Amit Sinha

First and foremost, I'm thankful to Darwin Deano, my SAP Leonardo mentor and a leader at Deloitte Consulting. The idea for this SAP Leonardo book started over dinner at a steakhouse in Atlanta. Thanks to Hans Thalbauer from SAP for welcoming the plan and being supportive of the idea. Both Darwin and Hans later chose the role of reviewer and connected me to my current coauthor team consisting of Vivek, Ganesh, and Pierre. I'm thankful to this team for the excellent and dedicated hard work required to write, shape, and finalize this book.

It has been a great experience to work with our publisher, SAP PRESS, but special thanks should go to our editors Meagan White and Hareem Shafi for their support and guidance from the conceptual phase to the end product.

I'm thankful to my career coaches Chris Verheuvel and Vadhi Narasimhamurti; their guidance has been instrumental to my learning growth and fulfillment in professional and personal life. The development of this book has also been supported by my colleagues and friends: Mohit Kakkar, Chandra Balasubramanian, and Rohit Fnu.

I thank them for their help and support through multiple discussions, system work, and manuscript development.

Gratitude is due to my family—my parents, my wife Surabhi, and my kids Ivan and Anaya—for their love and encouragement.

Amit Sinha, April 2019

Ganesh Wadawadigi

Writing this book has been an extremely fulfilling and enriching experience for me. First and foremost, I would like to thank my coauthors, Pierre, Amit, and Vivek; I really enjoyed our close collaboration and sharing of ideas. A very special thanks to Meagan White and Hareem Shafi from SAP PRESS for their patient and perceptive editing. Their continuous feedback and guidance in developing the chapters has been invaluable.

As SAP continues to rapidly innovate, our goal was to include the latest information at the time of this writing. For this purpose, I have the following colleagues to thank for sharing information on the latest product releases, providing research materials, and answering my questions: Alexander Schaefer, Alexis Lozada, Andreas Fichter, Bianca Luminita Duse, Chris Chan, Claire Remillard, Flavia Moser, Ginger Gatling, Guilherme Costa, Hannes Keil, Jens Krohn, Johann Dornbach, Keshav Rajpoot, Lars Olson, Lei Wang, Matt Creason, Matt Spohn, Mehmet Demirci, Melvi Pais, Merlijn Ekkel, Mike Fecek, Narjinder Pathania, Neil McGovern, Orla Cullen, Paulus Ng, Peter Mason, Petra Meyer, Poorya Farahani, Raghav Jandhyala, Raghavendra Deshmukh, Raimund Gross, Rainer Moritz, Renato Zadro, Richard Mooney, Sathya Narasimhan, Stefan Foerster, Steven Kim, Tom Chelednik, Torsten Zube, Ty Miller, Vadim Pavluk, Velin Ivanov, Viktor Kehayov, and Vinay V. I am also grateful for the management support I received from Hans Thalbauer, Martin Barkman, and Markus Rosemann.

Finally, I would like to thank my family—my parents, my wife Sravi, and my kids Akash and Anisha—for their support and encouragement.

Ganesh Wadawadigi, April 2019

Pierre Erasmus

Writing this book has been an amazing and exciting journey for me, and I would like to thank my coauthors: my dear old friend Ganesh, who has always been there for me throughout my career at SAP, and Amit and Vivek, my friends from Deloitte. It's been such a pleasure to work with Meagan White and Hareem Shafi from SAP PRESS for their endurance, feedback, and guidance.

I'd also like to thank my friends and colleagues for their support and help, especially Rob Enslin, Nadia Torres, Bernhard Schweizer, Priya Wenzel, Martin Barkman, Davide Pacchini, Michael Dietz, Francois Louw, Uwe Kuersten, Stephan Brand, Ken Pierce, Kevin Liu, Hans Thalbauer, Markus Roseman, Petra Diessner, and Tom Kurtz. I thank you for all your continuous support and assistance as we wrote this book.

Finally, I would like to thank my family—my parents Liz and Johan Erasmus and my brother Jacques and his wife Candice, with a special thanks to my partner Lehoa Nguyen.

Pierre Erasmus, April 2019

Vivek Vinayak Rao

When I was tapped to contribute to this book, little did I know that I was embarking on one of the most eye-opening and exciting journeys of my life. First, I would like to thank my coauthors Ganesh, Pierre, and Amit. It has also been a pleasure to work with Meagan White and Hareem Shafi from SAP PRESS, who deserve special thanks for their patience, feedback, and guidance.

I'd like to thank my friends and colleagues for their support and help throughout this process, especially Sadhalaxmi Vivek Rao, Sushant Chennapragada, Atanu Mukhopadhyay, Gautam Mylavarapu, Abhishek Sawant, Vikram Shirole, Abhishek Vinayak, Alok Gupta, Mansi Dixit, Rowin Masrani, and Veeru Teki. I thank you all for your continuous support and assistance.

Finally, I would like to thank my family—my mother Chitra, my wife Sadha, and my son Vedanth—for their support and encouragement.

Vivek Vinayak Rao, April 2019

PART I

Digital Transformation and the Intelligent Enterprise

Chapter 1
Introduction

"SAP Leonardo will unlock the full potential of the intelligent enterprise."

—*Bill McDermott, CEO, SAP*

In this chapter, we'll introduce you to SAP Leonardo and discuss its benefits and uses. You'll learn about digital transformation and how the intelligent technologies found in SAP Leonardo, along with SAP Cloud Platform, can enable your business to transform, modernize, and automate. The topics we discuss in this chapter will be expanded upon throughout the rest of the book.

1.1 Introduction to SAP Leonardo

The quote from Bill McDermott, CEO of SAP, that opens this chapter captures the goal of SAP Leonardo: using its capabilities to create an intelligent enterprise that effectively uses data assets to achieve desired outcomes faster with less risk, while empowering employees through process automation, anticipating and proactively responding to customer needs, and inventing new business models and revenue streams.

With breakthroughs in technological innovation in areas like data analytics, cloud computing, blockchain, machine learning, and artificial intelligence, business process operations in organizations are going through huge disruptions. Business process integration and automation, facilitated by ERP in the early 1980s, resulted in widespread computer adoption and productivity gains. The integrated data and processes through ERP applications, in general, matured by the early 2000s, with many departments working as a connected enterprise for different business functions. The evolution of the Internet allowed for collaboration with external entities, in addition to intra-organizational collaboration.

The Internet revolution further moved to mobile, cloud-based systems, and big data, and various organizations are currently at different phases of digital transformation. Digital transformation—along with the adoption of breakthrough technologies for data analysis, pattern recognition, automated decision-making, task automation, and intelligently connected people, processes, and things—is leading the way to intelligent enterprises. This shift will drastically change the way we live and work. For an intelligent enterprise, most repetitive tasks will be automated so that employees' attention can be devoted to the high-value tasks. Organizations following a strategic approach to digital transformation and the adoption of technological innovation have already started generating advantages in the market. According to research from the Forbes Insight team, 72% of CEOs around the world believe that the next 3 years will be more critical to their industry than the last 50 years. An SAP strategy paper concluded that 60% of an organization's tasks performed today could be automated in the near future, by 2025.

SAP Leonardo is SAP's solution for capabilities to help your business become an intelligent enterprise. SAP Leonardo integrates new technologies into SAP Cloud Platform using design-led innovation. SAP Leonardo makes SAP applications more intelligent and capable, enabling companies to achieve rapid innovation, which facilitates the scaling of new business models and the redefining of the business.

A connected enterprise with a mature ERP process can generate a huge amount of relevant data through business transactions. A further set of data is available from business partners and external sources. Add to this set the data generated by billions of customers on social media. Proper handling and analysis of this data can enable better decision-making, automation, and process optimization. SAP Leonardo provides data-driven capabilities for determining the best possible business actions in the least amount of time.

In the following sections, you'll learn about the technology component of SAP Leonardo and how it supports enterprise-wide processes. We'll also describe a recommended approach to adoption.

1.1.1   Technology and Components

SAP Leonardo is a methodology enabling rapid innovation and digital transformation and is comprised of the following:

- A core set of technologies (technical capabilities) focused on the Internet of Things (IoT), machine learning, analytics, big data, and blockchain technology

- Microservices and APIs that run on SAP Cloud Platform to help integrate SAP Leonardo capabilities into applications
- Applications powered by SAP Leonardo that provide machine learning, IoT, big data, predictive analytics, and blockchain capabilities
- Accelerator packages that can help you tackle problems without having to assemble pieces and parts on your own

As shown in Figure 1.1, SAP Leonardo's capabilities consist of following three groups:

- Design-led innovation
- Intelligent technologies
  - Internet of Things (IoT)
  - Data intelligence
  - Big data
  - Analytics
  - Machine learning
  - Blockchain
- SAP Cloud Platform, data management, and support for multicloud infrastructures

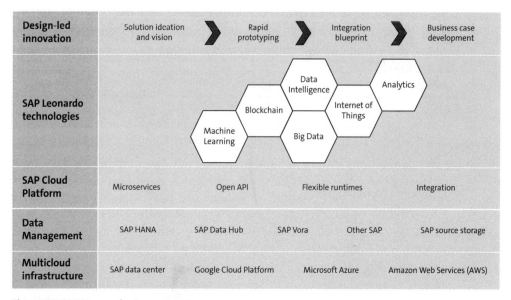

Figure 1.1 SAP Leonardo Components

33

Let's look at each of these elements, as follows:

- **Design-led innovation**

  SAP Leonardo innovation is governed by a design-led innovation approach with business users at the center while following a proven, design-led methodology. This methodology consists of a multiphase approach involving explore, discover, design and prototype, and deliver phases. This approach enhances the probability of success and increases value achievement through SAP Leonardo use cases and business implementation. Design-led innovation is managed with advisory and design gates to ensure the effort is aligned with the vision of the business.

  Design thinking enables business-led innovation in an agile environment based on customer collaboration involving building and validating a model prototype before further enhancing it. Design thinking aims for time-limited innovation cycles with guidelines for project phases and timelines. The project phases (explore, discover, design, prototype, and deliver) take the ideas, requirements, or opportunities learned from customer discussions to provide value-added results to the business.

  The explore phase is focused on identifying business opportunities through SAP Leonardo. User research is performed in the discover phase, which may involve mapping the process as-is and then ideating the to-be process. In the design phase, the best solution aligned to the identified business requirements is considered ready for building a prototype. The prototype phase allows for business validation and valuable user feedback, which will then be used for the actual product build and delivery.

> **Note**
>
> Additional details on the design-led innovation approach are discussed in Chapter 2, Section 2.4.

- **Intelligent technologies**

  The intelligent technologies enabled by SAP Leonardo include machine learning, blockchain, data intelligence, big data, IoT, and analytics. These technologies (individually or in combination) can be used as tools for business process automation and better decision-making. These technologies can be applied to different use cases with a broad range of objectives, such as automating repetitive tasks, identifying data patterns for actionable insights, supply chain transparency for better decision-making, automating account settlements, and identifying customers, to name a few, with a net impact of achieving higher efficiency, revenue, and profit. Each of these SAP Leonardo technologies is further described in Section 1.5 and covered in further detail in Part II of this book, from Chapter 3 to Chapter 8.

- **SAP Cloud Platform**
  As the foundation of an SAP Leonardo infrastructure, SAP Cloud Platform provides seamless integration of systems, things, and processes. SAP Cloud Platform is an open, extensible platform-as-a-service (PaaS) that provides core platform services, in-memory computing, and microservices to enable the digital transformation and to provide the capabilities needed for an intelligent enterprise. Through open standards, SAP Cloud Platform drives business agility with both flexibility and control. With SAP Cloud Platform as the foundation to SAP Leonardo, you and your partners can seamlessly integrate emerging technologies on SAP Cloud Platform to rapidly develop and deploy next-generation applications. We'll provide an overview of SAP Cloud Platform and its applications in Section 1.4.

- **Data management and multicloud infrastructures**
  Different SAP applications can be seamlessly integrated through SAP Leonardo technologies. More than 70% of transaction data around the world touches an SAP environment. This tremendous volume of data from different applications like SAP HANA, SAP Data Hub, SAP Vora, etc., along with any other high-volume, high-velocity data, structured or unstructured, can be processed, managed, and integrated by SAP Leonardo. Also, with support for a multicloud infrastructure, along with an SAP data center, you can choose any cloud provider, like Microsoft Azure, Amazon Web Services (AWS), or Google Cloud Platform. This flexibility allows for the colocation of new cloud applications alongside existing investments and help you meet local regulatory and compliance requirements.

1.1.2   Intelligent Enterprise Components

An intelligent enterprise powered by SAP Leonardo uses three components: the intelligent suite, intelligent technologies, and the digital platform, as shown in Figure 1.2.

SAP applications, with their built-in understanding of different business processes, can be used in association with your system of record to adapt intelligent technologies through the infrastructure of the digital platform. Intelligent suites like SAP S/4HANA (digital core), SAP Digital Supply Chain, SAP C/4HANA (for customer engagement), SAP Ariba (for network and spend management), etc. can be used with connected objects, which create data that can be staged on the digital platform for utilization by intelligent technologies like machine learning, artificial intelligence, analytics, etc.

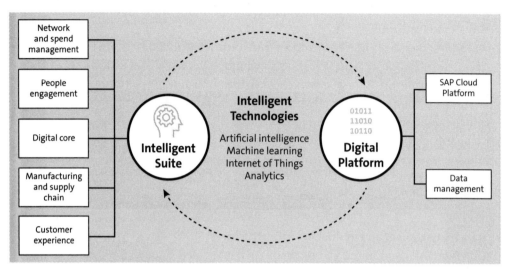

Figure 1.2 Intelligent Enterprise Components

Intelligent suites, as shown in Figure 1.3, normally use a system of record like SAP S/4HANA. The data available in the system of record can also be directly used by the SAP Leonardo for making an enterprise application intelligent. Figure 1.3 shows the system of record and the system of intelligence for an intelligent enterprise. The system of intelligence is provided through SAP Leonardo.

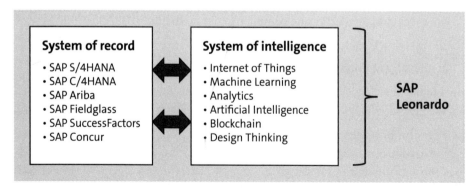

Figure 1.3 Systems of Intelligence and Record in an SAP Environment

1.1.3   Adoption Options

SAP recommends consuming SAP Leonardo in one of three primary ways:

- SAP Leonardo embedded in the SAP solution portfolio
- SAP Guided Outcomes
- Open innovation

An important advantage of adopting breakthrough technology through SAP is its embedded SAP portfolio products. SAP Leonardo technologies like machine learning, blockchain, AI, analytics, etc. work seamlessly with different SAP applications like SAP S/4HANA, SAP Ariba, SAP Digital Supply Chain, etc. Devices and sensors (IoT) can be used to capture real-time data for analysis, automation, and decision-making.

SAP Leonardo is adaptable and flexible enough to be used for any industry. SAP Guided Outcomes provides a defined set of business outcomes using products and capabilities from across the SAP portfolio. Its stated purpose is to make it easier for organizations to select the appropriate level of embedded intelligent technologies like machine learning or advanced analytics.

The open innovation option uses the openness and flexibility of SAP Leonardo to build specific solutions for your organization to resolve specific business problems and to harness value through cutting-edge applications.

As shown in Figure 1.4, the engagement track of SAP Leonardo leads to either industry accelerator services or innovation services. The preferred adoption option is one of the outputs of the explore phase.

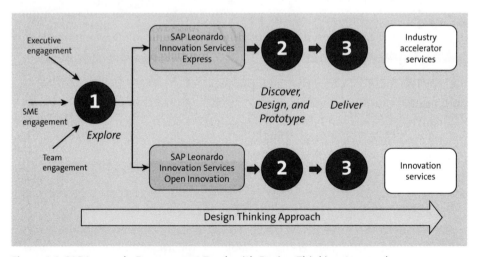

Figure 1.4 SAP Leonardo Engagement Track with Design Thinking Approach

Based on your requirements and recommended solution, either the express innovation or open innovation path can be adopted. The timelines of the projects will differ, depending on the option you choose, with innovation services requiring more time and effort than accelerator services.

Based on business requirements and identified value areas, your business can adopt one or a combination of these three options.

1.2   Benefits of SAP Leonardo

SAP Leonardo facilitates the synchronization, through intelligent connections, of people, things, and businesses, as shown in Figure 1.5. Intelligent machines have operated in silos for some organizations for decades. However, with SAP Leonardo, intelligence is spread across the organization through connected people, things, and business processes. Digital transformation supported by SAP Leonardo results in intelligent, nimble, and efficient organizations ready to disrupt current business processes and create future opportunities. Data from across the organization, from suppliers, and from customers can be made available to intelligent technologies like machine learning to generate real-time analytics in a collaborative environment so that real-time decisions can be made by machines or people. Such capabilities can help achieve higher revenue, higher efficiency, and higher profit.

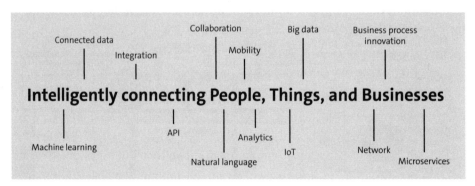

Figure 1.5 Intelligent Connections of an Intelligent Enterprise

Note

Multiple research reports support the benefits of digital transformation and automation through breakthrough technology adoption. The average value of the revenue increase for the selected group was 35%, with reduction in maintenance costs by 60% and higher worker safety of 10%.

The core definition of an intelligent enterprise powered by SAP Leonardo is made up of automated business processes managed through modern digital user interfaces. Digital user interfaces allow users to communicate through different channels (e.g. voice, smart device apps, etc.) and automatically manage processes in business applications with minimum support from actual users. Predictive analytics supported by machine learning and artificial intelligence algorithms can simulate and recommend the best possible decisions in areas like finance, supply chain, customer service, etc., thus improving decision-making and performance in your organization.

Another direct advantage of SAP Leonardo is how it can drive the digital transformation journey by making your organization ready for new ways of interacting with customers, managing and automating business processes, and reviewing product and service offerings in the new economy, all of which require working in a close-knit, always-on environment.

1.3 Digital Transformation

Digital capabilities of the current era have transformed the way we live, work, and conduct business. The scope of digital transformation has become much broader, touching the organization across the industry segments and is not limited to technology leaders like Google, Apple, Uber, etc. Digital transformation has redefined customer interactions, product development, business processes, and manual tasks.

Digital transformation is disrupting the traditional business model and redefining business leaders. Disruption offers opportunities for growth, efficiency, and profitability but, at the same time, is a business threat that can make an organization irrelevant to customers if not planned well. Digital transformation can be analyzed as a disruption that needs to be managed through process and workplace innovation, as we'll discuss in the following sections. We'll also take a quick look at some example use cases for digital transformation with SAP Leonardo.

1.3.1 Digital Disruption

Digital disruption in the current economic environment is related to market opportunities, threats, and the ways we develop and use products and services.

New Market Opportunities

The digital ecosystem has become crucial for revenue and profitability growth as well as to compete in the market. Many examples exist in which nimble organizations have used digital capabilities to reach the customers. For example, a relatively new organization, Uber created a new segment of business while an established organization, Marriott, could use digital capabilities to reach out to a new group of customers with a more efficient and automated process.

Digital transformation enables enterprises to be closer to their customers, gathering their feedback through different channels and using this information to deliver products with much higher success rates than products developed through older approaches. Digitally advanced organizations can reach out to a larger customer base with higher product agility and efficient service channels; these factors together enhance revenue through bigger market opportunities.

Dynamic Threats

Digital disruption in a particular industry can be detrimental to both the top-line and bottom-line of a company, along with threats to survival, if not managed properly. Many examples like Nokia, Blackberry, Kodak, etc. illustrate how digital disruption could create huge market segment losses due to the dynamic movement of the markets. Many of these organizations were not well prepared to deal with digital disruption. According to a Deloitte research of C-level executives around the world, only 14% of CXOs are "highly confident" that their organizations are ready to harness the changes associated with the new era.

Product and Service Digitization

We're moving from an era of disconnected products and services to a highly integrated world connected with digital sensor capabilities commonly referred to as the Internet of Things (IoT). This scenario impacts product and service development as well as delivery. For example, consider the case of product development in the automobile industry: Customers may expect a digital navigation system, which was once only available in luxury cars, as a standard feature just like other basic functions (engine power, safety systems, etc.). In fact, digitization has been taken to new levels where data is being collected from driving habits to offer service updates and innovative insurance policies. Another example is smart homes (i.e. with Wi-Fi-enabled thermostats) and smart household appliances (like refrigerators, washing machines, etc.), which collect data for efficient power consumption and the automatic replenishment of household items.

Shared Economy

One of the most important impacts of the digital transformation is the movement towards a shared economy. Companies like Uber and Airbnb have successfully adopted the idea of shared products and services with these organizations' revenue models based on services instead of one-time product sales.

Digital capabilities provide a platform that makes a shared economy efficient and workable. Although Uber, Airbnb, and Lyft are the most well-known pioneers in this area, more traditional industries are now getting into this space, thus resulting in a more efficient world with a smaller carbon footprint. For example, consider the disruption created by Trringo in the Indian agricultural sector through its tractor and farm equipment rental business. Due to the smaller land area owned per farmer, often, farmers found it difficult to own their own mechanized agriculture equipment. Trringo, a venture of M&M (Mahindra & Mahindra), has developed a digital platform to provide the tractor and farm equipment rental services required by the farmers. Efficient farming results in increasing the farm output, efficient machine usage, and overall productivity gain.

To be successful, the move to the shared economy requires a different approach to product development, planning, and customer interaction. You'll require a complete transformation of the organization and its processes. Although the sharing of the products and services has been present in many economies, the digital transformation, with its end-to-end visibility, easy-to-use apps, and optimization brought about by the cloud computing, is totally transforming the way we own, use, and share products. More and more organizations are joining the shared economy model and thus need to adopt the relevant digital transformation.

1.3.2 Business Process Innovation

The benefits of the digital transformation cannot be achieved by simply adding a technology layer to the business; the transformation requires the transformation of processes, systems, and people. A successful transformation differentiates itself by working on four factors:

- Transformation through the core to end to end
- Having customer at the center of transformation
- Leveraging breakthrough technology
- Talent and skill

Organizations following a piecemeal approach to digital transformation generally accrue minor benefits in terms of revenue and profit growth, but a well-planned transformation can be instrumental to your organization's success in the new marketplace. However, initial projects could still be small in nature, perhaps a proof of concept (POC) model, the success of which can be used to replicate the successful model across the organization based on a well thought-out plan for digital transformation starting from the digital core.

The transformation of the core spreads across the organization and must consider customer at the center. From enhanced customer experience, the digital transformation can govern internal processes and work through the collaborative network of suppliers and customers. Enhanced customer experience and process automation can be achieved through the breakthrough technologies of machine learning, artificial intelligence, analytics, IoT, blockchain, etc., and thus, leveraging and investing in these breakthrough technologies is important. The selection of the relevant technology or the group of technologies should be driven by the transformation plan. The most important enabler of success in this context is the availability of the right skills and talent, which can be achieved through retraining your existing workforce as well as through hiring or engaging external partners. A successful digital transformation journey, led with the design-focused approach of SAP Leonardo, can be achieved through these four factors.

Business process innovation needs to focus on the following four areas:

- **Customer experience**
  Digital business transformation must consider the customer experience at the center. Whether a customer is ordering a pizza, some farm equipment, or a car ride, customer experience is often the deciding factor for success in the digital ecosystem. Predictability, speed, and trust in the service can either generate a returning customer or a dissatisfied customer. Through the design-led innovation, SAP Leonardo focuses on the customer experience for the digital innovation system.

- **Real-time business**
  A digital ecosystem of customers, manufacturers, and suppliers works on real-time business information. SAP Leonardo facilitates actionable insights using real-time data from multiple sources including SAP and third-party applications, which allows businesses to run efficiently in a connected world.

- **Predictive insights**
  An efficient digital ecosystem can predict the outcome based on the connected infrastructure to automate the processes while gaining greater efficiency. An

example can be predictive asset maintenance in which, based on relevant operating or ambient parameters like temperature, vibrations, etc., the system proactively predicts required maintenance before a breakdown occurs. Taking this capability to the next level of efficiency would be to hold only a digital inventory of the maintenance parts and then use 3D printing to get the required component on-demand. The predictive capabilities provided by SAP Leonardo, along with a connected network, can help achieve the necessary business process innovation needed for an intelligent enterprise.

- **Cross-enterprise collaboration**
  Success in the digital world requires close collaboration with business partners. The involvement of partners, from extended supplier networks to the customers, is necessary to achieve end-to-end process visibility, efficiency, and control. Considering third-party service providers as the part of the collaborative network could be beneficial. Consider the example of a manufacturer with real-time visibility into changes in consumer demand at retail stores. Through connected processes, this company can sense demand at its distribution centers and direct its manufacturing plants to update its production and distribution plans accordingly, alerting its suppliers and logistics service providers and respond to the demand changes to maximize revenue and increase customer satisfaction. Such cross-enterprise collaboration can be realized with sensor devices, connected systems, and other SAP Leonardo capabilities.

1.3.3   Workplace Innovation

With the fast adoption of the digital transformation, the physical workplace now blurred into a digital frame with the realities of getting work done from anyone (direct employee or partners), anywhere, on any device. A digital workplace is the natural evolution of the physical workplace with the recent technological advancement and macro-level changes in the workforce and society. You would be hard-pressed to find a working environment without emails, conference calls supported by Internet applications, and mobile device connectivity. A digital workplace consists of a comprehensive ecosystem of the employees with the workplace and the technology in use to work. With time, a next-generation workforce, and next-generation technological advancements, the expectations of both employees and employers are changing, which must be planned with the evolution of the digital workplace to avoid the risk of falling behind.

Based on the recent research conducted by professional research firms, employee productivity is enhanced at the firms that adopt digital workplaces with the usage of mobile devices, easy-to-use apps, work flexibility, information availability, and seamless collaboration. In unprecedented ways, employees are communicating and collaborating with both internal and external stakeholders through multiple channels. Collaboration and information sharing in the digital workplace are much more than the emails and text messages. New tools of collaboration and connectivity are increasing productivity and employee satisfaction. A tremendous amount of change is expected with the further maturity of new technologies like 5G, data analytics, apps, IoT, and robotics. A clear roadmap is recommended to ensure value delivery and competitive advantage through digital workplace while still managing associated risks.

With SAP Leonardo's capabilities, supported by ease-of-use, app-based functionalities, end-to-end information collaboration in a secure environment can be used strategically for the achieving an effective digital workplace. The digital workplace strategy should be aligned with your digital transformation goals while considering the impact on the people, processes, and technology. In the old world, an organization's information infrastructure could be compared to a "fort." Strict controls ensured that information was retained within the boundaries of the organization and accessible to only the full-time employees who completed tasks. In the digitally transformed world, higher efficiency is achieved by collaboration with external parties like suppliers, customers, suppliers' suppliers, customers' customers, partner organizations, etc. Most of an organization's enterprise data is being moved from on-premise systems to the cloud. The fluidity required for enhancing efficiency, flexibility, availability, and predictability can be supported by the SAP ecosystem with SAP Leonardo and related infrastructure.

Some of the most important areas where we can see the digital workplace in action include the following:

- **Collaboration**
  The most common use of a digital workplace for employees to connect and work from different location without being limited to an office environment and a particular desktop while at the same time seamlessly communicating and collaborating with others. Productivity is achieved through this flexibility in space and time, and employees are empowered by having the right information in the right format in order to accomplish tasks on time.

  Agile enterprises require collaboration supported by an innovative workspace. In the current digital economy, organizations must be connected to information and knowledge sources. Collaboration in the current and future organizations must occur along different channels with both internal and external entities. The global work environment must support connectivity, allowing required flexibility for round-the-clock business operations as well as the real-time collaboration capabilities involving different parties to respond to customer requirements in the most effective manner.

- **Digital toolbox**
  Multiple tools, with ever-increasing availability with digital transformation, are available for developing a digital workforce. We recommend analyzing and adopting the required tools by area of focus, for example, productivity, communication, brainstorming, mobility, etc. Considering the fast pace of development in this area, this topic is fluid, requiring attention from your digital transformation leaders. The right tools for your employees can greatly enhance the productivity of the whole organization.

- **Governance, risk, and compliance**
  While collaboration and ease of information sharing are basic requirements in a digital economy, the underlying potential threat of data security cannot be ignored. At the same time, compliance requirements may need to be fulfilled. Thus, a proper governance structure is required for enabling the right control in the digital environment while still allowing for easy collaboration and information availability.

- **Business drivers for achieving measurable value**
  The most important business drivers for digital innovation systems are focused on revenue, cost, agility, and experience. The control framework for your digital workforce should aim to achieve the planned business drivers with the right mix of technology availability, process redesign, and workforce management. Workplace innovation can be further analyzed through the following four factors:
  - Workforce dynamics
  - Paradigm shifts in efficiency
  - Connected and collaborated work environments
  - Task automation

- **Workforce dynamics**
  Digital innovation and its related disruption are changing trends in employment, work approach, and technology. In the past, organizations focused on intrateam collaboration to enhance knowledge sharing, innovation, and productivity; now, the focus has shifted to include collaboration with external parties, partners, and

end users. The technology infrastructure, which was mostly used to process and handle the organization's ERP data, is now expected to work in a multicloud environment, processing information from a multitude of external and internal systems.

The leading organizations of the future will be distinguished by their ability to harness changes in workforce dynamics. Employees need a flexible work environment supported by advanced technologies and providing the insights required to make business decisions at their fingertips.

- **Paradigm shift in efficiency**
  The time has come for enterprises to reap the benefits of improved efficiency as the result of digital innovation. The digitization of content and the use of advanced technologies were pioneered recently by companies like Netflix, Facebook, Spotify, etc. to greatly enhance the customer entertainment experience. Similar innovations are now becoming mainstream, and other organizations are leveraging these innovations to enhance efficiencies and achieve productivity gains in their own organizations.

  For example, advanced technologies like machine learning algorithms, IoT, and image detection technology benefit manufacturing companies by helping identify manufacturing defects in products at the moment they occur in the production process, compared to previously when many days' worth of production output had to be scrapped due to late detection of defects, further down the supply chain. We'll discuss a multitude of examples throughout this book describing the potential efficiency gains for your enterprise through digital transformation.

- **Task automation**
  Many tasks currently being performed in the work environment can be automated. The repetitive tasks being performed by people, both in an office as well as in a factory environment will be automated as part of digital transformation. The human workforce will still be needed for higher value-adding tasks. For example, instead of the manual process of invoice matching, you could apply machine learning to perform the task, requiring human intervention only for managing exceptions, or, you could move from manual testing of products as they roll off an assembly line to robotic testing with automated visual inspection. Autonomous forklifts could take over the production floor. Numerous use cases across each industry illustrate how people could be relieved of repetitive and error-prone manual tasks and how using automation could achieve higher accuracy, efficiency, productivity, and cost savings.

1.3.4   Business Usage

Tremendous value can be harnessed with digital transformation by using SAP Leonardo and the related SAP family of technology products. The following are some currently implemented business use cases for SAP Leonardo in several different industries:

- A global consumer products company, with a presence in more than 200 countries, has deployed SAP Digital Boardroom, thus enabling the company to move from periodic reviews to reviews anytime, anywhere, in real time, resulting in actionable decisions to achieve business results.

- A leading industrial equipment manufacturer has connected customers, products, and installation of sensors and devices with a real-time review of work progress and actions on potential delays. Augmented reality allows for quick and easy approval checks by relevant leaders.

- A retailer is utilizing the data from a collaboration network on SAP Cloud Platform for real-time supplier scoring, benchmarking, report generation, and contract allotment.

- A leading company in the consumer products industry is using IoT devices on retailer shelves for managing and moving inventory from the manufacturing plant to the distribution center and from the distribution center to retail locations for replenishing shelves in the most efficient manner.

- A leading manufacturing organization is providing all its inventory, forecast, sales order, and production planning data to SAP Data Hub and is using machine learning algorithms to predict short-term demand by performing sensitivity analysis. Dynamic demand is used to produce the products aligned to the market demand, resulting in higher service rates at lower costs.

- An industrial goods manufacturer is utilizing a central data hub and additive manufacturing techniques to build spare parts on demand, thus reducing the cost of maintaining thousands of the service parts in inventory.

- An oil refinery is utilizing IoT devices to track atmospheric conditions like pressure and temperature in real time and to generate alerts when recorded values cross threshold values so that appropriate action can be taken in time. Costs and resources are saved with predictive maintenance when compared to reactive maintenance that only acts when breakdowns occur.

- A pharmaceuticals manufacturer is using a mobile app to track the health information of patients to make better and more specific therapy decisions.

- A car component manufacturer is using machine learning to predict maintenance requirements for their equipment. Predictive maintenance has drastically reduced machine breakdowns, avoiding losses in production and efficiency from sudden and periodic failures.

These examples illustrate just a few instances where SAP Leonardo and associated technology solutions were applied.

Note

Further detailed case studies are discussed in Chapter 14, where we'll discuss various examples from different industries.

1.4 SAP Cloud Platform

SAP Cloud Platform, the foundational platform for SAP Leonardo, is an open and flexible PaaS that allows easy extension of application development through easy-to-use apps. The platform provides in-memory capabilities, core platform services, and unique microservices for building and extending intelligent, mobile-enabled cloud applications. SAP Cloud Platform allows user-centric agile business application development for process automation, analytics, review, and control, which can drive business agility, allowing you to quickly build, extend, and integrate modern mobile-enabled applications to fulfill your business requirements in the digital world.

SAP Cloud Platform provides extensive integration capabilities with SAP Leonardo applications. Examples include the integration of connected assets, fleet vehicles, etc., through SAP Cloud Platform. Solutions like automated factory applications, automated warehouse operations, automatic procurement processes, etc., can be achieved by using different SAP technology solutions with SAP Leonardo and SAP Cloud Platform. Figure 1.6 shows a representation of the integration you can achieve through SAP Cloud Platform.

The business application and usage of SAP Cloud Platform through its capabilities can be grouped into the following three categories:

- **Create**
  Simple, personalized, and responsive user interface applications can be created on the SAP Cloud Platform using preconfigured design templates. SAP Cloud Platform can be used as the complete application development toolkit supporting prototype development to the build and deployment stages.

- **Integrate**

  Different application systems and data environments, both SAP and non-SAP, can be integrated through SAP Cloud Platform. Both on-premise and cloud-based application data are processed in a secure environment on SAP Cloud Platform, which also enables collaboration with both customers and partners. Further, data processing speed will not present a challenge due to SAP Cloud Platform's ability to process high volumes of data in real time.

- **Insight-to-action**

  Using the data on SAP Cloud Platform, SAP Leonardo can help convert insight into action using data from multiple systems and IoT devices. Real-time predictive analytics improves core business processes. SAP Cloud Platform provides a single platform for data management, predictive analytics, and visualization.

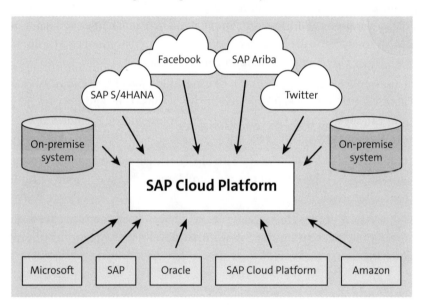

Figure 1.6 SAP Cloud Platform

SAP Cloud Platform provides the following four service categories, which we'll discuss in the following sections:

- Business services
- Platform services
- Data and storage services
- Edge services

1.4.1   Business Services

SAP Cloud Platform, in association with the SAP Leonardo and other SAP and non-SAP solutions, solves multiple business challenges and can add value to your organization through revenue gains, profitability gains, efficiency gains, and better user experiences. A few of the most widely used business services include the following:

- SAP Smart Business service enables predictive and embedded analytics as ready-reference SAP Fiori applications, without the need to write detailed.

- Key performance indicators (KPIs) and operational performance indicators (OPIs) can be visualized in apps, with threshold alerts to signal when manual attention is needed.

- SAP S/4HANA can provide the core capabilities for digital transformation by connecting your organization with common processes and data models while supporting daily operations. SAP Cloud Platform extends the capabilities and reach of SAP S/4HANA to meet the evolving needs of employees, customers, and business partners while simplifying processes for higher efficiency.

- Software-as-a-service (SaaS) offerings can be used build customized and collaborative services via SAP Cloud Platform and create a consistent and user-friendly application. The services that can be considered for integration include SAP SuccessFactors, SAP C/4HANA, SAP Ariba, etc.

- SAP Leonardo can be used to innovate with big data, analytics, machine learning, blockchain, and IoT to solve current business problems and create new opportunities for your enterprise.

- Business operations can be run on all types of devices at all the times through easy-to-use mobile apps using the full-featured development platform of SAP Cloud Platform.

1.4.2   Platform Services

SAP Cloud Platform is an enterprise-level PaaS, relieving organizations of tasks and effort required for maintaining the infrastructure. SAP Cloud Platform provides broad application development capabilities to extend, integrate, and build business-relevant applications for digital transformation. This PaaS service from SAP drastically reduces the total time required for the transformation; your organization can focus on creating mobile-ready, cloud-based applications without worrying about the underlying infrastructure.

Developed on open standards for flexibility in building solutions, SAP Cloud Platform provides a secure, reliable way to process and use data and applications. On this platform, the integration of processes and data is easily achieved between cloud-based applications, on-premise solutions, and third-party applications.

Many organizations have driven their digital transformation using SAP Cloud Platform with a multicloud architecture and Cloud Foundry technology. Cloud Foundry represents an *open source*, cloud-based PaaS on which your developers can build, deploy, run, and scale applications. SAP Cloud Platform, with Cloud Foundry technology, facilitates agile innovation using any programming language or service. SAP Cloud Platform and Cloud Foundry can provide you the freedom to choose your cloud infrastructure provider and the flexibility to colocate new cloud-based applications with existing applications while meeting local regulatory and compliance requirements. Organizations can choose a public cloud infrastructure to run SAP Cloud Platform, like Amazon Web Services (AWS), Microsoft Azure, or Google Cloud Platform. SAP handles the complexities of managing and operating the details of these infrastructure accounts.

1.4.3   Data and Storage Services

SAP Cloud Platform delivers data management and analytical services to build intelligent enterprises delivering real-time insights from data collected and managed from different sources. Companies can build competitive advantage by using SAP Leonardo intelligent technologies like machine learning and augmented reality. Both unstructured and structured data can be processed, providing real-time insights to achieve higher efficiency, productivity, and simplicity.

SAP Cloud Platform big data services is a full-service offering that meets the rigorous demands for reliability, scalability, and security needed for the digital transformation. SAP Cloud Platform is a secure solution for using Hadoop and Spark ecosystems and reduces the effort required to right-size production environments. SAP Cloud Platform Big Data Services includes deployment, automated operations management, scaling, monitoring, and support work. These services provide end-to-end coverage of the technical infrastructure, process, and people so that your organization can focus on getting the most out of the digital transformation work.

Key data management and storage services available in SAP Cloud Platform include the following:

- **SAP Cloud Platform, SAP HANA service**
  SAP Cloud Platform, SAP HANA service provides transactional and analytical

processing with advanced analytics capabilities. This service enables quick development of business-ready applications with state-of-the-art infrastructure and in-memory computing capabilities. The self-service capabilities such as backup recovery and updates are particularly handy.

SAP Cloud Platform, SAP HANA service also provides analytics. Numerous types of graphs and charts can be created on the fly for visualizing and analyzing your data and generating relevant insights. Geographical data can be illustrated with geospatial maps. Smart data integration and streaming capabilities facilitate predictive capabilities.

- **SAP Cloud Platform Big Data Services**
  SAP Cloud Platform Big Data Services can be used for machine learning algorithms as well as interactive business queries. The SAP Cloud Platform Big Data Services provide a performance-driven, robust big data framework using Apache Hadoop and Spark. With the solution subscription, SAP provides support for the big data operations team.

- **SAP Cloud Platform Document service**
  The SAP Cloud Platform Document service enables working with both structured and unstructured data. Unstructured data for business use can be in different formats (drawings, audio, videos, pictures), which are mostly available as documents. The SAP Cloud Platform Document service provides an efficient way to fetch the information contained in the document for the business purpose. Through the easy application integration capabilities, documents like computer-aided design (CAD) drawings, application logs, reports, assembly pictures, etc. can be accessed for determining the required information and generating insights from these unstructured datasets.

- **SAP Web Analytics**
  SAP Web Analytics is focused on providing business insights when using big data with sophisticated algorithms. These capabilities are available as predictive services and streaming analysis services. Predictive services use algorithms to predict future events, while the streaming analysis services help derive insights while presenting streams of live data in different formats like charts, graphs, etc.

- **SAP Data Hub**
  For data and storage services, SAP Data Hub is provided by SAP to solve the painful challenge of data integration in an increasingly diverse data landscape. SAP Data Hub optimizes data delivery from any source. The architecture of SAP Data Hub allows you to build data pipelines from different applications (cloud, on-premise, or hybrid) and enables orchestration processes to trigger workflows for moving

data to and from the SAP Data Hub and associated systems. A metadata repository can be built for discovery, profile, and search capabilities.

SAP Data Hub provides a universal and comprehensive view of your data from all data sources, covering end-to-end business processes and applications. While using data from enterprise applications and other applications, a self-service cockpit in the SAP Data Hub provides easy-to-use and easy-to-understand analytics. A variety of computational techniques can be performed by using SAP Leonardo intelligent technologies with SAP Data Hub to achieve the goals of an intelligent enterprise.

1.4.4 SAP Edge Services

An intelligent enterprise needs to receive information from a diverse set of physical objects, for example, a manufacturing line in a production plant, a robot in a warehouse, a truck transporting essential components, a wearable device being used by an employee at a supplier location, etc. With technical advancements in IoT and related economies of scale, a network of connected physical objects can provide data easily and cheaply. All this data is collected at the core, a central IT system used for storing, processing, and analyzing IoT data. However, in some situations, IoT devices at the edge cannot transmit the data to the core in real time for reasons such as limited or no network connectivity or the need to make real-time decisions locally, for example, at a site where safety incidents have been addressed right away. SAP Edge Services helps address such situations.

According to an IDC (International Data Corporation, a research firm) estimate, 40% of the data created by IoT is subject to edge computing, and the ratio of edge computing to core data processing is growing further with time. With the extension of the boundaries of an intelligent enterprise, given the increase need for collaboration in today's global economy, more and more IoT devices will be deployed at the edge.

As mentioned earlier, the use of edge IoT devices creates unique challenges for storing, handling, and processing information, such as the following:

- Bandwidth-constrained mobile communication link may limit capacity to transmit the information to core.
- Energy limitations for sensors of IoT could impede the data transfer to the core reliably or in the required manner.
- Internet communication breakage can occur in certain areas.

- Real-time decision requirements may not be possible where the time to send the data to the core and get the decision from the cloud is too long (e.g. a self-driving warehouse robot).

Edge processing, supported by SAP Edge Services in SAP Cloud Platform solves some of these challenges through an edge processing unit. An *edge processing unit* is a physical device, often called a *gateway*, connected to an edge IoT device (through a communication protocol such as Bluetooth, etc.) as well as to the core (through high-speed Internet). The gateway device used ranges from high-powered rack servers to smaller devices with embedded processors based on the unique requirements and business scenarios. The capability of storing, processing, and analyzing sensor data at the IoT gateway is referred to as *edge computing capability*.

Several different microservices are currently supported or planned by SAP Edge Services, as shown in Figure 1.7, which includes a representation of an IoT gateway. Device data is provided to a hardware device, which receives the data and moves the data to the core SAP Cloud Platform; this device is known as the *gateway edge*, being the entry point of the information.

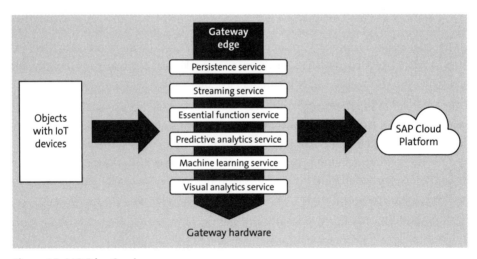

Figure 1.7 SAP Edge Service

The relevant microservices for gateway edges include the following:

- **Persistence service**
  For storing IoT data on the IoT gateway. The administrator can determine details about data relevancy, data aging, and data retention.

- **Streaming service**
  For analyzing IoT data streams. Automated events can be triggered based on patterns in the incoming data, for example, a user notification could be trigged by a threshold value.

- **Essential function service**
  Allowing essential business transactions to continue when the edge is disconnected from the core, for example, during the movement of an automated vehicle.

- **Predictive analytics service**
  Usage of predictive models for analyzing IoT data. The results can be sent to the core. The model can train itself and gets better with time.

- **Machine learning service**
  Applying machine learning algorithms for image and video analysis, the results of which are provided to the central ERP in use.

- **Visual analytics service**
  IoT data analysts can manually inspect the IoT data stored on the gateway, which provides the ability to dig into the details for the information not sent to the core based on the limitation. For example, an alert can be generated in the core based on the persistence and predictive service, the analysis of the alert can be performed through visually analyzing the detail data available in the gateway.

In summary, SAP Edge Services scale and extend cloud functionalities to the edge of the network. These services facilitate microservices at the edge with robust offline capabilities providing connectivity, insight, actions, and running business in the most efficient manner by using the IoT at the edge.

1.5   Associated Technology

The following intelligent technologies enable innovation in the intelligent enterprise. These technologies can easily be consumed in intelligent suite applications, as well as are offered on all multicloud infrastructures on SAP Cloud Platform. This approach provides SAP, SAP-developed ecosystems, and SAP partners with the flexibility and efficiency to develop and deliver solutions across standard products and customer-specific scenarios, using the following technologies:

- Big data
- Data intelligence
- Analytics

- Machine learning
- Blockchain
- Internet of Things (IoT)

The advantage that SAP provides for using these intelligent technologies are is that these capabilities are packaged, pretrained, and embedded in SAP applications; are delivered via SAP Cloud Platform to scale dynamically as managed services; and enable a modern and consistent user experience.

1.5.1 Big Data

In recent years, much research has been conducted by academic and professional institutions that show that firms who practice data-driven decisions are more successful in terms of profitability and growth when compared to organizations where leaders make decisions based only on instinct. Data-driven decisions, while based on multiple factors, essentially have one crucial element: data. Your organization probably has access to vast amounts of data generated through multiple business processes, from collaboration between entities (both internal and external), and in different business systems. This group of data in different formats, generated through different sources and transactions, is referred to as *big data*.

Big data elements, from perspective of organizational data, can be classified as structured and unstructured data.

Structured data has a defined length and format and is normally characterized by a number, date, and other defined attributes. For example, a delivery created in an ERP system against a customer sales order for a product is an example of structured data. Structured data is created by a system or a human processor. Commonly used systems like ERP, supply chain planning systems, customer relationship management systems, etc. generate an abundance of structured data daily. The advantage of working with structured data is the ease of processing and cross-referencing as provided by the inherent capability found in SAP products like SAP S/4HANA, SAP Integrated Business Planning (SAP IBP), SAP C/4HANA, etc. The cross-referencing of data through a common key allows end-to-end visibility and detailed analysis. For example, marketing campaign data from SAP C/4HANA can be used for supply chain planning, which can be further used for order execution and delivery in SAP S/4HANA. SAP Leonardo utilizes structured data from SAP and other legacy system and makes this data available for analytics.

Unstructured data does not follow a predefined format and can be in different formats like text, email, audio, video, number, etc. A vast amount of unstructured data is generated by social media networks and an organization's gateways to the customers and external entities. What makes big data complex is the presence of a vast amount of unstructured data. An analytics tool can be considered effective if, through smart solution design, the tool can access the ocean of unstructured data to find the pearls of wisdom to help the organization gain more customers, achieve higher-efficiency processes, and determine relevant product or service mixes. As with structured data, SAP Leonardo's capabilities, combined with the integration of SAP technology and ability to connect with the other systems, can glean insights from unstructured data.

In defining the characteristics of big data, Doug Laney, from Gartner, introduced the 3 Vs of big data: volume, velocity, and variety. Because of the digital transformation, the volume of the data generated multiplies every year. Capturing this huge volume of data for gaining insights and assisting the decision-making process could greatly benefit your organization. In addition to data volume, with the digitization of processes and the increase in the number and variety of points of interaction (websites, social media channels, point of sales data sharing, etc.), the velocity by which data is being generated is also growing exponentially. Finally, data in a variety of formats and types makes cross-referencing, analyzing, and processing the data difficult. To efficiently use the gains from big data, you'll need a system for collection and analytics that can process the volume, velocity, and variety of big data. SAP Leonardo comes with standard APIs for SAP Cloud Platform can help your organization effectively handle and leverage the volume, velocity, and variety of big data.

The difference between a highly successful organization and an average organization is often how they use and process data in analytical applications and in decision-making processes. Not just the quantity, but also the quality of the retrieval, collection, usage, and presentation of big data for generating insights and facilitating decision-making enhances the probability of success. Although many organizations now are collecting data at a massive scale, the actual usage of this data to derive useful information and thus draw insights is still rather limited. SAP Leonardo Big Data, along with the design thinking approach, can greatly enhance your ability to get to relevant information and the right insights. It provides both scalability and fast analytical processing power for use with big data.

Recently, many organizations have been confused regarding the handling of big data, the storage, processing, and usage of a divergent set of data coming through multiple channels. This complexity resulted in different departments working in silos with limited cross-organizational impact. For example, consider a sales team performing an analysis of a sales promotion campaign and a manufacturing team performing an analysis of plant efficiency in isolation, often accessing the same data. The disconnect between their decisions reached can result in an overall loss in revenue and efficiency across the organization. SAP Leonardo Big Data, in association with the SAP HANA Data Management Suite and SAP Cloud Platform, can help avoid such occurrences.

The data handling requirement of an organization is supported through SAP HANA Data Management Suite, which collects and integrates all the data in a secure and unified manner for operational and analytical processing. SAP Cloud Platform Big Data Services stores, processes, and analyzes information from a wide variety of sources with excellent operational performance and high computational capabilities. SAP Leonardo and SAP Cloud Platform services solve end-to-end data handling and processing requirements for an intelligent enterprise. The solution is equipped to acquire, transform, and store data from multiple sources like database systems, enterprise systems, data warehouses, Hadoop, etc. The available tools for data cleansing, transformation, and algorithm computation makes the quick journey from big data to managerial insights possible.

1.5.2   Data Intelligence

Data intelligence is the analysis of various forms of data to derive intelligence and insights for making and automating decisions. This analysis involves collecting, aggregating, and processing data to present information through analytics. The insights presented by data intelligence can be for different processes and areas like internal business processes, customers, suppliers, employees, etc. The output of data intelligence activities can be used to improve products, processes, services, customer interactions, sales, etc.

Datasets, as represented by big data to analytics, may require processing through different SAP Leonardo algorithms like clustering, segmenting, statistical modeling, etc. In addition to modeling, a large set of structured and unstructured data with the right representation on a graph can unlock tremendous business opportunities by pointing out the right analytics.

New advancements at SAP have widely influenced the areas of big data and data analytics. Easy and cheap storage of data coupled with in-memory computing allows an organization to handle unlimited amounts of data with an efficient processing methodology. Cloud computing has reduced the need for huge capital investments to make data-driven decisions.

Data analytics can help you make reliable decisions powered by insights from your data. Historical data, as well as the dynamic data generated through business processes, can be analyzed together to get the right insight for making business decisions. These data intelligence decisions can have a tremendous impact on organizational growth, especially through the following improvements:

- **New revenue channels**
  Usage of data intelligence to create new customer and revenue models to increase the top-line of your organization.

- **Efficiency**
  Usage of sophisticated machine learning models can enhance automation, leading to higher process and asset efficiency and ultimately growth in the bottom-line by reducing costs.

- **Customer interactions**
  The digital transformation and the insights achieved through business intelligence is transforming the customer experience. The impact involves both better customer experiences as well as better products, driven by your customers' requirements.

A comprehensive approach using SAP Leonardo Big Data and SAP Leonardo Data Intelligence provides the ability of thorough data analysis for customer interactions, internal business processes, logistics, supply chains, manufacturing, and market behavior through the analysis of competitors and macro-level market dynamics.

Note

Data intelligence is further discussed in detail in Chapter 6 of this book.

1.5.3   Data Analysis

Data analysis discerns hidden patterns, correlations, and insights by analyzing a large amount of data. With SAP Leonardo, dynamic insights can be generated so you can automate business decisions that had previously been totally manual or not possible. These insights are made possible by the tremendous speed and efficiency created by SAP Leonardo and its associated infrastructure.

SAP Leonardo Analytics provides across-the-board analytics capabilities that work together to analyze data from all sources. This solution uncovers issues and opportunity areas in the business, helps automate repetitive tasks, and provides insight for better and more efficient decision-making. Along with SAP Leonardo's other capabilities, SAP Leonardo Analytics can be further fortified by SAP Analytics Cloud and SAP Digital Boardroom.

SAP Analytics Cloud can access a divergent set of data and embed analytics directly into the business processes, thus enabling the conversion of insights to quick action. Equipped with data discovery, planning, and predictive analytics capabilities, SAP Analytics Cloud provides state-of-the-art visualization with role-based personalization. As a cloud application, SAP Analytics Cloud can be integrated with on-premise systems and supports mobile workforces as well as executive discussions in the boardroom.

SAP Digital Boardroom, built on SAP Analytics Cloud, connects to SAP systems and other data repository systems to monitor an organization's most important business metrics in real time. SAP Digital Boardroom makes boardroom communications and executive discussions much more efficient by providing ready-reference analytics for data-driven decisions, while providing a harmonized view of company operations across all lines of businesses that can be accessed on multiple devices.

Note

Analytics is covered in detail in Chapter 4 of this book.

1.5.4   Machine Learning

Machine learning applications incorporate capabilities for inferring knowledge through a computer program instead of basic memory-based learning. Imagine a program that could teach itself to improve its performance with time and usage is the basic essence of machine learning. Machine learning algorithms provide knowledge without being explicitly programmed to do so. Instead of just performing faster calculations with a predefined algorithm, these machines can learn to perform a task that traditionally had been limited to human intelligence or considered impossible. In traditional computing, a computer program is fed with a program and data for generating an output (e.g. calculating the total sales promotion cost and total sales in last quarter). With machine learning, a computer program is fed data and desired output to generate a program. This program can be used for prediction and output generation from another set of data (e.g. providing the previous promotion costs, sales increases, and other parameters as data to predict how much sales increase is expected in the next quarter while considering the future sales promotion budget).

A machine learning algorithm teaches itself to improve with data and iteration. The excitement around machine learning is based on two fundamental factors: First, machine learning allows machines to learn like humans, through deduction, and second, the capability and computational power of the computer allows it to perform calculations that are not possible by humans. A machine learning algorithm can discern hidden patterns in a dataset; this implicit pattern may not be identifiable to humans.

Even though these algorithms were previously known, the recent success of machine learning is based on advancements in the following areas:

- Advances in computational power and cloud computing
- Big data, the availability of tremendous amount of data
- Digital transformation
- Internet of Things (IoT), providing real-time data to algorithms
- Better algorithms through recent research and investment
- Open source flexibility allows you to use the native SAP model or bring your own custom model

Considering these factors for the success of machine learning, SAP's role, and the use of SAP Leonardo, seems obvious for machine learning applications. Enhanced with the SAP's data reach and easy APIs (application programming interfaces), vast amounts of data from SAP and other legacy systems can be made available to SAP Leonardo to process through SAP S/4HANA's inherently fast capabilities and through cloud computing.

The fuel that runs machine learning is data. A machine learning algorithm utilizes the available set of data as the training dataset. Based on the training data, the algorithm makes inferences about the process, and these inferences are used to make predictions about real data, also known as test or production data. A larger and richer dataset enhances the accuracy of the machine learning program's result. SAP Leonardo Machine Learning Foundation can work with both structured data (data as numbers and values, like sales, price, binary yes/no, etc.) and unstructured data (for example, a text in a tweet) to analyze for problem-solving.

Machine learning, empowered by the big data available to an organization, has its most widely used application in artificial intelligence. SAP Leonardo Machine Learning Foundation provides the technology for recognizing patterns and correlations in data. Consider the case of automatic fraud detection by a credit card company, or an oil company successfully predicting parts failure so worker's attention can be directed at the right time, or a consumer goods organization running a successful customer promotion plan. These business scenarios can be managed and automated by machine learning applications.

A machine learning algorithm can be categorized as supervised or unsupervised learning. In supervised learning, a data label is included with the data provided to the algorithms; in unsupervised learning, the data is provided without any labels. Consider a manufacturing organization's production line: Different images of the output product can be provided to the machine learning system with labels or categories to separate defective and nondefective products. Then, in the real time, the manufactured product's image can be provided to the algorithm as test data; the system sends a notification as soon as a faulty product is identified based on the learning it achieved through the training data.

In another case, a product's physical dimensions can be measured on the production line is provided to the machine learning algorithm as training data without any label. The algorithm can perform an analysis and, in the production environment, can flag a defective product in real time on the manufacturing line. The selection of either supervised and unsupervised learning is performed based on the business scenario, solution design, and availability of labeled training data. One variation of unsupervised learning is called *reinforcement learning*, which uses a reward/penalty system to train an algorithm based on the action taken by it. This kind of learning mimics the typical learning process of a child or a dog, who is trained for good behavior through rewards and penalties. The algorithms used in self-driving cars or in computer games are examples of reinforcement learning.

An effective machine learning algorithm can maximize the signal to noise ratio, thus enabling decision-making derived from both structured and unstructured data. This decision-making can be performed by a human or may involve machine learning integration with artificial intelligence in SAP Leonardo. SAP Leonardo provides various state-of-the-art machine learning algorithms with more than 90 native algorithms, as well as extension capabilities through open source R integration. SAP Leonardo, along with SAP applications and a robust technology stack based on SAP Cloud Platform allow you to create, run, and maintain intelligent applications on a common infrastructure, all in one place. The massive amount of data processed by SAP Leonardo in real time can reveal trends and patterns for making your business more efficient.

SAP Leonardo equips business users with the ability to run machine learning algorithms like a data scientist without having to write any code. Embedded into enterprise systems, machine learning lets you automate repetitive tasks and realize efficiency by unlocking new ways to perform the same tasks. With time, more innovative applications of machine learning algorithms are being discovered by businesses, including the following applications:

- Automating repetitive tasks through intelligent business processes (e.g. invoice matching, transaction execution, resume sorting)
- Digital representation and control of physical infrastructure, collecting data in real time and using machine learning algorithms to identify unusual activity
- Digital assistants and robots working on self-learning algorithms
- Pattern recognition to identify anomalies for business transactions like credit card fraud detection and unwanted deviations on the shop floor
- Clustering of customers, suppliers, employees, etc. to determine the right actions aimed at efficiency and effectiveness
- Manufacturing quality control by recording video and comparing images of the parts produced with the example correct and defective parts
- Image-based procurement, which means using an image to identify the right product from a catalog containing thousands of possible products
- Factory and site inspection using drones and image matching

In summary, machine learning is the crux of digital transformation and artificial intelligence. This topic is further illustrated in detail in Chapter 5 of this book.

1.5.5   Blockchain

A *blockchain* is a trusted ecosystem of shared data based on distributed ledger technology where secured information is recorded in a peer to peer network. Though blockchain was initially used for financial transactions as the underlying technology behind Bitcoin, many possible business applications may fundamentally change the way business is conducted. Blockchains can be applied for supply chain visibility, track and trace, customer relations, property titles, identities, logistics applications, supplier and spend management, etc.

The key differentiator of blockchain technology is the data ledger, which is shared across the network with trust guaranteed by the technology, without a central mediator. A distributed ledger of blockchain is a transaction database shared and synchronized across a network of computers in which each party owns an identical copy of the entire record, which is automatically updated as soon as approved additions are made. These additions occur through the consensus achieved by the underlying technology without the involvement of a mediator. For example, in a traditional money transfer process, say from a supplier to a customer, multiple third-party regulators like banks and other bodies may be involved. The same transaction in a blockchain environment can be performed in real time and without any cost or involvement by third-party mediators. Consider the potential applications of smart contract management of supplier and customers with end-to-end visibility of contract, order, delivery, and payment.

A blockchain is the chain of the individual data elements called *blocks*, connected through a fingerprint of digital data, called a *hash*. In the chain, only the last block can be added or modified through a combination of private and public keys controlled through hash values. Consensus is achieved through the distributed ledger across a multitude of computers. This property makes blockchains tamper-proof, facilitating various business applications. Consider an example in the food industry: Through blockchain technology, a chicken can be tracked from when it was just an egg, to the farm where it was raised, through the network as the chicken moves through the store before landing in a customer's basket.

In multiparty business process, blockchain is a new way of conducting business. Figure 1.8 shows an example of a consortium blockchain in which a consensus process is controlled by a preselected group of organizations and partner entities. This type of blockchain is called a *permissioned blockchain* and is most widely used in business contexts. Other examples of blockchains include public blockchains, private blockchains, and semi-private blockchains. In a *public blockchain*, anyone can read or send transactions and participate in the consensus process. Bitcoin (cryptocurrency) is an example of public blockchain.

A *private blockchain* is controlled by a single organization. Due to the limited control, private blockchains are mostly used for system building and proof of concept (POC) and not real-world business usage. A *semi-private blockchain* can be run by a single company that grants access to users, for example, a pharmaceutical company granting access to the consumer for information about the medicine or a buyer-seller relationship. As mentioned earlier and as shown in Figure 1.8, a consortium blockchain provides access to a group of corporations for a consensus process. The right to read and submit transactions can be predetermined and based on the role of the entity, which can be extended to individual end users too.

In essence, the basic elements of trusted ledgers have sparked a great deal of excitement in businesses because of the transparency and auditability provided by the blockchain technology. Multiparty collaboration in a secure environment adds value and efficiency in business transactions related to purchase, logistics, and customer service. Blockchain can also automate transactions based on predefined rules provided to the chain, using smart contracts, and can execute transactions based on validation performed by the chain.

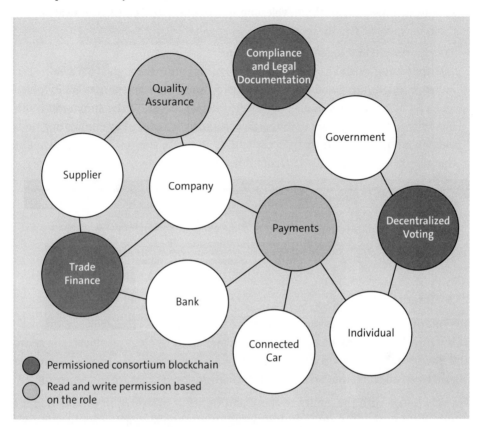

Figure 1.8 Distributed Ledger through Blockchain Technology

SAP is actively working augmenting various products for blockchain. Some examples include the following:

- **SAP Global Track and Trace**
  Allows real-time visibility of goods moving along the entire supply chain along with the storage condition of the goods. Augmented for blockchain, SAP Global Track and Trace can provide real-time visibility into storage and handling conditions, can detect counterfeit products, and can automatically trigger actions when required.

- **SAP Advanced Track and Trace for Pharmaceuticals**
  Augmented for blockchain, this feature can secure supply chains and instantly check the authenticity of a drug. This feature can help improve patient safety by preventing counterfeit drugs from entering into the supply chain, thus helping save lives, especially in the developing world where the pharmaceutical supply chain may not be strictly controlled.

- **Transportation and logistics management**
  Transportation visibility and process automation through blockchain can enhance freight, fleet, and logistics efficiency where multiple parties are involved and a lot of documents change hands, especially in cross-border shipments. With blockchain, efficiency can be gained, and costs can be reduced by eliminating middlemen who slow down the process and by facilitate the resolution of disputes that may result from a mismatch of information.

> **Note**
>
> Further details about and applications of blockchain technology are discussed in Chapter 7 of this book.

1.5.6   Internet of Things

The Internet of Things (IoT) involves physical devices connected over the Internet. This network of physical objects features embedded technology so objects can sense and interact with the environment and each other. A sensor on a transmission pipe owned by an oil company can provide information about pressure and temperature.

Physical things with the ability to sense and transmit information can be used for multitude of consumer and industrial applications. Applications of IoT have grown tremendously, supported by the low-cost availability of IoT devices.

> **Note**
>
> Gartner predicts that 20 billion things will be connected to Internet by 2020. According to research conducted by IDC, 30 billion things will be connected generating revenue of around $1.7 trillion for the ecosystem. One thing the experts do agree in is that this area is witnessing amazing growth. This growth potential can be seen by another projection expecting 1 trillion sensors by the year 2030.

Physical objects connected through a network and identified as IoT can transmit information without human intervention and must have the following eight design features:

- Sensors
- Internet connectivity
- Processors
- Energy efficiency
- Cost effectiveness
- Quality
- Reliability
- Security

With great strides in technological advancements, IoT technology has become more mature and efficient, while costs are also going down, from several dollars for a sensor to a few cents. With cheap availability of Internet connections across the globe, we're entering the golden period for the IoT devices!

More and more objects are being connected, interacting with each other for a better and more efficient world. In 2012, only 10% of new cars were connected to the Internet; connected cars are expected to represent 90% of new cars sold after 2020. Other than cost, processing speed is another important factor in the adoption of IoT. When you combine connected things with the sophistication and speed of SAP's platforms, SAP Leonardo offers excellent advantages, making IoT adoption a successful part of your digital transformation journey. SAP has been recognized as a visionary in this area with adoption examples in different industries ranging from agriculture to manufacturing, to retail to life sciences, etc.

Some examples where IoT applications have been enabled with SAP Leonardo include the following:

- **Smart irrigation**
  In a smart irrigation system, IoT devices that sense and transmit humidity data and data about other atmospheric conditions can connect to a central SAP system and guide real-time irrigation, thus enabling efficient water usage, better labor productivity, and higher yield.

- **Smart monitoring**
  Another example of a smart monitoring system can be found at an oil refinery, where an IoT device could sense and transmit pressure and temperature information to the central system. This IoT-enabled system can be represented through a digital twin, so that an operator can access the assets in real time through a handheld digital device. Any unwanted change in pressure or temperature is reported immediately to the operator, enabling him or her to take the right action at the right time.

- **Connected vehicles**
  Connected vehicles using IoT, SAP Cloud Platform, and SAP systems can automate fleet movements and material movements through connected robots and shop floor vehicles, which increases efficiency by reducing human error.

- **Smart home**
  Smart home solutions are based on the concept of connected home appliances through IoT interacting with each other to make decisions as required. Current in-progress applications include adjusting the temperature of the house based on a smart thermostat's ability to identify the presence of residents. Another concept is automated inventory control, for example, of food items (milk, bread, etc.) through the ability to check the inventory in the refrigerator and order products online for replenishment.

- **Drinking water monitor**
  IoT applications for drinking water warning systems are based on the noble concept of enhancing quality of life. A small sensor connected to the water monitoring system can sense and transmit, for example, the acidity of the water. Action can be taken immediately when acidity falls outside a specified, acceptable range.

- **Warning systems**
  For warning systems, an IoT device can be used to monitor and transmit data points that help predict natural disasters like earthquakes, tsunamis, etc. SAP Leonardo has been successfully used in the smart city projects in which authorities receive real-time information on disaster signals, providing ample time to act.

The combination of SAP Leonardo Internet of Things (SAP Leonardo IoT); SAP Cloud Platform; computing algorithms; and integrated systems of logistics, supply chain, warehouse, customer service, and transportation enable connecting assets, processes, and people through a digital core. The information captured can be used for analytics to identify patterns, outliers, etc. to automate decision-making.

Figure 1.9 shows the SAP Leonardo IoT Bridge, representing a connected organization and society with different parts such as the following:

- Connected products
- Connected assets
- Connected fleet
- Connected infrastructure
- Connected markets
- Connected people

SAP Leonardo IoT Bridge is supported by IoT business services and IoT technical services and is enabled by SAP Edge Services and device adapters.

Note

These topics, along with further details about IoT, is covered in Chapter 8.

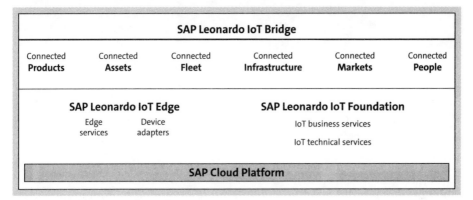

Figure 1.9 SAP Leonardo IoT Bridge Example

Figure 1.10 shows an example of IoT usage by a power company. With the help of IoT devices, information about a physical transformation can be available on a digital device, for example, live temperature, current, and voltage.

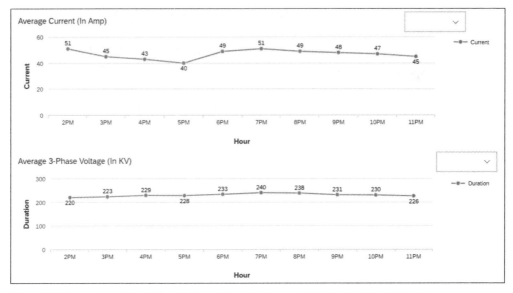

Figure 1.10 Example of Real-Time Information Capture and Display by the IoT Device

The information is provided for analytics through SAP Cloud Platform. Figure 1.11 shows analytics based on detailed information in an easily interpretable format. Any unwanted move is detected in real time and can be responded to, which results in reducing unwanted breakage, longer lifetimes, and better customer service.

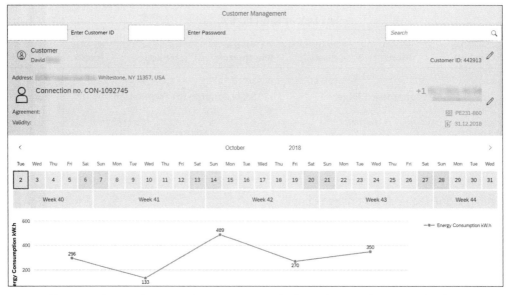

Figure 1.11 Energy Consumption Usage Example through IoT and Associated Infrastructure

Figure 1.12 and Figure 1.13 show a customer's energy usage, billed by the utility company, as generated by using the IoT device, related cloud infrastructure, and SAP Leonardo. With this detailed reference information, a customer can take actions to optimize energy usage, and the utility company can serve its customers in the most effective and optimized manner.

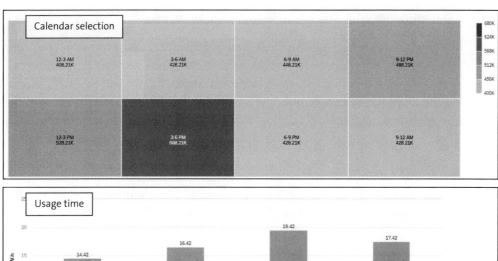

Figure 1.12 Analytics of Energy Usage by SAP Leonardo for Optimizing Use and Cost

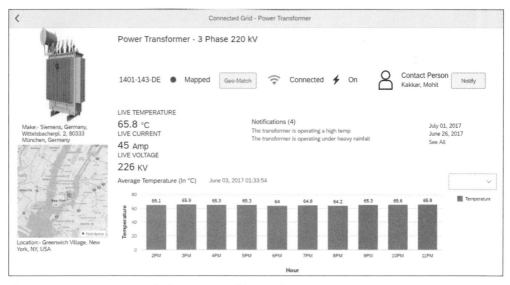

Figure 1.13 IoT Device Example for a Power Grid Transformer

1.6   Summary

SAP Leonardo's intelligent technologies can help your company transform business processes, deliver new products and services while collaborating with business partners, and create new business models through digital innovation. By taking a user-centric, design thinking approach, SAP Leonardo helps drive innovation on a scalable and open cloud platform. You can rapidly build applications using microservices and open APIs via SAP Cloud Platform, an open and extensible PaaS. With a powerful data management suite to process high-volume, high-velocity data feeds in real time using in-memory data management and integration technology and support for a multi-cloud infrastructure, your organization can outpace the competition while addressing your customers' needs with a highly engaged and productive workforce.

Chapter 2
Digital Transformation: Ecosystem and Approach

Successful digital transformation requires a collaborative ecosystem of people, processes, and objects. This chapter explores how you can achieve digital innovation by enabling intelligent connections throughout your organization.

Connected people and organizational collaboration are the keys to creating an intelligent enterprise with connected processes and connected data. We'll delve in detail into the expectations for the intelligent enterprise while sharing some examples of SAP Leonardo tools and associated products from SAP. The concepts explored in this chapter will be further detailed in Part III of this book where you'll learn how SAP Leonardo can be used to innovate in specific lines of business (LOBs). We'll delve in detail into intelligently connected people, things, and processes, as well as the use of the design thinking approach in this chapter.

Note that realizing an intelligent enterprise may require other SAP products in addition of SAP Leonardo products. For example, SAP Jam can be used for the enterprise collaboration, SAP Integrated Business Planning (SAP IBP) for supply planning, and SAP Ariba for procurement, while multiple other technologies could have logical connections with SAP Leonardo.

2.1 Intelligently Connected People

The digital transformation is here to stay as today we're more connected than ever before. The Internet has spread across the globe, technology touches almost every aspect of life, sensors have become economical, and power consumption and computing power have become cheaper. As a result, every "thing," ranging from factory equipment to the lightbulbs in your house, can now be connected and can share data.

That being said, in today's digital era, SAP strives to improve people's lives, work, and health by connecting people and communities and providing better lifestyle experiences and opportunities for organizations to evolve with new business models. SAP Leonardo intelligently connects things with people and processes across company boundaries, through business network solutions to enable unparalleled collaboration and improved productivity. Companies can connect to their ecosystems to increase engagement and collaboration, improve transparency, and create more value for their customers.

> **Note**
>
> As we look at specific industries, some areas where the concept of "connected people" can provide benefits include the following:
>
> - Help workers stay safe, linking them to their environment in real time and promoting safe practices and risk avoidance. Enable enhanced ways to collect and process real-time data to gain insights to increase safety and overall operational integrity when executing in the field. Use these insights to modify processes, fix bottlenecks, reduce downtimes, and collaborate with business partners to run better and safer.
> - Build a connected health network that breaks down existing silos to enable a network with the patient in the center to improve patient outcomes and lower healthcare costs.
> - Help patients realize better health outcomes with personalized healthcare options. Give healthcare providers access to a comprehensive and longitudinal patient dataset with personalized decision support.
> - Connect energy and security systems, along with smart appliances, to make home life more comfortable, efficient, and secure.
> - Leverage intelligence from a connected home so insurers can create other value-added services. Make customers' lives easier with real-time personalized products based on detailed information about usage behaviors and offer new services.

SAP Leonardo's capabilities support new networked business models, such as product-as-a-service offerings and value-added services. This approach involves the collaborative resolution of business and operational issues by connecting the right people with the right training and supplies at the right time and place to solve problems safely and reliably. For efficient usage of the technology, collaboration and easy-to-use interfaces are key, as we'll see in the following sections.

2.1.1   Collaboration

A digital workplace can be considered as a holistic set of workplace tools, platforms, and environments, delivered in a coherent, usable, and productive way. You can also consider a digital workplace as a place that empowers individuals, teams, colleagues, clients, and partners to share, communicate, and collaborate, which allows all stakeholders to perform their jobs more effectively. By collaborating with others, different departments or even different offices and skills can be pooled to make a project more successful. A collaborative workplace naturally cultivates a sense of community within an organization, with employees feeling almost like they're a part of a family. This connection compels employees to go beyond the expectations of their roles, absorbing as much organizational knowledge as possible and driving the business forward with informed and sound decisions.

Different forms of collaboration can be distinguished, depending on the parties involved. Figure 2.1 shows the distinction between internal, external, vertical, and horizontal collaboration. Internal collaboration occurs between departments or functions within an organization, while external collaboration occurs across the company boundaries, between independent organizations.

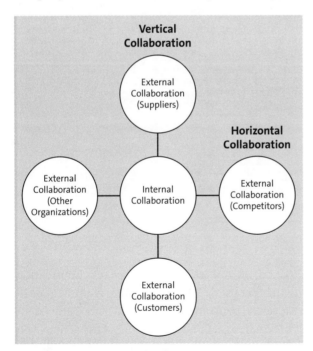

Figure 2.1 Types of Collaboration

Vertical collaboration refers to external collaboration with customers or suppliers, while horizontal collaboration could occur with other organizations such as R&D partners, competitors, or nonprofit organizations. A great deal of the research in supply chain management has focused on vertical collaboration, most likely given the focus on managing the forward and reverse flows of goods and information from suppliers to the final customer.

The SAP solution portfolio features robust capabilities to support inter- and intra-organizational collaboration. The core solution for collaboration is SAP Jam, which is an enterprise-level social media application that facilitates collaboration across user groups in an organization. Figure 2.2 shows an example of an SAP Jam collaboration page. Various boxes and information feeds on the user's homepage will appear based on the groups a user has been associated with. On the same page, information about open tasks and other notifications can be accessed through the application's buttons.

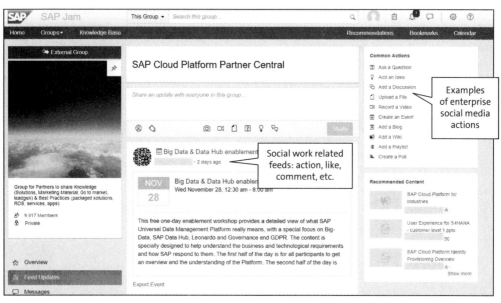

Figure 2.2 Collaboration and Enterprise Social Media Action in SAP Jam's External Group

Activities in the group, such as task updates and assignments, appear as information feeds. Users can share an update with other users, "like" an update, or comment on it. Multiple other work-related actions can be performed through SAP Jam. On the right side of Figure 2.2, you'll see a list of common action items. Some of the actions you can take include the following:

- Start a discussion
- Ask a question
- Create a poll to make decisions based on user votes
- Upload a file for sharing information with the closed group
- Add a task and assign it to a person for follow-up action
- Add a wiki/blog/discussion
- Invite a new team member to join the group

Task collaboration and management can be performed through the SAP Jam homepage by accessing the **My Tasks** and **Assigned to Other** options, as shown in Figure 2.3. An existing task can be modified, or a new task can be added and assigned. These activities are performed through intuitive buttons (e.g. a pencil icon for editing, dropdown options for changing statuses, etc.), as shown in Figure 2.3.

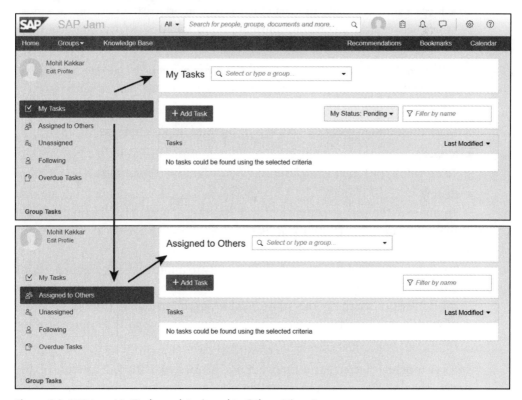

Figure 2.3 SAP Jam My Tasks and Assigned to Others View Page

2.1.2   User Interfaces

User experience (UX) is about the overall experience that a person has when using a product, whether a website or an application, whether on a mobile device or a desktop. For these applications, being easy to use and understand is of utmost importance. SAP considers this requirement in all their products, systems, and services. For SAP, the user experience must be as simple as possible so that the users can achieve their goals as easily as possible when interacting with the business application.

In our many years of experience, we have learned that the adoption of a technology is directly related to its ease of use. For a connected organization, a connected workforce is required, and for a connected workforce, supporting the connection between a user and the work should involve a simple and efficient user interface. With the SAP's recent focus on design thinking, SAP Leonardo-supported solutions should aim for an efficient and pleasant user interface.

To achieve a simple, easy-to-use, yet efficient user interface, the right balance must be struck between the technology, business needs, and desirability. To quote from SAP's user experience strategy:

> *Following these design principles, SAP will make superior user experience and design an integral part of the brand experience, just as the SAP platform has reconfirmed our reputation for innovation.*

To reach these design goals, SAP is focusing on three important areas:

- **New**
  To provide a consumer-grade user experience for new applications.

- **Renew**
  To improve the user experience of your existing applications, starting with the most commonly used business scenarios.

- **Enable**
  To enable customers by giving them the ability to improve the user experience of SAP software in ways that allow them to decide which business scenarios are most mission-critical for them. This strategy is further complemented by SAP's offering of specific user experience design services that aim to support customers in their future user experience endeavors.

SAP's view of how to create true innovation is manifested in the SAP Fiori user experience. The SAP Fiori concept and design principles are key components in SAP's design-led development process, which ensures the delivery of SAP Fiori innovation through all SAP products. The SAP Fiori user experience enhances cloud development and deployment in the cloud. Also, the SAP Build tool allows project teams collaboratively develop prototypes, engage end users for feedback, and jumpstart designs using one of the many prototype examples available in the gallery.

You can get references from SAP Fiori app recommendations analysis in the SAP Fiori apps reference library, shown in Figure 2.4, and identify the SAP Fiori apps that best fit your needs. The tool makes recommendations based on an app's relevance and readiness. Relevance describes SAP Fiori apps that are relevant for you based on the business processes you use, and readiness describes how ready your system is to use SAP Fiori apps. The analysis provides the following information:

- SAP Fiori apps that are relevant for the business processes you use
- SAP Fiori apps that are already installed and can be used without a system update
- SAP Fiori apps that can be used assuming a software update or database migration
- Installations required to use certain SAP Fiori apps

A prerequisite for using any of these apps is that the user must have an SAP ID (S-user).

With design thinking and the SAP Fiori app strategy, the focus of design has shifted from a functional scope approach to a user experience approach. You'll begin with a list of personas for whom you are designing and then design the logical groupings and arrangements for the tiles as needed, by persona.

You'll need to consider the following questions:

- Which tiles are used most often?
- Which tiles should be available by searching but not always be displayed on the screen?
- Which apps you should have links displayed, but don't necessarily need tiles?
- What do you want the user to see when they first log on?
- What are the important key performance indicators (KPIs) this user should be aware of?
- What key information can you show on tiles to your users to prioritize work and drive their behaviors?

Designing and finalizing SAP Fiori apps is an art as well as a science. Simple user experience considerations can highly enhance system usage and adoption. Tiles can add the most value when they contain dynamic content such is KPI data and micro charts. Figure 2.5 shows an example of the **Purchasing Analytics** group of apps in SAP S/4HANA. A terrible design decision would be hiding these tiles under the **Reporting** group, which would require users navigate to. Instead, the key information should be front and center, easily accessible with one click.

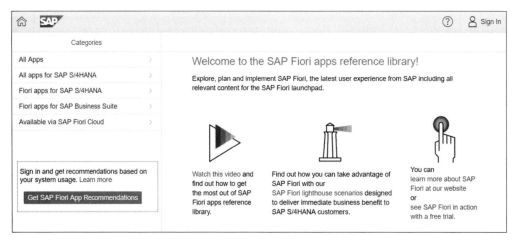

Figure 2.4 SAP Fiori Apps Reference Library Page

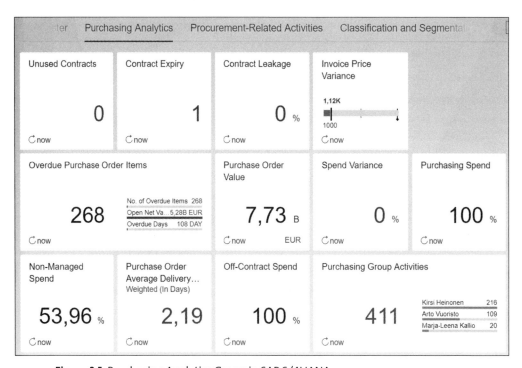

Figure 2.5 Purchasing Analytics Group in SAP S/4HANA

Plenty of SAP analytics tiles contain this type of content, and many more don't. Careful considerations must be made when designing tiles. Consider the **Production Engineering** tab in SAP S/4HANA, shown in Figure 2.6, where most of the 22 tiles have the same icon, which renders the icon useless as the user doesn't receive any specific visual information or detail. Simply by putting tiles in a group falls short of delivering the transformational user experience enabled by SAP Fiori.

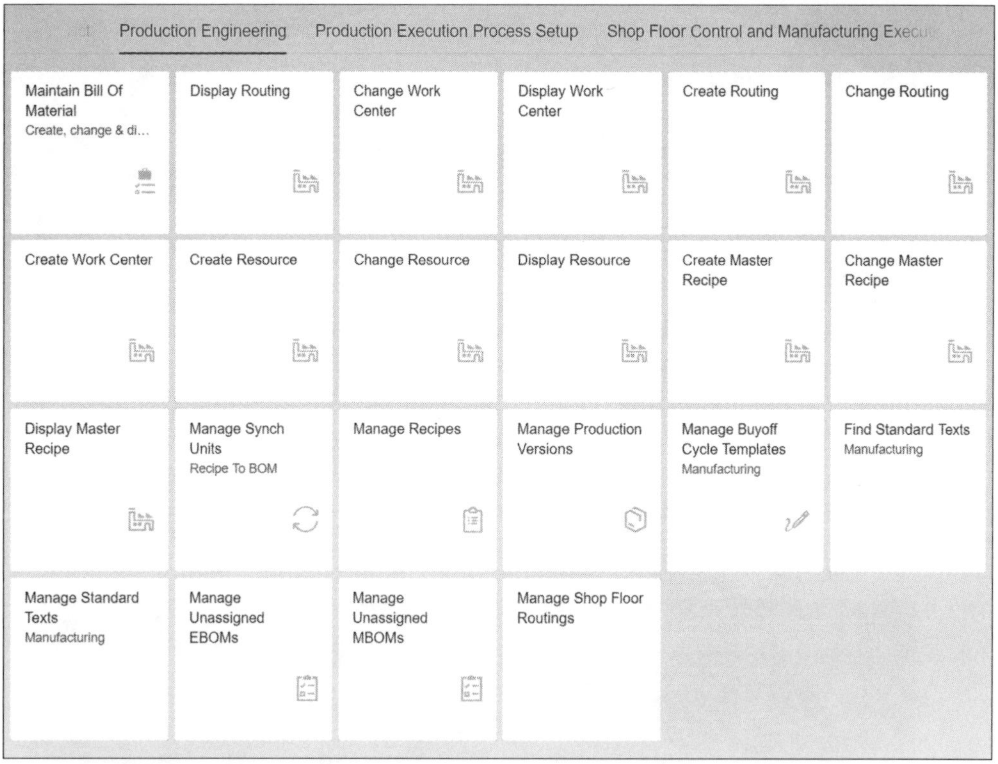

Production Engineering	Production Execution Process Setup		Shop Floor Control and Manufacturing Execu

Maintain Bill Of Material Create, change & di...	Display Routing	Change Work Center	Display Work Center	Create Routing	Change Routing
Create Work Center	Create Resource	Change Resource	Display Resource	Create Master Recipe	Change Master Recipe
Display Master Recipe	Manage Synch Units Recipe To BOM	Manage Recipes	Manage Production Versions	Manage Buyoff Cycle Templates Manufacturing	Find Standard Texts Manufacturing
Manage Standard Texts Manufacturing	Manage Unassigned EBOMs	Manage Unassigned MBOMs	Manage Shop Floor Routings		

Figure 2.6 Production Engineering Group in SAP S/4HANA

Building dynamic tiles and custom tiles can dramatically improve the launchpad's design and enhance user experience and productivity. An enhancement might be as simple as adding an image instead of an icon to bring the launchpad to life, or you might consider displaying dynamic values through KPIs and micro charts. Figure 2.7 shows a few examples.

Some tiles lend themselves easily to the addition of micro charts, as shown in Figure 2.8.

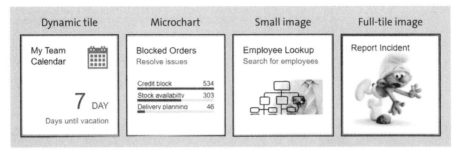

Figure 2.7 Custom SAP Fiori App Tiles

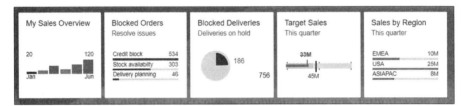

Figure 2.8 Standard SAP Fiori App Tiles with Micro Charts

When no useful chart or KPI makes sense to show, you can get creative with images, as shown in Figure 2.9. This screen displays the same **Production Engineering** group as earlier, but now with tile images and links. Now the user interface comes to life, and the application may even be fun to use.

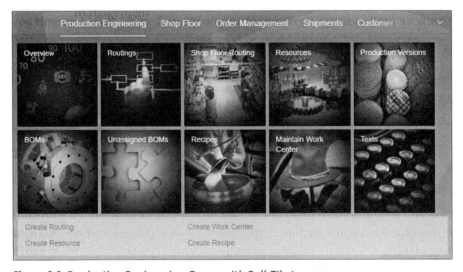

Figure 2.9 Production Engineering Group with Full-Tile Images

Building custom tiles and apps, although time consuming, can be very powerful. Figure 2.10 and Figure 2.11 show two examples, one for a mobile app and the other for a desktop version.

Figure 2.10 Custom Mobile SAP Fiori App

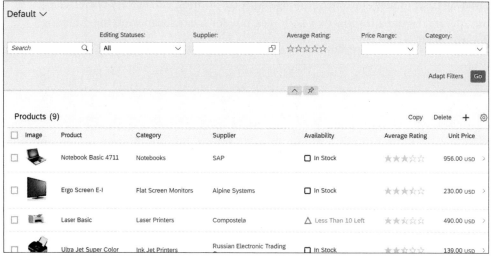

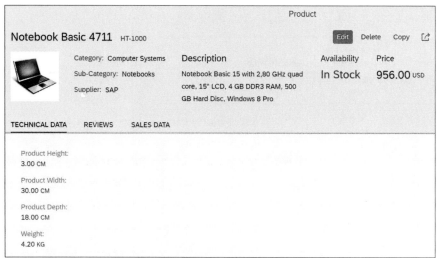

Figure 2.11 Custom Desktop View of an SAP Fiori App

To design such powerful and intuitive apps, we'll learn more about design thinking in Section 2.4.

2.1.3   Real-Time Analytics

SAP Analytics Cloud provides a unified experience for decision-making that allows users to discover, visualize, plan, and predict, all in one product. Everyone in your organization, whether in front of a customer or in the boardroom, needs the power to find new insights and act upon them.

The vision of an intelligently connected enterprise can't be achieved without intelligently connected people in the organization and related environmental infrastructure; more importantly, intelligently connected people must be connected through sharing of real-time data and information. This information sharing should be easy to understand through personalization of analytics with respect to the role and work of an individual in the firm.

The features of SAP Analytics Cloud are as follows:

- Discover, visualize, plan, and predict in one product versus separate point solutions
- Answer all your business questions whether you're in the boardroom or in front of the customer
- Access all data—big and small—to uncover new insights that enrich your analytics
- Experience a better way to analyze data that is designed around people, not engineering
- Anticipate and respond to new business challenges and opportunities without delay
- Navigate workflows seamlessly to find insights at the point of decision and to act in real time
- Trust your data is safe with the world's largest provider of analytics and enterprise applications
- Meet your specific business needs with application extensions that leverage an industry-standard cloud platform

For real-time analytics, SAP Digital Boardroom has received a lot of market traction with positive acceptance. SAP Digital Boardroom is a dynamic real-time presentation tool, enabling executives to find insights and address ad-hoc questions. While SAP Analytics Cloud has its own presentation capabilities, SAP Digital Boardroom offers a few enhanced features.

SAP Digital Boardroom uses line of business (LOB) data from SAP S/4HANA to provide executives with total transparency into the business in real time, thus providing instant data-driven insights and simplifying boardroom processes. SAP Digital Boardroom comes with powerful analytical capabilities and an intuitive user interface that can make full use of touchscreen displays. Your organization's top decision-makers can explore predefined metrics more quickly and easily—down to the line item level if needed—to fully understand business performance and address questions as they arise. Additionally, decision-makers can confidently analyze root causes, identify business challenges and opportunities, and simulate the impact of decisions while in a meeting, rather than having to defer decisions to collect more information.

The following list summarizes the functionality that SAP Digital Boardroom provides:

- Answer ad-hoc questions on the fly with powerful analytics and a simple, intuitive user interface
- Simulate the impact of finance and operations decisions and make decisions with confidence
- Uncover hidden insights and make better decisions faster with smart assistance features
- Use ad-hoc and what-if analysis to explore alternative courses of action and compare the impact of potential decisions
- Gain an understanding of the drivers and relationships in planning and simulation models
- Assess the sensitivity of information quickly and accurately
- Speed time-to-value with predefined queries, data models, visualizations, and best practices
- Use proven frameworks for corporate performance management
- Integrate seamlessly with SAP S/4HANA and SAP BW/4HANA as well as SAP SuccessFactors, SAP C/4HANA, SAP Ariba, and SAP Concur

A few example cases of the SAP Digital Boardroom, a corporate finance overview and a travel and expense overview, are shown in Figure 2.12 and Figure 2.13. We recommend that you to design and build with SAP Digital Boardroom while using SAP Leonardo's capabilities and considering the relevant performance parameters pertinent to your organization's processes.

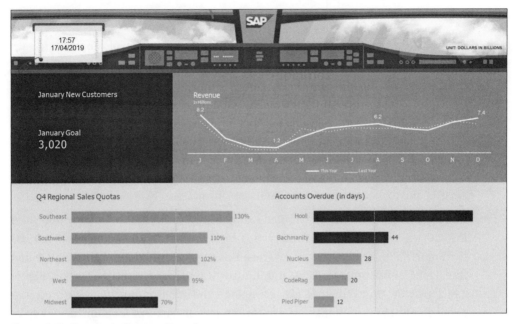

Figure 2.12 Corporate Finance Overview

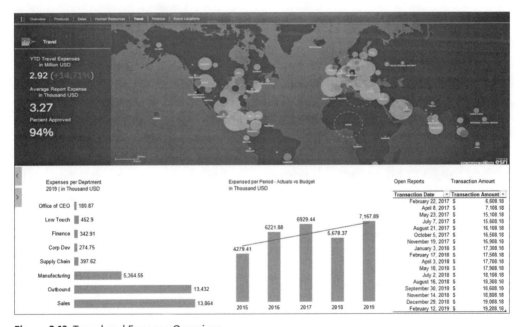

Figure 2.13 Travel and Expense Overview

2.2 Intelligently Connected Things

The massive number of connected devices ("things") and the explosion of data generated are changing the way we do business. SAP Leonardo is a solution portfolio that enables you to not only realize the digital transformation of existing end-to-end business processes, but also evolve new business models to run digitally. The Internet of Things (IoT) is on the top of the agenda for many companies. While the technology has existed for several decades, its use was limited. The evolution of network connectivity, big data management, analytics, and cloud technology now enables the convergence of operational and information technologies to make machines smarter and to drive end-to-end digital transformation.

Initially, IoT applications were limited to operational activities on the shop floor, and IoT data was not leveraged for enterprise use. With the evolution of Industry 4.0 and the industrial Internet, you can leverage this big data and develop responsive and intelligent applications for LOB- and industry-specific end-to-end processes. Figure 2.14 shows the SAP Leonardo IoT technology and solution portfolio. We'll go into detail about these solutions in the following sections (except for connected people, which was discussed in the previous section).

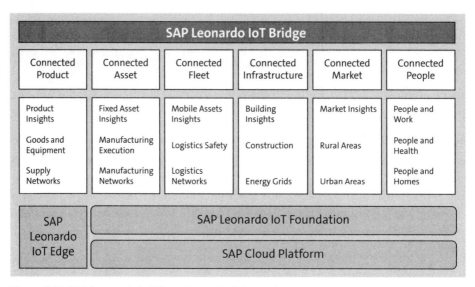

Figure 2.14 SAP Leonardo IoT for a Connected Ecosystem

2.2.1   Connected Products

Connected products enable end-to-end visibility for product-centric operations and provide the ability to optimize compliance, visibility, and service availability. As the demand for information and insight increases, we'll see a significant increase in the design, manufacturing, and delivery of smart, connected products across all industries. R&D can utilize data from sensors, connected products, and other big data sources to support the development of more reliable and desirable products that meet the target requirements, which will lead to increased demand and opportunities in the market and increased access to information for everybody. Some usage examples of connected products and associated values include the following:

- **Goods and equipment**
  - Connect, monitor, and control many customer-facing products.
  - Connect smart devices and products with core business processes and backend systems.

- **Product insights**
  - Design, manufacture, and distribute smart products to leverage sensor data from manufacturers and consumers.
  - Streamline and orchestrate design networks with intuitive design and collaboration tools to enhance product and project delivery. Manage internal and external development teams, capture their ideas, and reuse product and project data throughout your enterprise.
  - Increase efficiency in engineering and manufacturing with a single platform for design tool integration to provide a 360-degree product view (with total transparency across engineering disciplines) through a harmonized and intuitive user experience.

- **Supply networks**
  - Manage, control, and respond to changing conditions with a digital operations center for response.
  - Reduce planning cycle times and inventory levels and increase service quality by extending the supply chain to the business network.
  - Connect more easily with suppliers, customers, and outsourced manufacturers for enhanced collaboration across demand, supply, and inventory.
  - Optimize service and cost through collaborative planning of inventory, supply, and demand, while establishing a collaborative network with B2B connectivity for efficient supply chain collaboration.

2.2.2   Connected Assets

Connected assets enable the tracking, monitoring, analyzing, and maintaining of all fixed assets across a network. Connecting production systems and assets with manufacturing and maintenance business processes helps reduce operational and maintenance costs and increases asset uptime. Some usage examples of connected assets and associated values include the following:

- **Fixed asset insights**
  - Optimize asset performance throughout the entire lifecycle and build an app for asset network collaboration for better service and maintenance processes.
  - Move from a reactive to a proactive approach to maintenance by utilizing fixed asset insights for an end-to-end solution for predictive maintenance and service, from identification of emerging issues to procuring spare parts, scheduling, and executing maintenance.
  - Through an integrated asset network to collaborate between manufacturers, service providers, and end customers, serve assets that are both owned and operated as well as assets that are installed at customer sites and are covered by service contracts.

- **Manufacturing execution**
  - Connect, monitor, and tightly control manufacturing processes and operations by integrating business and manufacturing systems to enable lean, high-quality production on the shop floor.
  - Leverage manufacturing execution and industrial IoT to optimize manufacturing processes and have real-time visibility and transparency across multiple plants, vendors, and machine types and take real-time action to optimize efficiency.
  - Connect supply chain networks to manufacturing processes and operations while lowering total manufacturing costs via scalable, flexible, and cost-effective deployment options.

- **Manufacturing networks**
  - Efficiently address customer demands by connecting supply chain solutions with 3D printing/IoT capabilities, machine learning, and real-time operations insights through a global manufacturing network.
  - Identify and resolve any issues across the extended supply chain to increase fulfillment of delivery commitments, manage changes to existing and new product introductions, and share process improvement ideas across the enterprise.

2.2.3   Connected Fleet

A connected fleet enables the tracking, monitoring, analyzing, and maintaining of all moving assets, wherever they're located in the network. Businesses and public service organizations owning fleets of moving assets, for example, vehicles, robots, and forklifts can collect live telemetry and sensor data and integrate this information with the core business processes to improve services for and the safety of their operators, improve visibility to logistics, and provide better services to end customers. A connected fleet enables the creation of new business models and opportunities to reduce costs by leveraging IoT. Some usage examples of connected fleets and associated values include the following:

- **Mobile asset insights**
  - Collect, map, store, and analyze fleet/vehicle sensor data in real time.
  - Improve operational efficiencies by collecting, mapping, storing, and analyzing vehicle and sensor data in real time. The integration of telematics, enterprise, and customer data helps improve services and execution of the ordering process as well as the collection of goods and delivery processes. It creates the opportunity to optimize processes and create value through new business opportunities.

- **Logistics safety**
  - Perform comprehensive safety analysis of people and assets to reduce accidents and improve safety records.
  - Improve the end-to-end logistics safety record through analysis of vehicle conditions, environmental aspects, drivers' physical health, and driving behavior.
  - Manage the handling of hazardous goods through the integration to the environment, health, and safety solutions.

- **Logistics networks**
  - Maximize supply chain logistics strategy and comply with regulations across the global network.
  - Easily track inventory end-to-end with enhanced supply chain logistics.
  - Increase visibility into logistics to streamline goods flow in real time as well as boost visibility into supply chain logistics in yards and hubs through real-time management.

2.2.4   Connected Infrastructure

The connected infrastructure delivers new forms of operational intelligence to transform physical-infrastructure systems, improve service, drive economic growth, create more efficient and cost-effective operations, establish infrastructure compliance and risk mitigation strategies, create new infrastructure models, and provide opportunities for job growth. Transformation is driven by bridging sensors and control technologies embedded throughout physical infrastructure assets with information systems and business applications.

Some usage examples of connected infrastructure and associated values include the following:

- **Building insights**
  - Leverage real-time information to manage and maintain properties.
  - Ensure visibility across properties to optimize energy consumption, maintain facilities and equipment, and ensure improved customer satisfaction.
- **Construction**
  - Manage construction projects to deliver on time and within budget.
  - Leverage real-time data to manage projects end-to-end, ensuring that materials are at the right place, at the right time, and that usage of assets and equipment is optimized throughout the process.
- **Energy grids**
  - Optimize energy utilization by integrating processes and information by building an end-to-end energy grid that enables better transparency and better decisions.
  - Leverage predictive maintenance and analytical processes to optimize uptime and improve customer satisfaction.
  - Ensure visibility of all assets across the grid to enable improved performance and reliability.

2.2.5   Connected Markets

Connected markets foster local markets, cities, urban spaces, and rural environments with new products, services, data, businesses, and business models. Connectivity enables locally relevant innovation, production, deployment, and business formation at the right moment to meet the challenges of future and transform them into opportunities. Connectivity helps actualize global competitiveness, drive enterprises, power the knowledge economy, and cultivate a culture of innovation. A few examples of connected markets and associated values are:

- **Market insights**
  - Interact in a fully visible digital or physical marketplace to provide an excellent all-around personal experience.
  - Respond to the demands of consistent and seamless experiences, regardless of the constraints of time, space, and geography of today's hyper-connected consumers, citizens, and visitors.
  - Leverage beacons, mobile connectivity, identity, and security to provider hyper-personalized experiences to the consumers, citizens, and visitors in any market.
  - Provide an excellent all-around personal experience benefitting businesses to harness new modes of interaction to their fullest where one can interact in an all-knowing digital or physical marketplace.

- **Rural areas**
  - Transform agribusiness to evolve and grow to feed the world.
  - With a rapid increase in population and the shortage of natural resources, address agribusiness needs to transform and grow to, doing more with less and leveraging the wealth of digital information into business value now available.
  - Consume data from agricultural machines and equipment to increase farming efficiency and predictability and create transparent and sustainable food supply chains while managing price volatility.
  - Connect farmers and growers to global value chains through IoT and mobile technology, enabling the agriculture business to incorporate precision farming competence even in the most remote rural areas globally.

- **Urban areas**
  - Optimize energy, vehicles, and assets across the urban footprint.
  - Realize tremendous benefits for urban areas through automation blending seamlessly with the physical reality of urban spaces, for example, for traffic flow and management.
  - Improve the environment, health, and safety of public urban spaces across construction, services, and other smart city and government offerings like parking management and the management of physical infrastructure like buildings, lighting, parks, yards, ports, and other infrastructure that make up the modern-day urban landscape.

2.3   Intelligently Connected Processes

Organizations can harness diverse data driven by applied intelligence and human ingenuity to empower insight-led decision-making, superior customer experiences, and breakthrough business outcomes to excel in this new digitally focused world. Digital disruption, big data, and customer experiences are three challenges such companies face, in many ways the same problem viewed from different angles: How can organizations effectively onboard, integrate, and use data at scale to drive competitive differentiation and adapt to changing market and technological conditions?

This problem is addressed by integrated process and process automation while following the principles of design thinking. Microservices for machine learning, analytics, big data, user experience, and security, provided by SAP Cloud Platform, enhance this integration, which we'll discuss further in the following sections.

2.3.1   Integrated Processes

Together, SAP Leonardo and design thinking methodology create an effective combination that you can utilize for digital innovation and business-driven application development. Companies using SAP ERP or SAP S/4HANA can make the most of SAP Leonardo's integrated IoT, analytics, big data, blockchain, and machine learning technologies on SAP Cloud Platform. To succeed in today's hypercompetitive business environment, you'll need user-driven application development, new technologies, and integrated architectures.

SAP Leonardo offers significant benefits to companies still using traditional SAP ERP as well as companies moving to SAP S/4HANA. In the following sections, we'll look a few examples of integrated processes in action.

Demand Sensing

From the digital economy emanates digital demand signals, both structured and unstructured, from customers placing orders and making comments via social media on mobile devices. The ability to capture and analyze this new, unstructured sentiment data is key to getting closer to your customers to obtain a clearer picture of what is driving demand. Structured demand data provides the opportunity to improve both short-term and mid-term forecast accuracy through pattern recognition and predictive analytics. The challenge is to effectively capture, harmonize, and convert these huge volumes of raw data into something actionable.

Demand sensing uses actual current order data, along with recent history, to adjust forecasts for short-term horizons. The promotion planning capability gives you the option to either perform promotion planning in SAP IBP for demand or to integrate SAP IBP for demand with an external promotion planning system. Demand sensing allows for the short-term tweaking of execution plans (production, procurement, and logistics) to adjust to short-term changes, sensed as patterns, generated by the demand sensing algorithm.

You can integrate SAP Demand Signal Management for cleansed and harmonized point of sale data, also known as secondary sales, from your retailers, with demand sensing in SAP IBP for demand, as shown in Figure 2.15. With this tool, you can understand deviations that impact sales and understand those true demand patterns to help you minimize the movement of goods from one distribution center to another distribution center to cover short-term demand spikes. As a result, you'll improve customer service levels and logistics costs associated with expedited, cross-distribution center shipments. Overall benefits include minimizing inventory cost through improved forecast accuracy and lower safety stock at all points.

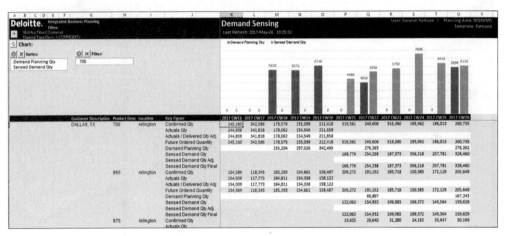

Figure 2.15 Short-Term Forecasting and Demand Sensing Example

With that, SAP Demand Signal Management enables manufacturers to perform the following actions:

- Analyze and improve their sales and brand performance
- Increase their trade promotion effectiveness
- Optimize inventory levels throughout the supply chain

- Successfully launch new products
- Get visibility into critical out-of-stock situations down to the level of individual stores and thus prevent lost sales
- Quickly spot market trends and deviations
- Respond faster to demand fluctuations

Connected Vehicles

SAP Leonardo IoT can be used for collecting, storing, analyzing, and processing telemetry data from vehicles. As shown in Figure 2.16, this solution enables you to collect data from your fleet vehicles to drive and improve business. By collecting data about driving habits, maintenance, and wear and tear, you can create new business models to improve the services you offer to your customers.

Figure 2.16 SAP Leonardo IoT for Fleet Management

The solution is flexible in its ability to process data for any vehicle and can be applied in a variety of situations, from international fleet management to warehouse planning. You can track wear and tear and preempt maintenance requirements, thereby

2

lowering costs and reducing vehicle downtimes. You can also use SAP Leonardo IoT alongside workshop management solution product like SAP EWM (Extended Warehouse Management), and SAP TM (Transportation Management), allowing you to automate your end-to-end vehicle maintenance process.

Fleet analytics (part of SAP Leonardo IoT) contains apps and business data that you can use to manage fleets, optimize availability, costs, utilization, and maintenance for whole fleets as well as for specific parts of a fleet. Coordinating vehicle utilization and keeping vehicles in working order are important jobs, and the main goal in fleet analytics is to help users achieve agreed-upon service levels. A key requirement of a fleet manager is to track and monitor fleet and driver operations. A few additional features to generate accurate, timely analytics and insights include the following:

- Track vehicle positions, routes, and conditions in real time
- Enable geofencing, alerting, and integrated scheduling of service appointments, as shown in Figure 2.17
- Perform manual or automated logging of activities based on predefined tasks or geofences
- Monitor driver behavior and create fleet scorecards

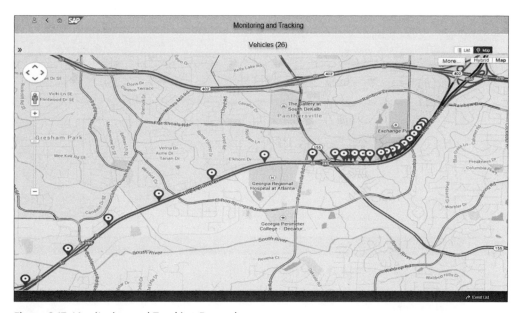

Figure 2.17 Monitoring and Tracking Example

The Monitoring and Tracking app (part of SAP Leonardo IoT) helps fleet managers and dispatchers monitor the last-known positions, previous and current trips, and related KPIs for vehicles in a fleet, as shown in Figure 2.18. Users can filter for specific vehicles in your fleet, view the master data for each vehicle, and see which properties were measured during a trip. A map view allows users to see the last-recorded position of the vehicles in their fleet with access to both previous routes for this trip as well as the current route that a vehicle has taken so far.

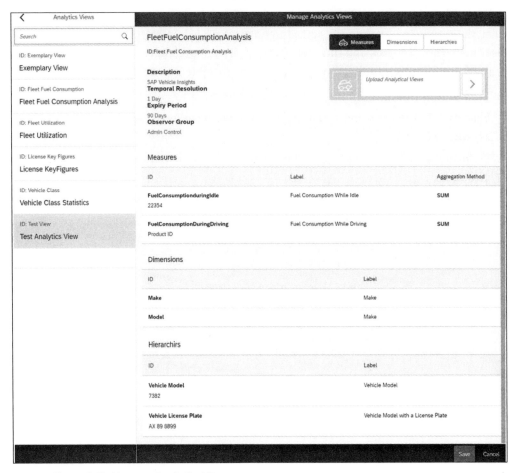

Figure 2.18 Manage Analytics View

Smart Factory

A smart factory is a flexible system that can self-optimize performance across a broader network, self-adapt to and learn from new conditions in real or near real time, and autonomously run entire production processes. A smart factory has several major features: connectivity, optimization, transparency, proactivity, and agility. Each of these features can play a role in enabling more informed decision-making and can help your organization improve production processes. Some sample applications of digital technology in integrated manufacturing processes are shown in Table 2.1.

Process	Sample Digitization Opportunities
Manufacturing operations	■ Additive manufacturing to produce rapid prototypes or low-volume spare parts ■ Advanced planning and scheduling using real-time production and inventory data to minimize waste and cycle time ■ Cognitive bots and autonomous robots to effectively execute routine processes at minimal cost with high accuracy ■ Digital twin to digitize an operation and move beyond automation and integration to predictive analyses
Warehouse operations	■ Augmented reality to assist personnel with pick-and-place tasks ■ Autonomous robots to execute warehouse operations
Inventory tracking	■ Sensors to track real-time movements and locations of raw materials, work-in-progress and finished goods, and high-value tooling ■ Analytics to optimize inventory on-hand and automatically signal for replenishment
Quality	■ In-line quality testing using optical-based analytics ■ Real-time equipment monitoring to predict potential quality issues
Maintenance	■ Augmented reality to assist maintenance personnel in maintaining and repairing equipment ■ Sensors on equipment to drive predictive and cognitive maintenance analytics
Environmental, health, and safety	■ Sensors to geofence dangerous equipment from operating near personnel ■ Sensors on personnel to monitor environmental conditions, lack of movement, or other potential threats

Table 2.1 Integrated Processes within a Smart Factory

The smart factory is an example of an intelligently connected process in which we do not have to wait for the testing at the end of manufacturing. Any quality issues are captured in real time through the connected process and are corrected.

2.3.2   Process Automation

SAP Leonardo Machine Learning Foundation delivers intelligent solutions that allow developers to consume, design, and scale machine learning in accordance with their requirements. Furthermore, SAP is continuously investing in machine learning abilities to help data scientists train their custom machine learning models as well as launch new machine learning services.

SAP recently introduced an extension of SAP Leonardo Machine Learning Foundation capabilities based on its updated SAP Conversational AI service that will allow you to develop increasingly complex corporate chatbots with ease. SAP also announced its investment in intelligent robotic process automation (RPA) with the aim of automating repetitive processes across its portfolio.

A few of the recent disruptive machine learning and IoT-enabled solutions that now with automated various processes are discussed in the following sections.

SAP CoPilot

SAP is taking the ERP to the next level where you can chat, ask questions, and give instructions just like you would with a personal assistant. So, the verbal information is exchanged with the SAP CoPilot, which in turn would encode, analyze, and would execute actions and present results in meaningful ways, in the form of reports and dashboards. The various features of SAP CoPilot include the following:

- Users can create notes while using the app; recorded details can be retrieved when the user returns to the same app later.
- Users can take, attach, and share screenshots. By clicking on the screenshot, the user can navigate to the app directly with the same filter parameters.
- Users can communicate with other users via text, gesture, or voice.
- Based on role or user requirements, users can display information on the screen like a monthly report, quarterly sales report, etc. Users can also generate business objects with minimal inputs.
- SAP CoPilot helps users make decisions or get insights for making necessary decisions.

- Starting with predefined logic or business rules and gradually learning from behavioral data, users can start getting recommendations about the next best actions to take.
- Users can invite other users to explore or investigate business objects outputs.
- Users can chat with each other in the same window and also schedule meetings.

Accounts Payable Service

The accounts payable service automates the accounts payable process by processing incoming invoices and extracting relevant information from existing financial systems using machine learning. The application offers an ever-expanding suite of services like invoice to record, which extracts information and posts the data to the general ledger, and vendor matching, which identifies an invoice and matches it against the vendor database to find the correct vendor ID.

SAP Cash Application

SAP Cash Application empowers you to focus on developing innovative strategies and growth plans with intelligent receivable matching automation that handles manually intensive financial processes.

Using SAP Leonardo Machine Learning Foundation capabilities, SAP Cash Application learns from accountants' past manual actions, capturing much richer detail of customer- and country-specific behavior, without the costs of manually defining detailed rules. Using SAP S/4HANA, new incoming payment and open invoice information are passed to the SAP Cloud Platform-based matching engine, and proposed matches are either automatically cleared or suggested for review by accounts receivable. Benefits of using SAP Cash Application include the following:

- Reduced days sales outstanding (DSO)
- Lower total cost of ownership (TCO) through efficiencies enabled by machine learning
- Enhanced quality of work related to accounts receivable
- Ability to scale shared services as the business grows
- Enabling a single, integrated environment with SAP S/4HANA on-premise, SAP S/4HANA Cloud, and SAP ERP 6.0

Robotic Process Automation

Robotic process automation (RPA) has matured over the last decade and is now used for enterprise-scale deployments. Intelligent automation, while still nascent, promises hugely transformative potential in the near future. To maximize the impact of robot-led automation, business leaders will need a solid understanding of the available tools and a clearly defined strategy for automating the enterprise.

RPA tools are best suited for processes with repeatable, predictable interactions with IT applications. These processes typically lack the scale or value to warrant automation via core systems transformation or if core systems transformation is not due to be implemented soon. RPA tools can improve the efficiency of these processes and the effectiveness of services without changing the underlying systems.

RPA software "robots" perform routine business processes by mimicking the way that people interact with applications through a user interface and by following simple rules to make decisions. Software robots can perform entire end-to-end processes with very little human interaction, typically to manage exceptions. RPA can be used to automate processes with following characteristics:

- Highly repetitive
- Prone to error
- Rules-based
- Time critical and seasonal

Traditionally, robots have been deployed for executing routine and repetitive tasks, requiring complex programming for setup and implementation, while lacking the agility to easily adjust operations. As autonomous robots become more sophisticated, setup times are decreasing, the robots require less supervision, and they can work side by-side with their human counterparts. The benefits are expanding as autonomous robots become capable of working around the clock with more consistent levels of quality and productivity, performing tasks that humans cannot, should not, or do not want to do. As the market for autonomous robots grows, the alignment of end-to-end supply chain operations will become more fluid. Currently, many companies that use autonomous robots have implemented them for targeted functions within the supply chain, piloting various robots to verify expected efficiency gains. As innovative companies grow and expand operations, robots that build robots could be the norm for more economically and efficiently optimizing manufacturing operations.

Production and manufacturing warehouses are witnessing a major shift from traditional human labor to an army of warehouse robots. While humans would not completely be removed from the picture, their roles will change. Rather than performing the tasks themselves, human resources will now be needed for giving commands and directions to the robots. The fundamental goal of AI is to create intelligent systems that think, work, and process situations in a human-like manner but in half the time humans take to complete specific tasks. Retailers are looking forward to robots in their warehouse as a means to reduce operational and logistical costs and to save on delivery times.

2.3.3   Microservices

SAP Leonardo business services includes a reusable microservices framework to enable you to rapidly build your IoT model and connect it with business context from backend systems by leveraging configuration-driven tools. SAP Cloud Platform provides end-to-end microservices for machine learning, analytics, big data connector, security, user experience, and backend integration APIs.

The reusable microservices framework allows you to rapidly build your prototypes and connect them with business contexts from backend systems and also leverage built-in configuration tools. SAP Leonardo IoT Bridge, for example, combines real-time data from connected devices with different business applications and microservices to implement an intelligent end-to-end process. Connected products for intelligent supply networks, connected fleet vehicles for intelligent logistics systems, connected assets for intelligent manufacturing networks are further examples of applications of the framework.

On SAP Cloud Platform, a wide variety of services can be used in your applications. Various versions of SAP Leonardo Machine Learning Foundation are available, as follows:

- SAP Machine Learning Foundation
- SAP Machine Learning Foundation Beta
- SAP Machine Learning Foundation Trial Beta

These versions are Cloud Foundry service contracts that, in the case of SAP Leonardo Machine Learning Foundation, bundle several machine learning services into one Cloud Foundry service contracts. You can use any of the versions, although the beta service will feature more machine learning services to choose from. The trial beta service is a beta service available on the trial edition account of SAP Cloud Platform Cloud Foundry. Be aware that the beta services are not production ready (some are even "alpha") and their APIs are subject to change without warning and may even disappear before graduating to the production-ready, non-beta service contracts.

To build apps, integrations, and extensions easily, you can leverage and consume pre-delivered content, which include APIs, prepackaged integration content, and sample apps.

2.4   Design Thinking

Have you ever played a video game and wondered how its creators made it so fun or looked at an awe-inspiring building and wanted to know how its architects and engineers planned it all? You see and use so many things every day that might make you curious about their creation. Well, in this section, you'll uncover some of the secrets behind all those well-designed products and learn how to think through, that is, learn a process for creative thinking and problem-solving called design thinking.

2.4.1   Design Thinking at SAP

Design thinking is a methodology or framework commonly used to innovate so that you can create useful and easy-to-use products and services. However, before we hit the high gear, let's ensure we understand some common terms and their meanings. So, what is "design thinking," and why does it matter? Design thinking is a human-centered process used to define and solve problems. It can be applied to any subject, industry, or field of study. Moreover, while it is a process, there are no hard and fast rules. It follows five basic phases that overlap and loop-back until you reach the desired outcome.

Design thinking was inspired by the natural way designers solve all kinds of design problems—by thinking outside the box and allowing ideas to flow creatively without setting limits by looking for the "correct" solution. Design thinking is a kind of a mindset, a way of thinking and looking at things: We look for an opportunity that motivates the search for solutions, create a process for idea generation, and then make ideas real. As practitioners of design thinking, we'll deepen our understanding of the problem or idea first, then use some techniques to generate ideas. Finally, we'll create something that is tangible and real. Although design thinking does not have any hard and fast rules, design thinking follows five core phases, as shown in Figure 2.19:

- Empathize
- Define
- Ideate
- Prototype
- Test

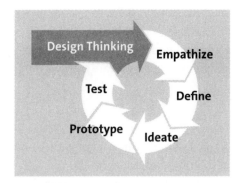

Figure 2.19 Design Thinking Approach

In the following sections, we'll describe each phase in turn.

Empathize

When designing a product, you don't just start building it right away. Instead, you should try to simulate how users will use the product before creating the final product, which requires empathy. Empathy is putting yourself in a position where you can feel what someone else feels. The goal of empathy is that, by paying attention to other people, you can discover problems worth working on. The objective is not to identify a solution for a project you're pursuing, but to understand the people involved in the project, what makes them tick and what's meaningful for them. If done well, you'll be prepared for the next step, defining problems and issues around their needs and using their insights.

Define

In the define phase, you'll take the insights from the previous empathize phase and combine them in meaningful ways to create a holistic overview of the problem that you want to solve and start coming up with ideas to solve the problem. Just writing and storing documents on hard drives is not enough because you'll never use this information again. Your goal should be bring data visibility to the team.

During requirements-gathering, we highly recommend you use color-coding for your different users and categories. With color coding, you'll more easily see common patterns and common insights from different requirements-gathering sessions, which will help you better understand the problems, wishes, and needs of your users.

Another important concept is the use of personas: descriptions of user for whom you are designing the solution. A persona is not an abstract definition of a user or an ice hockey fan; it is about a real human being, with a name, age, hobbies, etc. This process involves really describing your user in such a way that you can visualize this person and understand their concrete needs. These findings help you create a much more concrete problem statement.

Ideate

In this fun phase, you'll take all your insights and learning from the empathize and define phases and start working on ideas and solutions to address them. The main objective in this phase is to start working on as many ideas or solutions as possible, so later you have the chance to narrow down to a specific problem to solve.

Now, a common mistake during this stage is relying solely on brainstorming as the primary way to come up with new ideas. Often when organizations brainstorm, the process runs poorly, often resulting in an unproductive meeting, and other options are available. Ideation is a broader concept than simply brainstorming. Its goal is to generate as many unexpected options as possible to resolve the problem you defined in the earlier phase. How do you get as many unexpected options as possible to the problem that you identified? One primary strategy during ideation is to separate idea generation from idea selection.

Critical to successful ideation is to generate your ideas first, without any judgment and then evaluate and select the ones you want to test. Every strategy, whether brainstorming or something else, usually relies on this freedom, and only a few activities should be done intentionally or formally. One activity that you should undertake is bringing a diversity of perspectives to the table. If everyone in your group thinks the same way, chances are you will not get to unexpected places.

Second, to ensure you get to more unexpected places, we'll need to rethink brainstorming rules. For us, brainstorming should be more like a social covenant for how each member should behave when in the group. The brainstorming dynamic requires a delicate balance to get this diverse group of people to work constructively together and get to new places. If you are judging a lot of ideas too early, you may stifle open suggestions.

The third recommendation is to encourage wild ideas. What we've found is that, even if the wild ideas aren't worth that much on their own, they may inspire the team to think of other alternatives, and that other idea could be a really good idea. Fourth, we recommend aiming for a high number of ideas; the more ideas you have, the more likely some are good ideas. The last suggestion is to be visual. Sketching out your ideas visually provokes people to think differently.

Another type of ideation concept to aim for the long shot, or what you might call the most radical idea—something that sounds as impossible, but if you could do it, everything would change. What researchers have found is that, after you generate all your ideas, if you identify at least three concepts on these different criteria to move into prototyping, you have preserved your innovation potential. Thus, after generating as many ideas as possible, you should select multiple concepts to pursue. After the ideate phase, you'll move on to the critical prototype phase.

Prototype

During the prototype phase, you'll give shape or life to your ideas. A "quick and dirty" prototyping of promising ideas helps you not fall too much in love with your ideas. With your prototypes, you'll need to be open to feedback from users, including critical feedback. The prototypes will help you learn from and understand better what the best solution in the end could be.

A prototype could be a paper prototype, a physical prototype, a 3D model, or even a role-play. The main idea is to bring those solutions and ideas from your brain into real life where others can see them, touch them, and interact with them. To start, perhaps you'll draw a diagram called a blueprint and then start adding more details to it like the kind of materials, etc. Professional architects could even build a digital or physical 3D model so that details can be more closely studied and the design can be modified as needed. This approach to building models and simulating the end-product is called prototyping.

What's so great about prototyping? This process allows the team to study the eventual product more quickly and correct any potential mistakes in a timely manner before you've actually started "laying the bricks and pouring the concrete." In Section 2.4.2, we'll explain the SAP Build tool, used for prototyping and many other activities in detail, but during prototyping, we would take a storyboard describing an app for tracking sales orders, as shown in Figure 2.20, and build a prototype app, shown in Figure 2.21.

Figure 2.20 Track Sales Order Storyboarding Example

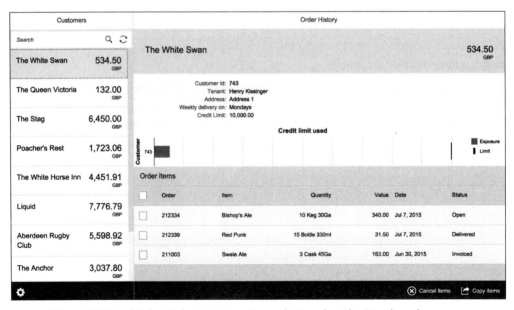

Figure 2.21 Track Sales Order Prototype Example Based on the Storyboard

Test

After prototyping, you'll move on to the last phase called testing or test. Testing is where you'll take those low-resolution, quick and dirty experience prototypes that you made earlier and put in front of the people you are designing for, checking what works and what doesn't. For testing, ask users to pay close attention and report on what worked for them and what didn't. Finally, as you run people through your experience prototype, you'll learn from feedback. You can adapt your prototypes and can go from one user to another user to gather additional feedback.

What should you do with all this feedback? In our experience, a good place to start is gathering this feedback and sorting them into categories. Were new questions raised through the feedback? What about new ideas that emerged when you ran those prototypes? Both new questions and new ideas are valuable for you to capture. As you run through the experience prototype, having a team member just observe and take notes and interview users could be valuable, and then, as a group, you can start sorting through and unpacking all the feedback you received. While reflecting on the feedback, you can decide what feedback to incorporate in your next prototype.

2.4.2   Approach

In this section, you'll learn how to bring your ideas to life by using SAP Build to create a high-fidelity prototype, which is a prototype that is as close to the real product in look and interactivity as possible without being fully built. The purpose behind all this work is so that you can let your target audience interact with as close-to-a-real thing to determine whether the design addresses their needs or still need some tweaks and fixes. A high-fidelity prototype is a key step in following user-centered design. Based on the feedback returned by your audience, you can cheaply and quickly improve the design and iterate through multiple cycles of development. As a result, prototypes are powerful tools for uncovering gaps in designs and for leading to a final, refined product.

SAP's UX strategy is to design and develop user-friendly applications according to SAP Fiori design principles. SAP Fiori applications adhere to this concept and can be deployed in the cloud or on-premise. SAP Build is a cloud-based collaborative design tool that provides the knowledge, tools, and inspiration you can use create beautiful apps that your users would love. You can use SAP Build to learn about design thinking, create interactive prototypes, get feedback from users, and jumpstart development without writing a single line of code. To begin, follow these steps:

1. Use Chrome web browser on a MacBook or PC laptop to access SAP Build at *https:// build.me.*
2. Click on the **Sign up for free!** link and then enter your email. Agree to the terms and condition and, finally, register with a valid email ID and associated password.
3. After logging in, click on **New Project** then **Create New Project**, as shown in Figure 2.22. Let's call the project "Smart Building" and add a description to create a project.

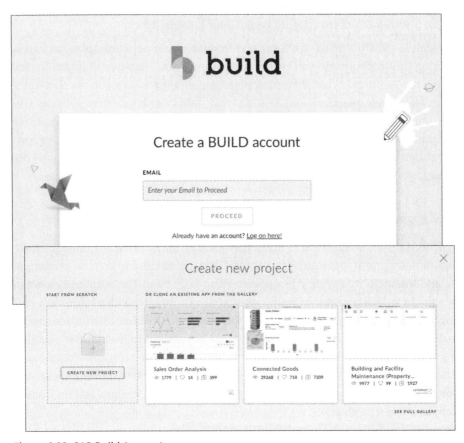

Figure 2.22 SAP Build Account

4. To create a *persona*, on the project's main menu, click on **Create a Persona**, as shown in Figure 2.23. It displays a persona form and you should complete the form as follows:
   - Click on **Upload** to upload an image from your machine. Crop the image as needed.

- Complete the data fields to the right of the image:
  - **Name**: of the persona
  - **Role & Organization**: at the company
  - **Quote**: a phrase that your persona will probably say, highlighting their most significant need or pain point
- Complete the info below the image by clicking on the **Add** button and then saving your input:
  - **About:** details about the persona's background, demographic, and work context, etc.
  - **Works with**: roles of colleagues and types of customers the persona works with
  - **Main Goals**: goals the persona need to accomplish to be successful at work
  - **Need**s: what the persona needs to reach their goal and why
  - **Job Responsibilities**: job responsibilities of the persona (including how often)
  - **Pain Points**: obstacles that prevent the persona from meeting their job requirements

Click on **Done** when you are satisfied with your persona (you can always come back and edit the details). You'll then be redirected to the persona summary page showing the persona's most important information.

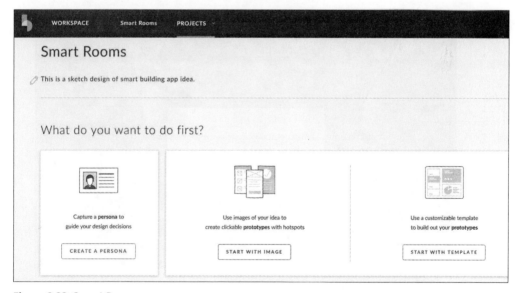

Figure 2.23 Smart Rooms

5. Now, you'll upload images to SAP Build and use these images in your prototype to create a low-fidelity design. Switch to using your mobile phone or tablet. Take a picture of the dashboard, occupancy, and meeting rooms. While still using your mobile device, go to your browser application and navigate to *https://build.me*. Log in and select the project name **Smart Building** from the dropdown menu and click on **Upload Images**. Navigate to your Photo Library, then upload the images that you took with your phone.

6. The study and review user feedback will be created in the SAP Build tool, as shown in Figure 2.24. Navigate to the second page of the prototype by clicking on **Meeting Room Occupancy** and then on the building info to open the third page. You can comment on each page. The more users click on the image, the more clicks you'll see in the heatmap later when reviewing results. Once finished, click **Done**, as shown in Figure 2.25.

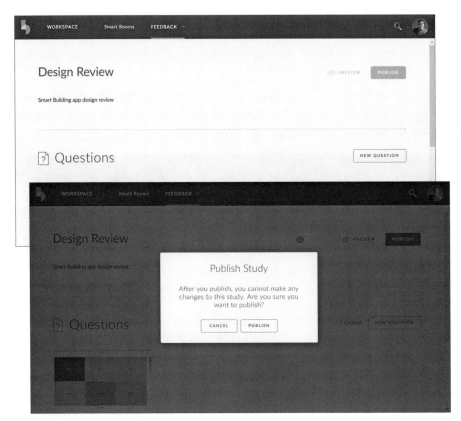

Figure 2.24 Creating a Study

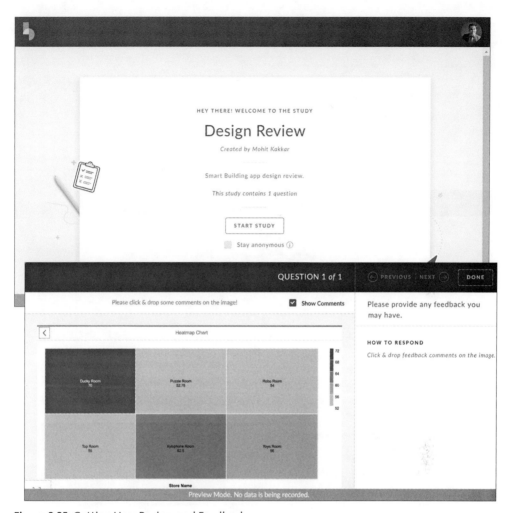

Figure 2.25 Getting User Review and Feedback

7. Next, we'll create a high-fidelity SAP Fiori master-detail prototype. Leave the existing prototype by clicking the **BUILD** icon in the top left corner, then clicking **New Project**. Check out more projects from the gallery by clicking **Go to Full Gallery**. Search for "smart" from the gallery and choose **Smart Rooms**. You can click on **TRY IT** to test drive this prototype in a new tab.

8. If you're satisfied with the prototype, go back to the previous tab and click **CLONE** to clone the app, as shown in Figure 2.26. Confirm the clone by clicking on **CLONE** and click **OK** when done.

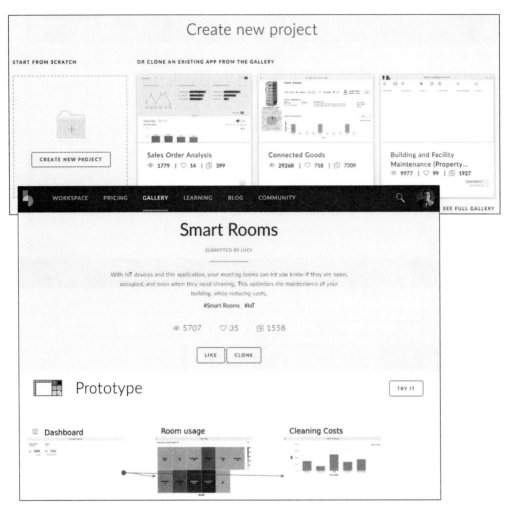

Figure 2.26 Clone the App

9. You'll be shown the project page of the cloned project. This project is now yours to modify further. Click on **GO TO PAGE MAP** then click on the first thumbnail to open UI Editor. Click on the plus sign in the top left corner and add a new **Responsive** page. Double-click on the header and rename the new page as "Occupancy Details." Then, click on **Edit Page**, as shown in Figure 2.27.

10. The data can be populated in the table, and charts can be customized according to user preferences, as shown in Figure 2.28. The final prototype can be published to the user group.

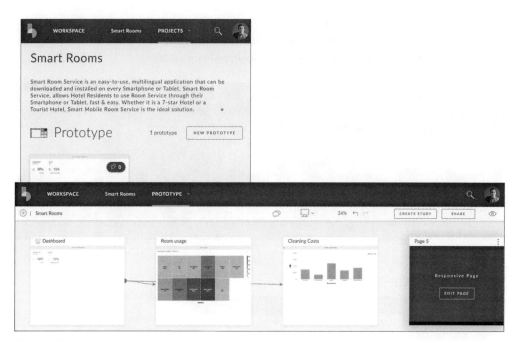

Figure 2.27 Cloned Project Page: Edit

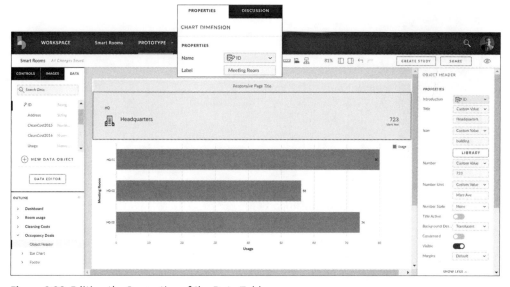

Figure 2.28 Editing the Properties of the Data Table

11. Finally, the build prototype must be imported into SAP Web IDE, by first going in to the SAP Cloud Platform cockpit, as shown in Figure 2.29 and then selecting the correct options under **Services**, as shown in Figure 2.30.

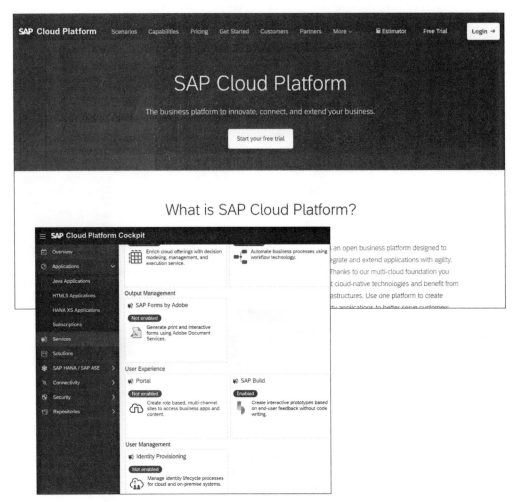

Figure 2.29 SAP Cloud Platform: Import

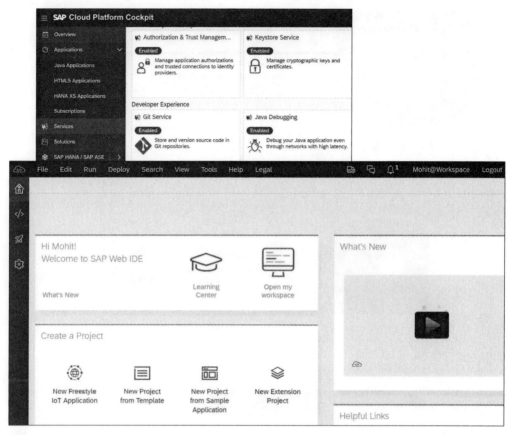

Figure 2.30 Importing into SAP Web IDE

12. Next, you'll need to go into SAP Web IDE and select **File • Import • Project From Template**, and then enter all the necessary information, as shown in Figure 2.31.

13. Finally, once you have it in your system, you'll just need to select **Run • Run as SAP Fiori Launchpad Sandbox**, as shown in Figure 2.32, and you're done!

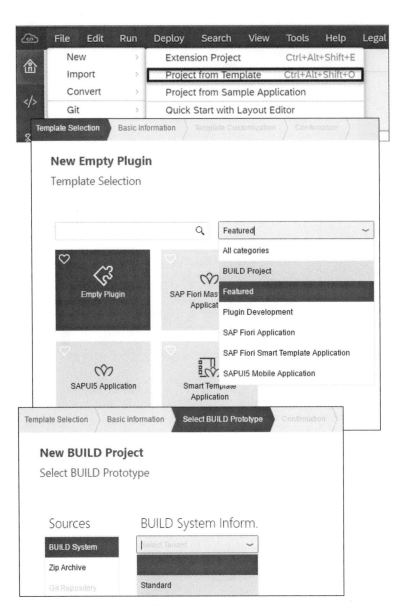

Figure 2.31 Import SAP Build Project

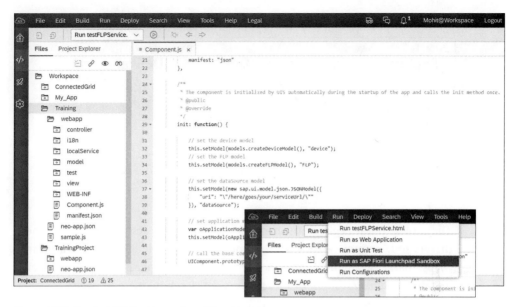

Figure 2.32 Run in SAP Fiori Launchpad Sandbox

2.4.3   Design-Led Development

SAP Leonardo offers a unique design-led development process to help you along your digital transformation journey consisting of four main phases: explore, discover, design and prototype, and deliver, as shown in Figure 2.33. The goal is to engage in a strategic conversation to identify the needs of business users and end users. Experts conduct a user-observation exercise to understand the current state of the business, resulting in next-generation business processes. You can gather feedback, validate, and iterate on the prototype before handing off the project for implementation.

Using this design-led approach, the solutions offered by SAP are human-centric. The key problems of your key users and other end users revolving around business problems are addressed. Another key feature of this approach is that this approach encourages all stakeholders to be involved in the entire process of designing the solution, which increases feelings of ownership in the solution, which encourages in solution adoption. The design thinking approach purposefully avoids looking at technology solutions in the beginning, and little focus is given to technology solutions overall. Instead, business problems and user concerns, the key factors to success with SAP Leonardo, are given primary attention.

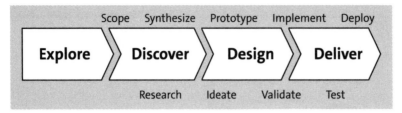

Scope   Synthesize   Prototype   Implement   Deploy

Explore 〉 **Discover** 〉 **Design** 〉 **Deliver**

Research   Ideate   Validate   Test

Figure 2.33 Design-Led Development Process

Design-led development involves four phases and three quality gates (commonly called design gates, or D gates), as follows:

- **Explore phase**
  The explore phase begins with an exploration workshop delving into the business drivers and commercial contexts for innovation and includes activities like threat maps, market evaluations, and feature wish lists. This phase is like the conceive and explore phases found in older product development methodologies.

  This phase is the initial phase of the approach where all business users, the IT department, and SAP solution experts are involved. Business problems, end-user concerns, and other issues related to business processes are discussed in detail. This discussion does not discuss IT problems and solutions for the business problem. The main goal is to understand the business problem and build a business case. During this workshop, the SAP team explores use cases and checks whether solution accelerators are already present to kickstart solution without wasting much time. User problems are prioritized, and worked is focused on these problems. The project can either follow an express track or a slower open innovation track from this phase.

- **Discover phase**
  The discover phase comes next and includes user research, insight synthesis, and participatory design workshops between the SAP team and your organization. The goals of this phase are to visualize an as-is process with you and understand the key pain points and tasks. Once these factors are understood, the team begins to codesign your to-be process with screen mock-ups to explain the concept.

  This phase involves two main activities—onsite user research and hands-on workshops to show as-is versus to-be process. This phase involves defining solutions on paper and building low-fidelity prototypes using the SAP Build tool. The main goal of this phase is to observe the users and the business process first-hand to understand business problems better. This participatory design workshop involves all the stakeholders, business, and end users, and help build a sense of ownership of the solution. By discussing the to-be process, the business is users are aware of the solution to expect, and with low-fidelity prototypes they can visualize the solution at a very early stage.

- **Design gates**
  Design gates are checkpoints to ensure the project team keeps the entire design process on track while following global SAP UX and SAP Fiori guidelines. A design advisory gate (after the discover phase and before the design and prototype phrase) will involve a detailed review of business use cases and UX solutions based on SAP best practices. This ensures a quality and feasibility check early in the design stage. The first D Gate ensures the solution fits with the SAP Fiori principles. The second D Gate checks for solution feasibility with adherence to SAP Fiori design principles.

- **Design and prototype phase**
  The design phase begins with the UX designer taking the insights learned from the discovery phase to produce an interactive, high-fidelity prototype, along with any other design artifacts that are required.

  This stage involves converting low-fidelity to high-fidelity prototypes as covered in Section 2.4.2. Several iterative steps may be required before an initial clickable prototype is created using the SAP Build tool, which helps the solution team develop prototypes, record feedback from users, and improve the solution. Using an agile process allows increased involvement from end users in this phase and increases opportunities to gather their feedback, which helps you address real business problems and developing solutions to address those problems.

- **Delivery phase**
  A final workable proof of concept (POC) is the outcome of the delivery phase. The POC is validated by end users and business users for desirability, usability, and feasibility. A technical blueprint is another outcome of this stage. Ideally, your high-fidelity prototype was so close to the real solution that, based on the feedback of the prototype, the final implementation, carried out by the solution provider or implementation partner, goes smoothly.

2.5 Summary

An intelligent enterprise is based on a highly collaborative ecosystem of people, processes, technology, and applications. In this chapter, you learned that intelligently connected people with internal and external collaboration channels are critical for realizing the goal of an intelligent enterprise. Work efficiency and system usage can be enhanced by adopting design thinking concepts and empathizing with end users, which can be applied to a broad range of tasks, from designing an SAP Fiori app to designing and building the solution model for an intelligent enterprise. The intelligently connected family of products, assets, fleet, infrastructure, markets, and people represent the nervous system of enterprise automation and intelligence. SAP Leonardo solution design and delivery is recommended to follow the design thinking processes of empathize, define, ideate, prototype, and test. Design-led development stages include the explore, discover, design, and deliver phases.

With the knowledge incorporated in this chapter, Part I of this book on the topic of digital transformation and the intelligent enterprise is now concluded. Now, we're ready to delve into the intelligent technologies that make the digital transformation possible in Part II of this book.

PART II
Technologies

Chapter 3
Big Data

Data is the currency of today's digital enterprise. Essential to your digital transformation journey is the ability to move, transform, integrate, and improve data quality—any type of data, from any source, at any frequency. You need an enterprise-ready, distributed computing solution to help uncover actionable insights from big data.

Big data is identified with the characteristics of 3Vs: volume, velocity, and variety. Volume refers to the large scale of data, running into multiple terabytes and petabytes; velocity refers to the speed at which the data is generated especially streaming data from sources like Internet of Things (IoT) sensors; and variety refers to the different types of data: structured, unstructured, and semi-structured. Companies now collect data along all these dimensions. Unlike in the past, when most of the data was largely transactional in nature, using a relational database paradigm to store, process, and consume data can't keep up with today's reality of big data.

Your IT strategy must keep up with the latest technological advances to reduce and bridge data silos, manage cloud as well as hybrid deployment strategies, leverage new data architectures like "data lakes" of unstructured data, and handle new types of data such as spatial and streaming IoT data.

In this chapter, we'll first introduce you to big data in general, looking at what big data is and why you need it. Then, we'll introduce the tools and products SAP offers to support this technology, while describing some industry-specific and line of business (LOB) use cases supported by these tools and products.

3.1 What Is Big Data?

Data has become central to any business, especially with the advent of big data from the influx of new sources like streaming data, social media data, and other types of unstructured data. While you may still rely on transactional databases that underpin your core business processes, new sources of data play an increasingly important role in your business in an unprecedented way. A universal data fabric is an architectural approach and set of data services to provide consistent capabilities and services that spans on-premise and multi-cloud environments and helps simplify the management of data integration and enable digital transformation for your organization. This universal data fabric answers questions that arise in the process, such as the following:

- Should I have different specialty databases for different types of data?
- Should each database operate in its own environment?
- How do I eliminate lag times arising from integrating these different environments?

Such an architecture also addresses the following requirements:

- **Performance**
  An infrastructure that delivers data at the speed your users and processes require and your business demands.

- **Freedom**
  As data is generated by your users, systems (both in the cloud and on-premise) and a variety of third parties, you need the data to flow unconstrained and seamlessly.

- **Data models**
  You'll need to model the data to your specific business goals. With big data, data discovery is critical for finding relationships and unearthing hidden insights.

- **Independence**
  You'll need to be able to scale; your computing power should not limit your data, and your data should not limit your computing power.

- **Low latency**
  Though data is being generated at an unprecedented rate, to keep up with the needs of your business, this data needs to be available for incorporation into transactions, automated processes, and analytics as soon as the data is created.

- **Governance**
  While ensuring data availability and usability needs, data integrity and security cannot be compromised.

- **Frictionless**
  Ensure seamless interoperability to combine structured data and new data sources as data is created without exposing the underlying complexity of the various data types.

In addition, a typical company's data management landscape will have evolved over the years to address the following individual business needs:

- **Enterprise data warehouses**
  Generally a single data warehouse to support the entire enterprise; this need arises from the requirement to connect processes across transactional applications and subsequently integrate the transactional processes with enterprise business intelligence.

- **Data marts**
  Allows you to draw data from multiple sources to optimize and support a business application or business needs. A data mart is often optimized to function operationally to answer business questions that need to be answered right away to take action.

- **Data lakes**
  Generally on a big data platform like Hadoop or Spark with the intent to store and mine all IoT data streaming from sensors across numerous locations, both within and outside your company, in its raw form. The data is then transferred from the data lake to a data warehouse or a data mart to organize and refine it, so it can be used for decision-making at all levels of an organization.

The SAP HANA Data Management Suite addresses these needs by enabling you to collect and combine all types of data, in real time, on a single platform. The SAP HANA Data Management Suite allows you to reduce data sprawl, analyze data in an instant, and solve previously unsolvable business problems, greatly simplifying your transition to an intelligent enterprise. As shown in Figure 3.1, the SAP HANA Data Management Suite enables secure, governed, enterprise-class applications and analytics by providing an open, hybrid, and multicloud-enabled solution suite that can orchestrate all your data in a trusted, unified landscape.

The SAP HANA Data Management Suite enables you to manage your data end-to-end, from capturing the data; to ingesting and processing the data; and, finally, to orchestrating, computing, and consuming the data. In the process, SAP HANA Data Management Suite can act as your decision factory by taking raw data, cleaning, and bringing it into a trusted format that can be used by applications, analytics, machine learning or a range of other uses. It acts as a development platform for your applications that need analytics on real-time transactions; for data governance, anonymization, and pipeline flow to protect and refine data across the landscape; for modeling across lines of business; for handling different data types and technology architectures; and for providing in-memory, multimodel analytics and data processing on a distributed computing framework.

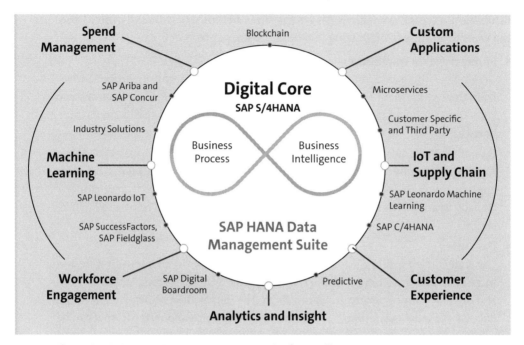

Figure 3.1 SAP HANA Data Management Suite for Intelligent Enterprises

As shown in Figure 3.2, SAP HANA, SAP Data Hub, and SAP Cloud Platform Big Data Services are key tools in the SAP HANA Data Management Suite for addressing big data needs, which we'll cover in the following sections.

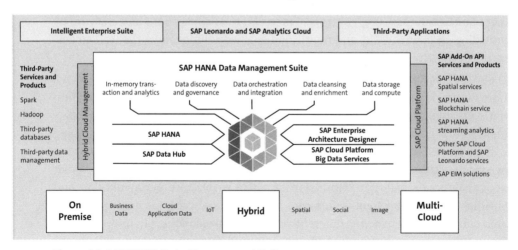

Figure 3.2 SAP HANA Data Management Suite

3.2   Universal Data Management Platform

SAP HANA, shown in Figure 3.3, provides you with a data processing architecture purposely designed to address today's data explosion so you can easily take advantage of new technology breakthroughs. You can run real-time analytics on live transactions without data replication by virtually or physically connecting to all data from any source. In fact, SAP HANA goes a step further and provides next-generation hybrid transactional/analytical processing (HTAP), with its unique ability not only to process operational analytics on structured data, such as business transactions, but also to apply advanced analytics processing, such as predictive machine learning or natural language processing on structured and unstructured data, for example, graph data, spatial data, text, document store, searches, and live data streams.

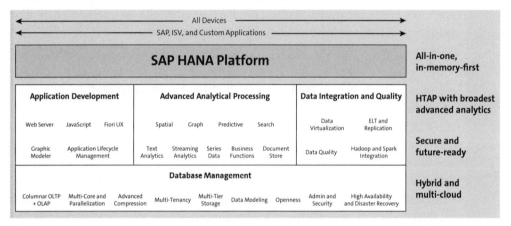

Figure 3.3 SAP HANA as a Business Data Platform for All Applications

SAP HANA also has built-in predictive libraries (SAP Leonardo Machine Learning Foundation) and integration to major machine learning frameworks such R, TensorFlow, etc. SAP HANA provides fast machine learning training, validation, and scoring as well as an automated framework to embed machine learning models into applications allowing developers and data scientists to move away from batch machine learning to real-time machine learning.

With built-in advanced analytics and multimodel processing, your application development architectures and IT landscapes will be radically simplified with SAP HANA. Logical data modeling eliminates the need for data stores and data marts, and you won't have to create separate data subsets and special purpose data repositories anymore. Instead, you can create virtual tables on the fly by pulling data from wherever it resides, and you can change virtual tables in response to changing business or technical requirements. As you develop applications, whether on-premise or in the cloud, openness is essential for fast innovation. SAP HANA supports both open and industry standards such as network protocols (OData); containerization (Cloud Foundry, Docket); security (SAML, LDAP, Kerberos); machine learning (TensorFlow, R); app servers (J2EE, Hibernate); and programing languages (Java, Node.js, Python), to name a few. Such capabilities help you achieve faster time to value and achieve immediate business results by allowing you to act on live intelligence from all your data.

SAP HANA's columnar, in-memory storage provides you the ability to achieve massive compression and computing performance. You'll get real-time performance metrics for analytics and transactions without complex tuning while avoiding data latency. You won't need to create and maintain indexes and aggregates anymore, as you would in relational databases, to fine-tune query and report generation response times. As a result, the time and effort needed to prepare the data for analysis will be greatly reduced, all while flexibility is enhanced for analysis.

SAP HANA offers advanced data security, including a privacy protection framework that supports data masking, encryption, anonymization, and authorization. Given compliance requirements like General Data Protection Regulation (GDPR) and the increasing threat of data breaches, anonymization is becoming increasingly necessary. SAP HANA provides sophisticated algorithms to anonymize data on the fly without altering the original data to ensure specific data points cannot be traced back to specific people. If you plan to share data from your SAP S/4HANA system with new applications you build on SAP HANA, you can automatically take advantage of SAP S/4HANA's authorization settings as already implemented, thus saving you time and effort. These features are key for preserving your customers' trust and for monetizing your data assets.

Finally, SAP HANA allows you to choose your own cloud provider, since SAP HANA is designed to run on major cloud platforms in addition to on-premise.

3.3   Big Data Operations Management

With a deluge of data, as shown in Figure 3.4, data often ends up in silos across the enterprise, resulting in distributed landscapes and manual, siloed data operations. Meeting the data access needs of the various LOBs can be a challenge. Lack of data transparency due to difficulties in managing and orchestrating data across distributed data landscapes and the risk and burden of enforcing compliance across a multitude of corporate and regulatory data policies can make innovating with big data a daunting task.

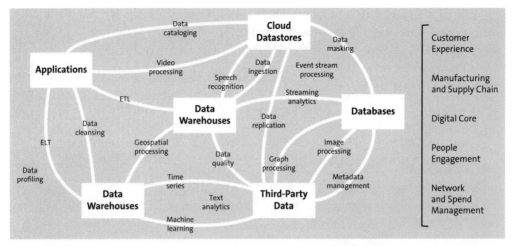

Figure 3.4 Data Deluge Makes Delivering Actionable Information Challenging

A streamlined approach to big data operations is needed to bridge the gap between disparate data sources and the consumption of this data by business processes in your digital core as well as all LOBs. As shown in Figure 3.5, regardless of where the data resides or where it originated, you'll need the ability to centrally orchestrate data and automate the end-to-end process of data discovery, refinement, enrichment, and governance so that you can deliver reliable and trusted data to different users and parts of your organization.

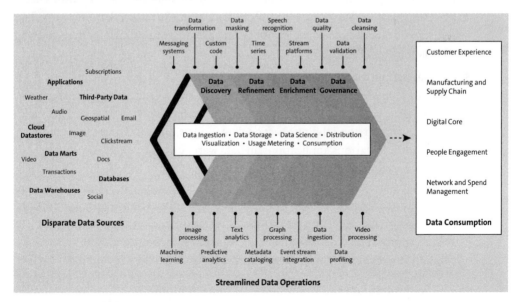

Figure 3.5 Streamlining Data Operations

SAP Data Hub, shown in Figure 3.6, is a multifaceted data operations solution designed to manage the ever-increasing distributed data landscape resulting from big data. SAP Data Hub helps you flexibly scale to orchestrate and automate the flow and refinement process of big data (structured, unstructured, streaming, bulk transfers, etc.), all in a single environment.

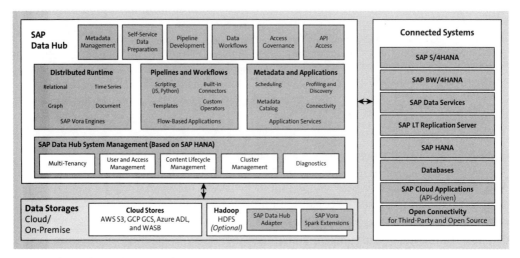

Figure 3.6 SAP Data Hub

To deliver intelligent data with the right context at the right time to the various users in your organization like IT administrators, data administrators, data stewards, data scientists, and business analysts, SAP Data Hub provides the following three building blocks, as shown in Figure 3.7:

- **Data landscape management**
  SAP Data Hub provides open and flexible end-to-end data landscape management. With a full view of your data landscape, you'll be able to orchestrate all data movements and understand their impact on data models. Data could reside on-premise, in the cloud, in various applications, in data warehouses, in data lakes, and in both SAP or non-SAP sources. Your data won't need to be physically centralized; instead, the orchestration of the data is centralized. You can leverage existing connections and integration tools as well as add new connections easily and flexibly. You can manage security settings for data access and enforce data policies to ensure appropriate data governance and security. A comprehensive view of systems and assets across the entire landscape helps you monitor your data.

- **Data pipelining**

  You can create, automate, and reuse powerful data pipelines to cleanse, conform, transform, ingest, refine, orchestrate, prepare, and enrich information from a variety of sources across your organization, all while leaving the data where it resides. You can define data operations processes by reusing existing code and libraries consisting of several predefined and customizable operations. You can understand the impact of quality problems on all downstream systems and applications to drive efficient and speedy innovations through the consumption of big data.

- **Data governance**

  Given the characteristics of the 3Vs of big data, delivering the right data to the right users with the right context at the right time is vitally important. Data profiling helps you analyze data to clarify its structure, uncover its relationships, determine deviation rules, and understand anomalies. Data profiling helps in data discovery so you can evolve data models more quickly. Metadata cataloging helps define, govern, and manage your metadata assets across enterprise systems with disparate sources.

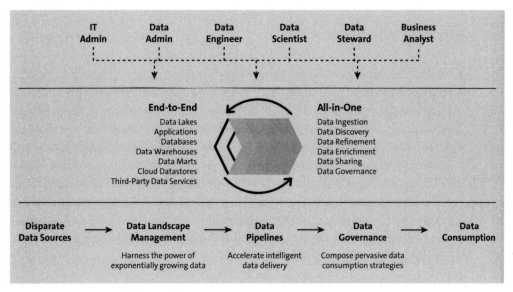

Figure 3.7 SAP Data Hub for Intelligent Data

SAP Data Hub has a cloud-native architecture and is designed to run in any environment—on-premise, cloud, or hybrid. SAP Data Hub can be installed on Kubernetes clusters provided by Google (Google Kubernetes Engine), on Microsoft Azure (Azure

Container Service), and Amazon Web Services (AWS). Apache Hadoop and embedded Apache Spark are optional components.

SAP Data Hub supports numerous data sources, for example, SAP HANA, SAP Vora, SAP Business Warehouse (SAP BW), Hadoop Distributed File System (HDFS), native cloud storage like Amazon S3, Google Cloud Platform, Google Cloud Storage, Microsoft Azure, ADL, and WASB. SAP Data Hub also supports several messaging systems like Kafka, Message Queuing Telemetry Transport (MQTT), NATS, and WAMP. Additional data sources can be connected via SAP Data Services.

With these capabilities, SAP Data Hub can help create value from your various big data initiatives at scale by supporting agile, data-driven applications and processes, for example:

- **Data science and machine learning data management**
  The use of machine learning on big data has vast applications across all industries, for instance, risk profiling in insurance, credit analysis and generating automated scoring models, predicting failures for automated preventive maintenance of assets, and fraud detection, to name a few. Typically, these applications start as data science projects where data scientists spend considerable time collecting, cleansing, and organizing data from various sources (structured, unstructured, streaming, etc.).

  SAP Data Hub can help you move from the prototype stage to production by identifying and refining all relevant data in a reliable and cost-efficient way. SAP Data Hub provides you with a single solution to process machine learning and advanced analytics algorithms using both SAP engines (SAP HANA Predictive Analysis Library, SAP Leonardo Machine Learning Foundation) as well as non-SAP engines (Python, R, SparkML, TensorFlow, etc.) to quickly operationalize machine learning outcomes back into enterprise processes to democratize their usage beyond your data science team. In addition, SAP Data Hub provides extensive data wrangling capabilities out of the box so that your data science team can spend less time collecting and cleansing the data and more time analyzing the data to create algorithms that help you rapidly innovate.

- **IoT data ingestion and orchestration**
  IoT-enabled devices provide you with real-world performance information that you can use to optimize your supply chain and logistics applications. You can perform on-the-fly, context-aware rerouting and replanning to adjust to changing business conditions, by using the concept of a digital twin to test outcomes and impacts of potential actions. As a result, you could provide better customer

service, create new revenue-generating business models, and/or initiate smart manufacturing by establishing predictive maintenance for your shop floor assets, etc. The challenge you'll need to overcome is integrating and analyzing vast amounts of raw data streams and events from disparate sources with low-level semantics and little or no business context. You must integrate IoT data with enterprise data stored in data warehouses, data marts, enterprise applications, etc. and be able to handle high volumes of data and complex computations. SAP Data Hub helps you meet the challenges of point-to-point integration and allows you to process disparate date from messaging systems, high-volume cloud storage, and enterprise applications with event-based pipelines and can execute thousands of pipelines in parallel at any time across highly distributed landscapes.

- **Intelligent data warehousing**
  As your business grows, you'll need to rapidly integrate and leverage new data sources with your existing traditional data warehouses, data marts, big data stores, and enterprise applications. Such situations can arise when you acquire or merge with companies or start big data projects like Hadoop. SAP Data Hub's capabilities can help you with these goals.

- **Governance and data cataloging**
  SAP Data Hub's centralized metadata catalog helps you effectively secure and govern an ever-increasing number of disparate data sources. This solution can crawl through your connected sources automatically to discover entities and their relationships. All the valuable metadata can be gathered and stored in a centralized information catalog so that you can search common data definitions and business rules in a seamless fashion regardless of how diverse and distributed your data source landscape is. The profiling capability helps you gain a deeper understanding of the source data so you can create meaningful pipelines.

- **SAP HANA cold data tiering**
  SAP Data Hub reduces total storage cost by optimizing integration from SAP HANA into various object storages like HDFS, Amazon S3, ADL/WASB, GSC, etc. You'll be able to offload older, less frequently accessed data to a much lower-cost storage options while still making this data accessible and usable whenever needed.

3.4   Big Data Services

Companies tend to start experimenting with leveraging big data by dipping their toes into Hadoop pilot projects. Soon, they realize the enormous benefits of big data, and these one-off pilots become larger-scale projects with large Hadoop and Spark big data clusters with multiple compute and storage nodes.

Since Hadoop runs in a distributed manner on multiple nodes, a host of complexities in this process often arise, including hundreds of Hadoop and Spark parameters to configure, troubleshoot, maintain, and upgrade; cluster parameters to fine-tune; and queries to modify to boost performance, among other things. In an on-premise approach, you'll need to consider the cost and lead time required to procure hardware; the effort required to manage the data center daily; the need to keep up with hardware and software installations and upgrades; the need to hire and train staff; and the burden of dealing with evolving computing and storage needs (e.g. data aging, training machine learning models, etc.).

Cloud-based big data platforms help you overcome all these challenges. These platforms help you future-proof your investment in a scalable data platform, allowing you to start small and grow your storage and computing resources over time by leveraging elastic computing and storage capabilities. You can easily onboard new big data sources like IoT, social media, mobile, etc. and quickly transition your proofs of concepts (POCs) to proofs of value at production scale. Last, but not the least, flexible, consumption-based pricing models allow you to efficiently allocate your capital.

SAP Cloud Platform Big Data Services, shown in Figure 3.8, provides all these benefits in a one-stop solution that includes hardware, software, data center operations, and support as well as integration with your SAP landscape. As a result, you can focus your efforts on building big data-driven applications to achieve the desired business outcomes and to reap the benefits of mining big data at petabyte scale.

SAP Cloud Platform Big Data Services run on infrastructure in data centers optimized for big data. These servers provide the right balance of computing power, memory, and disk storage for Hadoop and Spark workloads. The network provides bisectional bandwidth to support high volumes of interserver traffic while lightweight containers avoid the performance penalty common in virtual machines. SAP provides 24/7 operational support to keep your clusters healthy and running. The management tools found in the Unified Control Panel can provision your clusters, grow/shrink them as needed, and monitor them on an ongoing basis.

At the core of SAP Cloud Platform Big Data Services is Apache Hadoop and Spark, which can serve as a platform for you to build applications and run big data workloads. You can run your choice of big data tools on Hadoop like analytics, data exploration, custom applications, etc. Finally, the workbench is a server that acts as an edge or gateway node to access the cluster. SAP provides tools for data transfer from common data stores like local file systems or Amazon S3. A web-based portal can serve as a central access point for your administrators to manage users and view cluster usage.

Security is an integral part of the SAP Cloud Platform Big Data Services, which is SOC 2 Type II and HIPPA compliant. SAP enables Kerberos on the environment for distributed network authentication if needed.

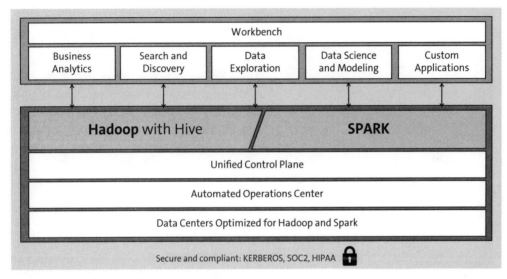

Figure 3.8 SAP Cloud Platform Data Services

With SAP Cloud Platform Big Data Services, you'll have access to fully managed and optimized big data operations for storing and processing structured and unstructured data, for training and scoring machine learning models, for running analytics, and for building IoT use cases, thus allowing you to minimize development and maintenance effort even while engaging in rapid innovation cycles.

3.5 Summary

Regardless of your industry, big data is a treasure trove of information, not only so you can intimately understand your customers' needs and behaviors, but also so you can innovate new business models and outflank your competition. As you embark on your big data journey, you'll need a sound technology strategy for storing, processing, and scaling your operations with big data as well as for helping your business users leverage big data to make well-informed decisions in real time. Both hardware and software considerations as well as integration tools for your enterprise data and analytics will need to be considered, as will data privacy and security, which are of utmost importance. Taking a cloud approach has numerous advantages, both from a cost perspective and from a scalability perspective, since big data has the power to radically transform your business.

Chapter 4
Analytics

The organizations that thrive in the digital economy are the ones that give all their employees, partners, and customers immediate access to the most relevant information they need to answer questions, understand the business needs, and seize new opportunities.

Analytics is a key pillar of SAP Leonardo's intelligent technologies that helps you build an intelligent enterprise. The ability to access and share timely, relevant, and trustworthy information is essential for driving confident and well-informed business decisions. Analytics tools need to be open for you to develop tailored analytical applications that fit your unique business needs, such as line of business (LOB) applications or industry-specific processes. These tools should be intuitive and easy to consume on any device.

As described in Part I, analytics is one of six SAP Leonardo intelligent technologies that can help drive innovation by optimizing your processes and resources. In this chapter, we'll cover how analytics can play a key role in achieving the digital transformation to improve business outcomes. We'll cover various SAP products for analytics under SAP Leonardo and their key capabilities to help you optimize, extend, and transform your business.

SAP provides a comprehensive set of analytics capabilities to help you transition to the digital age. In the following sections, we'll cover capabilities in business intelligence, planning and analysis, and predictive analytics that will empower you, with easy access to data exploration tools to drive smarter processes, model and manage the performance of your enterprise with fact-based decisions, and accelerate digital transformation with predictive analytics through insights embedded in your processes and business applications.

4.1   What Is Analytics?

Analytics is the process of evaluating, examining, and processing large amounts of data to find patterns, correlations, and insights. SAP Leonardo allows you to automate parts of the analytics process and the resulting business decisions to achieve dynamic insights.

SAP Leonardo Analytics provides across-the-board analytics capabilities that work together to analyze data from all sources. The analytics solution uncovers issue and opportunity areas in the business, helps automate repetitive tasks, and provides insight for better and more efficient decision-making. Along with the SAP Leonardo standard capability, the analytics solution can be further fortified by SAP Analytics Cloud, SAP Digital Boardroom, and other solutions.

Analytics should be embedded in all your business applications for in-context analysis, and function-specific analytics applications are needed to streamline your planning, budgeting, and forecasting needs. Figure 4.1 shows the typical maturity curve of user engagement versus use of analytics capabilities, broadly broken into using analytics to sense and respond, and predict and act. As you adopt advanced analytics capabilities, you'll leverage predictive analytics to move from understanding what happened and why it happened, to analyzing what will likely happen, and finally to using prescriptive analytics to assess what best could happen based on certain actions so as to optimize your decision-making and achieve your desired goals.

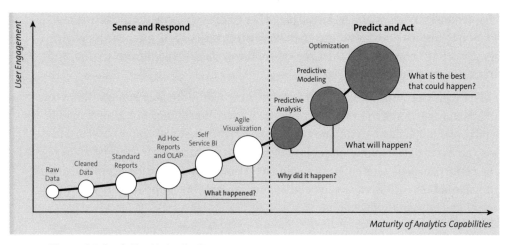

Figure 4.1 Analytics Maturity Curve

4.2   Business Intelligence Portfolio

SAP provides a comprehensive SAP Analytics portfolio, as shown in Figure 4.2. The SAP Analytics solution portfolio is composed of SAP Analytics on-premise solutions with business intelligence, planning, and predictive analytics capabilities as well as SAP Analytics Cloud, which provides a single platform in the cloud for all the analytics capabilities: business intelligence, planning, predictive, and application design.

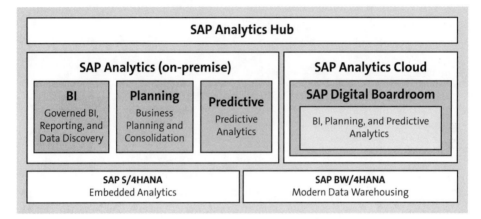

Figure 4.2 SAP Analytics Portfolio

Built natively on SAP Cloud Platform, SAP Analytics Cloud, as shown in Figure 4.3, supports data discovery, live data connectivity, data visualization, planning, simulation, what-if analysis, forecasting, and many other capabilities. To extend your existing analytics investments, SAP enables interoperability between the two to enhance your existing solutions and enables hybrid workflows with live data connectivity as well as import access to on-premise data sources, integration to SAP Analysis for Microsoft Office, and the import and export of planning models. SAP S/4HANA embedded analytics provide contextual analytics embedded in the SAP S/4HANA business processes, and SAP BW/4HANA provides modern data warehousing capabilities.

SAP BW/4HANA is designed to provide fast query performance with open and modern interfaces. Powerful transition tools are available to convert models, flows, and data from SAP Business Warehouse (SAP BW) to SAP BW/4HANA to reduce development effort. While SAP BW/4HANA simplifies data integration and offers comprehensive access to external systems, as shown in Figure 4.4, live connections to SAP BW/4HANA queries from SAP Analytics Cloud allow you to access these various sources of data for your analytics needs.

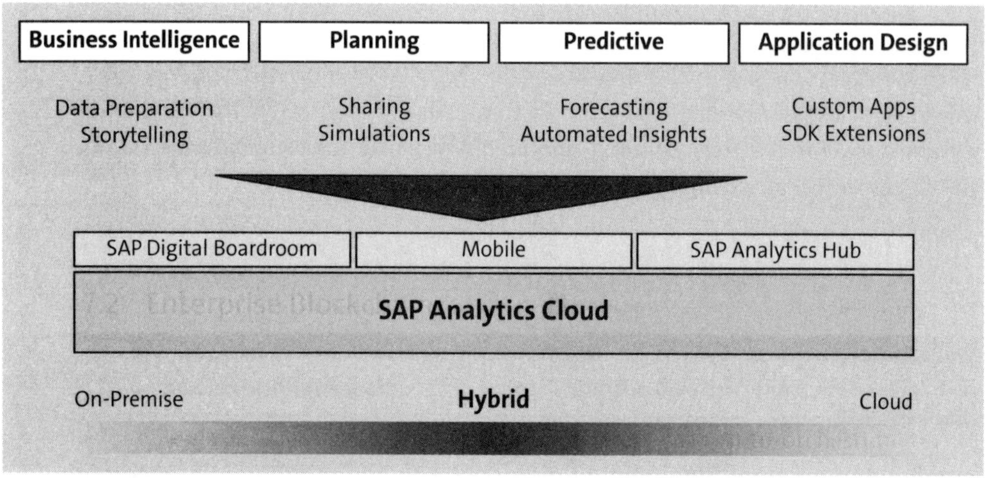

Business Intelligence
Planning
Predictive
Application Design
Data Preparation
Storytelling
Sharing
Simulations
Forecasting
Automated Insights
Custom Apps
SDK Extensions
SAP Digital Boardroom
Mobile
SAP Analytics Hub
SAP Analytics Cloud
On-Premise
Hybrid
Cloud

Figure 4.3 SAP Analytics Cloud

SAP BW/4HANA
SAP HANA Source System
ODP Source System
Big Data Source System
File Source System
SAP HANA
SAP EIM
Real-time replication
Direct access
Data load
Non-SAP Data
• Text
• Email
• RDBMS/Hadoop
• Social Media
• Structured
SAP Data
ODQ
• Extractors
• SAP Landscape Transformation
• SAP BW
• SAP Business ByDesign
• ABAP CDS
Big Data
HIVE
SPARK
SAP Vora
Hadoop
File
File

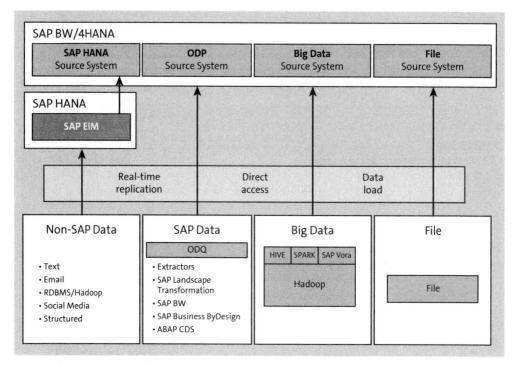

Figure 4.4 Comprehensive Access to all Data with SAP BW/4HANA

Finally, SAP Analytics Hub provides a cloud-based, single point of access for both on-premise and cloud analytics. SAP Analytics Hub provides a unified user experience, independent of content or deployment type, so that business users have a simple way to search for content, get information, and access analytics. Only metadata is stored, not the actual data, thus avoiding data duplication and redundancy, which would otherwise drive up your total cost of ownership (TCO). Content could originate from SAP Analytics Cloud, SAP BusinessObjects Enterprise, or other SAP or third-party sources.

In the SAP Analytics portfolio, flexible source data integration is available through live access as well as import access from on-premise sources. The data can be stored in on-premise databases, in cloud-based databases, or in personal files. You can enrich data and business metadata to prepare and serve up self-service data analysis through purpose-built data modeling and calculation applications. The live connection helps keep your data safe and secure behind your firewall so that no sensitive data is exposed to the Internet. You can use business metadata directly, without the need for additional modeling by leveraging existing security and data authorizations. Data import connections allow business users to model data, easily track and reverse data transformations if needed, and refresh data on demand or via an established data refresh schedule. Table 4.1 shows a partial list of the vast array of data connectors delivered by SAP, as well as by the SAP partner community, to cover your business needs.

Note

At the time of this writing, live connectors to SAP SuccessFactors and SAP Ariba and import connectors for Dow Jones DNA were planned to be delivered within the next six months.

Live		Import	
Cloud data sources	SAP Cloud Platform, SAP S/4HANA Cloud, SAP SuccessFactors, SAP Ariba	Cloud data sources	SAP Cloud for Customers, SAP Cloud Platform, SAP Business ByDesign, SAP S/4HANA Cloud, SAP SuccessFactors, Google Drive, Google Sheets, Salesforce, Dow Jones DNA

Table 4.1 Data Sources for SAP Analytics Cloud

Live		Import	
SAP data sources	SAP HANA, SAP Business Warehouse (SAP BW), SAP BW/HANA, SAP S/4HANA, universes in SAP Business-Objects BI	SAP data sources	SAP Business Planning and Consolidation (SAP BPC), version for NetWeaver, SAP Business Planning and Consolidation (SAP BPC), version for Microsoft, SAP HANA, SAP ERP, universes in SAP BusinessObjects BI, SAP BW, SAP BW/4HANA, SAP S/4HANA
Access via SAP HANA smart data integration for SAP Cloud Platform and SAP HANA	Apache Hive, Amazon AWS, SAP Vora, SAP Adaptive Server Enterprise, ESP, OData, Microsoft SQL Server, Spark SQL, Oracle, Teradata, MaxDB, IBM DB2, MySQL, Netezza, Facebook, Google+, Twitter	Other data sources	IBM, Microsoft SQL Server, MySQL, Netezza, OData, Oracle, CSV, Excel, Progress OpenEdge
Partner-delivered	APOS - DB2, Denodo, Microsoft Analysis Services, Microsoft Azure, Microsoft SQL Server, MongoDB, MongoDB Atlas, MySQL, Netezza, Oracle, Oracle Essbase, Oracle Exadata, Sybase IQ, Sybase SQL Anywhere, Redshift, Teradata, Google BiqQuery	Partner-delivered	APOS – Web Intelligence CDATA – QuickBooks, Microsoft SharePoint, NetSuite CRM & ERP, Oracle Marketing Cloud, MongoDB DataCirect Cloud – eloqua, Google Analytics, Microsoft Dynamics CRM, Hubspot, Marketo, SugarCRM

Table 4.1 Data Sources for SAP Analytics Cloud (Cont.)

To cater to the needs of an intelligent enterprise, intelligence needs to be embedded into every application to make your workflows and business processes smarter. Leveraging SAP Cloud Platform and a common data foundation with SAP HANA and SAP Data Hub, SAP Analytics Cloud provides out of the box integration to all line of business (LOB) applications from SAP, as shown in Figure 4.5. SAP also delivers free business content specific to various LOBs and industries. This content provides a quick and easy starting point to building your individual analytics scenarios and includes predefined stories, dashboards, and data models tailored to existing SAP data sources. You can easily connect the content to your own data and get started in SAP Analytics Cloud. Detailed documentation for key performance indicators (KPIs), models, and data flows are provided so you can understand how the dashboards are built and make the necessary adjustments to suit your specific requirements. You can access this content at *https://www.sapanalytics.cloud/learning/business-content*. In addition, SAP partners offer their SAP Analytics Cloud content, which you can access at *https://www.sapappcenter.com* by searching for "analytics cloud."

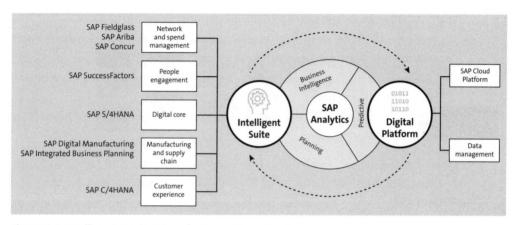

Figure 4.5 Intelligent Applications for Every Line of Business

SAP Analytics Cloud, a software-as-a-service (SaaS) offering, can complement your existing, on-premise deployments like SAP Lumira and the SAP BusinessObjects BI platform via a hybrid deployment. SAP Analytics Cloud is designed to access semantic data from SAP software like universes (from SAP BusinessObject BI), queries of SAP Business Explorer (SAP BEx) tools, and SAP HANA database views, in addition to traditional SQL sources. SAP Analytics Cloud also connects to cloud-based sources from SAP like SAP SuccessFactors, SAP Concur, SAP Fieldglass, SAP Integrated Business Planning (SAP IBP), SAP Business ByDesign, and SAP C/4HANA, as well as third-party sources. If your IT strategy requires on-premise business intelligence, you should use SAP BusinessObjects BI solutions and SAP Lumira.

4.3   Planning and Analysis

To keep pace with customer expectations, you'll need ready access to timely and reliable information, which requires alignment towards a shared objective with consistent

modeling and planning across all your organizational functions, while also addressing their individual needs, such as the following:

- Finance: Financial modeling and reporting, expense planning budget allocations, costing, preparing profit-and-loss, income, and balance sheets
- Sales: Territory, quota and commissions planning, sales forecasting, accounting segmentation, pricing, and quote management
- Marketing: Price and trade promotions planning and optimization, product prof-itability analysis, loyalty management, and campaign optimization
- Operations: Demand planning, inventory management, logistics optimization, warehouse management, production, and procurement planning
- Information technology: Project planning, asset management, resource utiliza-tion, cost allocations, network, and facilities optimization
- Workforce: Staffing needs, benefits analysis, pension planning, healthcare plan-ning, and facilities planning

In the following sections, we'll discuss various solutions in the SAP Leonardo portfo-lio of analytics solutions that provide the capabilities to address your planning and analysis needs.

4.3.1   SAP Analytics Cloud

SAP Analytics Cloud for planning consolidates data across applications and empow-ers planners to perform planning, budgeting, and forecasting with self-service and what-if simulation capabilities, as well as the ability to visualize the financial impact of their decisions with value driver trees. With role-based advanced analytics to uncover insights, you can share analytical results via desktops or mobile devices and resolve issues collaboratively. Smart Assist, a suite of augmented analytics features that use machine learning and natural language processing, augments intelligence to help discover insights and follow recommended steps. Smart Discovery pinpoints variances in data and allows you to drill down to their root causes. Smart Insights help identify the influencers of your KPIs so you can explore trade-offs for better decision-making.

The planning and analysis functionality in SAP Analytics Cloud allows you to avoid the inefficiency caused by standalone spreadsheets and data silos by linking across departmental boundaries and allowing everyone to discover, analyze, plan, predict, and collaborate together in one unified experience. By eliminating error-prone and manually intensive processes, you can shorten planning cycles and optimize the use of your valuable time and resources to focus on what truly matters to your business goals.

4.3.2   SAP Digital Boardroom

Every company expends significant effort in planning and analysis while preparing for executive boardroom meetings. Working off disparate sets of spreadsheets, reports, and static presentations, the information in which is likely outdated due to changing business conditions, makes it difficult to make sound, timely decisions. The management team needs visibility to the complete business strategy, as well as its individual components, and the ability to track and respond quickly to challenges that arise in individual business units. SAP Digital Boardroom, powered by SAP HANA and experienced through SAP Analytics Cloud, allows you to examine a range of potential scenarios and make timely and informed decisions using up-to-date data. As shown in Figure 4.6, SAP Digital Boardroom uses line of business data from SAP S/4HANA, the SAP HANA platform, SAP BW, and other SAP and non-SAP applications to provide a real-time view of your critical business metrics in one place.

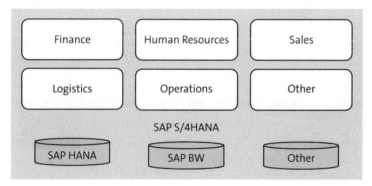

Figure 4.6 SAP Digital Boardroom

SAP Digital Boardroom is optimized to display on large, triple-linked touchscreens. You can also use SAP Digital Boardroom with a single screen and a projector. Business leaders can visualize and interact with all the critical metrics and drill down to the line item level to fully understand the business performance and address ad-hoc questions that arise, in real time. Confidently analyzing root causes, identifying business challenges and opportunities, and simulating the impact of decisions during the meeting, rather deferring decisions to collect more information, completely transforms the decision-making process. The integrated visualization, planning, simulation, and predictive capabilities of SAP Digital Boardroom can help you realize more value from your investments in SAP S/4HANA and achieve your digital transformation goals.

4.3.3   SAP Business Planning and Consolidation

While SAP Analytics Cloud for planning provides an SaaS solution to discover, plan, predict, and collaborate all in one place, SAP Business Planning and Consolidation (SAP BPC), with versions for SAP NetWeaver as well as SAP BW/4HANA, is an on-premise solution for unified planning, budgeting, forecasting, and consolidation that can handle complex workflows. SAP BPC eliminates standalone spreadsheets and helps improve the accuracy of plans and financial reporting with a centralized data store. With SAP BPC, you can run multiple what-if scenarios in real time. SAP BPC for SAP S/4HANA is based on the SAP BPC version for SAP NetWeaver but is embedded directly within SAP S/4HANA. Its benefits include real-time monitoring and analysis with access to master data and actuals in SAP S/4HANA, thus eliminating the need for periodic data replication. SAP BPC provides out of the box content for various reports, costing simulations, and sales planning scenarios. By leveraging the in-memory capabilities of SAP HANA, SAP BPC is a high-performance, highly scalable solution. The user experience is enhanced with SAP Fiori and SAP Analysis for Microsoft Office.

You can extend your investment in an on-premise SAP BPC solution with SAP Analytics Cloud in a hybrid scenario by using the native, bidirectional integration to move data and metadata between SAP BPC and SAP Analytics Cloud. This connection allows you to combine the best of SAP's mature and proven solution in SAP BPC with cloud-based capabilities for web-based reporting, visualization, collaboration, and predictive analytics in SAP Analytics Cloud.

4.3.4   SAP Profitability and Performance Management

To manage and measure profitability across multiple entities, SAP Profitability and Performance Management provides an on-premise solution for quickly allocating and analyzing costs and profitability with a variety of allocation methods to distribute costs and revenues and calculate funds transfer pricing on aggregated or individual instrument level. You can augment your profitability insights by minimizing data latency, redundancy, and reconciliation efforts with its strong integration with SAP BPC and SAP S/4HANA while leveraging the in-memory computational speed of SAP S/4HANA to evaluate results within seconds or minutes instead of hours.

4.4   Predictive Analytics

Data discovery and insights can be prone to human bias, and often data that is easily accessible or fits a hypothesis is chosen, which raises the question, can we trust these insights? With more data to deal with, uncovering key trends and patterns is an onerous task. Moreover, even when a new insight is uncovered, how do you decide the best course of action? As shown in Figure 4.1, you can augment your analytics journey with machine learning and predictive analytics to increase your ability to make the best decisions and influence the best outcomes by fully understanding what happened in the past and using these insights to predict what could happen in the future.

SAP Analytics Cloud makes machine learning simple for business users. Analytics augmented with machine learning can help automate data preparation, insight discovery, and insight sharing across users in your organization. Regardless of their understanding of statistics, analysts of all skill levels can build relevant visualizations into a story, draw attention to key insights and answer questions by creating their own predictive insights. You would start with data preparation and collection to automatically detect and correct data issues, rapidly apply necessary data transformations, understand data distributions, and detect outliers. Using natural language processing, you can simplify searches; automatically generate visual answers by identifying unique groups and trends; and enhance the visualizations with automatic, in-context explanations. By identifying key influencers and through pattern detection, you can simulate the impact on your KPIs by adjusting the values of key drivers. You can forecast future values based on historical data to predict the likelihood of future events along with explanations for every recommendation. You can publish real-time predictions from your latest data into business applications, plans, and stories.

For example, with SAP Predictive Analytics integrator, you can extend or create new predictive scenarios in SAP Analytics Cloud and publish these scenarios into SAP applications like SAP S/4HANA. SAP has developed several predictive scenarios with embedded machine learning and predictive analytics, which are delivered as templates in SAP S/4HANA and SAP C/4HANA. You can train these models with your own data and activate them for consumption through SAP Fiori tiles via defined user roles. Some of the predelivered predictive scenarios include the following:

- *Quantity contract consumption* uses machine learning to anticipate upcoming contract negotiations. Machine learning algorithms identify the contracts that are nearing the end of their terms and calculate the probability of the contract being consumed sooner than expected. This feature helps buyers by suggesting early and efficient renegotiations, which in turn may result in better prices for goods from suppliers.

- *Predict arrival of stock in transit* allows warehouse managers to predict the arrival of a shipment and classify its status into different classes. Early visibility to stock transport orders allows warehouse managers optimize and automate the business process of tracking stock in transit, thus leading to more reliable planning and scheduling. With the Materials Overdue – Stock in Transit application, users can get an overview of open shipments, allowing them to take action in case of delivery delays. Predictive application integration is used to provide predicted shipment dates for each goods movement.

- *Quotation conversion probability rate* allows sales leaders to improve sales forecasts with reliable predictions for achievable sales volumes by calculating the probability that a quotation item will be converted into a sales order item. The probability and net value of the quotation are used to calculate a total expected order value. This solution replaces the practice of manual calculation or the manual estimation of order probability with reliable predictions.

- *Payment block – cash discount at risk* allows accountants and purchasers to further automate and reduce exception handling situations in the invoice matching process. Unplanned additional costs in an invoice or quantity or price deviations trigger the automatic blocking of supplier invoices despite the highly digitized and automated invoicing process. This solution provides proactive visibility to issues requiring attention, with all the relevant information in one place, and helps you take advantage of cash discounts offered by suppliers in exchange for fast processing.

- *Smart alerts for profit and loss analysis* proactively informs the group controller of unusual business situations in revenue and cost accounts, decreasing the time required to investigate. The solution allows you to explore multidimensional data with filter combinations, detect unusual increases and decreases in single key figures, and get notifications on changes in trending behavior as well as track correlation changes between multiple key figures. Users can collaboratively examine these findings and add annotations.

- *Project cost forecasting* allows project managers to predict project costs ahead of time and reduce risks of budget overruns. Using machine learning in combination with reference class forecasting, i.e. by learning from past projects, project forecasts are derived based on facts rather than subjective criteria.

In addition, SAP also provides the following predictive scenarios:

- SAP Business Integrity Screening to enhance fraud alerts with predictive analytics
- SAP Tax Compliance to provide smart automation of compliance issue processing
- Opportunity scoring to increase win rates with predictive sales pipelines and revenue forecasting
- Dynamic adjustment and optimization of inventory buffers based on replenishment lead times
- Sales forecast prediction to forecast sales using predictive analytics
- Supplier delivery performance improvement using predictive analytics
- Estimate of project costs based on historical project data

These examples show how you can empower your workforce and management team with better decision-making capabilities and infuse intelligence into every business process to create better outcomes with embedded predictive analytics.

You can retrain these models directly within the application, and model debriefing enables you to verify the quality of the model. You can easily adapt these predictive use cases to create new ones based on your unique business needs. Smart Assist provides you intelligence and planning workflows by letting you ask natural language questions about your data by bringing conversational AI to analytics. Smart Predict, a self-service solution in the cloud, supports data ingestion, predictive model authoring, and model management in SAP Analytics Cloud, enabling business users to build custom models to meet their specific requirements.

While SAP Analytics Cloud for predictive analytics provides business users the ability to automatically analyze their data using machine guidance, SAP Predictive Analytics, an on-premise offering, is intended for more sophisticated business users or data scientists. SAP Predictive Analytics helps you manage the entire lifecycle of the predictive models, as shown in Figure 4.7. Data can be sourced from both SAP and non-SAP applications as well as other data sources. You can prepare predictive datasets and create, manage, and operationalize predictive models. The solution consists of predictive factory, a modeling tool, and, for SAP HANA customers, a native SAP HANA component called the Automated Predictive Library (APL).

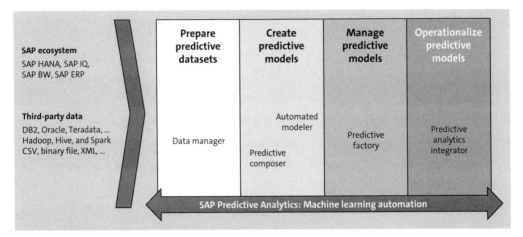

Figure 4.7 SAP Predictive Analytics

4.5   Summary

Analytics can play a key role in your company's digital transformation into an intelligent enterprise. With the ability to intelligently sift through the large amounts of data that is being generated, your employees can focus on high value-add tasks, and your workforce can become proactive, rather than reactive to changing business conditions. Not only can you provide the best value to your customers through your products and services, thus differentiating your company from your competition, you can continuously innovate and invent new business models by using your data to drive profitable decision-making in real time. Analytics can provide you the foresight to optimally deal with uncertainty in your industry and confidently drive strategic decisions.

Chapter 5
Machine Learning

Machine learning is a component of artificial intelligence (AI) that provides systems the ability to automatically and continuously learn to improve business understanding with the purpose of driving better outcomes.

Machine learning enables computers to complete operational tasks by learning from large sets of operational data, outcomes, or historical data rather than just being explicitly programmed to perform repeatable tasks. Machine learning often uses a library of complex algorithms to learn from large sets of big data derived from multiple sources. The general rule is that the more comprehensive the data available (for example, larger sets of historical data dating back further in time, more seasons), the more intelligent algorithms become (with better results and more accurate anomaly detection).

This chapter begins by introducing machine learning in general, explaining what the technology is and how it works. We'll then focus on the use of machine learning in the context of enterprise applications. Next, we'll look at SAP Leonardo Machine Learning Foundation, before moving on to the application of machine learning within existing SAP tools and products. In this section, we won't go into depth about each product in which machine learning can be embedded but rather, we'll elaborate on how machine learning can enrich these solutions. Finally, we'll end the chapter with a look at a brand-new offering from SAP: SAP Intelligent Robotic Process Automation.

5.1 What Is Machine Learning?

Data scientists use machine learning to explore, discover, and train algorithms to detect patterns in big data. The goal is to use machine learning to derive new insights and deliver new outcomes, through two categories of algorithms: supervised learning algorithms and unsupervised learning algorithms.

Supervised machine learning is often the starting point for beginners and more commonly used when the context, processes, or outcome are more descriptive or better known by humans. Examples of algorithms used by supervised learning are linear and logistic regression, multiclass classification, and support vector machines. In supervised machine learning, a data scientist takes the lead to decide the inputs and desired outputs to program the algorithm with an end design and expected descriptive result in mind. Therefore, with supervised learning, the algorithm's outputs are already known and require that the input data used to train the algorithm is already labeled. In this case, supervised learning can improve existing processes in terms of performance or efficiency with a focus on automation.

Unsupervised machine learning is closer to what we define as artificial intelligence and emphasizes the exploration of data through continuous learning. In this case, algorithms learn to identify anomalies and patterns in data without human intervention and train themselves through continuous data exploration. Today, we've only just started exploring the possibilities with unsupervised learning, which is often used for simpler use cases. However, this area shows much promise, and unsupervised machine learning may lend itself to solving much more complex problems that humans normally lack the capacity to solve.

In unsupervised learning, new data inputs are identified and relabeled with new categories. For example, IoT sensor data like friction, vibration, and temperature could all be identified as triggers/symptoms related to malfunctioning or incorrectly installed spare parts in machinery. Often, the inputs and outputs are unexpected and have changed over time as the algorithm learns or accesses more relevant inputs and delivers more valuable results. The outcome of unsupervised learning can result in creating new business processes and/or inspire a process change. In reality, a combination of both supervised and unsupervised learning is used for executing machine learning principles.

At a broad level, the output of a machine learning algorithm is based on the algorithm used with the training data. Typical modeling categories include the following:

- **Regression**
  Regression analysis is based on statistical modeling and is used for causal inferences. Regressions are performed through the usage of independent and dependent variables. Regression analysis determines the correlation between the outcomes by predicting the dependent variable based on the value of independent variables. For training data, values for both variables are provided. The model fits

a regression line, which can be used to predict the value on the test data. Figure 5.1 shows an example of a regression analysis where a regression line is fit for the dependent variable of sales revenue based on the independent variable values of the sales promotion budget and the new product research budget. This regression line can be used to predict future sales revenue based on the sales promotion and product research budget. SAP Leonardo Machine Learning Foundation and solutions like demand sensing include various sophisticated regression models for predictive analytics.

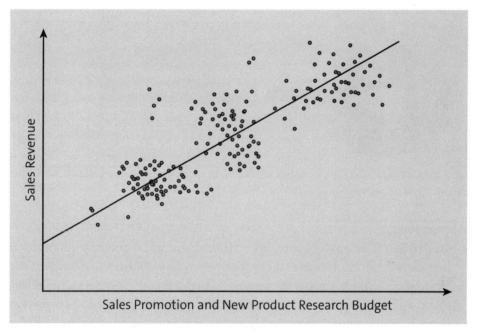

Figure 5.1 Machine Learning Regression Example

- **Classification**
  The goal of a classification model is categorizing an object into a group of preidentified categories based on its attributes. Thousands of fraudulent credit card transactions are now checked through machine learning classification models, where, based on attributes of the transaction, fraudulent transactions are flagged from thousands of transactions in real time. Another example, shown in Figure 5.2, is based on image recognition to identify a product. In this example, the asset maintenance team takes a picture of a worn-out part and feeds the image into the SAP Leonardo system.

Using the classification algorithm, machine learning can identify the critical part and monitors its current inventory in the plant from among thousands of the other parts. Then, through the integrated enterprise system, machine learning can offer the option to order additional quantities from inventory at the warehouse or to create a purchase order to procure from a supplier so that no production stoppages occur due to the part not being available in a timely manner. This example demonstrates the huge transformative potential of machine learning in inventory management for maintenance parts and the associated process efficiency gains.

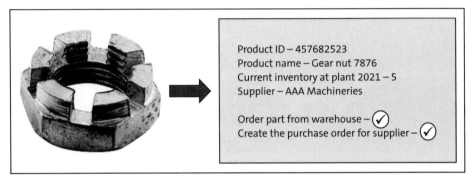

Figure 5.2 Machine Learning Classification Example

- **Clustering**
  Clustering is an example of unsupervised learning aimed at grouping a population into meaningful clusters relevant for business actions and decision-making. The expectation is that members of the same cluster or group will share more similarities than members of the other clusters. The number of clusters for a population size can be either provided to the algorithm or can be calculated by the machine learning cluster modeling algorithm. Figure 5.3 shows the example of a cluster algorithm output by SAP Leonardo in which for an online retail company, customers are grouped based on their yearly income and the yearly purchase amount. As shown in Figure 5.3, customers can be grouped into three separate identifiable clusters; these clusters can be used for targeted sales promotion programs, focused advertising, or creating upsell opportunities. Such intelligence enhances the effectiveness of sales and marketing budgets, creates revenue, generates opportunities, lowers the revenue-to-cost ratio for each customer, and generates long-term customer loyalty.

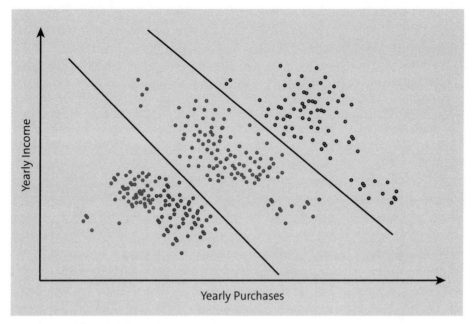

Figure 5.3 Machine Learning Cluster Example

Two types of machine learning approaches exist, as follows:

- **Embedded machine learning**
  This approach is appropriate for simple cases like trending or forecasting or for algorithms with low CPU/RAM/data demands. Data located in S/4HANA is sufficient for model training—no need for massive amounts of external data for training. The required algorithms are provided by SAP HANA (e.g. the Predictive Analysis Library, the Automated Predictive Library (APL), text analysis) and handled by the SAP Predictive Analytics integrator in terms of machine learning model lifecycle management.

- **Side-by-side machine learning**
  This approach is appropriate for deep learning cases like image or language processing or neural networks with high CPU/RAM/data demands. The machine learning logic resides in the SAP Cloud Platform while the business logic can be based on SAP S/4HANA or SAP Cloud Platform. Huge volumes of external data are required for model training, with a focus on processing unstructured data.

Figure 5.4 shows the architecture involved in machine learning; on the center left, you'll see an example of embedded machine learning used within SAP S/4HANA or applications whereby machine learning runs side-by-side, such as the case in the upper right corner where SAP S/4HANA machine learning applications use SAP Leonardo Machine Learning Foundation's business and technical services.

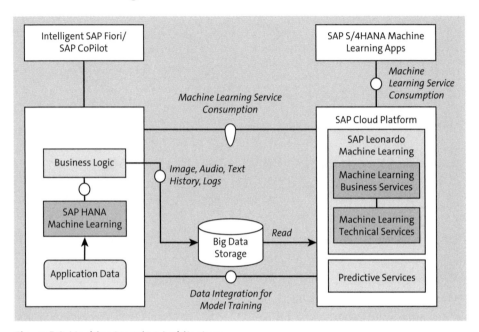

Figure 5.4 Machine Learning Architecture

5.2   Machine Learning Foundation

The solution of choice for building, creating, and testing machine learning algorithms for applications is SAP Leonardo Machine Learning Foundation, which provides users and companies the ability to build, test, execute, modify, and maintain algorithms.

SAP Leonardo Machine Learning Foundation is used for creating customized machine learning applications. Users of all levels, including novice beginners with no data-science skills, can use the toolset and library of existing templates and algorithms to experiment, edit, modify, and test, while advanced users can use the platform to create sophisticated algorithms. SAP Leonardo Machine Learning

Foundation can also connect multiple stakeholders, including developers, partners, and customers, to share machine learning technologies through the SAP Cloud Platform.

SAP Leonardo Machine Learning Foundation is a cloud-based product with a ready-to-use services library with prebuilt algorithms to train, test, and execute algorithms using custom data sources or multiple data sources. The ability to integrate third-party solutions and data sources for data flow streams, such as Google TensorFlow models, is also possible. The solution can help you easily develop and improve customized applications processes with machine learning rules and provides the option of using different data types with algorithms specializing in image, speech, text, and time-series data.

As shown in Figure 5.5, SAP Leonardo Machine Learning Foundation empowers end users to execute machine learning processes embedded through applications. Some capabilities are as follows:

- Developers can use reusable machine learning services to build into their applications.
- Data scientists can perform the training of models as a service by implementing their own models.

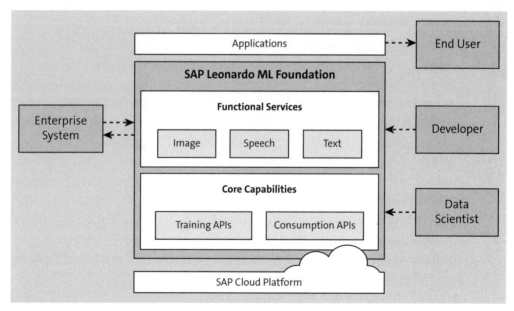

Figure 5.5 SAP Leonardo Machine Learning Foundation

- Retraining as a service can be used to customize or modify existing machine learning models.
- You can bring your own model and deploy existing results as a service.
- Services can be embedded into business applications.

Enterprise systems can serve as data sources via the cloud connector in SAP Cloud Platform Connectivity, or you can use SAP Data Hub to connect to an SAP S/4HANA or SAP HANA database system.

The main functional services in SAP Leonardo Machine Learning Foundation include algorithms for image, text, and speech processing. Customized machine learning services can be used with your own data using training APIs and custom models. You can also consume the services via REST APIs using the consumption APIs.

SAP Leonardo Machine Learning Foundation's image processing capabilities include the following functionalities:

- **Image classification**
  Classifies an image into generic categories, such as attribute types, color, size, image theme, etc.

- **Customizable image classification**
  Create a custom image classification service with your own data to recognize your own classification types.

- **Customizable image object detection**
  Create a service that localizes and recognizes custom objects in images.

- **Image feature extraction**
  Represents the content of an image as a vector, which can be used for search or finding pictures with similar content.

- **Optical character recognition (OCR) and scene text recognition**
  Processes document scans or images containing text and extracts texts and numbers.

- **Human detection and face detection**
  Detect pictures that show humans or human faces.

- **Face feature extraction**
  Represents a picture of a face as a vector, which can be used to find pictures with matching faces.

- **Multi-instance image segmentor**
  Partitions an image into multiple segments, typically used to detect boundaries or locate objects.

Figure 5.6 shows SAP Leonardo Machine Learning Foundation's image processing capabilities and examples of image processing microservices.

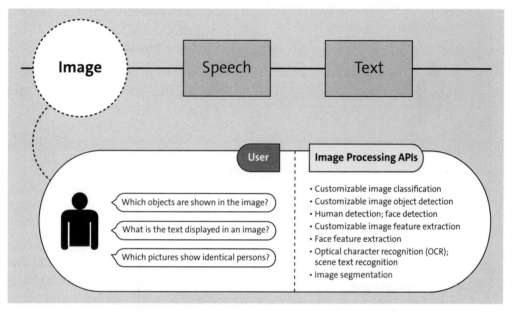

Figure 5.6 Machine Learning Image Classification

SAP Conversational AI is a platform to include capabilities for natural language processing technology. This platform can be used to create custom bots that can understand and communicate with customers and automate repeatable tasks efficiently. Industry-specific, off-the-shelf customer support bots make for quick and easy implementation. Speech capabilities include the following:

- Speech-to-text processing: Converting speech into text.
- Text-to-speech processing: Converting text into speech.

Figure 5.7 shows SAP Leonardo Machine Learning Foundation's speech processing capability and example microservices.

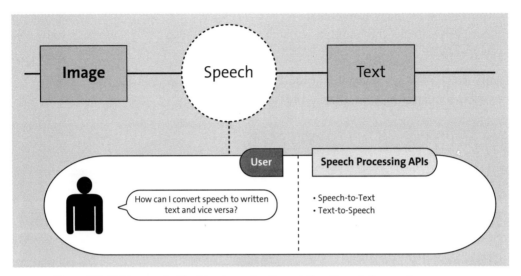

Figure 5.7 SAP Leonardo Machine Learning Foundation Speech Processing

Finally, text processing services include the following:

- **Topic detection services**
  Extracts topics and keywords from documents and assigns the documents to the most relevant topics.

- **Customizable text classification**
  Use custom text data to create your own text classification service.

- **Text feature extraction**
  Represent the content of a text document as vector, which you can be used for retrieving similar documents.

- **Language detection**
  Detects the language of a given text.

- **Translation**
  Translate texts into different languages, specifically suited for SAP-related content to provide accurate terminology.

Figure 5.8 shows SAP Leonardo Machine Learning Foundation's text processing capabilities and its related microservices.

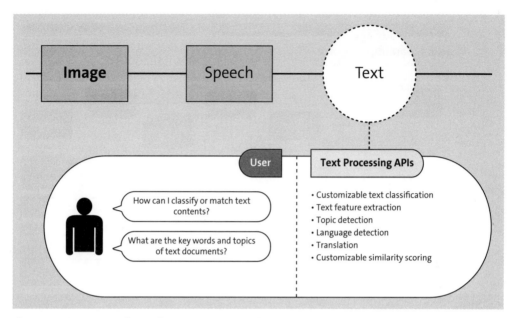

Figure 5.8 SAP Leonardo Machine Learning Foundation Text

5.3   Embedded Machine Learning

Machine learning technology is currently embedded in several SAP solutions, from the digital core to planning, execution, and innovation platforms, and will be embedded in additional solutions in the future. Figure 5.9 shows some areas where machine learning is planned to be embedded into existing solutions.

SAP Leonardo Machine Learning Foundation as a technology is presented as a toolkit to create applications or services or to be embedded into existing products. The three main categories are:

- Conversational experience, through SAP Conversational AI
- Intelligent applications and embedded solutions
- Machine learning and data science platform (SAP Leonardo Machine Learning Foundation)

In the following sections, we'll walk through a nonexhaustive sample of products and new capabilities derived from machine learning. Figure 5.10 shows a summary of machine learning process improvements by product.

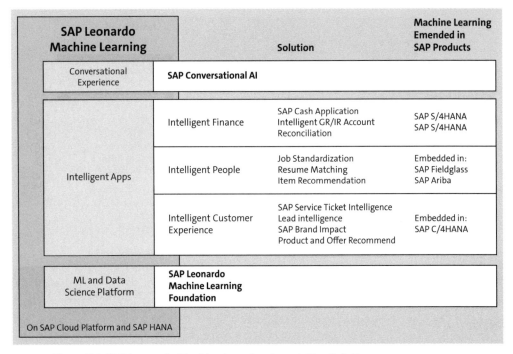

Figure 5.9 SAP Leonardo Machine Learning Foundation Solutions

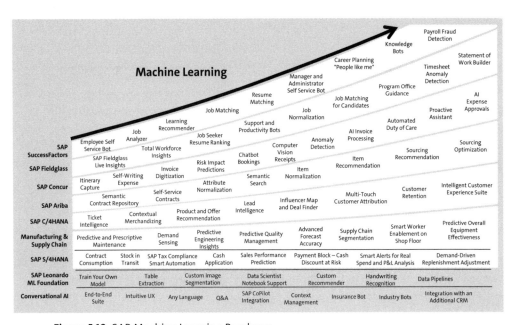

Figure 5.10 SAP Machine Learning Roadmap

5.3.1   Machine Learning with SAP Concur

SAP Concur has continuously looked for opportunities to reduce manual processes via machine learning and intelligence. The SAP Concur team started with eliminating the manual processes associated with expense reports. Using SAP Leonardo Machine Learning Foundation's image processing services, a user can take a picture of a receipt, and the service will automatically add the receipt to an expense report with the right amount, description, and expense classifications. The same capabilities were also used for other expense processes, invoice processing, and travel expenses. These processes now recognize receipt images and automatically create expense report entries via machine learning.

Expense processes automatically sense and process the text of a receipt, deriving currency, amount, dates, supplier, location, and the type of receipt to be included in your expense report. Some additional areas where SAP Concur is using machine learning are as follows:

- Concur Expense uses machine learning technologies in conjunction with Office 365 to enable users to create expense report entries directly from emailed receipts.

- Concur Detect uses machine learning to uncover expense fraud, errors, and compliance issues in real time, therefore auditing 100% of your expense reports.

- Concur Locate builds on machine learning to predict where employees are located through credit card data, itineraries, and other sources, enabling companies to help keep their employees safe in the event of an emergency.

- Hipmunk's Natural Language Processing (NLP) uses AI-powered travel search and travel bots to integrate with your calendar and provide travel advice and recommendations.

- TripIt leverages machine learning to give users a mobile interface experience by automatically integrating emails from travel bookings, Airbnb, Uber, flights, and hotel data.

- Concur Slack Beta allows users to type natural language commands into Slack, like "expense $5 to Uber" and populate expense reports in near real time.

- Concur Invoice uses machine learning to extract data from invoices and scale their managed invoice capture service. An area experiencing growth, higher-volume OCR extraction can be accomplished with lower technology and operational costs.

Figure 5.11 show the main capabilities for invoicing, expense, and travel associated with SAP Leonardo Machine Learning Foundation.

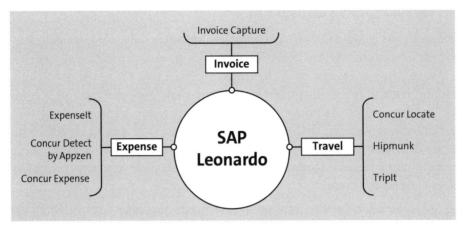

Figure 5.11 SAP Concur with Embedded Machine Learning Capabilities

5.3.2   Machine Learning with SAP SuccessFactors

SAP SuccessFactors is a cloud-based human resource (HR) management solution that covers multiple features, from payroll to employee engagement, scorecards, and performance management.

With SAP Leonardo Machine Learning Foundation embedded into SAP SuccessFactors, the following functional improvements were made:

- **People insights**
  The ability to use historical data provides the ability to simulate and predict what could happen next. Better understand your people, the organization, and how they behave and evolve. HR and management can analyze the effects of, for example, organizational change and determine what positive or negative effects certain actions have on employees, including providing flight risk predictions and influencer analysis.

- **Learning**
  Personalized learning recommendations can assist individual employees with a focused development path. In this case, all new personalized learning recommendations are powered by machine learning capabilities with SAP Leonardo. These targeted recommendations are based on taking what an organization knows about an employee, such as their learning history, and apply machine learning algorithms.

  Employees can maximize relevance by indicating topics of interest, which helps to focus the recommendation engine on delivering the best courses that match their preferences.

- **Service ticket intelligence**
  SAP SuccessFactors can now provide HR services with intelligent, automated processes which include capabilities to read, categorize, solve, route, and propose solutions for HR ticketing tasks. The SAP SuccessFactors digital assistant is a personalized HR resource for all employees, which enables instant access to information and actions across a broad range of HR activities though a conversational interface. In this case, machine learning speech services can be used to retrieve Q&A information via speech-to-text user interactions on mobile or desktop devices. These capabilities are now accessible through the SAP SuccessFactors solution as well as through other solutions like Slack and Microsoft Teams.

- **Recruiting**
  An intelligent job analyzer reviews and recommends the proper length of job descriptions and scans for gender bias to identify and recommend replacements for unconscious bias. Other suggested recommendations, such as salary band recommendations, can be based on a machine learning analysis of salary data by comparing salary to job difficulty.

- **Resume matching**
  Resume matching capabilities compare and pick appropriate applicants' resumes with open positions, based on skills, location, and experience. SAP Leonardo Machine Learning Foundation provides capabilities for finding suitable candidates based on job requirements for open positions. Scoring metrics and quantification scores with matching visualization assist managers to filter to a shortlist of suitable candidates.

5.3.3   Machine Learning with SAP Fieldglass

SAP Fieldglass Live Insights is a new machine learning-based solution to use data-driven insights and services to help decision-makers benchmark, plan, predict, and simulate talent processing.

The solution focuses on a recruiter's skills and soft skills, not just their previous job titles, by using machine learning algorithms. SAP Fieldglass is one of the world's largest source of transactional workforce data, which makes it ideal for machine learning services to derive new insights. These machine learning services now simulate primary and alternative suggested job locations and predict alternative roles based on the ideal talent you're looking to hire.

These machine learning services provide skills-matching algorithms provided by a rule-based engine that allows you to define which skills are most critical versus skills that are optional for the role. The machine learning service can then source millions of records to display alternative roles that best match the ideal skillset, using analytics. With this new insight, decision-makers can determine which skills are in short supply and determine a competitive salary for a job vacancy, including time to fill and candidates per role, for both permanent and talent options.

Executives can strategize by simulating and predicting in real time. SAP Data Network can assist with data-driven hiring decisions and help determine a corrective placement approach. Within a single view, decision-makers can see:

- Total cash to acquire a new hire
- Time required to fill a position
- Your successful hiring rates
- Alternative roles and locations for lowest total cash and shortest time-to-fill values

Machine learning can provide decision-makers with certainty and factual insights to make informative decisions, therefore enhancing confidence in their business case. SAP Data Network, live insights for workforce, is integrated with hiring processes running in the SAP Fieldglass solution, so once an decision-maker decides on an approach for hiring, the necessary workflows are triggered.

5.3.4   Machine Learning for Enterprise Applications

SAP delivers enhancements that enable companies to act on live data by integrating new intelligent applications using SAP Leonardo Machine Learning Foundation and predictive capabilities directly into the digital core. In this section, we'll only showcase a few, selects example of new enterprise applications created through the use of machine learning:

- **SAP Cash Application**
  You can consult the SAP Cash Application to see the number of invoices to be processed. This application uses machine learning to automatically clear matching payments with invoices. If the payments cannot clear automatically, the algorithm suggests the best-fitting invoices.

- **SAP Brand Impact**
  SAP Brand Impact is a product that uses machine learning image recognition services to analyze brand logos within videos to determine their exposure in terms of time and the position they appear on the screen, like upper right or lower left.

- **Digital sales and after sales services**
  The next enterprise machine learning application is designed to replace spare parts and broken products. You can upload a photo of the broken product and use the machine learning image feature extraction algorithm to determine a similarity score. Also, the image feature extraction algorithm can be used to analyze product catalog images using the feature vectors database to derive similarity scores. You'll then be presented with several materials or products with the highest similarity scores. The product can then be selected and ordered.

- **Legal document classification**
  This application can identify and rate legal documents relevant for product design and development. Typically, legal documents are available on the publicly accessible servers of governments with over 1,000 legal changes at any given moment. This feature can determine if a new legal change is relevant or important. Missing a legal change can have severe impact on your company.

  The solution leverages several SAP Leonardo Machine Learning Foundation text analysis services: language detection, text classification, similarities coding, and text feature abstraction. With integration of these services, new laws and regulations can be immediately detected once documents are published and determined to be relevant. The overview page shows a quick preview of all the legal documents with an assessment of their relevance appearing on the top to the left of the document.

  The details of the document show relevance and similar documents while highlighting the importance of the paragraph. The machine learning algorithm's confidence in detecting relevant changes is shown in the intensity of the highlighting. Darker blue indicates more relevant. The machine learning text processing services used in this case are the text feature extraction and text feature classification algorithms. Finally, the solution provides users with a reduction in time, effort, and risk.

5.4 Robotic Process Automation

Robotic process automation (RPA) accelerates the digital transformation of business processes by automatically replicating tedious actions that have no added value. RPA is available in two main types:

- **Unattended**
  Fully automated process, where robots are working autonomously with human supervision only

- **Attended**
  Partially automated process, where robots are coworking with human beings, also called robotic desktop automation

RPA solutions automate repetitive tasks traditionally performed by humans without modifying existing business systems. Some typical RPA activities include the following:

- Extract data through various connectors, for example, Excel files, PDFs, external apps, websites, third-party apps, and enter this data into a finance system
- Log on to enterprise instances, collect purchase requisitions, and distribute to shared service center (SSC) teams
- Download various reports, which can be collated and saved in shared drive
- Check ticket inboxes in a Shared Service Center and route tickets to bots
- Search invoices by reference number in various ERP instances

RPA can impact almost any line of business in just about any industry. Think of situations where someone must access multiple systems or manually process artifacts according to a set of rules. Let's look at a few examples:

- **Procure-to-pay**
  Many procure-to-pay processes (P2P) span multiple systems including ERPs, CRMs, banks, and logistics companies—systems not easily integrated. You can process invoices with computing power and connect to multiple backend systems while saving time, improving accuracy, enforcing policies, and allocating resources to high-value activities. With RPA, invoices from third parties can be processed with computer vision and connected to multiple backend systems, which saves time, improves accuracy, and easily allows the enforcement of procurement policies.

- **Insurance claims processing**
  Insurance claims processing is another example of too many manual steps. You can access a dozen or more disparate systems, process unstructured data, interpret text, make decisions, offer suggestions, and track progress in real time.

- **Access and bring data together**
  RPA can automatically connect to disparate systems, interpret text, make decisions, and track progress in real time. You're creating more data than ever, all spread across many systems, and bringing that data together for reporting can be

time-consuming. RPA can automatically access these systems; get the data (whether via an API or a manual extraction, for older systems); bring the data together; and based on an understanding of the data, decide how to disseminate the report. RPA can be set up to know that, if certain data sources contain too many error log entries, the report must go to a different distribution list. The options for access and bringing data together include the following:

- Access legacy systems, Excel files, third-party portals, websites, etc.
- Bring together data from disparate systems and generate regular reporting
- Intelligently determine dissemination based on content status

Current RPA systems in the market interact with systems like a user. You're replacing the person using a laptop with a bot, and many times, this bot is interacting with other bots. These bots use the same UI as a person, but you'll need to ask some of the following questions:

- What happens if the UI changes?
- What happens when the system is updated? System maintenance becomes a risk.
- A person can easily relearn, but what about an RPA bot?

These bots typically scrape the UI of systems, like a web crawler looking at webpages. This approach may reduce the manual nature of the previous process, but now, the process is far more complex. That complexity means that an inherent risk exists even updating or upgrading your systems. If one piece changes, the entire thing could break.

When SAP automates systems, the actual APIs behind the UI are being used. Updating the system and breaking the UI has no risk to the bot because the APIs stay stable.

SAP's intent is to deliver an intelligent, integrated automation suite so that you don't spend time and effort resolving deployment/tool issues rather than leveraging the potential of RPA. If the basic expectations of RPA are fulfilled as promised, great opportunities can be opened up for analyzing the process-level data that a process is executed on and for formulating a suggestive/prescriptive mode of process modeling, with self-driving robots unleashing the complete potential of RPA. In this scenario is where SAP's strength of integration and the significance of SAP Leonardo Machine Learning Foundation are more relevant than ever.

SAP has launched the SAP Intelligent Robotic Process Automation solution where RPA is the "hands" and the "legs" of the robot, whereas SAP Leonardo Machine Learning Foundation acts as the "brain" that makes decisions, and where conversational AI can play an interfacing role to receive and disseminate instructions digitally. Figure 5.12 shows the three groups of capabilities: interact, execute, and optimize.

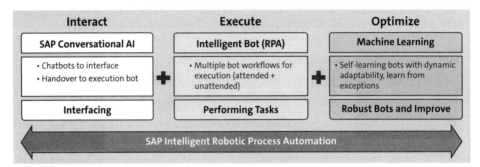

Figure 5.12 SAP Intelligent Robotic Process Automation Scope

The solution has the following key modules:

- Modeler for graphically designing bot workflows
- Repository for storing individual process steps as well as for reusing steps during the design phase
- Runtime environment for managing robot deployments in various virtual/on-premise/hybrid environments
- Monitoring tool for an overview of the robots in action, including work completed, progress, service-level agreement fulfillment, risk mitigation, etc.

Figure 5.13 shows the key modules found in SAP Intelligent Robotic Process Automation.

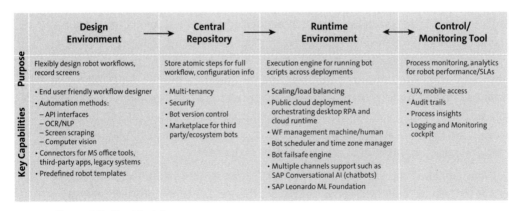

Figure 5.13 Key Modules

SAP aims to realize their vision for SAP Intelligent Robotic Process Automation in multiple phases. With phase 1, SAP intends to deliver the core solution with four critical components: design, repository, runtime, and monitor. This SAP S/4HANA-focused release will include SAP S/4HANA-specific preconfigured content out of the box and will include the ability to integrate with SAP S/4HANA APIs, machine learning services, and SAP Conversational AI. In phase 2, SAP intends to extend SAP Intelligent Robotic Process Automation for the wider SAP portfolio, including SAP SuccessFactors, SAP Concur, etc., depending upon how use cases are prioritized. Phase 3 move towards cognitive modes after gaining some experience through multiple robot deployments. Thus, SAP can make robots more and more AI enabled with a prescriptive mode that can remodel processes and can self-correct.

5.5 Summary

Machine learning technologies enable computers to complete operational tasks by learning from large sets of operational data, outcomes, or historical data. Machine learning opens up a dialogue around using automated machine-driven to repurpose human effort to more high-value tasks, while automation focuses on areas characterized by a high degree of repetition.

SAP Leonardo Machine Learning Foundation as technology is present as a toolkit to create new applications, services or embedding machine learning into existing products. SAP Leonardo Machine Learning Foundation is used for building, creating, and testing machine learning algorithms for applications. Machine learning in enterprise applications delivers enhancements that make have made it easier than ever for companies to run on live insights by integrating new, intelligent applications using SAP Leonardo Machine Learning Foundation and predictive capabilities directly into the digital core.

Chapter 6
Data Intelligence

Data intelligence is a toolset that a company can use as a differentiator to derive accurate, time-dependent insights so that appropriate, deliberate, and impactful decisions can be made to drive outcome-based results.

Data intelligence is the way we analyze, visualize, use, consume, process, collect, and store data and insights inside or outside an organization to improve business outcomes. One goal of SAP Leonardo Data Intelligence is to consume data to ultimately create what is known as the intelligent enterprise. This transformation requires the intelligent use of informed insights for better decision-making, improved and streamlined operations, and even automated processes so you can focus on higher-value tasks.

Data intelligence is a vital component of SAP Leonardo technologies. Data intelligence is often considered part of data mining, analytical reporting (tactical or strategical use of informed insights), or business processes (operational use of data).

Data intelligence also includes the use of external data such as demographics, environmental, compliance, legal, competitor, social media, or supplier data to improve positioning or extend operations. Data intelligence can be used to explore external business environments like industry trends, markets, and other competitive factors. Data intelligence is also supported by combination of artificial intelligence (AI) and machine learning to explore and derive new insights.

In this chapter, we'll start by discussing what exactly data intelligence is and what you can use it for. Then, we'll move to two areas supported by SAP Data Network, powered by SAP Leonardo: data-driven business and data monetization. Finally, we'll look at data-as-a-service (DaaS) using SAP Data Hub.

6.1   What Is Data Intelligence?

Data intelligence is often incorrectly referred to as "business intelligence" or "analytics." Even though similarities exist between these solutions, their key differences are significant.

Primarily, data intelligence is processed data used intelligently to generate insights to make better decisions, especially for endeavors like investments, and is part of a solution that also includes data mining, analytics reporting, and data intelligence embedded into business processes.

Data intelligence is also a service that allows an enterprise to provide its own data in the form of data-as-a-service (DaaS), which we'll discuss in more detail in Section 6.4. In this area, data intelligence can help your organization join data together, aggregate your data in a number of ways, and anonymize your data. This data can then be used for commercial consumption, either by your own organization or sold to a third party.

Business intelligence and analytics, on the other hand, are the processes of understanding a business process and the data associated with that process. Business intelligence and analytics include data structuring, data storage, and data sourcing to make the data useful for a business's practices. Business intelligence and analytics also involve gathering unstructured data such as customer insights, social media content, or e-commerce and merchant records. Organizations also use the insights from this data to improve customer service levels.

Data intelligence has several data analysis techniques for deriving new insights for better decision-making, as follows:

- **Descriptive**
  This technique is used for reviewing and examining the data in such a way as to understand and analyze business performance. Providing more meaning and description to enrich your understanding of business outcomes, not just enrich your understanding of the data.

- **Prescriptive**
  Used for developing and analyzing alternative knowledge that can be applied in the courses of action. A prescriptive technique offers options or a course of action to take to increase value. An example of a prescriptive outcome could be a task for replenishing a certain brand/product that a retailer has indicator is off the shelves.

- **Diagnostic**
  Used for determining the possible causes of particular occurrences. Often referred

to as "root cause analysis" because this technique determines the root cause of a problem or issue.

- **Predictive**
Used for analyzing historical data to determine future occurrences. A predictive technique estimates future needs.

- **Decisive**
Used for measuring the data adequacy and recommending future actions to be undertaken in an environment of multiple possibilities. Data can be used to make strategic and financial decisions like managing the lifecycle of assets or for right-sizing assets.

SAP Leonardo Data Intelligence is closely connected with other SAP Leonardo technologies, particularly big data and machine learning.

6.2   Data-Driven Business

Organizations can be driven by data in many different ways. Some companies are metrics-driven; they focus predominately on and track predefined key performance indicators. Some companies are completely data-driven, and others use data to drive a more conventional business, while still others use data to enhance or optimize business processes. SAP Leonardo technologies allow data-driven companies to harness insights across the organization and implement these insights to create competitive advantage. Being data-driven is much different discipline than traditional business models. You'll need a researcher's mindset, with the curiosity to explore fully the business or the market and the willingness to be guided by these new insights.

An organization that is completely data-driven competes solely by transforming information into a monetizable asset. These businesses effectively create revenue streams through their platforms to adapt information sharing into a means of value exchange. Consequently, these companies benefit from extracting some kind of fee layered on top of the basic costs of a transaction.

A prime example is Airbnb, which is a two-sided marketplace for customers (individuals looking for temporary housing) and goods/services providers (people with space available for short-term rentals). The company basically partners with the providers, collects their information, and makes that information available to the customer pool. A customer selects a provider and executes the transaction, and then a negotiated commission is transmitted back to the company. The company, however, does not own any of the assets (the rental properties); the assets are owned and managed by the providers. Uber and eBay follow a similar model.

As shown in Figure 6.1, SAP's digital platform unlocks data-driven intelligence and innovation in the following ways:

- SAP HANA's in-memory database can be used for data management to address both structured and unstructured data as well as for data storage and processing.
- SAP HANA powers SAP applications as the foundation of high-performance data warehousing and analytics.
- SAP Data Hub provides data orchestration and metadata management across heterogeneous data sources.
- APIs and microservices deliver deep data and process integration.
- SAP API Business Hub constitute a customer and partner ecosystem for building innovation and leveraging APIs and business services (*https://api.sap.com*).

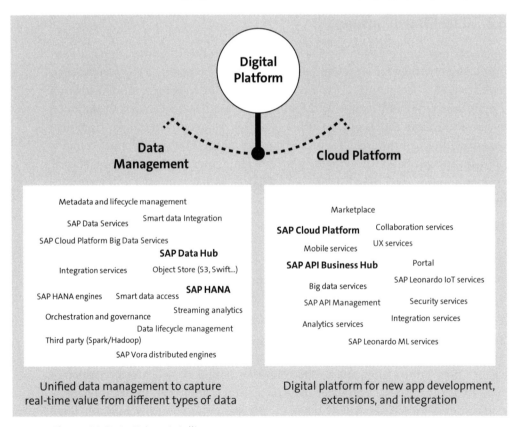

Figure 6.1 Data-Driven Intelligence

One of the biggest tools that can be used for data-driven business, however, is SAP Data Network, live insights for workforce. With this tool, you'll take millions of records from your cloud-based businesses and then aggregate and anonymize this data to deliver real-time benchmarks and ready-to-consume insights. In this way, you'll have full transparency into the business and generate new insights and unfiltered facts about how your business is operating and performing. These data-driven services are built by SAP for you to subscribe to and consume. These services can be modified to meet your specific needs and often act as building blocks for developers and consultants.

With connected workforce data, you can use insights from these services to help your recruiting managers attract the best talent by using transactional data enriched with external datasets as well as machine learning-enabled skill-matching to simulate, predict, and implement various contingent and permanent hiring scenarios in real time.

A combination of internal performance data and external market data within an industry often bring new unexpected or expected insights. Often, these expected insights simply validate existing strategies, while unexpected outcomes often challenge and possibly force a change in existing strategies.

6.3   Data Monetization Strategies

Organizations are expanding their ability to use big data to improve decision-making; by itself, this data is limited in value until the data is processed to support decision-makers as they turn informed insights into opportunity.

Few companies have mastered the ability to continuously execute actions based on informed insights to drive the opportunity and revenue streams. Informed insights can also determine vulnerabilities or R&D opportunities to create innovative more competitive services and products. Data monetization offers opportunities for organizations that can proactively execute on market indicators. The way an organization reacts to insights and market indicators is often reflected in its business strategy. Business models change often due to new insights and newly discovered information. Companies need to be conscious and strategize the leadership hired and developed, as the success of yesterday will not be reproduced in the market of today.

SAP Leonardo Data Intelligence can be used for delivering outcome-based results to your organization through data monetization. SAP Data Network, live customer cloud, is a private, end-to-end data network for monetizing commercially valuable insights found within your data. SAP Data Network, live customer cloud for data monetization consists of your company's own data combined with the data of your company's particular industry ecosystem and enriched by trusted, supplemental third-party data. This network is powered and secured by SAP but controlled by you.

SAP Data Network, live customer cloud, industrializes the process from ingesting raw customer data; to data processing (cleansing, enrichment, anonymization, aggregation); through extracting insights; and all the way to packaging this data into a consumable data-as-a-service (DaaS).

SAP Data Network, live customer cloud, allows you to perform the following activities:

- Share data with third parties while remaining compliant
- Evaluate datasets for quality, completeness, and depth
- Combine existing enterprise data with additional dimensions like geospatial, demographics, weather, or movement data
- Create bidirectional apps within your system
- Monetize your apps based on either usage or subscription
- Control your own data ecosystem
- Collect customer data
- Embed predictive modeling into processes using machine learning

Together, these capabilities help you to leverage your own data to learn how to enhance your customers' experience or break into new markets. These capabilities can also help you use your data to develop new revenue models, either directly or indirectly.

> **Note**
>
> SAP API Management can also be used for data monetization. You can expose and monetize existing APIs using metering within the system, which would charge your customers based on their usage or via a subscription (usually monthly).

6.4   Data-as-a-Service

Data-as-a-service (DaaS) is a cloud strategy for orchestrating the efficient and timely sourcing of operational data. DaaS instinctively delivers on the idea that valuable data should be provided instantly to users on demand, from anywhere and of any type of source or format. Mission-critical data at a single location should be accessible, usable, and modifiable by multiple users via a single update point. SAP Leonardo, using SAP Data Hub as part of its foundation technical and business services, can be used as a DaaS solution to accelerate and orchestrate the use of big data.

SAP Data Hub is a DaaS solution that operates across a complex and heterogeneous enterprise landscape while driving informed business decisions. The central building blocks for SAP Data Hub are as follows:

- SAP Data Hub distributed runtime
- SAP Data Hub modeling perspective
- SAP Data Hub cockpit

SAP Data Hub integrates with SAP Data Services to route, move, and process the data. SAP Data Hub's workflows facilitate data pipelines, and SAP Data Hub's governance capabilities, with integration to SAP Information Steward and SAP Master Data Governance (SAP MDG) provide governance and monitoring.

SAP Data Services uses a rule-based engine to process and transform your data. SAP Data Services jobs include workflow processes to orchestrate and run jobs, alongside with SAP Information Steward, for governance and monitoring.

Both data architects and data scientists can access and consume all the available data dispersed across the enterprise, whether in hot or cold storage, to produce actionable insights that enable intelligent, data-driven processes and applications.

SAP Data Hub describes how the data landscape is managed and can instigate business transformation. SAP Data Hub reduces landscape complexity and provides a single simplified solution for data propagation, pipelining, and governance across the landscape. SAP Data Hub centralizes data via governance by leaving the data where it resides, thereby reducing complexity and total cost of ownership (TCO) to avoid unnecessary data migration. Figure 6.2 show the SAP Data Hub architecture with open integration.

SAP Data Hub addresses three key challenges:

- **Governance**
  In a unified view, SAP Data Hub helps you track and trace how data is used by your users and understand the impact of future changes throughout the data value chain. Benefits include:

- Easily create and enforce access policies.
- Conduct lineage and impact analysis to see where data came from and how changes to the data impact data models and results.
- Easily understand systems and assets across the full landscape.

- **Pipelines**

  Distributed "pushdown" processing executes pipelines quickly, where the data resides, without centralizing data, so you can accelerate and scale data projects quickly. Benefits include the following:

  - SAP Data Hub allows you to create powerful data pipelines that leverage advanced capabilities like big data processing and machine learning.
  - These pipelines can be triggered by changes in data, so that your business is more responsive to opportunities and threats.

- **Data sharing**

  You can leverage existing connections and integration tools, while adding new connections easily and flexibly. With SAP Data Hub, each system's data catalog is registered to the SAP Data Hub, which makes adding new systems over time and leveraging them quickly with existing systems easier. Therefore, you'll be able to more easily orchestrate data movements across the landscape.

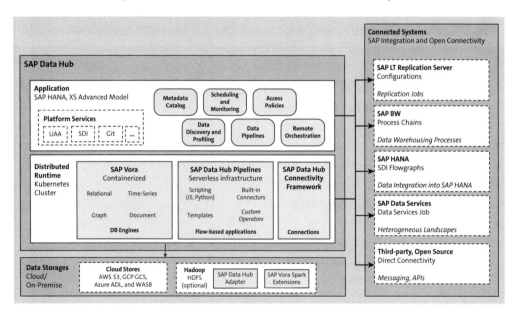

Figure 6.2 SAP Data Hub

Figure 6.3 shows how SAP Data Hub can be used for comprehensive data management.

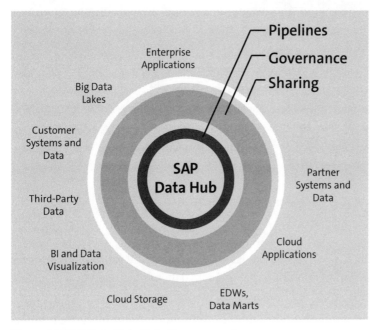

Figure 6.3 SAP Data Hub: Data Management

SAP Data Hub also has an open architecture to help you manage a modern, hybrid landscape. SAP's goal is to make information available across the data landscape, no matter where the data resides. Data could be stored in the cloud or on-premise, with data from SAP systems like SAP HANA or non-SAP systems like cloud-based storage (Amazon Web Services) and Hadoop. SAP Data Hub also is intended to help drive, not just analytics, but also application development and master data management.

SAP Data Hub offers a highly visual environment for creating and extending data models, thus allowing you to accelerate and scale your data projects, since more of your users can create or refine data models more quickly.

SAP Data Intelligence

SAP Data Intelligence, released in Q2 of 2019, is a unified integrated solution that offers a data science frontend and lifecycle management to manage artificial intelligence needs. Its stated goal is to combine the power of the open source community and SAP machine learning with enterprise reliability and scale.

SAP Data Intelligence extends SAP Data Hub capabilities such as addressing the missing link between big data and enterprise data, governing complex modern landscapes, productizing complex data scenarios, and additional capabilities dedicated to the design and the operationalization of artificial intelligence processes. Some key capabilities include:

- Ability to access any data source: cloud, on premise, IoT, SAP, and non-SAP.
- Automatically index and crawl any available data asset to find it with ease.
- Manage the design of the project, giving access to the right tools, offering artificial intelligence as a service, and making models deployments seamless and simple.
- Automate low value tasks, surfacing model performance and lifecycle that is automatically managed so IT.

6.5   Summary

Data intelligence focuses on processed data used intelligently for future endeavors like investments as part of a solution that includes data mining, analytical reporting and data intelligence embedded into business processing.

In this chapter, we discussed how the SAP Data Network can help you create new revenue streams and new business models from your own data. With SAP Data Network, live customer cloud, and SAP Data Network, live insights for workforce, you can take records from your cloud-based businesses to deliver real-time, ready-to-consume insights. SAP Data Network, live customer cloud, is a private, end-to-end data network managed by SAP. We also discussed how SAP Data Hub can help you refine and orchestrate big data across a heterogeneous enterprise landscape to drive digital business decisions.

Chapter 7
Blockchain

Blockchain is positioned to become the primary system of trust, and many believe that blockchain is an opportunity that will improve compliance across multiple stakeholders.

Although some of the technology underpinnings of blockchains like cryptography, distributed ledger technology (DLT), etc. are decades old, interest in blockchain has risen dramatically in recent years, especially with the meteoric rise of cryptocurrencies like Bitcoin in 2017. Blockchain has garnered a lot of attention, not only in the press but also from analysts and companies across industries, both private and public sector, including governments across the globe. Blockchain promises companies an efficient way of removing intermediaries, enhancing control and ownership of your own data, and leveling the playing field by adding a layer of transparency. These capabilities, among other capabilities, make blockchain applicable to a vast array of use cases in a variety of business scenarios. Blockchain promises to act as a key enabler of digital transformation and the creation of efficient and intelligent business networks.

In this chapter, we'll cover SAP's approach to blockchain technology as well as explore examples of specific use cases to give you a taste of the vast applicability of blockchain as well as to illustrate how blockchain data can be combined with enterprise data to further enhance value.

7.1 What Is Blockchain?

Blockchain is a distributed ledger, a decentralized database that is replicated across a peer-to-peer (P2P) network. Transactions are grouped into blocks, and each block is linked to its predecessor block using cryptographic hashing (i.e. the hash of the preceding block is included in the new block). This linking of the blocks is what inspired the name "blockchain." The recording of blocks is achieved through a consensus mechanism whereby blocks are verified before being recorded on the distributed ledger using a consensus mechanism, resulting in each node on the blockchain network having the exact same copy. This process is referred to as *mining*. Two important underlying principles are at work here. First, the blocks are immutable: No individual participant of the blockchain network can change the contents of a block without breaking the link. Second, since each node contains a copy of the entire blockchain, created through the consensus mechanism, digital trust is created between the participants even when they don't know each other, simply because they can all see the same data on their copy of the distributed ledger.

Cryptography, with use of keys (public and private), provides secure access to the data by participants of the blockchain network.

Also, smart contracts (if available), which consist of codified logic representing a set of business rules, can be used to process certain types of events on the blockchain. Smart contracts can be a powerful mechanism for optimizing processes and eliminating the need for intermediaries. Smart contracts execute on the blockchain and act as decision points. Smart contracts can help speed up intercompany processes, make processes efficient, increase transparency, provide autonomy by eliminated intermediaries, and eliminate error-prone manual steps, all of which creates substantial opportunities to save costs.

Several open source blockchain platforms and protocols are available. The main differences among them are the hashing and consensus algorithms used for, for example, proof or work, proof of stake, Kafka, round robin, atomic broadcast, Istanbul Byzantine fault tolerance, etc.; the availability of smart contracts (Bitcoin and Multi-Chain do not support smart contracts but Ethereum, Hyperledger, and Quorum do); and type of cryptography and hashing algorithms used for data privacy and encryption (e.g. zero-knowledge proofs, public and private key pairs, etc.).

Blockchain provides distributed, immutable data storage with integrity checking built-in. Unlike a traditional database, which has create, read, update, and delete (CRUD) operations, data can only be read from or written to a blockchain. Once written, data cannot be changed (i.e. updated or deleted). When dealing with large amounts of data, commonly this data is stored off-chain, and a hash of that data is stored on-chain, guaranteeing that the data cannot be modified while allowing one to manage the data volume stored on the blockchain.

Variations of blockchain exist: public or permission-less blockchains, private or permissioned blockchains, as well as semi-private or shared permissioned blockchains (consortiums) where only verified participants are permitted to validate blocks.

Figure 7.1 shows a partial list of blockchain platforms. While anyone can join a public blockchain (like Bitcoin or Ethereum), as well as read or write data to the blockchain while maintaining their anonymity, permissioned blockchains on the other hand are closed to a network of participants with restrictions on who can participate in the network. Examples of permissioned blockchains are Hyperledger (an open source initiative), MultiChain (a fork of Bitcoin), and Quorum (a fork of Ethereum and an open source initiative driven by JP Morgan). User authentication and authorization is needed in private blockchains.

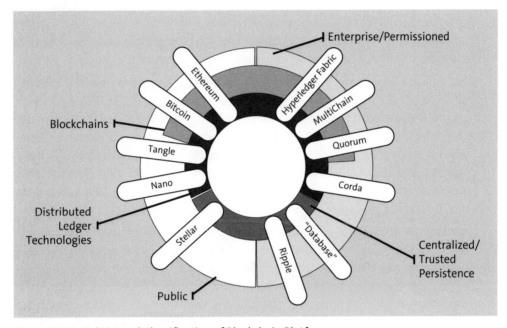

Figure 7.1 Partial List and Classification of Blockchain Platforms

Various use cases for blockchain exist, and you'll need to select a blockchain platform accordingly. Use cases for blockchain span various industries, such as financial services, utilities, consumer products, agriculture, retail, healthcare and pharmaceuticals, high-tech, utilities and energy, media, law, engineering and construction, real estate, insurance, etc. In addition, cross-industry uses cases are prevalent in logistics and international trade, supply chain and manufacturing, procurement, and finance. Blockchain uses are also present in the public sector and in governments, for example, for recording property ownership, voting, proxy management, citizen identity management, etc.

SAP has been working on blockchain technologies for several years and, at the time of this writing, holds leadership roles in various blockchain organizations and consortiums, actively contributing to and driving initiatives in the adoption and usage of blockchain technology. SAP is a premium member of the Hyperledger Foundation, hosted by The Linux Foundation, an open source, collaborative, cross-industry effort to advance blockchain technologies for business. SAP is also a member of the Blockchain Research Institute, a global, independent, thinktank to identify strategic implications and opportunities for blockchain for business, government, and society. SAP is on the board of directors and a working group member of the Blockchain in Transport Alliance (BiTA), which aims to drive standards and enable the adoption of technologies like blockchain by identifying the most applicable business processes transformations and to create technical standards for them.

SAP is also a member of Alastria, a Spanish consortium focused on the establishment of a semi-public, independent, permissioned, and neutral blockchain network. Finally, SAP is a founding vice-chair member of The Chinese Trusted Blockchain Alliance, which aims to advance R&D in blockchain technology, improve standards and governance, and drive cross-industry adoption. Through these activities and initiatives, SAP's goal is to influence and contribute to the development of open standards and to understand market needs to develop innovative solutions and help companies in their digital transformation journey.

At the time of this writing, SAP also has several industry blockchain consortiums and blockchain co-innovation initiatives to work closely with its customers and collaboratively discuss blockchain use cases as well as engage in proofs of concepts (POCs) to understand the value that blockchain can bring to business networks in supporting digital transformation initiatives. The Industry Consortium is a multilateral framework between SAP and SAP customers to discuss challenges that may be solved by blockchain, and each member has equal rights to the generated output. In contrast, a co-innovation agreement is a bilateral agreement between SAP and an SAP customer to participate in a hands-on blockchain POC to validate SAP products augmented with blockchain, and SAP exclusively owns the IP of all productized outcomes.

As you explore multiparty use cases for blockchain, there are many situations in which you should use a multistage approach. For example, your revenue streams may depend on peer-to-peer content consumption. Similarly, you may want to address challenges arising from limited transparency or need more efficient ways to audit your assets through their lifecycles. Perhaps you need to create frictionless settlements or facilitate multiparty agreements. Such an approach could serve as a basis for a multiyear strategy, beginning with the optimize stage to improve existing processes, followed by the reimagine stage to disrupt and create new business processes, and finally the revolutionize stage where you'll create entirely new network-based business models on blockchain.

These use cases will require an end-to-end technology landscape, as shown in Figure 7.2, but you'll be able leverage the open and technology-agnostic approach of SAP Cloud Platform combined with SAP Leonardo technologies like Internet of Things (IoT), machine learning, analytics, and big data. You'll also be able to extend your investments in existing business applications by making them blockchain-ready. Such a holistic approach will ensure that the business value you gain from the use of blockchain technology today is future-proof and can be extended as blockchain technologies continue to evolve.

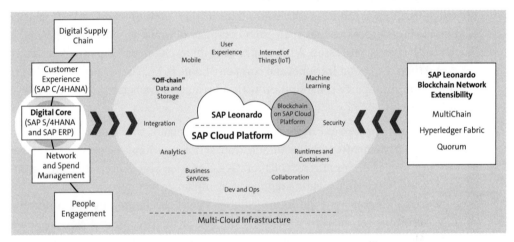

Figure 7.2 Connecting to the Blockchain Ecosystem End-to-End

However, as blockchain technology continues to mature, some areas that dictate the speed of adoption will need to be considered, such as the type of blockchain (i.e. public, private, or consortium) or performance scalability of the consensus procedure to validate the blocks and access to off-chain data as the blockchain network grows. The security of the entire system, from the source of the data (e.g. smart meters and IoT-enabled devices), to data gateways, to the blockchain application itself must be considered. Interoperability of different blockchains must be achievable since use cases and participants will likely span across multiple blockchains.

A governance structure to coordinate and incentivize participation will be needed for operating a blockchain network. Development and implementation of smart contracts (including when regulations and compliance authorities are involved),

technical roadmap for accommodating enhancements, rules and operational procedures for off-chain and on-chain data management are some other areas to consider
in the application of blockchains. Lastly, given regulations like General Data Protection Regulation (GDPR), you'll need to determine how data protection requirements
related to personal data can be implemented in the blockchain if personal data is to
be processed and stored on the blockchain.

7.2   Enterprise Blockchain

SAP's current focus is on permissioned blockchains, also referred to as enterprise
blockchains. A value-generating blockchain would require the blockchain protocol
itself with all its capabilities (discussed later in this section) to orchestrate one or
more business processes that span cross-company boundaries with touch points to
internal business processes. As a result, each blockchain participant must think
beyond their own organizational and company boundaries. The value of blockchains
is rooted in multiparty collaboration with information transparency, security, and
auditability.

Cross-company processes can thus become more efficient, as digital trust is created
between all participants with immutable transactions, without the need for a central
authority, and as decentralized, collaborative scenarios are orchestrated with minimal risk and fraud while meeting regulatory compliance mandates. Overall costs can
be reduced with none or fewer intermediaries as well as eliminating or automating
time-consuming reconciliatory steps via the use of smart contracts. New business
models can evolve with decentralized business scenarios across company boundaries by utilizing data transparency on the blockchain.

SAP recognizes that, depending on your use case, your specific need for a specific
blockchain technology will vary. Further, since blockchain technologies are fast
evolving, you'll need the flexibility to exchange blockchain technologies based on
your future needs while shielding the business solutions you've already developed.
Thus, SAP has taken a blockchain technology-agnostic approach.

Figure 7.3 shows SAP's technological approach to blockchain on SAP Cloud Platform.
Application integration services provide for the integration of existing on-premise
SAP solutions to blockchain capabilities. In the following sections, we'll look at some
foundational services before moving on to discussing the blockchain services themselves.

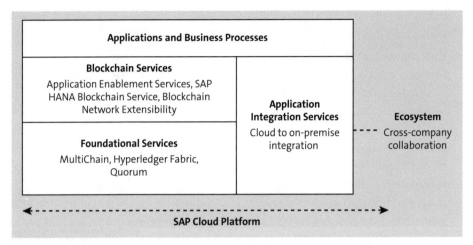

Figure 7.3 SAP Cloud Platform Blockchain

7.2.1   Foundational Services

At the time of this writing, the following SAP Cloud Platform Blockchain services are available as part of its foundational services. SAP plans to continue developing additional blockchain protocols as they reach enterprise-scale maturity:

- **Hyperledger Fabric on SAP Cloud Platform**
  Hyperledger Fabric is an enterprise-scale blockchain framework hosted by The Linux Foundation with several components such as consensus and membership services. Using Hyperledger Fabric nodes with Hyperledger Fabric on SAP Cloud Platform allows you to grant network and channel permissions to participants using secure service keys, thus allowing you to control access to the blockchain. You can provision private channels and deploy and analyze Chaincode for smart contracts. Hyperledger Fabric on SAP Cloud Platform gives you a choice of pluggable consensus algorithms like Practical Byzantine Fault Tolerance (PBFT), Raft, or Kafka.

- **MultiChain on SAP Cloud Platform**
  MultiChain, a permissioned blockchain, is a fork based on the Bitcoin protocol and is proven for production readiness with enterprise-grade features. It is suitable for scenarios that do not require application logic on blockchain like data storage and retrieval, and asset transfer during an asset's entire lifecycle—issuance, transfer, exchange, escrow, reissuance, redemption, destruction. MultiChain on SAP Cloud Platform allows you to implement "cloud-to-cloud" and "cloud-to-on-premise"

collaboration. You can explore data on a MultiChain node or network using the MultiChain dashboard.

- **Quorum on SAP Cloud Platform**
  Quorum is an enterprise-focused, open source version of the Ethereum distributed ledger and smart contract platform and is available as an Early Adoption release at the time of this writing. Quorum provides both transaction-level privacy and network-wide transparency, customizable to your business requirements while providing speedy transactions with high throughput of private transactions within permissioned setups. The zero-knowledge security layer allows for cryptographically assured private settlement of digitized assets. All public smart contracts and transactions are shared in a single complete blockchain of transactions validated by the network nodes. Private contracts and transactions are integrated by committing payload hashes to the public chain while the private state is only seen by the authorized nodes. Existing Ethereum smart contracts remain network-transparent on Quorum out of the box. Therefore, the state of the private smart contract is known to and validated by only parties on the contract as well as approved third parties, like regulators.

7.2.2   Blockchain Services

The various blockchain services shown in Figure 7.3 will be discussed in the following sections.

Application Enablement Services on SAP Cloud Platform Blockchain

SAP Cloud Platform Blockchain application enablement services allow you to integrate blockchain capabilities into your business applications. As shown in Figure 7.4, using these services, applications can be developed and adapted to integrate blockchain capabilities without using blockchain technology-specific coding and thus isolate the business application from a specific blockchain technology.

The time stamp service, proof of state service, and proof of history service help you accelerate your blockchain projects by taking a blockchain technology-agnostic approach.

The time stamp service securely stores, on request, a time stamp to prove that the specific key was known at a specific time. The time stamp service can be used for scenarios where object states require the verification of a time stamp, for example, if you needed to prove that a document, such as a bid document for a specific tender, existed in a specific state at a specific moment in time. The consuming application builds a hash function, effectively a unique fingerprint, over the entire content of the document, and then the calculated hash value is saved via the time stamp service to the blockchain. In the future, anyone who receives the same document can compute the hash value again and validate the time stamp for this hash value with the service. Any changes to the document result in a new hash value.

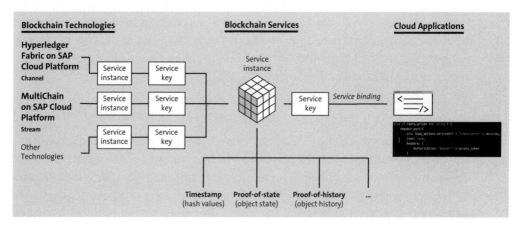

Figure 7.4 Application Enablement Services on SAP Cloud Platform Blockchain

The proof of state service allows you to securely store JSON objects in a complete state via an API call to a given key. The proof of state service can be used for scenarios where the complete state of an object is stored (usually, once). For example, let's say that a business manages the end-of-year financial records for each of its subcompanies or subsidiaries on the blockchain. Records can be stored via the proof of state service in a complete state on the blockchain with each subsidiary using its own company key. When, for example, periodic tax accounting takes place, the exact records of the subsidiary can be recalled exactly as they existed at the close of business for the last financial year or tax period. Another example is storing of public equipment safety certifications on the blockchain with each inspection organization using its own organization-specific private key. All inspection records can be retrieved and examined as needed at any later point in time.

The proof of history service allows you to record updates or changes to a business objects' attributes (JSON formatted storage) for a specified key and recall the history of those changes upon request. The proof of history service can be used for scenarios where you would like to keep a record of delta updates to an object. For example, a manufacturing business could use machinery operated via a digital twin system in the cloud. Each time an attribute of the machinery is changed in the cloud-based system, this information can be stored on the blockchain. When the spin speed of a machine used to mix paint has changed, for example, the change can be recorded on the blockchain via the proof of history service. If an error occurs in production, the audit trail (the details of the revisions to the attributes of the machinery) can be retrieved and reviewed. Another example is in device management where the included software version needs to be recorded for assets like smart meters. Each time an attribute of the smart meter is changed in the smart meter, this change can be stored on the blockchain. If an error occurs in billing and in the case of security reviews, the audit trail (the details of the revisions to the attributes of the smart meter) can be retrieved and reviewed.

All of these services run in Cloud Foundry and are agnostic to the underlying blockchain network (i.e. a Hyperledger Fabric channel or MultiChain stream).

SAP is continuing to extend blockchain services for setting up trusted digital identities and for establishing object provenance across companies, among other things. An identity service would help integrate existing corporate identity infrastructures with blockchain to accommodate the different needs and characteristics needed in decentralized ledgers. As a result, you could use your existing business users and roles for blockchain use cases to establish trusted relationships with business partners and overcome the blockchain's pseudoanonymity. A business object service would help you easily integrate blockchain applications to establish a complete documentation of materials across a multitiered network and ensure immediate propagation of provenance-related information to all network participants using the immutable and shared data layer that blockchain provides. A business object service would provide you secure and seamless tracking of objects to help cover uses cases in supply chain, logistics, manufacturing, and production where multiple business partners are involved.

SAP HANA Blockchain Service

The SAP HANA Blockchain service help you integrate blockchain data into SAP HANA. As you leverage blockchain to establish digital trust and transparency across your business network, you'll need to continue to streamline your internal business processes. For example, as you gain supply chain transparency by extending order processing information to suppliers, you can streamline your sales and operations planning (S&OP), demand and inventory management, and manufacturing and production operations. Through the integration of business and blockchain financial transactions, you'll be able to perform comprehensive financial analyses.

With the SAP HANA Blockchain service, blockchain transactions can be accessed using standard APIs and standard SQL interfaces without needing to learn blockchain technology, thus lowering the barrier to innovation. You can run real-time analytics on data from both traditional and blockchain transactions and combine machine learning and spatial analytics with blockchain data, while creating a single, unified view of your business.

As you build your intelligent enterprise, you'll rely on a variety of data like IoT sensor data, graph data, geospatial data, and a variety of unstructured data, combined with internal data. As shown in Figure 7.5, the SAP HANA Blockchain service helps you include blockchain data into the SAP HANA database to achieve your goal of an intelligent enterprise via digital transformation.

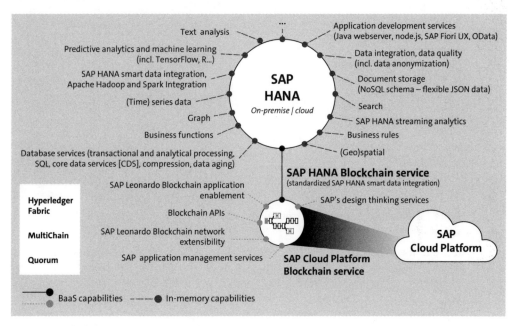

Figure 7.5 Blockchain Integration with SAP HANA

Blockchain Network Extensibility

To foster open business collaboration, SAP has adopted an open and protocol-agonistic approach to allow you to connect with different architecture layouts with blockchain network extensibility. As a result, you can have blockchain nodes spread across regions and geographies as well as embed on-premise components and have different infrastructures and architectures.

As shown in Figure 7.6, you can set up distributed ledgers in any of the three architectural formats: First, you could connect an external node where a single blockchain node is integrated into a network while remaining at a different location like at a regulator or on-premise (close to your SAP ERP or SAP S/4HANA system), or second, you could create a multicloud environment where the blockchain node is provisioned on SAP Cloud Platform but is connected to a multipartner blockchain network operating across different cloud operators. Finally, you could "bring your own network" by participating in a multipartner blockchain network operating across different cloud providers on an SAP stack (business process, application, blockchain services on SAP).

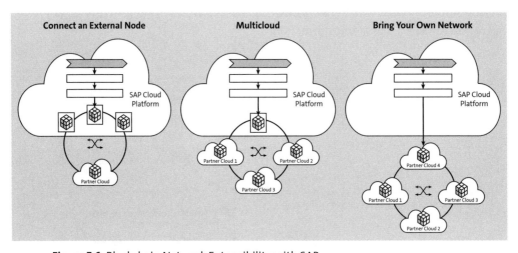

Figure 7.6 Blockchain Network Extensibility with SAP

In the following sections, we'll walk through some blockchain use case examples in different industries and lines of business (LOBs).

7.3   Blockchain for Industries

The technology approach described in the previous section rests on two fundamental considerations for pursuing an optimal approach to multiparty processes using blockchain. First, being agnostic in terms of blockchain platform and protocol means you can select what suits your needs, and second, utilizing an abstraction layer between the technology-enabling layer and the business process layer eases integration and application development, as shown in Figure 7.7. SAP recognizes that, in your business network, not all participants will work on the same cloud platform and technology stack. SAP's blockchain technology allows you to focus on value-adding and business-relevant processes to establish digital trust across all participants while reducing technological barriers to entry in realizing your goals.

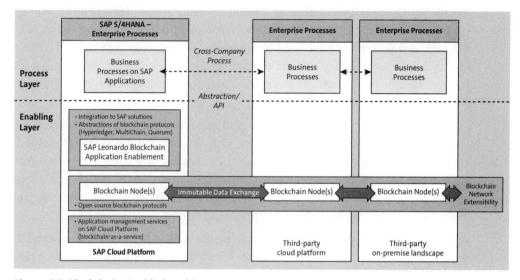

Figure 7.7 Blockchain-Enabled Multiparty Enterprise Processes

The following sections contain industry use cases for blockchain, but is by no means an exhaustive list.

7.3.1   Consumer Products, Agribusiness, and Retail

Food traceability, better visibility into product provenance to better handle recalls and eliminate counterfeit products from entering the supply chain, sustainable farming, and ensuring fair trade practices in farming and fishing are some of the many relevant uses cases for blockchain in the consumer-packaged goods, agribusiness, and retail industries. With traceability across a multitiered supply chain, blockchain can help avoid the high costs associated with regulatory noncompliance. Blockchain can facilitate traceability downstream to end consumers as well as upstream to mills, farms, or fisheries with participation from farmers, agents, buyers, traders, multiparty and multistep production facilities, distributors, and logistics providers.

At the time of this writing, several projects are under way. SUSTAIN is a palm oil industry-initiated consortium of palm oil producers, nongovernmental organizations (NGOs), and customers. The objective of SUSTAIN is to use blockchain to prove palm oil provenance and restore trust in palm oil sustainability credentials. A mobile app helps farmers, agents, and truckers to log all activities in the blockchain.

Another project underway is to trace fish from origin-of-catch to retail consumption by leveraging blockchain to provide traceability to all stakeholders in the multitier supply chain. While the goal is promoting sustainability and fair trade, blockchain will also provide real-time catch information for fishermen with analysis of fishing results to increase overall yield. End consumers could use a mobile app to scan a QR code on a product's packaging to learn who caught the fish and be assured of its quality and authenticity.

Food quality and waste are global issues. Studies have shown that 1 in 10 individuals fall sick every year due to poor food quality, 420,000 people die each year from food-borne diseases, and 30% of the food produced is spoiled or wasted. To help address such issues, SAP launched the farm-to-consumer blockchain POC initiative with ten companies as part of the SAP industry consortium. The objective is to enable data sharing across the supply chain and improve end-to-end visibility for all.

At the time of this writing, SAP has announced a beta program for SAP Logistics Business Network, material traceability option. Using the MultiChain blockchain protocol, the solution will provide the provenance for multiingredient food products across a multitiered supply chain. Currently, food supply chain stakeholders individually record product information and share this information only if necessary with their direct business partners. Using a blockchain solution, network participants could create trust and transparency between themselves; increase speed and operational efficiencies (i.e. for recalls via upstream and downstream provenance and batch genealogy); and enhance food safety while supporting provability of sustainability and compliance.

7.3.2   High-Tech

The high-tech industry has practiced outsourcing for decades, from design to manufacturing and production. The industry has been dealing with short product lifecycles and rapid innovation cycles while new technologies are embedded in products in multiple industries at a rapid rate. The high-tech industry requires that companies work with multiple business partners across the globe. Several blockchain use cases exist in the high-tech industry, such as verifying supplier certification when employing third-party testing laboratories, preventing theft and unauthorized use of intellectual property, etc.

At the time of this writing, SAP is working on a POC with several customers on using blockchain to safeguard the supply chain network by preventing counterfeit products from entering the supply chain. Counterfeit products like semiconductor chips can lead to billions of dollars of lost revenue and increase the risk of a company's brand image being damaged. In addition, counterfeit products can lead to financial liabilities and criminal penalties, for example, in cases such as automobile seat belts that use semiconductor chips. A counterfeit chip could risk public safety due to malfunction.

The multitier supply chain in the scope of this POC consists of original equipment manufacturer (OEM) negotiating specifications with component manufacturer for components that they ship to electronic manufacturing services (EMS) providers who then procure parts from approved distributors to assemble, test, and ship the product to the end customer. During tight supply situations, the EMS often purchases parts from other sources, which is typically when counterfeit chips enter the supply chain. With blockchain, the component manufacturer would register the components to be used in the distributed ledger, the EMS would register their purchase information on the blockchain, and the OEM can retrieve and verify all the information regarding the components in the product on the blockchain to ensure their authenticity.

For the high-tech industry, blockchain can help a multiparty network to ensure compliance checks, trace the provenance of parts, and trigger an alert system to immediately notify all parties in case of product issues so a targeted recall process can be initiated. Blockchain can help build a digitally trusted high-tech ecosystem with immutable, secure, and shared data across the participants and optimize and automate processes.

7.3.3 Utilities and Energy

Optimizing processes such as billing, master data management, and procedures for changing electricity suppliers are some areas where blockchain-based solutions can automate and increase processing speed while lowering costs. With electric vehicles on the rise, the need for a nationwide charging station infrastructure has arisen. Blockchain smart contracts can be used for billing and payment processes when electricity is purchased for electric cars at a public charging stations or when participants make their own private charging stations available to other electric vehicle drivers. In case of peer-to-peer energy trading and certification of energy products, blockchain can serve to authenticate the generation source, track electricity offered or consumed, and assure that incorrect values are not immutably written to the blockchain. Smart contracts can automate threshold prices or sources of electricity (e.g. green energy) as well as the associated parameters for billing. Blockchain can also help establish electricity trading without intermediaries, thus reducing overall costs to end customers.

7.3.4   Life Sciences

As a regulated industry with region-specific compliance mandates as well as multiple business partners involved (manufacturer, wholesaler, carrier, hospitals, contract manufacturers, etc.), blockchain can be quite relevant for the pharmaceutical and life sciences industry. Multiple parties need access to same information, and no central owner exists. Blockchain provides secure access to information as well ensure the immutability of information stored on the blockchain. Furthermore, end consumers also need access to the information as well their individual information (e.g. patient health records), which can be securely stored and shared among the required parties (e.g. doctors and hospitals) on the blockchain. Smart contracts on a blockchain can improve data transparency in clinical trials as well as facilitate reporting to government authorities for reimbursements. Rebates and chargebacks involve multiple parties and complex contract terms. Blockchain can improve the speed and accuracy of the process and reduce operational costs.

In a multitiered supply chain, blockchain can document batch genealogies as products flow through the supply chain. If any issues arise with one or more batches, a batch containment or recall can be immediately propagated across the network. This capability has tremendous business value as it helps better manage the risk from recalls, minimize product loss, and most importantly protect the safety of the patients. In case of a cold supply chain, where products like vaccines and medicines must be maintained in temperature-controlled environments during storage and transportation, IoT sensors can log data onto the blockchain.

Regulatory authorities can be provided secure access to blockchain data for demonstrating compliance with regulatory requirements. Analytics and machine learning combined with blockchain data can be used to recognize patterns and systemic issues, analyze scenarios, and predict potential points of failure across the value chain, which can help reduce costs and better manage risks.

Blockchain can help track and monitor product provenance across a multitiered supply chain for accurate and timely returns, which can be a huge issue for the industry as it tackles the effects of fraud and revenue leakage. In the case of scaleable returns, the Drug Supply Chain Security Act mandates companies in the US must both identify and verify saleable returns starting by November 2019. To address this need, in a coinnovation project with seven companies, pharmaceutical manufacturers, and distributors, SAP built a POC using Multichain on SAP Cloud Platform.

SAP provides SAP Information Collaboration Hub for Life Sciences, option for U.S. supply chain for this purpose. Upon batch release or upon shipping, an EPCIS (Electronic Product Code Information Services, a GS1 standard to share traceability data) message will be created and sent to the SAP Information Collaboration Hub for Life Sciences. The product identifier will be extracted from the event message and written into the blockchain with the key data being hashed to prevent unauthorized access. A user at a US wholesaler checking a saleable return could scan the barcode of a pharmaceutical product that contains the exact same data. This data would be hashed and verified against the hashes stored in the blockchain. In the future, this functionality could be extended to an end consumer or a pharmacist who scans a barcode on a product package with a mobile app. The app would decode the barcode and create a hash of the barcode's content and verify the existence of that exact hash on the blockchain to check its authenticity. This feature will help build consumer trust in the brand and ensure patient safety against counterfeit drugs.

7.4   Blockchain for Lines of Business

While the previous section covered industry-specific blockchain use cases, several uses cases for specific lines are relevant across industries, for example, manufacturing, 3D printing, spare parts management, procurement, logistics, finance, etc. All these use cases have characteristics of multiparty collaboration with limited visibility and lack of trust, which can lead to process inefficiencies, misuse, fraud, theft of intellectual property, and disputes. Blockchain technology can address these needs with its ability to facilitate immutable data sharing across all participants while providing process automation with the use of smart contracts. A sample list of blockchain uses cases are covered in the following sections.

7.4.1   Procurement

Supplier management is a complex process today. Buyers work with multiple suppliers, and suppliers work with multiple buyers, in a multitiered supply network. Onboarding new suppliers is a lengthy process for buyers as they need to ensure that the supplier information is current and accurate for validating their claims and certifications. Various compliance and risk requirements need to be checked, like ISO certification; labor and fair trade practices; conflict minerals usage; sustainable, green, LEED, and renewable energy usage claims, sanctions, and watchlist-related information, etc.

In addition, company and financial information must be verified to conduct business with a supplier, information must be passed on to secondary and tertiary suppliers, if needed. Multiple teams across legal, audit, risk, finance, supply chain, and procurement departments need to be involved, and they all need access to various information. Similarly, suppliers will have the same needs in relation to their own suppliers. Given the huge supplier network available on SAP Ariba, SAP is investigating how to bring suppliers, buyers, third-party content providers, governments, standards bodies, and certifiers together and to augment SAP Ariba with blockchain to share supplier information on the blockchain. Some information can be public and available across all players in the network, while other information can be maintained as private and can only be shared with certain players to address their specific needs.

7.4.2 Logistics

Given the global nature of supply chains, cross-country shipments of goods are an inherent part of the process. The end-to-end process today suffers from a great deal of inefficiency given that numerous participants must be involved as goods move from sellers to buyers or to consignees, such as freight forwarders, logistics providers, port authorities, customs, agents, brokers, banks, etc. Further inefficiencies stem from the need to exchange several documents during the process like letters of credit (LCs), commercial invoices, packing lists, export declarations, export customs clearances, bills of lading, import declarations, release orders, import customs clearances, pickup instructions, etc. These documents are transmitted over fax, via emails, or even hand-delivered. Often, these documents are paper-based, involving a lot of manual handling. Such a slow, error-prone process suffers from limited or even no visibility, which leads to delayed shipments; fraud; high costs; and an enormous amount of time, effort, money, and resources spent reconciling disputes and discrepancies. Blockchain for international trade, with integration to enterprise processes, promises to revolutionize the international trade process as it exists today by addressing all these shortcomings and by providing complete visibility and digital transparency to all participants in the blockchain network.

Working with its customers in a coinnovation project, SAP has developed a POC using Hyperledger Fabric on SAP Cloud Platform to model the end-to-end process as four phases: initiate trade, initiate shipment, shipment delivery, and trade settlement. Smart contracts were used to specify which parties needed to be involved at each step, specify which documents needed to be provided and by whom, provide secure visibility to these documents with digital signatures, and ensure all prerequisites were satisfied for a trade to move to the next phase. In the future, with integration to SAP Transportation Management, SAP Global Trade Services, SAP S/4HANA, and SAP Global Track and Trace, as well as the ability to integrate information from third-party applications, blockchain has the potential to provide significant value in terms of cost savings and process efficiencies for all parties involved in international trade.

7.4.3   Finance

Several use cases for blockchain technologies in finance are relevant, and at the time of this writing, SAP is looking at augmenting SAP S4/HANA with blockchain. For example, payment fraud is a serious threat in international payments, but the approval process to change suppler master data account is a tedious and error-prone process but susceptible to hackers and social engineering attempts. Supplier data can be stored as a hash on the blockchain, and at the time of the payment run, that data can be cross-checked against the data found in SAP S/4HANA to ensure its accuracy. Multiparty collaboration on such an immutable, single source of truth, with built-in alert mechanisms, can help all involved parties to gain transparency. Your account information, as well as your supplier relationships, can be kept private, and any tampering of data will be immediately visible and preventable.

Another use case for blockchain in finance is in optimizing days sales outstanding (DSO). Revenue recognition requires that the chance of collection be "probable" or "reasonably expected" according to accounting rules, and for certain types of contracts, revenue is recognized only when an invoice is paid. For the services industry, considerable delays can result because of disputes over the invoice. By sharing open items on a blockchain, the parties won't need to wait for the net payment terms in the contract, and buyers can accept an open item prior to the net payment date. In this way, a vendor can recognize the revenue much earlier while a buyer can continue to make payments per the agreed-upon dates. In a similar fashion, a buyer, who is likely a vendor for another customer, can in turn leverage blockchain in a similar fashion to reduce its own DSO. Once the movement of cash is no longer the way revenue recognition is triggered, the actual payment may be unnecessary with regard to multiparty accounts receivable/accounts payable netting. Instead of all parties paying through the bank, data on the blockchain can be used to net revenue amounts against credit owed by a buyer as well as against credit owed by third parties.

With the visibility and security provided by blockchain, a vendor may decide to allow credit-worthy customers to accrue amounts owed for longer periods. Blockchain can also be used for accounts receivable (AR) factoring. If your company, for example, has difficulty in finding loans to grow their business, you can engage in selling your AR (called *factors*) to third parties, at a discount to obtain funds. Silent factoring can be initiated by a vendor without your knowledge, whereas reverse factoring would be initiated by you, the customer. A vendor can sell its open items to a factorer at a discount either before or after the buyer accepts the liability. Blockchain reduces the risks involved in factoring by eliminating fraud and increasing transparency for the parties involved. This mechanism can help small vendors or vendors with poor credit ratings to access cheaper financing because financing cost is highly correlated to risk and blockchain minimizes risk.

Another variation of this use case is using blockchain for third-party collections. If a vendor posts an invoice on the blockchain, but the invoice is disputed by the buyer, the vendor can turn around and sell its accounts receivable for the disputed invoices to debt collectors. Blockchain can help reduce the effort involved in third-party collections and increase transparency.

Other use cases like processing letters of credit (LCs) and requests for quotations (RFQs) go hand in hand with the international trade and procurement areas described earlier in this section.

Letters of credit often involve a lengthy process of back-and-forth exchanges between multiple parties: the buyer, the seller, banks, customs, logistics service providers, freight forwarders, inspectors, etc. A large degree of paper-based reconciliation and validation had to be done manually, slowing down the receipt of goods and payments. Letters of credit using smart contracts on blockchain can help reduce costs, prevent fraud, and facilitate faster payments by providing transparency into the shipment statuses, inspection results, and required documentation, as per the terms of the purchase order, on the shared ledger thus automating the effort for the bank's review and approval.

RFQ processing in procurement involves a buyer initiating an RFQ and suppliers creating and submitting bids. A considerable time lapse before the decision deadline leaves room for manipulation and possible collusion between a buyer and a supplier if confidentiality is not maintained, which often results in expensive lawsuits when suppliers challenge bid awards. With a blockchain-verified RFQ process, a hash of each submitted bid can be stored on the blockchain, maintaining information on who opened a bid and when. With blockchain, trust and transparency is enhanced by an established audit trail open to all involved. The time stamp service in SAP Cloud Platform Blockchain described in the previous section can be used to achieve these objectives.

7.5 Summary

As discussed in this chapter, the use of blockchain technology must span across organizational boundaries and requires the willingness to share data between all the participants. Network nodes can potentially be distributed across different cloud infrastructures or exist as on-premise blockchain nodes. Cryptographic algorithms create a hash of a block of transactions, which is then stored in a distributed ledger using consensus algorithms that automatically resolve concurrent write access to achieve a consistent state across the distributed ledger. The blocks are immutable and can only be read from or written to the distributed ledger, which creates digital trust and a high level of transparency between all the network participants since all participants will have identical copies of the same data, although private sharing of data is possible to protect trade secrets like product recipes and contractual agreements between two parties.

The choice of a blockchain technology, whether Hyperledger, MultiChain, Quorum, or others, will depend on the nature of the use case and the capabilities needed. Blockchain can enable many high-impact use cases across all sectors, and the combination of blockchain data with enterprise data can be a powerful catalyst for innovating new network-based business models. The data immutability and transparency aspects of blockchains lend themselves to many use cases, such as ensuring product authenticity, providing visibility into product provenance, ensuring sustainable sourcing, promoting fair trade, encouraging adherence to fair labor practices, providing value-added services to citizens, and protecting intellectual property, to name a few.

Chapter 8
Internet of Things

The use of sensors, devices, and data to improve business processes is not a new phenomenon, but the Internet of Things (IoT) has been gaining new recognition as a key pillar of digital transformation. IoT has the potential to revolutionize enterprise optimization.

Connectivity is the core capability of the Internet. In our everyday lives, we're likely to use the Internet to connect with other people and with information, but the Internet can also be extended beyond ourselves and our computers to connect other things. As a concept, the Internet of Things (IoT) refers to the idea that every physical thing can be connected into a vast communication network. In an enterprise context, these "things" are likely devices and machines equipped with sensors that collect and exchange data. We can leverage this data to educate the "things" and make them smarter through built-in machine learning or use the data to inform predictive analysis.

We've never had more data at our fingertips. As more and more "things" are connected, you can access real-time data and unlock new potential from deeper and more frequent insights, enabling wider visibility into business processes, optimized planning, and better decision-making.

In Chapter 3, you learned about big data—the currency of the digital enterprise—and in Chapter 5, you learned how this data can be used to train SAP Leonardo algorithms and artificial intelligence to solve business problems. But how is data collected from enterprise assets? How can this data stored and processed? How can SAP Leonardo help extract value from this data?

In this chapter, we'll explain what IoT is and its place in Industry 4.0. You'll learn about SAP Leonardo's IoT portfolio and the range of services and applications it provides to help enterprises use IoT to transform their business processes.

8.1   What Is the Internet of Things?

The Internet of Things (IoT)—sometimes referred to as the Internet of Everything—is an ecosystem of physical objects that have been equipped with sensors and connectivity technology to enable them to transmit data. This data can be collected and analyzed to provide variety of insights about a device's real-time status, health, lifecycle, location, and surrounding conditions. Devices are also able to respond or react to changing conditions. For example, an IoT-enabled thermostat can collect and transmit data about a home's internal temperature and can be configured to switch heating and cooling systems on or off, based on temperature fluctuations.

By making inanimate devices smarter in this manner, you can simplify and automate a variety of workflows, which is especially useful for enterprises where increased insight is always beneficial, and can help businesses develop more efficient and transparent processes. Automation and smart operations in particular are cornerstones of digital business models. IoT can connect equipment, machinery, vehicles, buildings, and cities—just about any type of enterprise asset.

Although not a new technology, IoT is more accessible than ever. The price of devices and data storage has dropped significantly. Big data technology has made it possible to stream data from thousands of devices directly or indirectly into the cloud. Cloud solutions enable a lower total cost of ownership (TCO) and enable the centralization and harmonization of multiple data sources and formats. Different connectivity technology options also allow the application of different use cases with a feasible return on investment (ROI)—for example, LTE and narrow band IoT connectivity, which allow for low-cost, low-band tracking. These advancements have enabled enterprises to move from pilot IoT processes towards productive applications of the technology. IoT can now be used to improve asset utilization, increase efficiency, reduce costs, and or even disrupt entire industries, pushing businesses to adopt new business models.

Multiple industries can benefit from IoT technology. For example, commercial farming and agriculture have become more industrialized and technology-driven through automation. Precision farming has been made possible by monitoring livestock and land. Livestock can be monitored for vital signs and conditions, such as temperature and humidity, with the aim to improve the quality of livestock conditions to ensure growth. Sensors can be put into the ground where crops are growing to monitor the conditions of the ground, applying more or less water and pesticide depending on the exact required amount needed, making soil conditions more predictable and improving efficiency. Tractors and harvesters could run autonomously, ensuring precision movement on fields. Agriculture business is changing where asset vendors lease harvesting services versus farmers buying the assets. Usage-based billing could be applied to reduce the capital expenses required by farmers. Remote commercial farming is also possible.

Utilities, oil companies, and the construction industry can all improve their remote service operations by connecting their distant plants and assets so that predictive maintenance, work manager tasks, and service times can be managed remotely for critical operational assets.

Manufacturing operational assets can be monitored across multifunctional operational teams, such as asset vendors, operators, service stakeholders, thus creating a single asset network view across an ecosystem. IoT sensors can monitor operationally critical assets and ensure that machinery is always operating correctly by comparing a machine to its digital twin and alerting you to any deviation found.

IoT data can be used in any industry to improve core operations such as financial and asset management decision-making and lifecycle management of fleets, machinery, and equipment. IoT can also be used for larger economies and ecosystems such as smart cities. IoT sensors combined with traffic systems can improve the flow of time-dependent traffic and change traffic flow conditions, such as the direction of dynamic traffic lanes, which change as traffic patterns change during the day. Fleets can easily identify open parking and loading spots and reduce traffic obstructions. Buses and maintenance fleet can be equipped with sensors screening road quality and detect road vulnerabilities to trigger maintenance repairs.

SAP Leonardo brings this IoT framework and technology foundation to SAP, making it possible for you and your partners to take advantage of IoT services and solutions on a shared and consistent platform.

The SAP Leonardo Internet of Things (SAP Leonardo IoT) platform consist of three main areas:

- **Applications**
  SAP Leonardo provides IoT applications, developed to be reusable and modular for specific industries and lines of business. You'll learn more about this area in Section 8.3.

- **Foundation and platform**
  SAP Leonardo provides a foundation of business and technical services to enable IoT in SAP landscapes called SAP Leonardo IoT Foundation. These services can be

built into new applications that run on SAP Cloud Platform and SAP HANA and leverage the capabilities of both. You'll learn more about this area in Section 8.4.

- **Edge computing**
  SAP Leonardo enables secure edge processing for IoT applications, making it possible to process, store, and analyze IoT sensor data on the *edge*—that is, near the data source instead of in remote data centers. This feature enables sensor- and device-agnostic ingestion of IoT data. You'll learn more about this area in Section 8.5.

Figure 8.1 shows the different components of SAP Leonardo IoT.

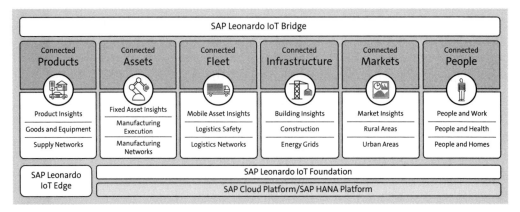

Figure 8.1 The SAP Leonardo IoT Innovation Portfolio

These pillars of the SAP Leonardo IoT platform work together. SAP Leonardo Machine Learning Foundation and SAP Leonardo IoT Edge are both built on SAP Cloud Platform, to enable them to connect products and manage large data streams. Business-specific IoT applications analyze the data and link business logic with business processes to enrich these processes with real-time sensor data.

The platform includes microservices and an API marketplace that enable development teams create new IoT applications. These solutions can then be used as templates for new projects. Developers can create digital twins, reusable application services, and apply predictive algorithms while consuming IoT services. Other parts of the SAP portfolio can also be integrated to create more robust IoT solutions. When used with SAP S/4HANA, SAP Leonardo helps digitize business processes and generates value for businesses using IoT, as shown in Figure 8.2.

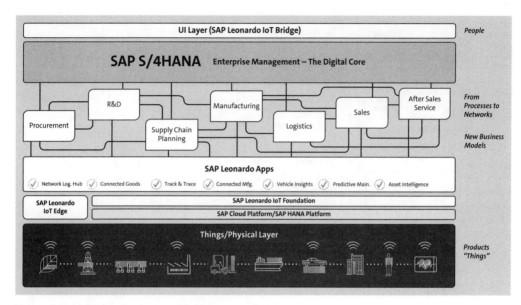

Figure 8.2 Digitizing Business with SAP Leonardo IoT

Let's explore these interactions more in the next section.

8.2   Reference Architecture

The SAP Leonardo IoT reference architecture defines the foundation for holistic end-to-end IoT solutions that enable digital transformation. Figure 8.3 shows a general overview of this architecture.

This architecture ensures flexibility in connecting and managing real-world assets, providing logic at the edge, managing, and processing massive amount of data; facilitating analytical and machine learning capabilities; and building a strong connection to individual business processes. The integration of processes and data (in both an information technology context and an operational technology context) is a particular strength of SAP's overall portfolio.

In the following sections, we'll briefly describe the building blocks of SAP Leonardo IoT's reference architecture.

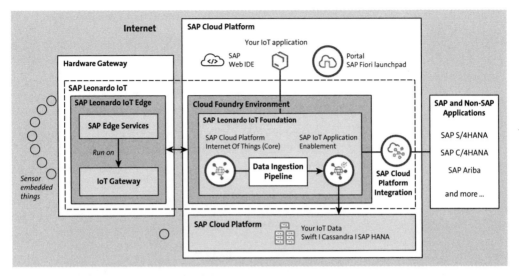

Figure 8.3 SAP Leonardo IoT and Edge Networks

8.2.1   Connecting Assets and Processing on the Edge

SAP is well-positioned to connect assets and equipment along the supply chain due to its long history of offering and running shop floor and factory solutions. When combined with technology that creates direct connections between assets and cloud platforms for IoT, SAP solutions can support a variety of industry-specific communication protocols. For example, tools like SAP Plant Connectivity can interact with the OPC Unified Architecture (OPC-UA), a machine-to-machine communication protocol that enables automation. SAP Leonardo IoT Edge enables additional protocols and offers an open plug-in concept to extend out of the box protocols and meet industry-specific needs for connecting additional assets. As a result, SAP landscapes not only support bidirectional asset connections but also deeply integrate these connections into business processes.

These connection capabilities are enhanced with SAP Data Hub, a data orchestration solution that helps SAP Leonardo bring data processing directly to data at the edge. SAP Data Hub provides capabilities for processing incoming IoT data using rules, events, and transformations. Additionally, some machine learning capabilities can also be executed through SAP Data Hub, which allows you to process data in real time, based on the same algorithms and rules you would apply to IoT data processed in the cloud. This functionality is particularly useful in scenarios where reaction time is key—the more quickly you need to react, the less time is available to communicate and act via a cloud-based solution. Even in situations where time is available for sending and processing data in the cloud, SAP Data Hub can use transformation and filtering capabilities to reduce the amount of data that needs to be sent from the edge to the cloud.

Once in the cloud, SAP Cloud Platform offers an optimized and scalable environment for SAP Leonardo IoT asset connectivity and edge data processing. A number of IoT services provide integration points for connecting assets, directly or via SAP Leonardo IoT Edge. These services can handle both sending data from the edge to the cloud and controlling connected assets from the cloud. These services also provide key IoT protocols like the Message Queuing Telemetry Transport (MQTT) and the ability to send signals, software components, and firmware updates to the edge.

The combined features of SAP Leonardo, SAP Data Hub, and SAP Cloud Platform allow SAP to manage the complete lifecycle of edge components and assets. SAP also drives a partner-centric approach for asset coverage and integration by enabling partner device management solutions through IoT services. These devices and assets are managed by a partner's device cloud. Data can still be integrated into SAP Cloud Platform and used with all SAP Leonardo solutions.

8.2.2   Data Processing and Storage

Once device data reaches SAP Cloud Platform, IoT services provide basic rule-processing and data-filtering capabilities. Then, this data can be handed over to a message broker, which ensures high throughput, scalability, and resilience and also decouples device data from both producers and consumers.

In general, handling the massive amounts of data IoT scenarios produce, including processing the data, storing the data, and enabling dynamic access the data, can be a challenge. Operations to process rules, compute events, and cleanse data are essential. SAP Data Hub comes into play again here, by providing a flow-based pipeline solution. Each pipeline consists of various flexibly configurable operations. Each operation has controlled data input and output and provides clearly defined capabilities to handle data—for example, individual operations can read and write data from the message broker, SAP HANA, or data lakes. A complete development environment is also available so that you can enrich the pipeline with additional steps, including specialized operations. Operations can be simple transformations, embedded Apache Spark executions, or user-provided code in a range of languages. The pipelines are implemented using a container approach, making them highly scalable in serverless scenarios. Since this pipeline concept is so flexible, you can complete all data process-ing logic for standard applications through SAP Data Hub.

Once SAP Data Hub pipelines process data from the message broker, the data is stored in a data lake. A *data lake* consists of an object store for the affordable storage of large amounts of raw data. This layer is often called the *cold store*. On top of this layer, a more flexible and scalable approach to expose the data is required. In SAP Data Hub, the SAP Vora layer provides a highly scalable persistence layer and is there-fore the foundation of a data lake. The key element is the disk engine, which is responsible for storing warm IoT data on nodes with local spinning disks and SSDs. Since replicas are provided as well, this data layer is resilient and highly scalable on commodity hardware. Higher-value engines are provided as well, for example, the time-series engine for IoT, which handles and computes time-series data.

On top of SAP Vora, SAP HANA forms a unified access layer to IT and OT (operational technology) data. As a result, all data residing in SAP Vora is accessible via SAP HANA, providing transparency to application developers. All of SAP HANA's capabilities can be used to connect data from SAP's business solutions with IoT data. This connectiv-ity is a key differentiator of the reference architecture and a key element for driving the digital transformation in companies, where connecting existing business pro-cesses and data with new capabilities coming out of IoT scenarios is essential.

The combination of SAP HANA, SAP Vora, and a cheap object store we described in this section ensures cost-conscious handling of mass data without losing the flexibil-ity to combine data from various sources into new end-to-end IoT scenarios.

8.2.3 Analytics

After processing, IoT data must be enriched with semantics to draw conclusions and take action. Integration with analytical and machine learning capabilities is key. The data lakes we discussed in Section 8.2.2—a combination of SAP HANA and SAP Vora—can be accessed by SAP's analytical solution stack, including SAP Analytics Cloud. You can use these tools to analyze data, create analytical dashboards, and understand data insights.

For predictive and automated scenarios, SAP integrates SAP Data Hub and the data lake with SAP Leonardo Machine Learning Foundation. As a result, you can access both raw and enriched data to train machine learning algorithms. Both SAP Data Hub and SAP Leonardo are based on a highly scalable and flexible container approach. Trained algorithms can be provisioned into the machine learning execution infra-structure in SAP Cloud Platform.

8.2.4 Reusable Business Services

Many SAP Leonardo scenarios will be a mixture of out of the box and prebuilt SAP solutions combined with your own custom developments. For this reason, SAP offers a platform-as-a-service based on the Cloud Foundry. Cloud Foundry is an open initiative to provide an industry-leading platform for the development of microservice-based solutions. SAP's Cloud Foundry platform provides a number of solutions out of the box, such as the data integration services we've been discussing, SAP Cloud Platform Integration for process integration, SAP Fiori for user interface development, mobile services for connectivity, and collaborative solutions for project management.

SAP Leonardo applications are built with reusability in mind. Applications are comprised of a variety of business services, to complement SAP Leonardo IoT's technical offerings (like device management and connectivity). These business services are called SAP IoT Application Enablement and include location services, authorization services, thing registries, UI templates and controls, time and time-series APIs, and more. You'll learn more about SAP IoT Application Enablement in Section 8.6.

8.3 Applications

SAP Leonardo is a solution portfolio that enables companies, not only to realize digital transformation of existing end-to-end business processes, but also to monetize new digital business models untethered from physical limitations.

SAP Leonardo IoT combines adaptive applications, streaming analytics, device management, big data management, and edge computing connectivity in packaged solutions across lines of business (LOBs) and industry use cases, ranging from connected products, assets, and infrastructures to vehicle fleets, markets, and people. The SAP Leonardo IoT portfolio has been segmented into five distinct areas:

- Connected products provide visibility into product operations and usage, thus allow you to proactively use product data to improve product designs by sharing data to R&D, operational streamlining such as automated order supply, preventive maintenance, or supply chain visibility.

- Connected assets represent machinery associated with manufacturing, often associated with productivity. Sharing machine performance data allows maintenance, operators, and decision-makers reduce cost and increase asset uptime.

- Connected fleets goes far beyond just telematics therefore track, monitor, analyze, and maintain all moving assets, within a supply network but also include optimizing supply chain operations asset management and right-sizing of fleets.

- Connected infrastructures concern physical infrastructure, such as buildings or transportation infrastructure such as roads and rail, to effectively monitor operations and proactively predict failures before they occur. Operational efficiencies are gained in terms of cost, service-level improvements, and lowering the likelihood of noncompliance.

- Connected markets focus on how IoT can be used to improve operations for local markets, smart cities, and agriculture for both urban and rural areas. Efficiency for both compliance and conservation is often the goal while improving or finding alternative advancements towards the appropriate use of natural resources and assets; the reduction of emissions, congestion, and energy usage; and the improvement the environment.

- Connected people concerns the ability to improve people's lives in terms of health, emergency response, work safety, customer experience, convenience and belonging to communities. With new insights organizations can evolve operations into new operational models.

Table 8.1 lists additional application areas that specific SAP Leonardo IoT applications can address.

Application Areas		Applications
Connected Products	Product Insights	<ul><li>SAP Engineering Control Center</li><li>SAP Product Lifecycle Costing</li><li>SAP Ariba Sourcing</li></ul>
	Goods and Equipment	<ul><li>SAP Connected Goods</li><li>SAP Integrated Business Planning (SAP IBP) for response and supply</li><li>SAP Billing and Revenue Innovation Management</li></ul>
	Supply Networks	<ul><li>SAP Supply Chain Control Tower</li><li>SAP Global Track and Trace</li><li>SAP Ariba Supply Chain Collaboration</li></ul>

Table 8.1 SAP Leonardo IoT Application Portfolio

Application Areas		Applications
Connected Assets	Fixed Asset Insights	■ SAP Predictive Maintenance and Service ■ SAP Work Manager ■ SAP Ariba Supply Chain Collaboration
	Manufacturing Execution	■ SAP Manufacturing Execution ■ SAP Manufacturing Integration and Intelligence ■ SAP Plant Connectivity
	Manufacturing Networks	■ SAP Manufacturing Integration and Intelligence ■ SAP Global Batch Traceability ■ SAP Global Track and Trace ■ SAP Leonardo IoT for SAP Distributed Manufacturing
Connected Fleet	Mobile Asset Insights	■ SAP Leonardo IoT ■ SAP Predictive Maintenance and Service ■ SAP Asset Intelligence Network
	Logistics Safety	■ SAP Connected Parking ■ SAP EHS Management
	Logistics Network	■ SAP Global Track and Trace ■ SAP Yard Logistics ■ SAP Extended Warehouse Management ■ SAP Networked Logistics Hub ■ SAP Vehicle Network
Connected Infrastructure	Building Insights	■ SAP Real Estate Cockpit ■ SAP Enterprise Asset Management ■ SAP Customer Energy Management ■ SAP Ariba Procurement
	Construction	■ SAP Project Management ■ SAP Global Track and Trace ■ SAP Yard Logistics
	Energy Grids	■ SAP Asset Intelligence Network ■ SAP Manufacturing Integration and Intelligence

Table 8.1 SAP Leonardo IoT Application Portfolio (Cont.)

Application Areas		Applications
Connected Markets	Market Insights	▪ SAP Customer Activity Repository ▪ SAP Connected Goods
	Rural Areas	▪ SAP Leonardo IoT ▪ SAP Predictive Maintenance and Service ▪ SAP Connected Agriculture
	Urban Areas	▪ SAP Networked Logistics Hub ▪ Intelligent traffic management ▪ SAP Connected Parking
Connected People	People and Work	▪ SAP Knowledge Workspace ▪ SAP Jam
	People and Health	▪ SAP Connected Goods ▪ SAP Connected Health
	People and Homes	▪ Connected homes (insurance)

Table 8.1 SAP Leonardo IoT Application Portfolio (Cont.)

SAP HANA capabilities, together with core SAP Leonardo technical services and SAP Cloud Platform, ensure that these applications can be deployed in real-world situations where high-velocity big data is required, alongside the ability to stream analytics and run predictive scenarios.

8.4   Platform and Foundation Services

The core platform service underpinning SAP's approach to IoT is SAP Leonardo IoT. This service intelligently connects things, people, and processes to optimize IoT deployments, speed up decision-making, and supports the adaptability you need to change quickly. SAP Leonardo IoT also provides decision-making tools at the edge, leading to significant optimization of your processes at the core of your business.

SAP Leonardo IoT's key features include the following:

- **Protocol support**
  SAP Leonardo IoT supports a wide array of IoT connectivity protocols including MQTT, a lightweight messaging protocol that simplifies publishing and subscribing.

- **Device management**

  SAP Leonardo IoT also supports comprehensive device management, from on-boarding devices to decommissioning devices, with messaging functionality and remote device control as well as the scalability required to collect, preprocess, and manage high volumes of sensor data via the cloud or at the edge.

- **Compliance**

  SAP Leonardo IoT enables you to address regulatory, environmental, industrial, and safety compliance for IoT devices and processes. This service can meet IoT-related guidelines and regulations for privacy and data security, product safety, and energy efficiency as well as other legal, procedural, and documentation requirements.

- **Security**

  SAP Leonardo IoT also covers operational security for IoT devices, accommodating security standards such as X.509 for public key certificates and supporting multitenancy for connected devices to enhance privacy through role-based information access.

- **Edge processing**

  SAP Leonardo IoT automates processes and connects objects and devices with streaming analytics at the edge of your network for greater speed and better communication, as shown in Figure 8.4. Discussed at greater length in Section 8.5, the edge processing capabilities of SAP Leonardo IoT lets you ingest data regardless of connectivity, latency, or device protocol concerns. You can perform local streaming analytics and send aggregated measures over specified time windows or locally evaluate rules and trigger immediate local commands.

  The service scales to support and connect large numbers of IoT devices. Lightweight databases for edge devices let you capture and store data locally on your equipment, or on SAP Cloud Platform, and synchronize that data for use by other applications. You can also connect and secure unconnected, or "dumb," devices.

- **Dashboards**

  SAP Leonardo IoT and other SAP solutions work with SAP Cloud Platform Internet of Things capabilities to open up opportunities for generating insights.

  For example, SAP Fiori provides a consumer-grade user experience for mobile and IoT-enabled devices. Flexible dashboards enable you to provide a personalized, role-based experience that's responsive to the needs of individual users. People can use dashboards and the SAP Fiori UX to tap the analytics power of the SAP Cloud Platform Internet of Things service for predictive analysis and machine learning functionality, extending data retrieved by SAP Leonardo IoT. SAP Cloud Platform Internet of Things automates decision-making to streamline processes, while real-time alerts can trigger intervention as necessary.

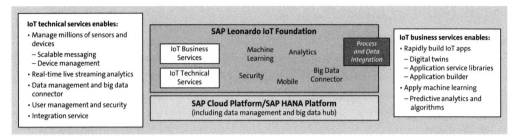

Figure 8.4 SAP IoT Leonardo Foundation

8.5 Edge Computing

Edge processing is the idea of using devices deployed at the edge of an IoT network to process data and take action without transmitting data back to the business enterprise via the cloud. This approach can dramatically improve IoT efficiency and effectiveness by circumventing common cloud network challenges associated with high-bandwidth requirements, intermittent connectivity, data latency, power consumption limitations for sensors, and security risks.

SAP enables edge computing with SAP Leonardo IoT Edge. This offering includes a containerized IoT gateway that sits in close proximity to edge devices in an IoT network to manage the onboarding, provisioning, and management of edge devices.

SAP Leonardo IoT Edge also includes edge services that run on top of the IoT gateway to help manage the edge environment, such as the following:

- **Business semantics service**
  Provide business context on the edge for critical business functions, despite intermittent connectivity, thus helping to reduce costly downtimes, increase worker productivity, and improve operational efficiency. For example, you can use this service to automatically create maintenance work orders to ensure uninterrupted business process flows. This service also extends cloud computing to the edge for line of business (LOB)-centric business scenarios, such as logistics, warehousing, and asset management.

- **Policy service**
  Centrally define, set, and distribute local data policies from the cloud to local edge nodes. Take, for example, a policy requesting only data when an exception arises to a predefined temperature threshold. All temperature data is processed at the edge, based on the local policy, with only the exceptions are sent back to the cloud for valuable insights.

- **Persistence and streaming service**
  Analyze IoT data streams in real time based on business logic, storing data locally and transmitting only anomalies via the cloud to keep performance high and costs low. For example, you can monitor an average temperature from multiple sensors in 1-minute increments and trigger alerts only when dangerous spikes emerge.

In short, SAP Leonardo IoT Edge provides the ability to collect, filter, and aggregate raw data and enrich this data with business context, when needed at the edge. SAP Leonardo IoT Edge can then transform data into meaningful insights, enabling events, alerts, and activity without need to submit all the raw data to the cloud.

8.6 Application Enablement

SAP IoT Application Enablement allows you to extend and create personalized IoT applications. The service features rich semantics, an extensible data model, and functionality for digital twins, which use data from sensors for modeling, monitoring, and diagnostics. Users can rapidly build IoT applications, create reusable application services, and apply predictive algorithms.

You can build web and mobile applications with SAP's development environment, the SAP Web IDE. Also, the SAP Cloud Platform SDK for iOS combines powerful native apps for iPhone and iPad with cutting-edge capabilities from SAP HANA to give designers and developers tools for building iOS apps for iPhones and iPads based on SAP Cloud Platform.

Developers can compose apps quickly thanks to the SAP API Business Hub, a directory of SAP software APIs, which can incorporate blocks of SAP software functionality within custom-developed apps.

The SAP Cloud Platform Workflow service enables a low-code approach to creating workflow-based applications and extending standard cloud applications. The service lets you make process changes quickly to increase enterprise agility while reducing development costs. User-friendly functionality enables greater participation from various lines of business in building more optimal flows.

With the help of SAP Cloud Platform Internet of Things and SAP IoT Application Enablement, you can securely connect with a magnitude of devices over a broad variety of protocols to derive business-relevant data. The IoT service provides you with full flexibility to decide where and how to process IoT data—either at the edge of your network or on SAP Cloud Platform. You can leverage SAP IoT Application Enablement to feed this data into IoT applications, enabling real-time IoT analytics or interactions with core business processes.

The main features of SAP IoT Application Enablement include the following capabilities:

- **Connect**
  Connect IoT devices with SAP Cloud Platform IoT services. SAP Cloud Platform Internet of Things can be used to connect devices to SAP Cloud Platform so that you can use data from these devices in your applications. The feature includes lifecycle management at scale for IoT devices from onboarding to decommissioning. Securely connect to remote devices over a broad variety of IoT protocols. Collect and process sensor data at scale already at the edge or in the cloud and store it on SAP Cloud Platform for use by other applications

- **Enable**
  Microservices secure, access, and organize data with an extensible "thing data" model. The thing model allows flexible modelling and provides out of the box REST endpoints for create, read, update, and delete (CRUD) operations on things and for CRUD operations on thing data through property set types.

- **Manage big data**
  Data storage capabilities can provide you with deep insights at affordable costs. These capabilities support multiple infrastructure-as-a-service (IaaS) offerings to avoid vendor lock-in. You can enable applications with automated, dynamic data storage. Microservices can automate big data storage with advanced data aging capabilities.

- **Build**
  Application development tools drive scale and consistency and achieve value faster. You'll be able to build IoT applications quickly and efficiently to drive scale and consistency and achieve value faster. This section consists out of:
  - IoT developer experience: Set of tools, content, and knowledge helping customers and partners to build great apps faster

- UI development: Web-based development environment, storyboards as rapid development perspective, IoT templates and UI components, thing modeler, rules modeler, KPI modeler and tenant management
- Mash-up services, API composition: Data collection for user interfaces (REST/OData)
- Business logic: Process automation with event and API-driven application flows
- Application services: Thing model as central service for business semantics, business partner authorization, partner microservices, and your own microservices

8.7 Summary

In this chapter, you learned what the Internet of Things is and the technologies SAP Leonardo uses to help enterprises use IoT technologies to make their processes smarter. We discussed a host of technologies that help make IoT capabilities a reality, from SAP Leonardo IoT and SAP IoT Application Enablement services, to SAP Data Hub, SAP HANA, and SAP Cloud Platform.

The SAP IoT Leonardo portfolio empowers business by connecting the emerging world of intelligent devices with people and processes to achieve tangible business outcomes.

PART III

SAP Leonardo Business Processes

Chapter 9
Products and Inventory

Digital transformation requires keeping your customers at the center of your attention. In this chapter, we'll discuss how advanced analytics, machine learning, and the Internet of Things (IoT) can bring intelligence to integrated business processes especially for designing compliant products, predicting demand, and maintaining an optimal inventory to profitably fulfill customer demand.

In today's customer-centric, networked economy, ensuring the right product is available at the right location, at the right time, in the right quantity, and at the right price is ever more important for you and your business. While all companies try to keep pace with rising levels of customer demand and with the increasing number of choices available to customers in the market, innovative companies lead the pack by setting the bar higher. These companies leverage technology to establish and grow their brand identity and usurp market share. Industry boundaries are blurring, and traditional businesses are changing the way they operate—new business models are evolving that require close collaboration with a network of business partners:

- Companies are augmenting their wholesale model with a direct-to-consumer model.
- Same-day deliveries are shrinking to same-hour delivery.
- Physical inventory is being replaced with digital inventory through the use of additive manufacturing.
- Product offerings are transforming into solution offerings through the use of technologies like IoT and blockchain.

Providing superior customer service levels for products and associated services is a universal goal that requires constant striving to achieve, even though, in such a hypercompetitive market, this task can be daunting. You'll need to adopt a demand-driven outlook and have visibility into all aspects of demand for your products, from a design-to-operate approach, with minimum latency from insight to action.

You'll need to ask yourself a series of questions to assess your readiness for the necessary digital transformation:

- How can you best capture new product ideas from all internal and external stakeholders that will address your customers' current and future needs?

- How can you uncover trends and derive a detailed understanding of products through the entire lifecycle from inception, design, engineering, production, operations, sales, maintenance, and service to end-of-life to improve the quality of the products?

- How can you derive real-time insights into product state, inventory, and consumption to drive demand-driven replenishment?

- How can you improve service levels based on real-time product usage and performance data and predict the likelihood of desired outcomes by driving insights into product design?

- How can you increase customer intimacy by a better understanding of product consumption patterns and key demand influencers?

- How can you develop robust yet flexible demand plans across the entire planning horizon while considering various sources of demand signals?

- How can you segment demand and recognize patterns to focus resources on the most profitable products?

- How can you establish optimal inventory targets at every level of the supply chain to meet or exceed customer service levels while reducing working capital?

In this chapter, we'll cover common capabilities in SAP's intelligent technologies, covered throughout Part II, that can help you address these questions and help you build a competitive edge by profitably driving customer acquisition and retention while providing higher levels of customer service. Section 9.1 covers the holistic view needed for product and project lifecycle management and describes how analytics can help drive insights to action in the design process. Section 9.2 covers the entire spectrum of demand that you'll need to consider during planning to respond to your customers' needs utilizing both internal and external demand signals and describes how machine learning can not only automate planning process but also improve plan quality. Section 9.3 covers how multistage inventory optimization helps account for supply chain variability to establish the appropriate inventory levels to profitably meet customer service levels. Finally, in Section 9.4, we'll cover how IoT can be used to operationalize sensor data by connecting enterprise edge networks to the core and create opportunities to establish new business models.

9.1 Digital Product Management

In recent years, a significant and disruptive shift has taken place in the market. Customer demand for new, highly functional, smart, and personalized products has been on the rise. Digital product management must be the heart of your product development process as you aspire to sell product experience and product performance, not just widgets, to your customers. Your goals should be to design and deliver products or pursue projects that will help you win market share, satisfy customers' needs, and meet quality and regulatory requirements.

Product lifecycle management can no longer exist as a siloed, standalone process. Customers' needs for individualized products require accelerated design cycles with continuous feedback loops from the design, manufacturing, sales, and service functions in your company. In addition, you'll need to establish close collaboration with your customers and the ecosystem of your trading partners.

SAP's portfolio of cloud-based, industry-specific solutions can enable the required digital transformation journey. SAP Leonardo capabilities, combined with SAP S/4HANA as the digital core, provide an intelligent, integrated, and visual product innovation platform with built-in compliance.

SAP solutions can help you develop new products quickly and go to market more quickly than your competition, by integrating the product development process across functional silos. With compliant product lifecycle management, you can facilitate effective collaboration across various functions, streamline the ramp-up process, and develop products that comply with the regional necessary regulations. With visibility into product costs throughout the process, you can continuously monitor and reduce costs and protect revenue margins while developing innovative products that preserve and grow your brand value. With portfolio and project management solutions from SAP, you'll gain better insights into your product development processes and help ensure your budgets are on target by allocating your resources optimally. With product and project insights, SAP solutions provide the necessary flexibility and visibility that your project and engineering teams need to collaborate effectively across your extended supply chain network to establish an innovative product development process.

9.1.1 Compliant Product Lifecycle Management

Compliant product lifecycle management helps you maintain a detailed understanding of your products through their entire lifecycle. The required data can come from smart connected products with embedded software or IoT, or from live connected systems and repositories. As shown in Figure 9.1, data collected at each of the following stages of the lifecycle is used to analyze product performance and institute continuous improvements in the product design:

- As designed: product portfolio and costs
- As configured: options and compatibility
- As built: production processed and delivery
- As maintained: in-situ updates
- As operating: collect data in action and from the operating environment

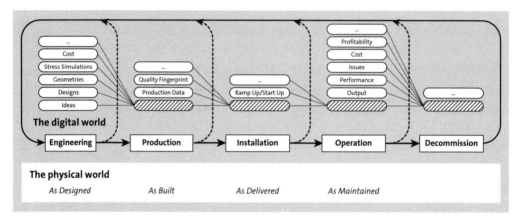

Figure 9.1 Stages in a Product's Lifecycle

Combined with SAP S/4HANA and SAP Leonardo intelligent technologies, the core building blocks of compliant product lifecycle management are:

- **Requirements management for intelligent product design**
  This enables efficient definition, structuring, and management of customer requirements management in a requirements-driven product development environment. A single multidisciplinary product definition across the enterprise helps reduce development errors. Traceability and impact analysis of requirements helps you fully understand the implications of any requirement changes. In addition, SAP Leonardo Machine Learning Foundation helps you design smart products with capabilities like anomaly detection and influencer analysis. Future releases of SAP S/4HANA are planned to provide requirement acquisition capabilities from social sentiment feeds using machine learning.

- **Collaboration across the extended enterprise**
  Ability to rapidly design new products with visual handover of bill of materials (BOM), routing, and visual work instructions to manufacturing as well as sharing engineering changes including software version upgrades with the SAP Asset Intelligence Network. In order to incorporate insights from product usage to further improve product design, SAP S/4HANA Cloud for intelligent product design, powered by SAP Leonardo, brings live product data from the field to help designers analyze detailed performance and usage data. This feature is facilitated by integration with SAP Leonardo IoT and SAP Leonardo IoT Edge.

- **Integrated product development**
  Enhanced computer-aided design (CAD) integration of market-leading authoring tools with SAP Engineering Control Center supports cross-discipline product definition for complex products with mechanical, electric, and electronics components, including management of embedded software versions. The personalized user interface in SAP Fiori apps helps maintain multiple BOMs in an intuitive and easy way.

- **Integrated recipe development**
  SAP Fiori-based apps for product developers help create accurate recipes through the ability to view, create, and edit multiple recipes simultaneously. In addition, users can run live reports to analyze recipes. Managing accurate recipes helps avoid breakdowns in subsequent enterprise processes like procurement, production, service, and compliance management.

- **Product costing**
  To meet target costs and manage the impact on the bottom line, SAP Product Lifecycle Costing helps calculate costs and identify cost drivers. Especially useful during the early stages of new product development, you can easily simulate and compare alternatives while in the design phase.

- **Advanced variant configuration**
  A configuration engine leveraging SAP HANA helps handle complex, costly, and labor-intensive, multidisciplinary definition of individualized products. Variant configuration requires interaction with engineering, sales, planning, and distribution functions, and an SAP Fiori-based UI provides a simulation environment for creating BOMs with machine learning algorithms to support configuration and classification scenarios. Machine learning capabilities are being planned in SAP S/4HANA to support the automatic classification of documents.

■ **Product safety and compliance**

For global marketability, checks with changing compliance requirements and improved regulatory and functional coverage is required. The SAP Product Stewardship Network and the SAP EHS Regulatory Documentation OnDemand content service provide real-time product compliance processes with analytics embedded into core business processes. All product compliance processes are covered, including product marketability, chemical compliance, safety data sheets, and label management as well as dangerous goods management. Machine learning capabilities enable intelligent compliance management. You can connect directly with your suppliers and customers to receive and provide product sustainability information.

With these capabilities, you can orchestrate an end-to-end product design lifecycle, as shown in Figure 9.2. With SAP solutions, you can accelerate product innovation with requirements-driven product development processes while actively collaborating with all stakeholders and leveraging actionable insights across the extended enterprise.

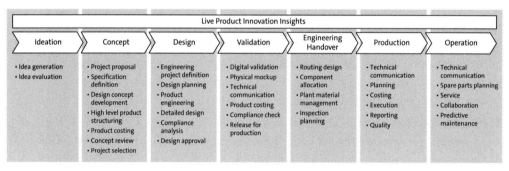

Figure 9.2 End-to-End Product Design Lifecycle

Tightly integrated processes across business functions are key to successful digital transformation. With a holistic, end-to-end approach to compliant product lifecycle management as part of your design-to-operate strategy, you can deliver personalized products in this era of Industry 4.0 while keeping your customers as the top priority.

9.1.2   Intelligent Enterprise Portfolio and Project Management

To make effective investments for long-term growth in revenue, capture market share, and increase profitability, you'll need to intelligently manage your portfolio and your projects. You'll need to make decisions about where and how much to invest and decide how to match your investments to the objectives aligned to your growth strategy. Thus, you'll need to allocate the right resources to the right projects and balance risks against performance as you continually monitor your end-to-end project portfolio management process.

This approach is applicable to any type of project, such as the following:

- **Capital projects**
  Large, long-term projects that are common in asset-intensive industries like utilities, oil and gas, chemicals, etc.

- **Innovation projects**
  Where the R&D organization is looking to build and launch new portfolio of products into the markets.

- **Information technology projects**
  Where the IT organizations are addressing large number of requests for new IT solutions or maintaining and supporting large installations of technology applications.

Project organizations in all these types of projects typically have many stakeholders and participants, and data is usually spread across multiple systems in various formats, including Excel and Word documents, data repositories, emails, etc. With no single consolidated view and lots of manual processes in each stage, as shown in Figure 9.3, managing the end-to-end process efficiently could be a daunting task.

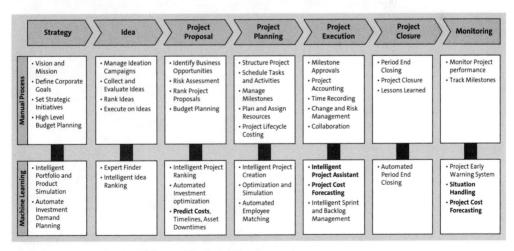

Figure 9.3 Enterprise Portfolio and Project Management

SAP Portfolio and Project Management for SAP S/4HANA provides a single source of truth for immediate and instant access to all project participants, internal as well as external to the enterprise. With the role-based user experience of SAP Fiori apps and real-time project analytics, the various business functions can perform their tasks in an integrated manner while using insights from analytics to drive the necessary actions.

In addition, as shown in Figure 9.3, intelligent technologies from SAP Leonardo bring a new generation of user experiences. Predictive analytics can help users focus on outcomes rather than look at the past. Intelligent assistants using bots can empower users to focus on what matters. SAP CoPilot extends the graphical user interface with a conversational user interface and provides a powerful tool for managing projects. Interacting in natural language with the user interface changes the user experience paradigm completely; all stakeholders gain enhanced access to project information via voice or chat using natural language processing capability of SAP CoPilot. Figure 9.4 shows an example where you can query all the projects of a project manager.

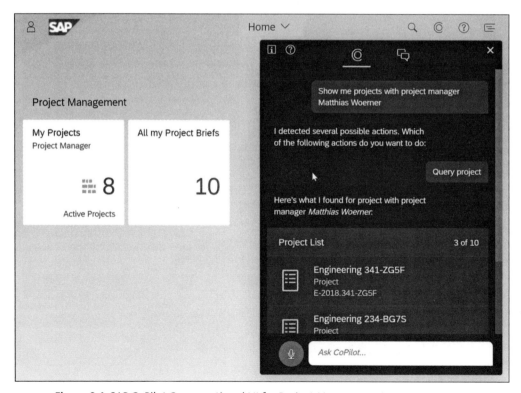

Figure 9.4 SAP CoPilot Conversational UI for Project Management

A conversational UI can more efficiently tackle project issues by identifying them and reaching resolution. For example, from Figure 9.4, you can invite various project stakeholders to conversations and collaborate with them within the business context of the project, all by using voice or chat. SAP CoPilot also provides the ability to jump to the project in the application directly while keeping the context in the conversational UI. In upcoming releases of SAP S/4HANA, additional skills will be added for querying financial data for your project.

By utilizing machine learning, you can reduce the number of mundane tasks, eliminate errors introduced by manual steps, and increase business agility in various areas like helping predict and visualize overall project costs. You can intelligently forecast project costs based on historical data using machine learning, simulate scenarios, etc., which not only reduces the effort involved in project cost planning and forecasting but also improve the accuracy. You can optimize your R&D expenses with less budget overruns and better investment decisions based on more realistic expectations. Figure 9.5 shows planned and actual costs and commitments for a project as well as the predicted cost and predicted cost range. Using the intelligence from machine learning, the estimated planned cost is lower than what is predicted, and the project will likely run overbudget.

From the screen shown in Figure 9.5, you can drill down into the prediction details, as shown in Figure 9.6. In these details, you'll see the cumulative planned and actual costs and commitments over time and overlay of the lower, upper, and average predicted costs.

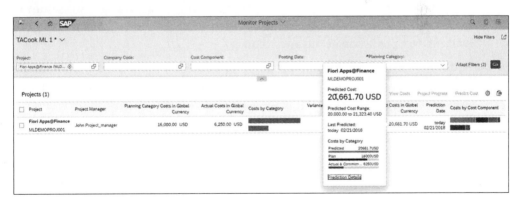

Figure 9.5 Project Cost Prediction Using Machine Learning

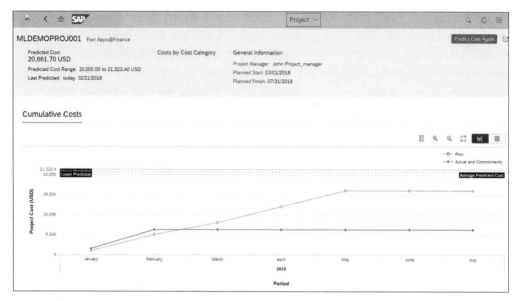

Figure 9.6 Project Cost Prediction Details

New machine learning algorithms are planned to be included in future releases to enhance cost prediction, for example, cost prediction by timeline, cost prediction by general ledger account, etc. As shown in Figure 9.6, you'll be able to simultaneously view the graph, not only the planned costs versus actuals up to the current time, but you'll also be able to compare planned project costs with projected project costs along with upper and lower predicted costs in varying time periods in the future. In addition, you'll be able to view similar projects to help with cost prediction, which will enhance prediction details and accuracy.

With these machine learning capabilities, you can gain better control and uncover better insights during your product development processes and ensure project budgets are on target while improving the allocation of resources. With lower total costs for new product development and accelerated time to market with improved resource utilization, as well as highly efficient development teams, you can deliver a broader product portfolio and create a competitive edge in the market.

9.1.3   Product and Project Insights

In today's era of digitization, to bring innovative and high-quality solutions to market faster, you'll need to embed intelligence into your design process. You'll need a

360-degree view of the live status of the entire design process. You'll also need strong collaboration capabilities both with internal and external participants as well as an active feedback loop with actionable insights to reuse product- and project-related data from downstream sources into the design process. These capabilities will help you eliminate non-value-added work during product development, provide real-time information to engineers and product developers, share and update design information with internal and external stakeholders with minimum latency, and ensure that you have accurate set of requirements to realize your planned business outcomes.

SAP S/4HANA Cloud for intelligent product design helps achieve the objective of accelerated product innovation with instant collaboration and actionable live insights across the extended enterprise along with integration to SAP on-premise applications. This solution also provides capabilities to collaborate with all parties involved.

The Live Product Cockpit, shown in Figure 9.7, provides users easy access to all the relevant information from various sources, so they can take the necessary actions quickly while leveraging usage feedback. This feature enhances transparency into development progress and provides insights into requirements, including collaboration capabilities with 3D product representations.

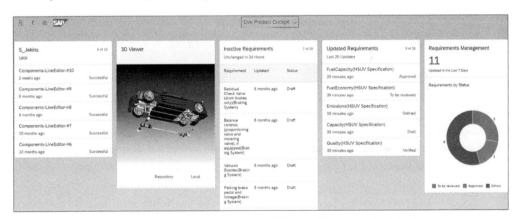

Figure 9.7 Live Product Cockpit: SAP S/4HANA Cloud for Intelligent Product Design

The SAP Fiori apps for the Live Product Cockpit, as shown in Figure 9.8, allows users to define and manage SAP Fiori cards, including editing card properties, changing their configuration, and previewing and updating card content.

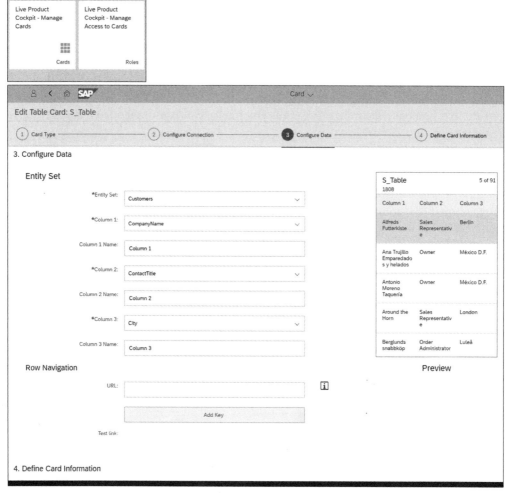

Figure 9.8 Managing SAP Fiori Cards: SAP S/4HANA Cloud for Intelligent Product Design

SAP S/4HANA Cloud for intelligent product design facilitates multifaceted collaboration across the extended enterprise. Users can create collaboration workspaces and invite participants and assign them authorizations based on roles. In these workspaces, content is securely stored and shared across devices, and you can leverage a built-in 3D viewer to collaborate on live product data, create workflows with an integrated inbox to review work items, and directly launch collaboration shared folders with integration to content management interoperability (CIMS)-supported repositories, for example, to upload documents directly from the Document Management System (DMS) to a collaboration workspace or to update document changes seamlessly.

Figure 9.9 shows your inbox. This workflow-based collaboration page shows a status on the top, along with a due date and description, and provides links to various documents. You can also post comments as you engage in ongoing collaboration activities with other stakeholders across the extended enterprise. Various team members can share documents, product data, and design models as well as post comments to initiate action and follow through with each other, while all participants can view all the latest information, including the most recent actions and comments.

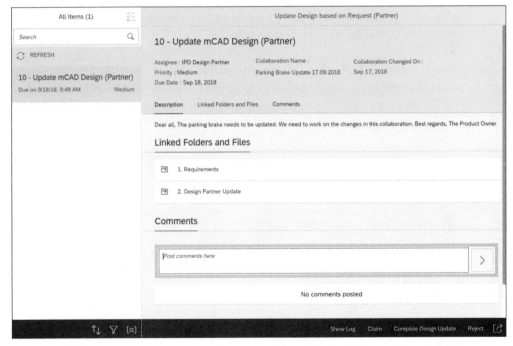

Figure 9.9 In-line Collaboration via Messages in SAP S/4HANA Cloud for Intelligent Product Design

Figure 9.10 shows work items active on a collaboration workspace, including the overall status and description of work items, with details such as due date, priority, status, etc.

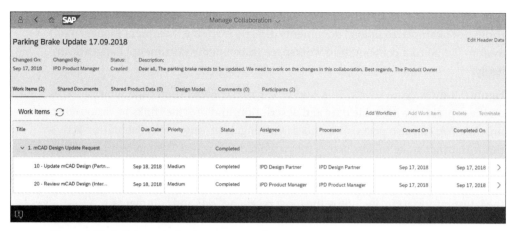

Figure 9.10 Collaboratively Managing Work Items with Various Stakeholders in SAP S/4HANA Cloud for Intelligent Product Design

Figure 9.11 shows the **Shared Documents** tab. Integration to corporate repositories makes maintaining a single version of truth in a complex, multiparty collaboration process easier. As a result, you'll achieve quicker turnarounds and be responsive to internal and external customer needs.

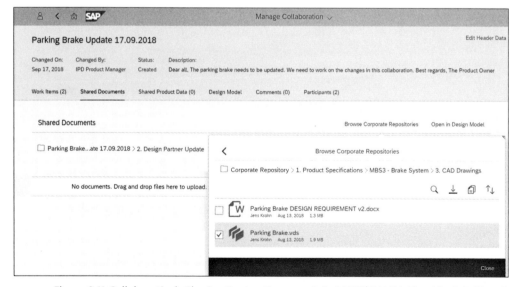

Figure 9.11 Collaboratively Sharing Design Documents in SAP S/4HANA Cloud for Intelligent Product Design

Users can also create and manage ad-hoc work items within a collaboration workspace like adding, editing, deleting, or terminating a workflow or ad-hoc work item. Further, users can define their own workflows in a collaboration workspace using the SAP Web IDE with public standard APIs or SAP Cloud Platform Workflow, and can use OData APIs to integrate with the collaboration workspace capability to enable, for example, cFolder uses cases, integration with SAP S/4HANA applications, project and portfolio management, engineering change management, etc. Using the standard Requirements Interchange Format enables you to exchange requirements between your partners.

SAP S/4HANA Cloud for intelligent product design, with its collaboration capabilities, provides a centralized requirements management solution for your engineering teams. You can ensure that all requirements are met, and you can quickly identify the impact of any changes in requirements. With products with embedded software, you can include software components in the engineering BOM, maintain representations of software versions, support conflict and redundancy checks for constraints, and ensure that all software in the BOM is compatible with other BOM components, as shown in Figure 9.12.

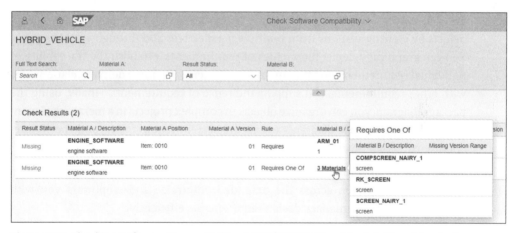

Figure 9.12 Checking Software Compatibility: SAP S/4HANA Cloud for Intelligent Product Design

SAP S/4HANA Cloud for intelligent product design also helps you develop complex products in interdisciplinary teams with model-based systems engineering by allowing architecture designers capture and manage system architecture, analysis, and design, for example, a wheel brake system, as shown in Figure 9.13.

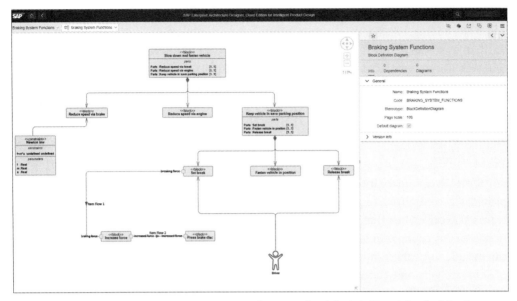

Figure 9.13 Architecture Designer: SAP S/4HANA Cloud for Intelligent Product Design

You can detect issues and omissions early in the design cycle and reduce system defects by viewing systems from multiple perspectives and through visual analysis. You can graphically depict hierarchies of requirements, establish the traceability of individual requirements to other modeling elements, examine derived relationships with other requirements, and support the reuse of requirements. Finally, using the package diagram, you can organize objects in complex projects in a hierarchical manner and create use case diagrams to capture system requirements and specify preconditions, actions, exceptions, and postconditions.

These capabilities in SAP S/4HANA Cloud for intelligent product design facilitates real-time collaboration across the extended enterprise and empowers you with actionable insights to manage design requirements efficiently.

9.2   Demand Management

As discussed in the previous section, incorporating real-time information from downstream processes and collaborating with all your internal and external stakeholders are of paramount importance for product design in today's era of digitization. These capabilities are equally relevant and must be incorporated in your demand management processes as well to understand, generate, and shape demand for your products in the market. You'll need real-time information, not only from your traditional sources like inventory on hand, orders, shipments from your own manufacturing plants and warehouses, and sales histories from your regional sales units, but also from your distribution and logistics providers as well as channels that sell your product to the end consumer, for example, the retailers, including their distribution centers and individual stores.

Furthermore, in today's hyperconnected world, you can also incorporate demand-influencing information from sources like social media, weather, economic data, etc. into your demand management process. In fact, understanding the entire downstream demand network, as shown in Figure 9.14, and getting information in real time from disparate sources, in different formats, and in different time granularities and then utilizing this information in your demand management process is critical.

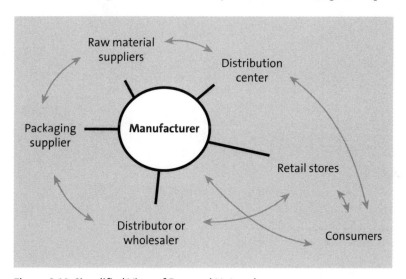

Figure 9.14 Simplified View of Demand Network

Such an approach will give you a competitive edge for overcoming issues like lost revenues due to product being out-of-stock, lost sales to a competitor due to a product not being available in the assortment at the store, etc. In fact, when you consider additional aspects like successfully launching new products, efficiently phasing out of old products, entering new markets, understanding and countering your competitor's moves, a traditional approach to demand management is not adequate. Your demand management process needs to be holistic, capturing demand from all downstream sources, beyond your company's four walls and systems. You'll need the ability to handle all time granularities of demand and seamlessly plan across them. For example, as shown in Figure 9.15, while sales and operations planning looks at demand with a strategic view in time buckets of years and months, consensus demand planning operates on monthly and weekly time buckets of demand. This traditional demand planning process needs to be extended to cover demand sensing and include the ability to capture demand signals in more granular time buckets from downstream sources to utilize them across the entire demand planning spectrum.

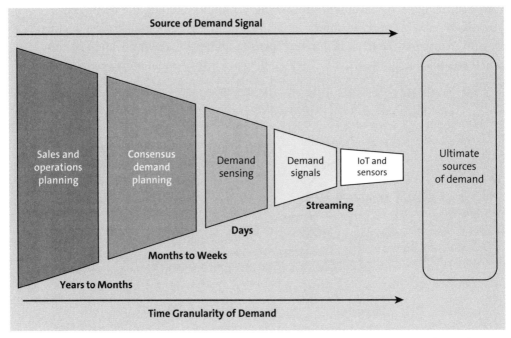

Figure 9.15 Holistic Demand Management Covering the End-to-End Demand Signal Spectrum

In the following sections, we'll cover the three main pillars of a holistic demand management process, which consist of consensus demand planning to help drive accurate long- and mid-term forecasts, demand sensing to create short-term forecasts to drive better fulfillment and inventory reduction, and establishing a single source of truth with high-fidelity demand signals from your demand network to help provide visibility and generate the insights necessary to facilitate an intelligent demand response.

9.2.1   Consensus Demand Planning

A consensus demand plan is one of the key inputs to help drive your company's plans for revenue growth, market share, and product and customer profitability. Various functional business units are involved in providing input, and hence, you'll need a streamlined approach, as shown in Figure 9.16, with the flexibility to quickly adjust to changing market and competitive trends as needed. SAP Integrated Business Planning (SAP IBP) for demand provides you with such an approach, providing capabilities that are lacking in traditional demand planning processes applications, capabilities like embedded, rich analytics for insights as well as the ability to run simulations for what-if analysis.

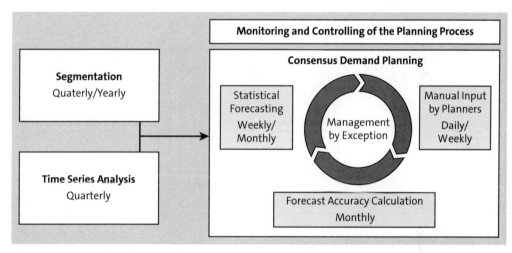

Figure 9.16 Streamlined Approach to Consensus Demand Planning with SAP IBP for Demand

In addition, you can use machine learning to incorporate added intelligence to your demand planning process. SAP IBP for demand puts you on a path towards fully automating your demand management process with an overarching framework for monitoring the progress and status at every stage while providing you with an ability to incorporate planner judgment to override and fine-tune your demand plans via the familiar and popular Microsoft Excel user interface.

The demand planning process also needs to be closely integrated with your sales and operations planning, response and supply planning, demand-driven replenishment, and inventory planning processes. Unlike traditional solutions, SAP IBP provides a common data model across all these processes to facilitate coordinated planning via a common user interface.

Two key inputs to forecast optimization in the consensus demand planning process come from demand segmentation and time-series analysis. SAP IBP for demand helps you perform these functions on a regular basis to help drive robust demand plans.

Setting up demand segmentation profiles in SAP IBP for demand helps you define ABC and XYZ segments. ABC segments your demand based on measures like profitability, revenue, and sales volume. These measures can be at any level like brand, product category, or product group and defined for a time period. Likewise, XYZ segmentation is based on demand volatility using measures such as forecast error. Demand segmentation helps you focus your efforts on the right products, as shown in Figure 9.17. You would want to focus more of your demand planning efforts on the boxes marked in red or orange for a higher return on investment.

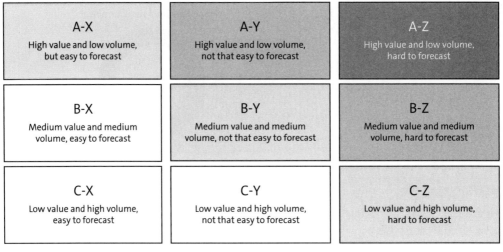

Figure 9.17 Demand Segmentation

Time-series analysis helps you achieve increased automation in forecasting, generating high-quality, robust forecasts, thereby increasing planner productivity. By constantly monitoring, measuring, and refining your approach, you can select the optimal forecasting algorithms and the necessary parameters. These choices are shaped by your understanding of the data, identifying patterns to seek out trends, correlations, and seasonality and detecting anomalies so you can optimize and automate your forecasting process. This capability is key as demand for your products is influenced by many factors, and you'll need to generate robust demand plans, which in turn drive your supply, inventory, production, distribution, and fulfillment plans.

In consensus demand planning, while the statistical forecasting is executed in weekly and monthly time buckets on a weekly basis, planners continue to manually fine-tune the forecasts daily. Forecast accuracy is typically calculated on a monthly basis, and adjustments are made accordingly. The consensus demand planning process enabled by SAP IBP for demand, as shown in Figure 9.18, is developed around a management by exception paradigm.

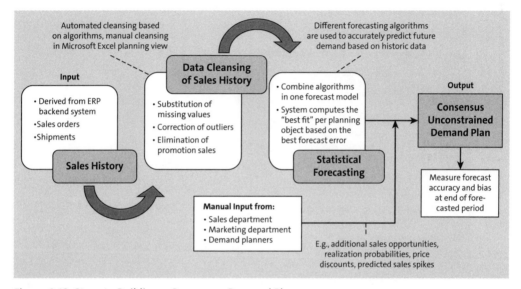

Figure 9.18 Steps to Building a Consensus Demand Plan

The first step in the process is to load the input data, like sales and shipment history and master data, into SAP IBP. To create a good forecast, data cleansing is performed using automated data cleansing algorithms to plug in missing values, correct outliers, and remove demand uplift created due to promotions or one-time events. Several outlier correction algorithms including machine learning techniques are available.

A planner can further examine and perform manual corrections in a familiar Microsoft Excel environment. Next, time series analysis, as explained earlier, identifies which forecasting algorithms fit the demand pattern of the product since the forecast accuracy of the algorithms varies by the type of demand pattern, whether it is constant, seasonal, sporadic, or trending. Figure 9.19 shows the choice of various forecasting algorithms available to the planner. Depending on the scenario, the planner can select a combination of these algorithms.

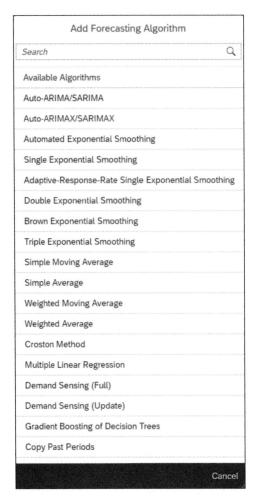

Figure 9.19 Choice of Forecasting Algorithms in SAP IBP for Demand

SAP will continue to extend the choice of forecasting algorithms in future releases. A machine learning technique called a gradient boosting decision tree is also available as part of forecast modeling. As shown in Figure 9.20, to maintain ease-of-use, only parameters that significantly impact the forecast accuracy or runtime performance are exposed to the planner.

Best fit selects the algorithm with the best accuracy based on the model fit error through training and testing, as shown in Figure 9.21.

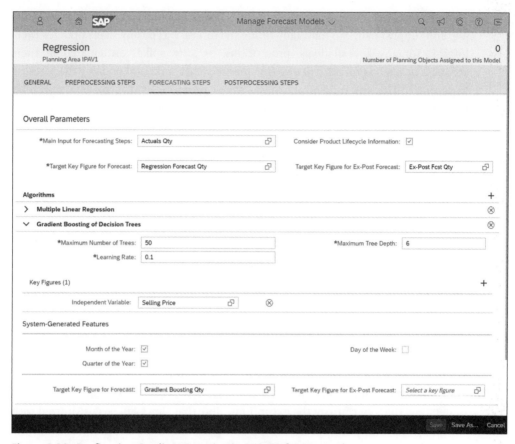

Figure 9.20 Configuring Gradient Boosting in SAP IBP for Demand

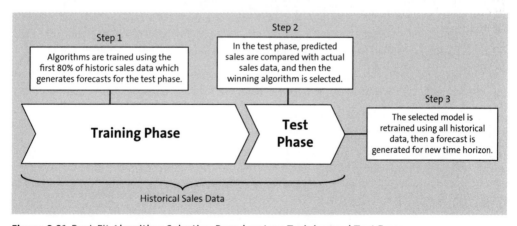

Figure 9.21 Best-Fit Algorithm Selection Based on Low Training and Test Error

Once the statistical forecasts are generated, various stakeholders from sales, marketing, and supply chain can manually refine the forecast. Typically, sales updates their forecast for any special deals, promotions, or sales spikes anticipated in their accounts or regions for a particular time period, and marketing updates the forecast to accommodate any marketing campaigns or promotions that are planned to be launched. The final consensus demand plan is ready to feed to the supply and inventory planning processes.

To monitor forecast performance and improve forecast accuracy, you can define appropriate forecast accuracy goals and measure quality and bias in the various forecasting steps involved in creating a final global consensus demand plan. This process helps instill continuous improvement towards your goal of achieving forecast optimization and automation. SAP IBP for demand provides you standard error measures like mean percentage error (MPE), mean absolute percentage error (MAPE), mean square error (SQE), root of the mean square error (RMSE), mean absolute deviation (MAD), error total (ET), mean absolution scaled error (MASE), and weighted mean absolute percentage error (WMAPE), as well as analytics and dashboards to easily visualize and analyze the results.

The management by exception paradigm is a powerful capability in SAP IBP for demand. This paradigm is based on real-time alerting based on thresholds you define such as the forecast bias being too high, or the forecast accuracy being too low, or the planned promotion uplift being larger than planned etc., and actionable analytics to understand the root cause of the exceptions. Note that alerts can be customized with machine learning in SAP IBP, as shown in Figure 9.22. Static rules work fine if the thresholds for exception conditions are known and if the data is generally consistent, but typically this is not the case in the demand management process. A lot of variability is involved in demand planning because demand patterns change. Using machine learning can help adjust your processes to changing data patterns by providing manageable and relevant alerts to the planner.

Using the case management capability in SAP IBP, you can handle exceptions and drive the resolution of issues via collaborative actions, for example, specifying what steps need to be taken, who is responsible for implementing them, and by when. In addition, what-if simulation capabilities in SAP IBP for demand help you make informed and timely decisions during the demand management process by simultaneously simulating multiple demand plans and comparing them side-by-side using key performance indicators (KPIs) while using embedded analytics with drilldown capabilities.

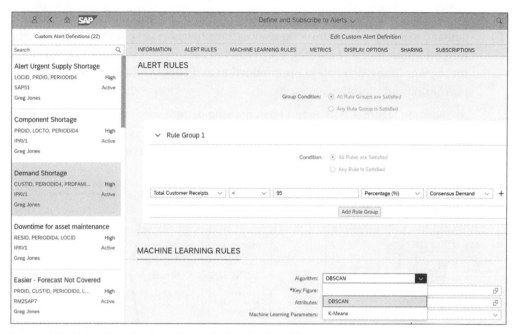

Figure 9.22 Using Machine Learning to Define Custom Alerts

9.2.2   Sensing Short-Term Demand Patterns

The demand planning capabilities described in the previous section can help you establish a streamlined process to better forecast demand across your product portfolio. The demand plan covers the mid- to long-term horizon, typically with telescoping time buckets—weekly in the near term, extending to monthly further out in the planning horizon. In the near term, you'll still have to deal with market volatility, which could be caused by any number of factors. For example, a new product or promotion you introduced in the market could have been wildly successful, and your products are flying off the retail shelves, resulting in demand outstripping the planned supply (from your consensus demand plan). Alternatively, a competitors' product could be outselling yours due to raving customer reviews about it on social media, or unexpected weather conditions could negatively impact your planned sales in a particular region, thus resulting in your unsold products sitting at distribution centers and retail stores.

In such situations, you must quickly adjust inventory deployment across your regional distribution centers or, depending on the lead times, even adjust your production and packaging operations to ensure the right amount of stock in your channels.

Demand sensing using pattern recognition-based machine learning in SAP IBP for demand can help you address these situations by generating accurate, short-term forecast for the next 4 to 8 weeks, which you can use to adjust your inventory deployment plans, transportation plans, production and packaging sequences, and other purchasing and allocation decisions.

As shown in Figure 9.23, demand sensing using pattern recognition-based machine learning augments your consensus demand planning process covered in the previous section with short-term forecasts by considering various inputs.

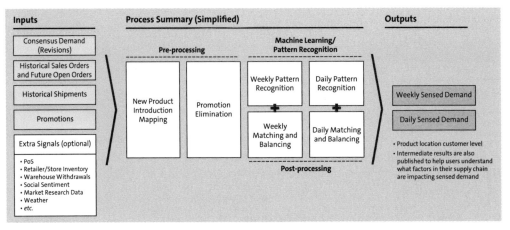

Figure 9.23 Demand Sensing Using Pattern Recognition-Based Machine Learning

The optional extra demand signals that demand sensing can consider may be internal like warehouse withdrawals as well as external from downstream sources like retailer point of sale (POS) data, social media, and weather. Figure 9.24 shows the inclusion of two downstream demand signals—point of sales (customer store sales quantity) and social sentiment. The point of sales data feeds, which first needs to be cleansed and harmonized, would come from SAP Demand Signal Management, which we'll cover in the next section.

Figure 9.25 shows the results of demand sensing in the Excel frontend of SAP IBP for demand. The left part of the screen shows the various demand signals, including point of sales data, considered in generating a sensed demand representing by the green bars. Notice that the consensus demand indicated by the black line is much lower. The zoomed view to the right shows that the machine learning algorithm in demand sensing recognizes the demand patterns whereas the consensus demand underestimates the demand (open orders and forecast).

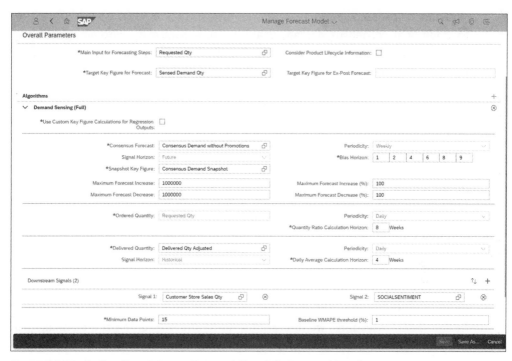

Figure 9.24 Including Downstream Demand Signals in Demand Sensing

Figure 9.25 Demand Pattern Recognition with Point of Sales Data Using Machine Learning

Note that pattern recognition-based machine learning can also be a useful addition to traditional consensus demand planning processes even without considering downstream demand signals. For example, often, many products in your portfolio may be underforecasted for several periods in a row due to the use of equal split or fixed quota mechanisms, or you may have other products and customers having cyclical ordering patterns, resulting in undersell and oversell patterns. In these situations, demand sensing can understand the underlying patterns and adjust future forecasts accordingly.

Improved short-term forecasts with demand sensing for fast-moving items help you drive timely deployment and transportation decisions, resulting in fewer stockouts and expedited shipments. The higher forecast accuracy not only leads to improved planner productivity but also leads to lower safety stocks and higher customer service levels, which ultimately leads to building a competitive edge and garnering market share.

9.2.3   Incorporating Demand Influencing Factors

In the previous sections, we discussed ways to streamline demand planning processes for the mid and long term and using demand sensing to extend these capabilities to accurately forecast short-term demand to respond to near-term demand changes and volatility. As shown in Figure 9.15, a holistic approach also needs visibility and an understanding of the entire downstream demand network. In today's world, sources of demand data are exploding, and companies have quick and easy access to numerous sources of demand, consumption, and demand influencing data. The traditional approach of using order and shipment history, along with sales and marketing plans, as major inputs into the forecasting process will not suffice in today's volatile demand environment. To be competitive and profitable, you can't wait for your customers to place orders or even anticipate those orders. You must proactively create and shape demand by leveraging all sources of downstream demand signals and demand-influencing data like weather data, competitor data, IoT data, demographic data, events, consumer sentiments, distributor data, market share data, and point of sales data from retailers.

You must incorporate all this data and create high-impact strategies to strengthen sales, revenue, and relationships with distributors and retailers by completing the following tasks:

- Quickly identify developing out-of-stock situations and taking mitigating actions by monitoring inventory levels across the demand network to reduce inventory carrying costs; benchmarking store performance to optimally allocate sales force; and increasing forecast accuracy by including granular, high-fidelity point of sales into the demand planning process

- Improve promotion effectiveness by ensuring the performance of participating stores while a promotion is running, ensuring on-shelf availability during promotion execution and leveraging insights into the promotion's performance by utilizing sell-in and sell-out data

- Monitor market trends and analyze your market share by making use of competitor data and point of sales data and identify root causes for any decline in market share to proactively take corrective actions

- Ensure the success of new product launches by tracking their daily progress, monitor and ensure stock availability in your channels, and matching consumer sentiment to sales to optimize your demand response

These tasks require a "demand source of truth," a high-performance and scalable repository of big data to handle the volume, variety, and varying time granularity of demand signals. Such a solution can serve as a foundation for your supply chain, sales, and marketing teams to generate insights via a variety of analytics, for example, descriptive (what happened last week, yesterday); predictive (given the current situation, what might happen); and prescriptive (how to avoid unforeseen or undesirable situations). A solution should provide you valuable downstream demand information that typically doesn't exist in your current enterprise business applications that can be integrated with planning processes like demand and promotions. Finally, a solution should provide you the intelligence to better engage with your business partners and end consumers.

SAP Demand Signal Management, powered by SAP HANA, provides such an enterprise-scale solution. The bulk of the downstream demand signals, typically where companies start their digital transformation journey to become more customer-centric, lie in data from distributors, retailers, and syndicated data subscriptions from companies like Nielsen Holdings and Information Resources, Inc., as shown in Figure 9.26. A simplified flow of goods and transactions is shown on the top; a typical downstream network is much more complex with many distributors, retailers, and retail store locations spread across regions and countries. Though some of the information, like demand from each node in the demand network, percolates up to the manufacturer, the information is aggregated at each node, thereby losing granularity and richness. Moreover, this information may be several days old by the time it reaches you.

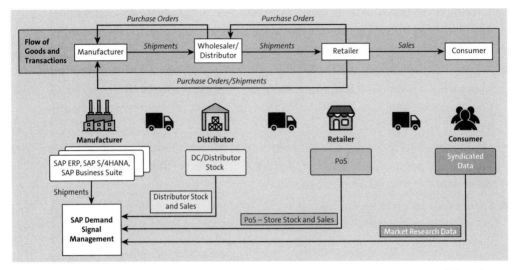

Figure 9.26 SAP Demand Signal Management Ingesting Downstream Demand Signals

Other information, like the stock situation at each node in the demand network, may not even be available to you, thereby inhibiting your ability to get a true picture of customer demand. SAP Demand Signal Management provides the capability to ingest stock and sales data directly from each source, along with competitor information, and to combine this data with internal enterprise data, like shipments and promotions, to provide a complete downstream view in near real time. Armed with timely market insights, your supply chain, sales, and marketing teams can execute the high impact strategies described earlier, drive better decisions, and rapidly respond to demand fluctuations to stay ahead of your competitors.

Figure 9.27 shows the key capabilities of SAP Demand Signal Management. Interfaces allow you to ingest data from retailer and distributor systems, for example, in CSV (comma-separated value) files as well as market share databases from syndicated data providers that you may subscribe to.

An extensible data model allows you to accommodate the various data formats used by these sources. The entire data management process, which is at the heart of SAP Demand Signal Management, uses an exception-driven paradigm with a process control and monitoring framework, allowing you to manage large volumes of data at scale. An extensible business rules framework allows you to extend the rules and algorithms to manage quality validation, harmonization, and enrichment.

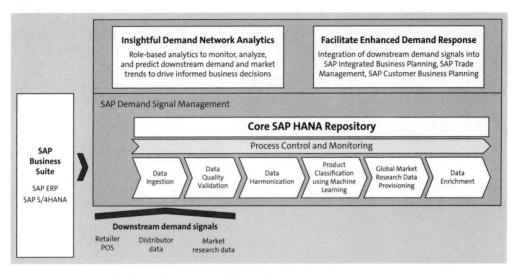

Figure 9.27 Key Capabilities of SAP Demand Signal Management

Harmonization allows you to link the source's product and location taxonomy to your own so that you can interpret and act upon the demand signals, as well as communicate with your partners using their nomenclature. This critical step enables SAP Demand Signal Management's capability to automate this process and is key to eliminate error-prone, manually intensive process. The data enrichment process includes algorithms to compute key performance indicators (KPIs) like out-of-stock, out-of-shelf, lost sales, etc. from the ingested demand signals.

Along with stock and shipping data from your distributors, SAP Demand Signal Management also allows you to ingest BOMs from distributors if any repackaging of products is being performed by them before shipping downstream to the retailers, for example, bundling individual products into buy-one-get-one-free packages. Using this information, you can accurately analyze the point of sales data of the repackaged products you receive from the retailers versus the individual products you shipped to the distributors. Further machine learning services can automate the classification of your customers' and competitors' product hierarchies and attributes to match your internal representation using predictions at each level of the hierarchy, with confidence scores, as shown in Figure 9.28.

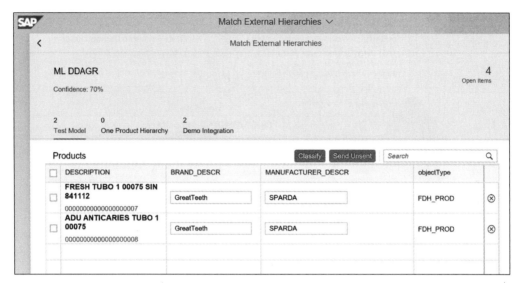

Figure 9.28 Matching External Hierarchies Using Machine Learning in SAP Demand Signal Management

Another powerful feature is global market research data provisioning. Since syndicated data providers provide market share data at different points in time during a month, for different countries, and for product categories, SAP Demand Signal Management can extrapolate and time split this information to generate a global market share status at any point in time during the month. Using this information, guided analytics for market performance management can then help your marketing team analyze market share relative to your competition, perform root cause analysis, and take corrective measures.

You can derive benefits from such a curated repository of demand signals in the following ways:

- **Insightful demand network analytics**
  Since SAP Demand Signal Management is built on SAP HANA, you can use your business intelligence tool of choice to develop role-based analytics to help monitor and analyze your downstream demand and market share in real time. Figure 9.29 shows an example of visualizing market share in SAP Analytics Cloud.

  You can sense and respond to demand signals by understanding what happened given the current stock situation and given the sales in the downstream supply chain by using purpose-built analytics as well as self-service analytics. As you build proficiency in utilizing demand signals, you can move from visualizing historical data to predicting and responding by using predictive analysis and modeling to understand what might happen or what is the best that could happen given the current downstream demand and stock situation in each of your channels.

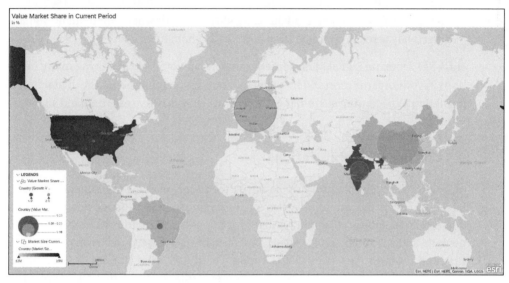

Figure 9.29 Market Share Analysis in SAP Analytics Cloud

Some examples are using cluster analysis to group stores with similar characteristics to fine-tune your demand shaping strategies; key influencer analysis to identify key influencers like number of promotions, average out-of-stock occurrences, sales revenue, etc. which may be affecting sales performance and determine what actions need to be taken; using POS data and demand influencing variables like weather, events, etc. to forecast sales quantity at the store/SKU level and predict potential stockouts to prepare your customer logistics operations in avoiding any negative impact to sales revenue.

- **Facilitate enhanced demand response**
  SAP Demand Signal Management provides integration of the cleansed and harmonized data into various SAP applications like SAP IBP, SAP Trade Management, and SAP Customer Business Planning. Traditional demand planning and promotions planning and optimization processes do not utilize downstream demand signals. By integrating these signals into these processes, you can enhance your demand shaping and sensing capabilities to better position yourself to serve the evolving customer demand patterns and optimize your promotions, forecasts, and inventory

deployment strategies to maximize revenue opportunities and capture market share. Furthermore, as you leverage downstream demand signals in SAP Trade Management to optimize promotion tactics, and in demand sensing in SAP IBP for demand to create short-term forecasts, the integration between the two solutions themselves further advances your capability to use downstream demand signals collectively across your marketing and supply chain functions.

Thus, SAP Demand Signal Management can play a pivotal role in serving many functions in your organization and in laying the foundation required for the digital transformation to becoming customer-centric by utilizing downstream demand signals.

9.3   Inventory Optimization

Managing the right inventory levels across the supply chain is fundamental to your business. Given the capital investment in inventory, you must develop the right strategies to deploy and maintain safety stock targets so that you can profitably meet demand and customer service levels. Several aspects will need to be considered. The first and foremost is where in the supply chain and what quantity of inventory should you hold to optimally meet customer demand, given that the demand is inherently variable. With the complex supply chain structure, this question is a challenging in and of itself. And in the era of digitization where you might have multiple fulfillment channels, from traditional brick-and-mortar stores to online stores, you'll need to be able to handle variability in demand across all channels, while still shaping demand through promotions and pricing tactics to build market share.

Second, given the complex supply chain structure in which you are collaborating with multiple suppliers and have manufacturing sites spread across geographical locations, you'll need to account for variability in supply as well. A third challenge arises if you must account for product design-related issues, especially when you offer smart or personalized products to your customers or manufacture make-to-order or engineer-to-order products. Lastly, while your product portfolio grows, your inventory strategy also needs to account for product obsolescence, product servicing needs, product replenishment, storage capacity constraints, and varying lead times. So, managing inventory boils down to an intricate, ongoing balancing act between the need to reduce inventory carrying costs to meet profitability goals and the need to improve service levels to meet market share and customer service targets.

In the following section, we'll discuss how you can use SAP IBP for inventory to master the various types of uncertainties that you'll encounter at every level of your supply chain, including demand variability; supply uncertainties; and variability in costs, lead times, and service levels. SAP IBP for inventory allows you to optimize safety stock globally and simultaneously across all your products and locations in the supply chain. Multistage inventory optimization capabilities allow you to improve your service levels with lower investment in buffer stock. You can establish an ongoing process to better manage your inventory, rather than viewing inventory management as a static, once or twice yearly process. You can integrate inventory optimization process with your sales and operations planning, demand planning, and supply planning processes. With exception management and what-if scenario analysis capabilities, you can empower your planners to achieve better and faster decision-making by simultaneously evaluating different plans and immediately assessing the impact on customer service levels and working capital investment. With embedded analytics to visualize your supply chain network and powerful predictive analytics to quickly gain insights into inventory drivers, you'll be able to carry less inventory to buffer against risk and handle inherent uncertainties in your supply chain.

9.3.1 Accounting for Inherent Variabilities in the Supply Chain

Holding the right amount of safety stock in order to lower your inventory carrying costs, reduce stockout issues, and meet customer service levels boils down to understanding and accounting for the variabilities inherent in your supply chain. Demand variability stems from various factors like forecast errors, forecast bias, unanticipated spikes in demand, intermittent or seasonal demand, unexpected customer response to promotions, etc. Similarly, from a supply perspective, variability is introduced due to lead times, short or delayed supplier shipments, production constraints, supplier constraints, temporary disruption of supply sources, etc. In addition, production lot sizes or warehouse batch sizes may be set independently of the consideration of having the right safety stock needed at any point in time.

As shown in Figure 9.30, given the complex nature of a supply chain structure with multiples stages (both internal and external), and with each stage dependent on one or more stages (both upstream and downstream), these variabilities are magnified, making determining the right safety stock needed to meet the desired service levels challenging. SAP IBP for inventory considers all these aspects and optimizes your inventory at each location, for each item, for each time period. This solution takes inputs from the consensus demand planning process, like forecasts generated while considering outliers, promotions, seasonality, etc., as well as forecast error and forecast bias information (as discussed in the previous section), computes the optimal safety stock at each node for each time period, and then feeds that input to the supply planning process. Inventory targets from SAP IBP for inventory are also available to SAP IBP for sales and operations.

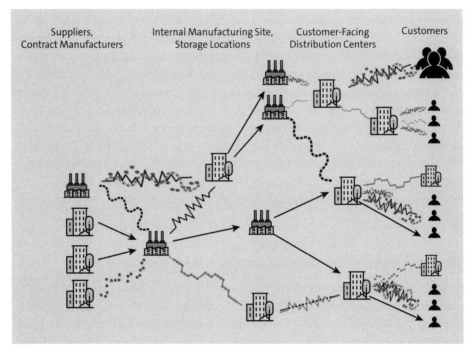

Figure 9.30 Complex Interdependencies between Various Stages of the Supply Chain

If you are bringing to market highly individualized products and moving towards a "lot size of one" using demand-driven material requirements planning (DDMRP), you can use SAP IBP for inventory. SAP IBP supports DDRMP, which leverages lean concepts and pull-based inventory buffers. SAP IBP for inventory can help you decide where to place these buffers and how much stock needs to be maintained in these buffers and dynamically adjust your inventory to meet customer demand. SAP IBP for inventory's DDMRP application supports the first two components of DDMRP as defined by the Demand Driven Institute: strategic inventory positioning and buffer level recalculation. The *recommended decoupling points (solve)* operator uses heuristics to recommend decoupling points, decoupled lead time, lead time and variability categories, and buffer levels. The *calculate DDMRP buffer levels* operator allows users to load their own decoupling point decisions and run scenarios for recommended decoupling point outputs. The DDMRP algorithm also generates decoupling point reason codes to help users understand the decoupling point recommendations. An SAP Fiori app allows users to compare decoupling point scenarios.

9.3.2 Establishing Multistage Inventory Targets

SAP IBP for inventory allows you to achieve multistage inventory optimization. Using stochastic algorithms, you can consider the entire supply chain holistically and simultaneously include all interdependencies as well as the variabilities discussed in the previous section to arrive at the safety stock required at each stage, for each item, for each time period in order meet or exceed targeted service levels. Such a holistic approach overcomes the inefficiencies common in traditional, siloed, single-stage inventory planning processes.

As shown in Figure 9.31, if planners at each stage work independently of each other, overbuffering may occur at each stage, resulting in excessive inventory stock. The multistage optimization approach used by SAP IBP for inventory eliminates such overbuffering because safety stock levels at each stage are calculated while considering the potential impact on the adjacent stages. The result determines the most efficient inventory targets needed at each stage of the supply chain to minimize working capital and inventory carrying costs while reducing risks due to supply chain uncertainties as you strive to meet your customer service targets.

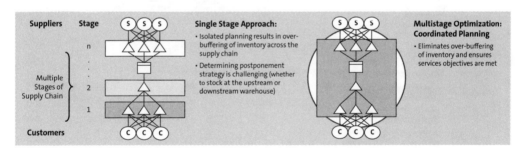

Figure 9.31 Single-Stage versus Multistage Inventory Optimization

9.3.3 Meeting Customer Service Levels

SAP IBP for inventory provides your managers and planners the visibility they'll need to evaluate the tradeoffs between investing in working capital to hold inventory and meeting customer service level objectives. Powerful embedded analytics provide the ability to easily analyze complex inventory-related data from across multiple stages of your supply chain.

Figure 9.32 shows one such example. In SAP IBP for inventory, a planner can view target working capital by product family, target cycle stock, and pipeline stock and recommended safety stock at the finished goods level, with visibility into safety stock drivers like variability in demand, supply, and service levels across product families. Users can review heat maps of forecast errors across product family and location as well as visualize all the tiers of the supply chain from an inventory optimization perspective. Such powerful embedded analytics capabilities are available throughout SAP IBP. The integrated nature of SAP IBP makes decision-making seamless across all these functions. With the ability to easily personalize these dashboards, your planners and managers alike can easily adapt them to their individual needs and focus areas. They can set up alerts for any deviations that occur from the set thresholds. They can adapt an exception-driven planning paradigm centered around root cause analysis to build an agile supply chain to deliver high customer service levels at the lowest cost.

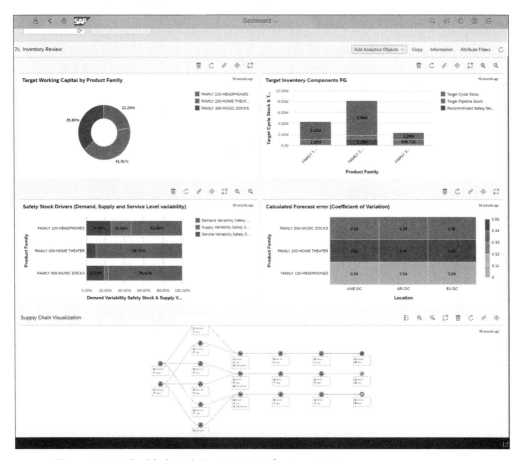

Figure 9.32 Embedded Analytics in SAP IBP for Inventory

SAP IBP also allows you to create and compare what-if scenarios, another powerful capability. Figure 9.33 shows an example of a what-if scenario analysis in SAP IBP for inventory. Planners can work in a familiar Microsoft Excel environment and compare various scenarios side-by-side. In this example, a baseline plan is compared with two other plans, one with a higher service level and one with a lower service level, along with a plan with a lower forecast error. The planner can easily view various key figures at various stages of the supply chain, for example, recommended safety stock for each scenario with the corresponding safety stock value, days of supply, and working capital.

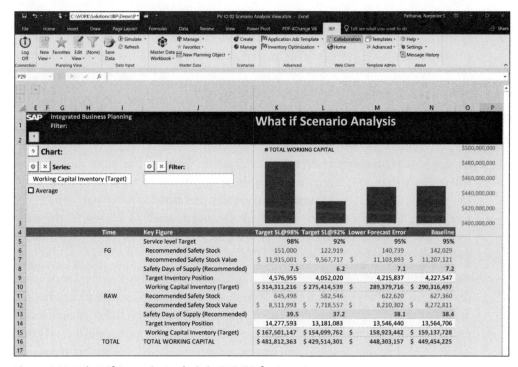

Figure 9.33 What-if Scenario Analysis in SAP IBP for Inventory

Based on this analysis, a planner can then make well-informed decisions about which plan to implement knowing the tradeoffs involved. As a result, your company can always have the right inventory in the right amount at the right location to meet customer demand and not have to engage in last-minute expedited shipments, thereby lowering costs and increasing profitability.

9.4   Connected Products

In previous sections, we covered how SAP Leonardo's intelligent technologies and business applications can facilitate your digital transformation when it comes product design, managing demand for your products, and optimizing inventory to meet customer demand. These important capabilities will be required to operate in a hypercompetitive market where business processes span an extended ecosystem of partners and where maintaining customer service is your top priority. In this section, we'll cover how SAP Leonardo's intelligent technologies can help you achieve your vision in delivering highly individualized product and product experience to your customers by leveraging IoT, machine learning, and analytics to track product performance and usage through the entire product lifecycle. These capabilities will help you increase your customer focus as well as open new go-to-market strategies and "as-a-service" business models by intelligently leveraging the large amounts of data generated at the edges of your extended enterprise.

9.4.1   Network of Digital Twins

As you strive to adopt the digital transformation required for your supply chain where you design and manufacture products and assets to meet your customers' unique needs, meet specific industry regulations, and strive to provide customer specific service level agreements, you'll need to equip yourself to address all the challenges associated in the design-to-operate process. SAP's network of digital twins addresses these needs.

As shown in Figure 9.34, a *digital twin* is a virtual representation of a physical product or asset that is always synchronized with business data, product information data, asset master data and sensor data. Using intelligent technologies like machine learning, predictive analytics, IoT, and edge computing, the digital twin provides real-time or near real-time information, enabling an entire ecosystem of manufacturers, suppliers, asset operators and service providers to proactively monitor, improve, and optimize customer service. The network of digital twins enables collaborative, end-to-end digital transformation at every stage—as-designed, as-configured, as-procured, as-built, as-delivered, as-installed, as-operated. With an integrated business context and a native collaboration environment across all internal and external stakeholders, you can use SAP's network of digital twins to not only enhance your product and service offerings but also enable new business models.

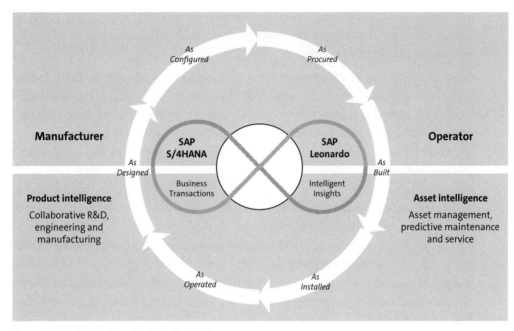

Figure 9.34 SAP Network of Digital Twins

The digital representation is enabled by SAP solutions, including SAP Predictive Engineering Insights, SAP Predictive Maintenance and Service, and SAP 3D Visual Enterprise. In conjunction, SAP solutions including SAP S/4HANA, SAP Engineering Control Center, SAP C/4HANA, SAP Manufacturing Integration and Intelligence, and SAP Manufacturing Execution support end-to-end business processes from design, production, maintenance, and service. A scalable business network for collaboration is supported by solutions such as SAP Ariba, SAP Asset Intelligence Network, and SAP Leonardo IoT for SAP Distributed Manufacturing. In Chapter 10, we'll go into more detail about specific solutions in manufacturing and asset management leveraging networks of digital twins.

9.4.2 Connecting IoT Sensors to the Enterprise

In today's digital economy, an increasing number of devices can be connected using IoT sensors. A variety of types of sensors are available with varying functionalities and prices to suit your needs like sensors to monitor temperature, vibrations, humidity, fill levels, etc. You can leverage IoT to maximize the value of your customer-facing and revenue-generating business assets used to deliver goods and services. You can do so across industries, both in a business-to-business (B2B) context as well as in a business-to-consumer (B2C) context.

In B2B scenarios, products are stored in containers, tanks, and silos in various industries like consumer products, wholesale distribution, agriculture, mill products, chemicals, and oil and gas. These business assets are typically spread across production sites and across storage locations in the supply network, as well as close to the customers' point of consumption. In B2C scenarios, product refrigeration units like coolers and product dispensers like vending machines and coffee makers might be located in large numbers across locations like retail stores, public transport stations, sports venues, etc. In all these scenarios, without the use of IoT, monitoring the correct storage conditions of the product to ensure product quality can be challenging as can monitoring the location of the business asset itself to ensure its proper utilization. It can also be challenging to monitor the product consumption rate to optimally replenish inventory and prevent stockouts, the consumption pattern and customer interactions to fine-tune product offerings, etc. SAP Leonardo IoT, along with machine learning and analytics, addresses these needs.

SAP Leonardo IoT uses sensor data to provide real-time insights on product inventory, product state, and storage parameters so you can ensure product quality and trigger timely replenishment. SAP Leonardo IoT provides contextual alerts to identify and address operational deviations like temperature or inventory levels using predetermined thresholds with configurable business rules. With geofencing, you can monitor and ensure that devices are located at their intended location. SAP Leonardo IoT, with integration of the sensor data with SAP business applications, adds business context, and triggers business actions like generating a service ticket or a replenishment order. We'll discuss these capabilities further in the next section.

As shown in Figure 9.35, SAP Leonardo IoT provides end-to-end integration from the sensors at the edge of the extended enterprise to the enterprise system, with flexible options to integrate the sensors attached to your IoT-enabled business assets. The integration mechanism can be chosen based on your business situation. You can stream sensor data to SAP Leonardo IoT directly with SAP Leonardo IoT Edge, or via SAP Edge Services using a gateway, which would be used in cases where multiple devices are located at a single location like a warehouse, distribution center, or production facility or via a third-party device cloud provider of your choosing.

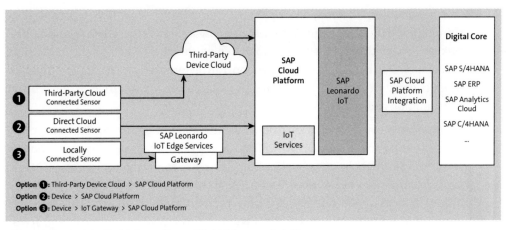

9

Figure 9.35 End-to-End Integration with SAP Leonardo IoT

9.4.3   Operationalizing Sensor Data and Establishing New Business Models

With an increasing number of devices being connected, one of the biggest challenges is managing all the IoT data being generated and deriving business value from that data. Not only can this data provide real-time visibility but can also uncover valuable insights to help drive better business decisions by increasing transparency and reducing uncertainty across the value chain. These insights can also help your company be responsive to your customers' needs and help you reimagine new business models.

With the power of analytics, you can provide innovative and intuitive user experiences with embedded analytics through sophisticated visualization and analytic tools to enhance user interactions as they sift through the vast amounts of data generated by IoT devices. Dashboards can provide a bird's-eye view of all the devices a user is responsible for and visualize key information on device status, including alerts and notifications. With the map overview, users can select and apply different overlays such as weather, temperature, revenue generated, etc. for additional context and further insights. Users can drill down for deeper root cause analysis and get a 360-degree view of all operational parameters at a single device level. Users can also analyze trends and trigger business actions when any anomalies are detected.

The entire user experience can be personalized to suit the user's individual role. Further, by using the power of machine learning, users can derive further insights from the sensor data, for example, using anomaly detection to detect problems in product storage conditions that may affect product expiration dates. Outliers in product consumption and utilization can be identified to trigger contextual alerts as well as forecast stock depletion rates to take timely replenishment actions to ensure product availability. Further, influencer detection can determine which factors influence product quality the most, like temperature and humidity, to drive better product consumption and usage.

Finally, with prebuilt integration to SAP business applications like SAP S/4HANA, SAP ERP, SAP Analytics Cloud, and SAP C/4HANA, you can convert insights into action by integrating IoT data to drive business processes like campaign optimization, inventory replenishment, etc. As a result, you'll be able to respond to changing market conditions and customers' needs in real time. Figure 9.36 shows an example where you can use SAP Leonardo IoT to monitor inventory levels in silos that are spread across multiple locations. To ensure adequate inventory levels are maintained as your customer draws product from these silos, SAP Leonardo IoT can be used, not only to monitor the fill levels at each silo, but also to integrate sensor information into an order-to-cash business process to trigger replenishment orders, which in turn may trigger procurement orders to your suppliers. This end-to-end integration eliminates inefficient manual processes for monitoring the silos, thus preventing out-of-stock or overstock situations and automating the fulfillment process while reducing costs. Thus, using IoT can not only increase your business agility but also allows you to build new as-a-service business models.

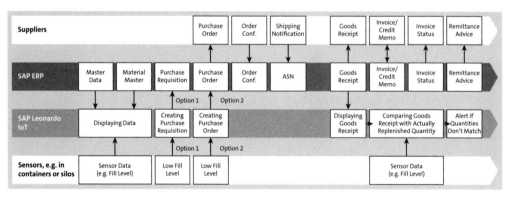

Figure 9.36 Inventory Monitoring and Automated Replenishment with SAP Leonardo IoT

Through real-time monitoring of usage and consumption, you can move from offering your customers a capital expenditure (CapEx)-based business model to an operational expenditure (OpEx)-based, pay-for-outcome, model. For example, instead of

selling packaging machines to your customers who may ship products to their customers, you can provide IoT-based packaging machines that can remotely monitor
the consumption of packaging material and thus the usage of the packaging machine
and charge by the number of boxes shipped. With IoT sensor data, you can proactively monitor the status and utilization of the machine to ensure it is in optimal
working condition and thus eliminate the cost and lead time to repair machines
while also avoiding downtime. Such innovative business models can not only help
you drive more business and set yourself apart from the competition but also offer
an attractive financial model for your customer with a pay-as-you-go service.

9.5 Summary

Building an intelligent enterprise requires a laser focus on your customer, which
means that products should be designed with customer needs in mind, and customer
demand should be planned accurately, considering all sales channels. Inventory will
need to be positioned optimally across all tiers along the supply chain, and demand
will need to be sensed and serviced in an agile and proactive fashion. For these tasks,
you'll need efficient collaboration both within and across company boundaries and
the agility to respond to changing business conditions in a cost-effective manner to
drive profitability and brand loyalty.

Chapter 10

Manufacturing and Assets

SAP Leonardo can be used to automate processes, improve asset uptime and safety, reduce maintenance costs, and make manufacturing more efficient overall. In this chapter, you'll learn how to use SAP Leonardo technologies to optimize manufacturing processes and assets.

One of the most exciting areas of growth as the result of new technologies in supply chain management, with great impacts on how we manufacture our products and use our assets. With Industry 4.0, manufacturing is now more efficient and automated, sometimes even called "smart manufacturing."

In this chapter, we'll get into detail about smart manufacturing and the usage of assets in an intelligently automated enterprise supported by SAP Leonardo. We'll discuss how digital manufacturing operations are achieving the goals of factory automation. Asset management has developed a new approach to management through predictive maintenance, which we've detailed in this chapter. In the last section of this chapter, we'll explore the concepts behind and the usage of digital twins in manufacturing.

10.1 Smart Manufacturing Optimization

We're in the middle of the Fourth Industrial Revolution, also referred to as Industry 4.0, which relies on smart connectivity and the integration of advanced production and operational techniques with smart digital technologies to create an intelligent digital enterprise. A digital enterprise represents an interconnected and autonomous system, which receives real-time data from the physical world, analyzes the data, and uses the data to make intelligent decisions and take actions. Industry 4.0 can help your organization overcome common challenges and opens the door to new opportunities.

Fully connected processes and systems present huge opportunities for businesses, not just with monitoring processes in a linear fashion (recent standard practice) and reacting to events. Now, companies can learn along the way and feed these insights back into the process, learning from what they see and adjusting accordingly in near real time or in real time. The real-time information presented to business operators leads to smarter decisions; better-designed products, services, and systems; more efficient use of resources; and a greater ability to predict future needs.

Manufacturers require production agility and visibility across the entire supply chain to optimize and drive value throughout their operations. Manufacturers need to collect, analyze, and extract intelligence from the deluge of data captured from sensors, equipment, and machines. Based on the volume, velocity, and criticality of the data collected, you may manage processes at the edge of the network or engage in processes centrally in the cloud.

Factory automation refers to the equipping of cutting-edge manufacturing facilities with the building blocks of a smart manufacturing system. In the following sections, we'll go into detail about factory automation and its building blocks.

10.1.1   Factory Automation

Automation in manufacturing is not a new concept. We've seen automation on the shop floor where assembly operations are automated for production efficiency. However, *smart manufacturing optimization* goes beyond just automation, representing a leap forward from the traditional automation to fully connected and flexible systems. Traditional factory automation restricts itself within four walls of the factory. Smart automation starts with automation within the factory and expands to providing visibility and automation across and beyond the supply chain. For example, an oil production company could implement smart manufacturing optimization to enable its production planners to have visibility into demand across various distribution centers. If production output fails to meet planned quantities, the planner has the tools available to determine whether to produce less or to extend the production run to meet changing demand by considering costs, profitability, order fill rates, and other business and process key performance indicators (KPIs).

Smart manufacturing optimization provides various benefits at the organizational level as summarized in Table 10.1. These benefits can be achieved at the business operation level by gaining operational efficiency and reducing waste or increasing growth in business.

Organizational Impact	Key Objective	Organizational Transformations
Business operations	Productivity improvement	■ Maximize asset utilization ■ Minimize downtime ■ Drive labor efficiency
	Risk control	■ Component availability ■ Mitigate geographical and operational risks
Revenue growth	New revenue opportunity	■ New products and service offerings ■ Customer and geographic extension
	Growth of revenue	■ Cross-selling opportunities ■ Aftermarket opportunities

Table 10.1 Benefits and Value Drivers of Smart Manufacturing Optimization

Let's look at each key objective in more detail next:

- **Productivity improvement**
  Your organization can achieve improvements in productivity by maximizing asset utilization and minimizing downtime. Sensors placed on the critical units of an assembly line can gather data in real time and predict the likelihood of failure. As a result, this asset could be maintained proactively, before it actually breaks down. Predicting the failure of an asset can lead to huge savings for a company. The tools available for detailed scheduling and for the constant monitoring of the production progress provide stability in production and drives both direct and indirect labor efficiencies.

- **Risk reduction**
  A shop floor manager's primary concern is safety. Industry 4.0 can help to reduce safety-related accidents by implementing operation and digital technologies to avoid accidents. In addition, you can ensure the availability of raw material on time, reduce the risk of production stoppages, and manage recalls and warranties effectively. From the business and revenue growth perspective, companies can see incremental revenue benefits and new revenue prospects.

- **Incremental revenue opportunity**
  Organizations can strengthen customer relationships and deepen their understanding of customer insights. For example, a shoe and apparel manufacturing company could gather real-time customer behavior at various outlets and online

sales, which could help sense demand and determine the factors that drive the interest towards specific products. Promotions can be planned based on real-time customer interest at the store, which can then be shared with manufacturing to ensure adequate production and ensure that the right product mix will be available to meet customer demand.

The aftermarket revenue stream for manufacturing companies can be a long-term source of income, and this revenue can be increased by constantly monitoring the health and usage of the machines at customer sites and collaborating with them to maintain the performance of the equipment.

- **New revenue opportunity**
Organizations can benefit from new business models emerging out of deploying smart technologies. For example, a tool manufacturing company traditionally focuses on the assembly of equipment at the customer site and provides customer support as needed. Smart technology advancements in the equipment connectivity space have made following a product-as-a-service model possible. Now, the organization can rent machine tools instead of selling them and thus create a new revenue stream based on usage.

10.1.2   Building Blocks of a Smart Factory

The concept of connectivity and how connectivity gets converted into actionable insights can be explained by the physical–digital–physical data (PDP) transfer loop shown in Figure 10.1. PDP forms the building blocks of a smart factory or smart enterprise. The first step in this loop is capturing sensor data from physical assets and creating digital twins from this data ❶. A digital twin is a digital parallel to a physical asset.

The sensor data sent from the physical asset can be visualized, and alerts can be generated based on actual performance ❷. Data feeds from multiple machines and assets can be consolidated, which helps us gain insights from the collective performance data.

After the data consolidation, the data is sent to machine learning or predictive algorithms where actions to take in real world are generated ❸. Based on this feedback, physical assets can be updated, thus stabilizing production.

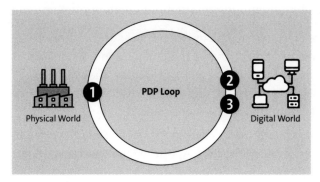

Figure 10.1 Physical–Digital–Physical Loop

10.2   Digital Manufacturing and Operations

Now that you have some background on Industry 4.0 and smart manufacturing optimization, let's further explore the concept of the smart factory, which basically digitalizes manufacturing operations. A smart factory uses a constant stream of real-time data from connected production and operating systems to learn and to adapt to changes in the production environment as well as in customer demand. A smart factory can integrate data from system-wide physical, operational, and human assets and, with the digitalization of assets, can drive improvements in production, maintenance, inventory tracking, and other activities across the manufacturing network.

A smart factory is a flexible system that can self-optimize performance across a broader network by self-adapting to changing environmental conditions in real time. The true potential of the smart factory is realized in its ability to evolve and grow along with the changing needs of an organization like changing customer demand, changes in the market, expansion into new markets and regions, and using more responsive approaches to manufacturing operations. Powerful computing and performance capabilities along with smart connectivity technology has made previously unachievable goals now possible.

In the following sections, we'll first provide a general introduction to the characteristics of a smart factory. Then, we'll introduce you to the Smart Shop Floor tool (built by Deloitte and leveraging SAP Leonardo) and its architecture. Next, we'll discuss the five main functions that this tool provides in greater detail: the shop floor control tower view, material availability, the floorplan view, predictive maintenance, and dynamic routing.

10.2.1   Characteristics of a Smart Factory

The implementation of smart factory technology doesn't need to be identical for every company. Your company must meet unique requirements in asset efficiency, labor efficiency, or raw material availability. For one organization, the availability of components may be a crucial factor while for another the availability of a skilled labor force to perform complex setup changes is more critical.

Regardless of the industry or company, some characteristics of a smart factory can apply to all companies, like the connected system, optimized process, transparency in operations, and proactive prediction. Let's look at each of these characteristics next:

- **Connectivity**
  An important aspect of a smart shop floor, connectivity forms the fundamental basis of data in a smart factory. Smart factories require that underlying processes, equipment, and material inventory to be connected so that data can be streamed in real time to make timely decisions. Integration of data from operations and business systems, as well as from suppliers and customers, enables a holistic view of upstream and downstream supply chain processes, driving greater overall supply network efficiency. Connectivity is an important characteristic that connects two different functions like production and product development.

- **Optimized processes**
  A smart factory strives to optimize the production processes, both inbound and outbound. Network and production optimization helps create a reliable, predictable production capacity utilization by improving asset uptime and efficiency. An optimized shop floor is characterized by highly automated production and material handling with minimal human interaction.

- **Transparency in production**
  Real-time metrics and tools are available to support quick and consistent decision-making. Transparency and visibility to customer demand enable planners to make changes to the production schedule to meet demand on time, which improves customer satisfaction. Transparency into raw material availability data is also important for making decisions about production runs and customer commitment.

- **Proactive prediction**
  A smart shop floor reads real-time equipment data and predicts the likelihood of failures in the future, which helps shop floor managers schedule maintenance in

advance and avoid machine breakdowns. Safety monitoring and real-time visibility into supplier quality issues are important aspects that drive efficiency.

- **Agility**
  Detailed scheduling of production orders while taking changeovers into consideration ensures the production schedule suffers minimum downtime. Real-time production progress and visibility into product demand help the factory be agile and react optimally to changes in demand and schedules.

SAP Leonardo has provided a suite of services that can help you develop enterprise asset management capabilities and achieve the smart shop floor. The concept behind the smart shop floor primarily focuses on production efficiency by leveraging connectivity and computing efficiency. In the next section, we'll get into the details of a shop floor tool that leverages SAP Leonardo.

10.2.2   Smart Shop Floor Overview

The Smart Shop Floor tool leverages the technical capabilities of SAP Leonardo and helps manufacturing organizations predict machine failures or resource shortages so that proactive action can be taken to avoid disruptions in manufacturing.

This tool helps production managers solve common challenges and ensures that resources are available on-time so that the production output is not negatively impacted. SAP Leonardo provides an opportunity to customize the dashboard to meet your business's specific needs.

Shop floor managers face multiple business challenges, such as the following:

- Lack of operational visibility in real time can prevent production managers from taking action before production issues arise. Real-time visibility into the production progress and into the availability of resources helps planners take proactive steps to prevent failures.

- Because of the high cost of maintenance when equipment fails unexpectedly, production often comes to a halt, and service personnel must be summoned to address equipment failure, leading to higher costs than predictive maintenance.

- Lack of real-time access to the health status of equipment makes repair versus buy decisions difficult.

- Poor planning and forecasting results from the lack of a detailed planning tool that looks into the material availability, stock-in-transit delays, and other resource availability issues that can lead to production delays and impact productivity.

- Low data quality adds to costs due to manual data fixes and results in poor visibility for making timely decisions.

- Production losses are incurred due to a lack of real-time order balancing capability when an unexpected downtime of resource occurs.

- Labor availability plays a critical role in manufacturing processes that rely on manual packaging processes. Real-time visibility into labor helps planners schedule the production orders in advance.

The Smart Shop Floor tool is a mobile-friendly application and can be launched on various devices including desktop, tablet, and phone. This flexibility can be quite beneficial to a production manager, who might access the app from his office desktop, and a production supervisor, who is constantly on the move. Both users can get the same real-time access to shop floor information. The functional capabilities of the Smart Shop Floor tool are as follows:

- **Internet of things (IoT) connectivity sensors**
  IoT sensors can be placed in strategic locations on the shop floor to collect data points on asset performance and production progress. IoT sensors are the nervous system of the smart shop floor. The sensor data collected forms the base for making business decisions.

- **Beacon-based guided shop floor navigation**
  Beacon-based shop floor navigation helps shop floor managers leverage the power of mobility. These users can use handheld tablet devices to view relevant asset information as they physically move closer to an asset. This capability helps plant managers detect issues related to the health status and performance of assets as they move around the shop floor.

- **Production asset health monitoring and predictive maintenance**
  The smart shop floor leverages the power of SAP Predictive Maintenance and Service and alerts users when anomalies are detected. Built on SAP Cloud Platform, real-time sensor IoT sensor data is used for predictive analysis.

- **Production planning and tracking**
  Graphical scheduling board-based production planning and detailed scheduling helps sequence and plan production orders.

- **Raw material availability checking and purchase order tracking**
  On-time availability of required components ensures uninterrupted production and the availability of finished goods to meet the demand on-time. Though

production planning assumes the availability of components and plans production sequences accordingly, during execution, the unavailability of components can impact asset utilization and production. A smart shop floor features real-time visibility into the inventory at the manufacturing site from the ERP system and can also receive real-time feeds from vendors about orders in transit. In the food processing industry, for example, we could install IoT sensors in our trucks so that we can receive real-time status updates about the arrival of products and updates about quality inspections and about readiness for consumption.

- **Replanning and dynamically rerouting production orders**
  A smart shop floor is not only an analytics tool that reports on what went well or poorly in the past; it also helps you take action on what needs to be done in situations where issues arise. In this area, machine learning can add value by learning the desired action taken during a particular situation and repeating this process when the situation occurs in the future. For example, if one of our drilling machines breaks down, the machine learning algorithm can look for a similar machine that can perform the same operation and reroute the process to that machine, which ensures uninterrupted production so that customers are served as promised.

- **Dynamic and real-time reporting**
  Real-time analytics and reporting capabilities help you gather information on the performance of assets and production processes and provide the visibility for senior management into overall equipment effectiveness.

The Smart Shop Floor tool utilizes the power of IoT connectivity to monitor various parameters for asset and material availability. A representation of a smart shop floor technical architecture is shown in Figure 10.2. Physical sensors are connected to various pieces of equipment and linked to SAP Cloud Platform. These sensors receive data from various sources to provide real-time visibility into asset availability, raw material availability in the shop floor warehouse, in-transit raw material availability, and updates on customer order changes. The sensors deployed in this solution are beacon proximity sensors, temperature and vibration measurement sensors, and GPS position sensors.

The sensor data that is captured is streamed in real time into SAP Cloud Platform where we can build analytics applications to automate action and trigger real-time alerts.

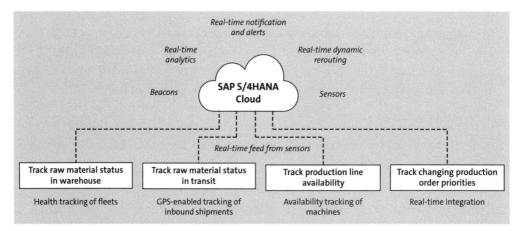

Figure 10.2 Smart Shop Floor Technical Architecture

10.2.3   Shop Floor Control Tower

The **Shopfloor Dashboard**, shown in Figure 10.3, can be launched from the shop floor control tower, and production managers can choose which plant for which information should be visualized. The dashboard consists of visuals showing various KPIs and a notification window that displays work orders in progress as well as any critical notifications that require action.

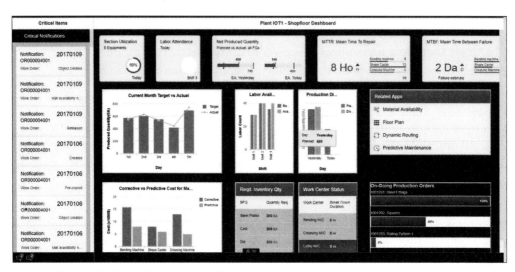

Figure 10.3 Control Tower Example

The equipment notifications are generated from SAP Predictive Maintenance and Service. Critical notifications that require immediate actions are displayed on the dashboard. As shown in Figure 10.4, for example, **Lathe machine-1** is the most critical equipment with the highest probability of failure. Production supervisors can act on the notification by proactively scheduling maintenance service.

Figure 10.4 Smart Shop Floor Notification Example

Various charts can be configured in the shop floor control tower. All these analytics graphs can be configured to meet specific business needs of a shop floor at a consumer packaged goods (CPG) manufacturer. With no restrictions on analytics capabilities, these visualizations can be configured to meet your specific business needs.

The graphs shown earlier in Figure 10.3 can also be configured to enable drilldown capabilities. The following charts are currently configured in our example control tower:

- **Section utilization**
  This chart shows the percentage of manufacturing equipment currently operational. Users can drill down into a detailed view of actual machines that are down from this graph.

- **Labor attendance**
  This chart provides visibility into a number of employees checked in for a shift. This chart helps you plan work according to the availability of labor. In addition, a graph shows the planned versus actual labor requirement and graph immediately highlights any labor shortage and prompts the user to take action.

- **Asset availability KPIs**
  KPIs related to asset availability are displayed such as mean time to repair (MTTR), mean time between failures (MTBF), and the difference between corrective versus preventive cost for maintenance. All these KPIs are calculated from various pieces of equipment and aggregated based on the aggregation logic.

- **Gantt chart**
  On production progress, the Gantt charts show the planned versus actual production quantity and status of ongoing production orders.

Finally, material availability is shown for components that are required for today's and tomorrow's planned production. The dashboard view covers the production process holistically by showing KPIs related to asset availability, labor, and material availability.

10.2.4   Material Availability

The **Material Availability** section of the Smart Shop Floor tool shows details at a plant level like in-house stock of semi-finished goods, in-transit stock, and delayed stock due to transportation issues, as shown in Figure 10.5. Users can further drill down into details about materials that are delayed and the production orders that are impacted as a result.

Semi-finished goods that are produced in-house and raw materials procured externally are displayed in a graph. The sidebar shows a list of purchase orders currently in transit. Details about these orders can be displayed by clicking on a specific order.

A KPI chart on means of transport shows the usage ratio of various means of transport (road, rail, ocean, and air). Materials that are shipped out by air can be planned to use other cheaper modes of transportation in the future.

Figure 10.5 Material Availability Example

10.2.5   Floorplan View

The floorplan function can be utilized by beacon proximity sensors where the details of an assembly unit or piece of equipment are displayed as soon a user comes in close proximity to the physical asset on the shop floor. Production supervisors can also investigate the details remotely by manually selecting the assembly line.

As shown in Figure 10.6, the floorplan function is the analytical view of the backend of the SAP Predictive Maintenance and Service system. The health status that is continuously monitored in SAP Predictive Maintenance and Service can be pulled over into the floorplan function. Users can investigate work orders that are planned and in-progress. The utilization pie chart shows resource utilization along the production line for a defined period of time.

The health status of your equipment is gathered in real time from the sensors attached to the equipment. In this case, the equipment's health is assessed by measuring temperature and vibration.

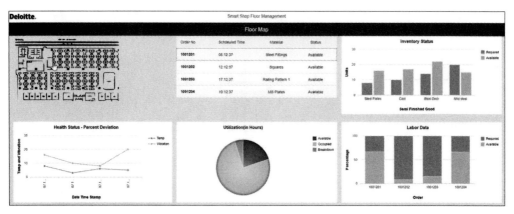

Figure 10.6 Shop Floor View Example

The real-time temperature and vibration values of multiple machines belonging to the same model can be viewed together, as shown in Figure 10.7. Various algorithms can be deployed to detect anomalies, when recorded values cross a threshold for "normal" behavior.

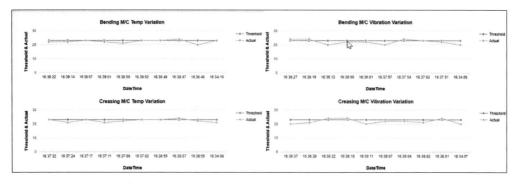

Figure 10.7 Real-Time Equipment Health Parameter Value

Further, users can drill down into details about each piece of equipment or a group of equipment and display the result of predictive maintenance. As shown in Figure 10.8, notice how the top half of the screen contains important KPIs about the equipment, like open notifications (that require action), mean temperature variance, mean vibration variance, and damage/action analysis.

The bottom half of the screen shows a table of individual pieces of equipment and the results of the machine learning algorithms for predicting failure. The algorithms calculate the time to possible failure with a degree of confidence.

Figure 10.8 Shop Floor Predictive Maintenance Example

A production manager can perform root cause analysis on equipment breakdowns, which helps to take corrective actions and avoid future failures. The analytics charts shown in Figure 10.9 illustrate what the primary root cause of failures were in the past, for example, wear and tear or poor maintenance, and the action that was taken to fix the machine. If the action taken is a only temporary solution, then this chart shows whether any further follow-up action needs to be taken on these assets.

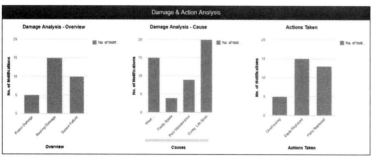

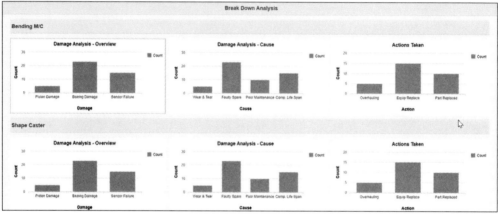

Figure 10.9 Equipment Damage and Action Analysis Example

10.2.6   Dynamic Routing

The capabilities of the smart shop floor do not end with reporting failures and recording actions taken in the past. A smart shop floor also helps you take corrective action during unplanned downtimes. The landing page of this function, shown in Figure 10.11, illustrates the asset utilization of machines under each hierarchy like benders, creasers, and lathes. Users can easily locate the overutilized machines, displayed in red, which require action.

In the next step, a production planner can drill down into a detailed view of broken resources to investigate the production orders impacted by the associated downtime. As shown in Figure 10.10 and Figure 10.11, the **Welding** machine system is impacted, and the asset is overutilized because of unplanned downtime. The drilldown function helps you get into the details, where you'll see that **Welding Bots WD01** needs corrective action.

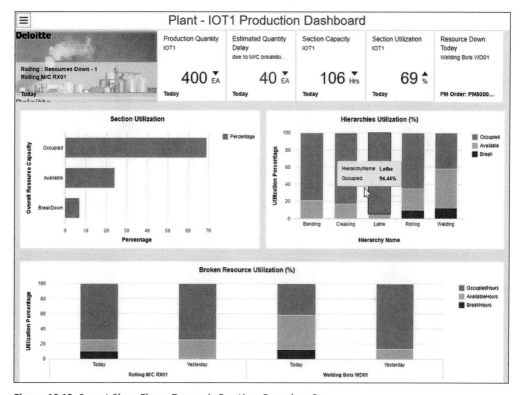

Figure 10.10 Smart Shop Floor: Dynamic Routing Overview Page

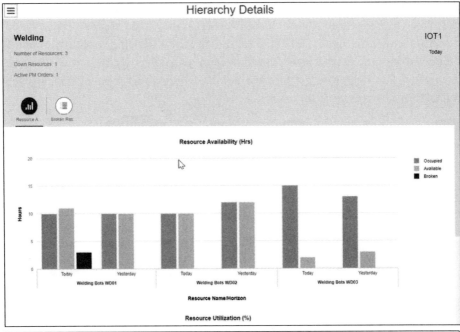

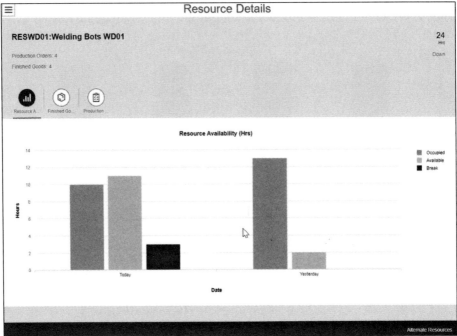

Figure 10.11 Hierarchy Level Asset Utilization Example

Once the workstation that requires attention is identified, planners can take one of two actions: identify an alternate workstation where the production order can be scheduled or postpone the order into the future on the next available workstation, as shown in Figure 10.12. In this case, **Welding Bots WD01** has capacity available, so we'll reroute and reschedule the order using this resource to avoid or reduce production delays.

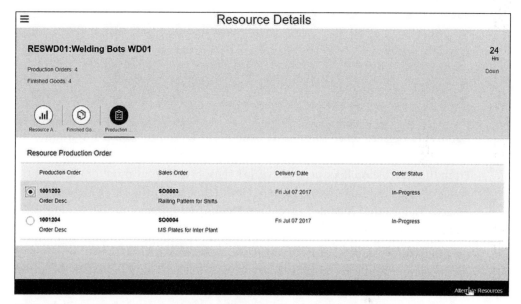

Figure 10.12 Rerouting Production Order to an Alternate Resource Example

10.2.7   Production Planning and Detailed Scheduling

A smart shop floor can be further enhanced by integrating SAP S/4HANA Manufacturing for production planning and detailed scheduling (PP-DS). PP-DS embedded in SAP S/4HANA is a production planning tool that helps you investigate the details of the orders planned at a work center and sequence them to meet each order's due dates and minimize delays due to machine downtime.

PP-DS embedded in SAP S/4HANA provides a robust, detailed scheduling board, shown in Figure 10.13, that helps to visualize production orders sequenced at any production resource down to the second. The solution can sequence orders by optimizing setup times to minimize delays and costs. Production planners have a lot of options to manually adjust the production schedule as needed.

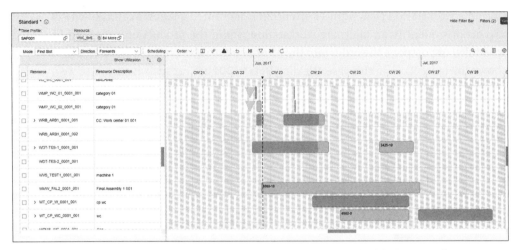

Figure 10.13 Detailed Scheduling Board Example in PP-DS Embedded in SAP S/4HANA

From the smart shop floor perspective, IoT sensors help your monitor the real-time status of your assets and planned orders. PP-DS embedded in SAP S/4HANA can be leveraged to adjust the schedule to avoid production disruptions and plan semi-finished and raw materials in advance.

In summary, the smart shop floor can play a critical role in a manufacturing environment. Planners can use real-time data, and machine learning models can be trained to act when a specific situation occurs repeatedly. In most situations, the system can take actions automatically without manual intervention, which frees up a planners' time so they can to focus on root cause analysis of past failures and the corrective action taken to prevent future occurrences.

10.3   Digital Asset Network and Operations

Production asset availability and efficiency plays an important role in manufacturing optimization. Enterprise asset management (EAM) is the process of managing the lifecycle of physical assets by documenting, continuously monitoring, and predicting failure and by undertaking MRO (maintenance, repair, and overhaul) inventory management and automation of business processes through collaboration. EAM plays a key role in asset-intensive industries like heavy engineering, energy, aerospace and defense, government, utilities, and more. EAM is not restricted to just monitoring asset health and corrective action on physical assets. The scope of EAM is much broader, encompassing asset standardization, predictive maintenance, managing an ecosystem of network of assets, creating insights from asset performance, and MRO planning.

As part of asset standardization, EAM focuses on maintaining an accurate, detailed database of the assets, documents, historical events and notifications, and regulatory compliance.

SAP provides a suite of EAM solutions that can seamlessly integrate with the digital core. As shown in Figure 10.14, asset central foundation is an IoT-powered application that supports the SAP Asset Intelligence Network, SAP Predictive Maintenance and Service, SAP Asset Strategy and Performance Management, and SAP Predictive Engineering Insights. This solution also provides various functionalities across IoT applications and ensures seamless integration and data consistency across systems.

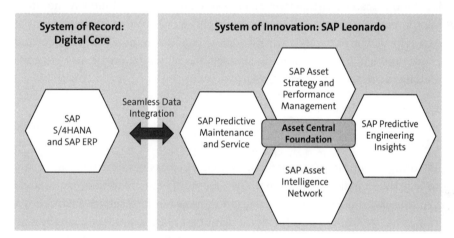

Figure 10.14 Enterprise Asset Management Systems in SAP Leonardo

In more detail, each product is as follows:

- **SAP Asset Intelligence Network**
  This solution is an asset collaboration platform that brings together various stakeholders of a physical asset like the manufacturer, the operator, original equipment manufacturer (OEM), service provider, etc. By bringing stakeholders into a digital ecosystem, companies can solve complex and predictive spare parts availability issues by collaborating with each other. This solution also provides an opportunity for service providers and asset manufacturers to improve their own product and service efficiency.

- **SAP Predictive Maintenance and Service**

  This solution, as mentioned earlier, continuously monitors the health of your physical assets and predicts failures. SAP Predictive Maintenance and Service uses statistical methods and machine learning techniques to predict failures before they occur, resulting in maintenance activities being scheduled in a cost-effective manner.

- **SAP Asset Strategy and Performance Management**

  This solution helps you define and plan maintenance execution strategies for improved asset performance. While defining the strategy for execution, the solution holistically investigates the historical performance of the assets and insights from the network and takes a decision based on collective intelligence.

- **SAP Predictive Engineering Insights**

  This solution creates a virtual twin of a physical asset and continuously monitors the sensor parameters you define to gain insights on performance. Digital twins of assets help you proactively identify issues, conduct remote diagnostics, and improve products. This solution can also serve as a foundation for new business models like a product-as-a-service, on a pay-per use basis.

In this section, we'll focus solely on the SAP Asset Intelligence Network. However, later sections in this chapter will go into detail on the other EAM solutions supported by SAP Leonardo.

Manufacturing organizations manage thousands of pieces of equipment and spare parts to keep the shop floor operational. The volume of equipment to be maintained and their associated documents, like warranties, sales orders, service instructions, operating manuals, etc., can be difficult for plant managers to process. Even the simple assembly of a manufacturing machine usually contains a heterogeneous mix of parts supplied by various vendors. During installation, these vendors provide documentation and drawings that need to be stored in your backend system for future consumption. A plant manager needs his or her team to consolidate all information and make sure the organization has all the necessary details like maintenance frequency and other critical functioning parameters to ensure seamless production.

Plants face challenges in maintaining the equipment details, warranty information, parts lists for nonintegrated systems, plus the manual effort required to maintain data in a variety of systems across the organization, thus making collaboration in a single platform practically impossible.

The SAP Asset Intelligence Network aims to solve this problem by providing a common platform to maintain details about your assets and providing a collaboration platform. This solution provides a repository of equipment models that can be shared between multiple business partners, resulting in a common definition of machines that delivers new business models and true operational excellence. The SAP Asset Intelligence Network brings together manufacturers, service providers, and operators of the assets across regions to collaborate around shared equipment information to maximize availability, improve efficiency, and create new business models, as shown in Figure 10.15.

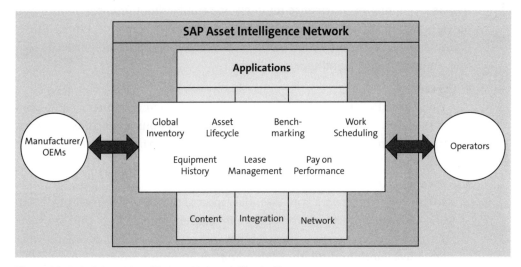

Figure 10.15 SAP Asset Intelligence Network Illustration

The SAP Asset Intelligence Network is a cloud-based solution built on SAP Cloud Platform with a central repository for all the assets, providing both tools to visualize these assets and a collaboration platform for various stakeholders.

Operators and manufacturers can use the same platform for sharing information. The SAP Asset Intelligence Network is a great repository for holding details about asset lifecycles, lease management, equipment history, global spare parts inventory, benchmarking, and work scheduling. In addition, the SAP Asset Intelligence Network can be used to implement a pay-per-use service model for assets. All asset-related information is stored in a shared model database, thus providing an opportunity to standardize equipment and parts list.

Service providers, manufacturers, and operators are all on the same network, which results in collaboration opportunities because the manufacturer can get real-time usage data and an operator can get updated information directly from the manufacturer. The SAP Asset Intelligence Network provides role-based access to restrict access to sensitive information.

The SAP Asset Intelligence Network is a key component of digital twins, which we'll discuss in more detail in Section 10.5. Digital twins help visualize real-time operating information of assets, which helps the operator to detect anomalies and communicate to the manufacturer on the same platform. Once access is provided, OEMs can monitor equipment performance remotely and troubleshoot problems, which also provides the opportunity for manufacturers to improve the performance of their products. Digital twins on the SAP Asset Intelligence Network are supported by content, network, and frontend apps, as follows:

- **Content**
  A cloud portal of standardized content that defines and documents equipment and models is shared and stored for consistent definitions among business partners. Data standardization is a prerequisite you'll need to perform in order to reap the benefits of the SAP Asset Intelligence Network.

- **Network**
  A robust backend network is an essential aspect of the SAP Asset Intelligence Network. All business partners who operate in different parts of the world can share information on the network. Since this network must be secure, and SAP provides a secured channel for network collaboration.

- **Frontend apps**
  The SAP Asset Intelligence Network provides a flexible, functionally rich set of frontend apps for visualizing data. The apps are created on the SAP Cloud Platform. Your users can use the standard functionalities provided, or custom analytics and visualization can be built.

Figure 10.16 shows an example dashboard on the SAP Asset Intelligence Network. On this customizable screen, users can add information of interest to your organization. SAP 3D Visual Enterprise provides a 3D visualization of the asset, which can be particularly helpful for procuring spare parts and installation.

The SAP Asset Intelligence Network provides a simple onboarding functionality for adding equipment, OEMs, and spare parts vendors for collaboration.

Figure 10.16 SAP Asset Intelligence Network Dashboard Example

10.4   Predictive Maintenance

Different maintenance strategies are followed in manufacturing environments like the run to failure strategy, preventive maintenance, and predictive maintenance. The *run to failure* strategy means waiting for a part to fail completely and then replacing that part. This strategy is not advisable for high-value assets, the failure of which will cause a production disruption. Even with low-value assets or spares, an inventory of spare parts must always be carried since failure is unpredictable. With a *preventive maintenance* strategy, maintenance is scheduled in a time-phased manner or based on the frequency of asset usage. This strategy ensures an asset is taken care of frequently, but a company might end up spending a lot of money in procuring spare parts and undertaking service to avoid production disruptions. Also, this strategy cannot identify problems between inspections. Predictive maintenance tries to solve these problems by predicting failures before they occur.

Predictive maintenance is a data science-driven approach of continuously monitoring the health parameters of an asset to predict the probability of failure, which helps your organization plan service in a cost-effective manner without disrupting production flows. Predicting failures before they occur could potentially save thousands of dollars a day depending on the industry. With the advent of cost-effective industrial IoT sensors, you can monitor system health continuously.

Companies often resort to nondestructive testing methods to monitor the health of an asset. Nondestructive testing includes physical sensor technologies like infrared sensing, acoustic, laser-aided computer visual detection, vibration and sound level measurements, temperature, and humidity. SAP Leonardo IoT enables IoT sensors to continuously feed measurement data to SAP Predictive Maintenance and Service, which can ingest and analyze this data to create alerts, notifications, and service requests and of course to predict failures.

Additive manufacturing, commonly referred as 3D printing, can play a crucial role in predictive maintenance and can be utilized to optimize efficiency, as we'll discuss in the following sections.

10.4.1   On-Demand Spare Parts through 3D Printing

SAP Predictive Maintenance and Service helps you identify anomalies in asset performance and predict failure. An anomaly results in creating a work order for fixing the production asset, which results in the need for spare parts. Maintaining an inventory of spare parts has historically been a burden for suppliers and asset operators. Storing spare parts that are seldom used is expensive, and sometimes, service providers don't always have ability to produce the spare parts perhaps because of their own outdated technology. Additive manufacturing using 3D printing is an emerging technology to meet this challenge.

Companies see the innate business value of 3D printing and its impact on the supply chain. Transitioning to on-demand manufacturing can result in cost savings by eliminating or significantly reducing inventory requirements. Digital files also provide the ability to quickly produce new, updated designs at little to no additional cost. Businesses that utilize 3D printing service providers deal with less risk and have more control because you can use a single manufacturing method for a variety of parts.

Using 3D printing for spare parts addresses following business challenges that many companies face:

- Customer demand may spike for a variety of spare parts, requiring short delivery times. An inventory of spare parts that are not often needed is generally not inventoried. However, when an asset breaks down, the spare part is required immediately so that the production can resume.

- Additive manufacturing technology is progressing at a rapid pace. More and more parts can be 3D printed, which pushes spare parts manufacturers to leverage the technology.

- Increasingly, spare parts manufacturers moving towards 3D printing technology gain a competitive advantage because they can meet the demand of their own customers quickly.

By implementing 3D printing for spare parts, your company can gain many benefits, like an optimized spare parts inventory, reduced spare parts delivery costs and lead times, higher customer satisfaction, and fewer production disruptions due to asset breakdowns.

10.4.2   Building Blocks of Predictive Maintenance

SAP Predictive Maintenance and Service can be viewed as an add-on tool to your maintenance execution system that continuously monitors and predicts failures. SAP Predictive Maintenance and Service can seamlessly integrate with SAP ERP, SAP S/4HANA, and other execution systems. Master data can also be transferred from the execution system to create the model and the hierarchy.

As shown in Figure 10.17, the execution system and SAP Leonardo system form the two boundaries of SAP Predictive Maintenance and Service. SAP Leonardo Machine Learning Foundation provides the technical support to pull asset health parameters in real time. Then, SAP Predictive Maintenance and Service can seamlessly integrate with your execution system for notifications and work orders.

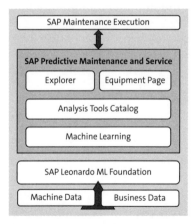

Figure 10.17 SAP Predictive Maintenance and Service Components

The machine learning service in SAP Predictive Maintenance and Service ingests sensor data from various pieces of equipment and performs the defined action as trained in the model. Real-time data and the ability to train models are integral to the successful use of machine learning. The analysis tools catalog provides building blocks you can use to create dashboards of equipment.

The SAP Predictive Maintenance and Service explorer page is the entry page for monitoring the health status of a group of machines. Various analysis charts configured using the analysis tool catalog can be viewed on this page. Drilldown functionality enables you to navigate from the overview dashboard page to the individual equipment page.

The equipment page provides the consolidated view of equipment consisting of highlights of the equipment, structure and parts, documentation, and monitoring.

Implementing the asset central foundation also incorporates a set of standardization practices into your organization. Asset names are organized in a taxonomy with different levels and hierarchies. SAP is licensed to use ISO 14224 to define classes and subclasses of equipment. To create a collaborative environment for asset maintenance, following industry standards is important so that data sharing is seamless between various stakeholders.

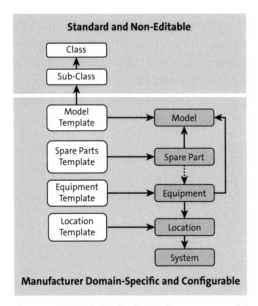

Figure 10.18 SAP Predictive Maintenance and Service Data Model

In the following sections, we'll investigate various levels in which the equipment is classified and named. Templates are common across the levels. For every level (i.e. model, equipment, location, spare parts), a template can be created and reused in multiple instances. For example, a model template for a machine that makes paper can have attributes like paper feed speed, run speed, energy consumption range, etc. One template can be used to create multiple models of the papermaking machines using the SAP Predictive Maintenance and Service data model, as shown in Figure 10.18.

Class and Subclass

Industry standards in SAP Predictive Maintenance and Service are made possible by the class and subclass templates. To use this level, you'll need to activate the SAP Asset Intelligence Network. The currently available class and subclass templates are based on ISO 14224, which collect and exchange equipment reliability and maintenance data. This level is a standard set provided by SAP, and the users cannot make modifications. However, all levels below the subclass can be configured to meet your company's specific needs.

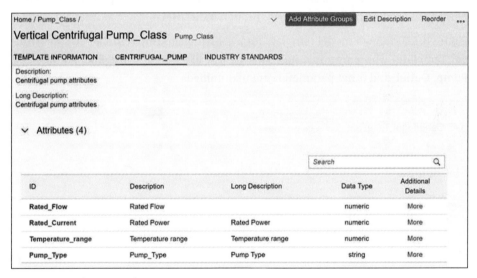

Figure 10.19 Class Template

Various attributes can be assigned to the class. Attributes are the characteristics or specification of the asset. In the example shown in Figure 10.19, the **Vertical Centrifugal Pump_Class** is the class, and the attributes defined under the class include

Rated_Flow, Rated_Current, Temperature_range, and **Pump_Type**. Attribute groups, a logical group of similar attributes, can also be defined under a class.

Let's take the example of a drilling machine. Different attribute groups can be created, like relevant speeds, temperature, and motor and drill bit specifications. Attributes defined under an attribute group are inheritable, which reduces data maintenance efforts when configuring multiple models.

Model

A model represents the maintenance and specification information of a physical asset. The attributes defined in the class are inherited by the model. A model template can be created so you can create multiple models quickly. For example, a centrifugal pump template can be created once. In a process, for example, in the oil and gas industry, hundreds of centrifugal pumps might be installed.

The actual values of the attributes are maintained in the model. Indicators can be represented in the model. Indicators represent the measurement values that indicate the discrete or tolerance range of an attribute. Just like attributes, groups can be created for indicators where a set of indicators can be logically grouped. Industry standards for a model can also be defined through indicators.

Figure 10.20 shows a model template for a centrifugal pump template (**OC Centrifugal Template**) where multiple indicator groups like **Pump_Drive_End**, **Pump_Inlet**, **Pump_Outlet**, and other parameters are maintained.

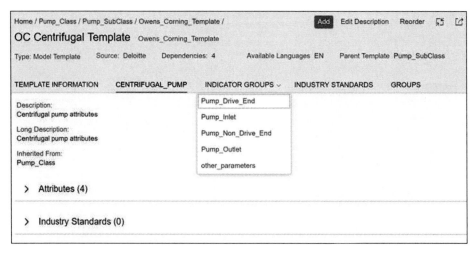

Figure 10.20 Model Template Example

The indicator **Pump_Drive_End** shown in Figure 10.21 represents a group various indicators under it like vibration range (horizontal, vertical, and axial). The indicator range definition forms the basis on which parameters are monitored.

Additional information like installation instructions, service instructions, environmental compliance, and spare parts documentation can also be attached to the model.

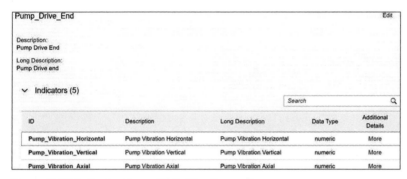

Figure 10.21 Indicator Group Definition Example

The attributes and indicators defined in the model template are pulled into the model, and the values are maintained in the model. Documents attached to the model template, which may be common across different models, is inherited by the model. In some machines, the characteristics or parameters can vary based on usage. The model definition (an example of which is shown in Figure 10.22) can maintain time-based attribute values and can track changes in parameters.

Figure 10.22 Model Definition Example

Equipment

Equipment represents an instance of a model installed on the shop floor. For example, in a packaging industry shop floor, conveyor systems may be installed in multiple assembly units. The specification of the conveyor belt model can be common across various instances of the conveyor systems installed. One model for the conveyor system is created, and multiple equipment instances are created to represent the individual installations on various assembly lines.

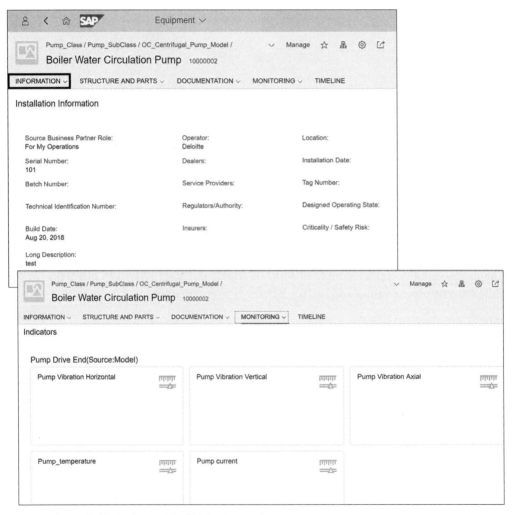

Figure 10.23 Equipment Definition Example

Equipment definition also has the ability to save installation information, warranty information, and equipment serial numbers. This serialization of equipment is an important step towards standardizing assets within the organization. An equipment definition example is shown in Figure 10.23.

Location

Location corresponds to a virtual representation of the physical location where the piece of equipment is physically installed. A location need not be the factory itself but can represent a location within the factory like assembly area A, the electrical room, the cooling station, etc. By providing the GPS coordinates of the location where the actual equipment is installed, a group of machines can be viewed on a map.

Spare Part

Just like a model, a spare part can also be defined with critical information to help in the ordering of the spare parts. A spare parts template configures the attributes and parameters related to the spare part. Typically, only critical spare parts are modeled in SAP Predictive Maintenance and Service.

Groups and System

Groups are defined to logically group objects for reporting, while a system is a set of interrelated assets, generally equipment that interact with each other and work together. For example, in a manufacturing environment, an assembly unit is a collection of multiple pieces of equipment that work as a group.

Master Data Integration

SAP has provided master data synchronization capabilities between SAP ERP (or SAP S/4HANA) and SAP Predictive Maintenance and Service. A new piece of equipment can be created, or existing machines can be synchronized with SAP Predictive Maintenance and Service system as shown in Figure 10.24.

As soon as a piece of EAM equipment is created in SAP Predictive Maintenance and Service, data synchronization can be performed. This synchronization can also be performed manually with Transaction AIN_EQUI_SYNC. Equipment master documents stored in the Document Management System (DMS) can be synchronized with the SAP Predictive Maintenance and Service system.

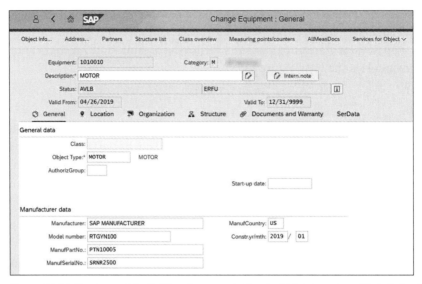

Figure 10.24 Equipment Definition Representation in SAP Integrate with SAP Predictive Maintenance and Service

10.4.3   Digital Dashboard

The SAP Predictive Maintenance and Service explorer page features a dashboard view of the system where various analytics graphs can be visualized in the group. The analysis tool catalog provides various analytics tools like 3D charts, alerts, equipment lists, equipment locations, and health status overviews.

In the indicator's definition, you can define the dimension of the indicator and the threshold relevancy of the parameter. Indicator values can be from measured values, or these values may be calculated based on the measured parameter value. If the indicator values are aggregated from a different system, these values can be aggregated in the indicator and monitored for deviations from the defined threshold limits.

On the equipment page, real-time monitoring charts can be viewed. As shown in Figure 10.25, the pressure value from the **Boiler Water Circulation Pump** is being continuously monitored, and the values are displayed on the chart. The upper and lower horizontal lines represent the threshold values of the indicator that is measured.

When the values of a monitored parameter exceed the threshold values, the system can be configured to generate alerts. As shown in Figure 10.26, pump pressure has spiked and breached the upper threshold value at 9:20 am. A critical alert was created as a result. Based on these rules, notifications can also be created based on the alert.

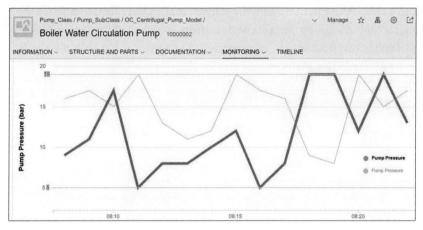

Figure 10.25 Chart Based on Real-Time Monitoring

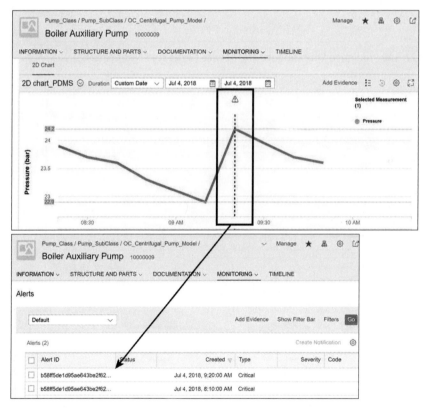

Figure 10.26 SAP Predictive Maintenance and Service Alert Example

Typically, in a shop floor environment, the sensors that capture the parameters feed to SAP Digital Manufacturing Insights system from which SAP Predictive Maintenance and Service can read values. Alternatively, the sensor values can also be fed directly into SAP Predictive Maintenance and Service.

Figure 10.27 SAP Predictive Maintenance and Service Generated Notification

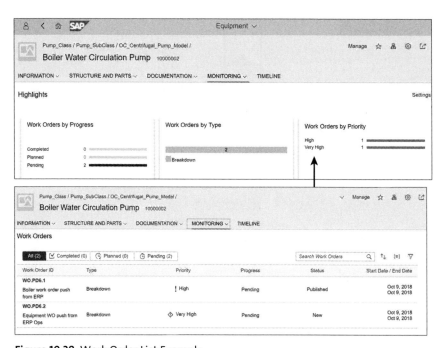

Figure 10.28 Work Order List Example

Notifications created in the SAP Predictive Maintenance and Service system can be integrated with SAP Enterprise Asset Management (SAP EAM). Users can create notifications without an alert as well. Just like notifications, work orders can also be created in SAP Predictive Maintenance and Service and integrated with the execution system. SAP Predictive Maintenance and Service can receive work orders created in connected systems.

SAP Predictive Maintenance and Service catalog tools provide you with the ability to view notifications and work orders in a consolidated view as shown in Figure 10.27 and Figure 10.28.

10.4.4   Machine Learning Service

The machine learning service in SAP Predictive Maintenance and Service provides a framework and tools for predicting equipment failure. The results of machine learning, like the probability of failure, health statuses, and anomaly scores, can be visualized on the SAP Predictive Maintenance and Service explorer page. The various building blocks of SAP Predictive Maintenance and Service machine learning service are shown in Figure 10.29.

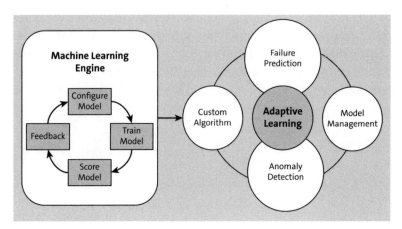

Figure 10.29 SAP Predictive Maintenance and Service Machine Learning Engine

In the machine learning environment, you'll need configure, train, and score machine learning models to attain accurate and desired results. Historical equipment data, gleaned from many years of operation, forms the basis of machine learning. Typically, in organizations, building a robust digital core forms the foundation of prediction. The first step of the process is configuring a model, usually involving a data scientist identifying a suitable algorithm that meets a specific business case. Next, you'll feed the model historical equipment performance data, which includes both normal conditions and failure conditions. The model can be scored by feeding test data into the model. Depending on feedback, the model will be improvised further until the desired results are achieved.

Let's look at a hypothetical example in the meat processing industry where the assembly unit cleans, cuts, and packs meat. The meat cutting and processing section of the assembly unit is the critical component. Multiple moving parts are involved, and temperature is maintained by a cooling unit. The company has installed different instances of the same model at various locations, and each machine is functional for about ten years. Let's assume the company has recorded data about both failure and normal conditions of the machine during this period. First, a model is built by taking data from operations from 2005 to 2015. Then, the model is tested by feeding in the actual data from the years 2015 to 2018. If the model can predict past failure with a probability of success, then this model can be deployed for future predictions. If the model needs further smoothening and improvisation, then you'll go through an iterative process of model enhancement.

Two types of predictions can be made by SAP Predictive Maintenance and Service: anomaly detection and failure prediction. An anomaly refers to outliers and exceptions detected when compared to the normal working conditions of the machine. Failure predictions are made by reading input variables and correlating these values with historical failure events. The health status predictions made by the algorithms are displayed on the SAP Predictive Maintenance and Service explorer page, as shown in Figure 10.30.

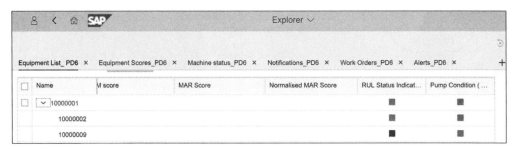

Figure 10.30 SAP Predictive Maintenance and Service Explorer Page

Model management helps data scientist create, train, and score models by helping with various kinds of analysis on the input data.

SAP Predictive Maintenance and Service provides the following seven machine learning algorithms out of the box. Before using the machine learning service, you must understand these algorithms and use the one that fits the specific use case of the equipment:

- **Anomaly detection with principal component analysis**
  Principal component analysis (PCA) is deployed for anomaly detection based on the sensor data collected from different points on a piece of equipment. A conveyor system in an assembly unit may be quite long, in some industries, miles long. Multiple motors may power the conveyor system, and these motors need to execute in synchronization. Sensor data from these motors can pull in parameters like rotations per minute (RPM) and temperature. This algorithm immediately detects whether any anomalies arise in the data. While deploying this algorithm, you'll need train and score the model for momentary spikes in data. These sporadic anomalies can be normal, requiring the historical data must be smoothened.

- **Distance-based failure analysis using earth mover's distance (EMD)**
  EMD calculates anomalies by comparing the sensor data with normal functioning data. To configure the model, you'll need historical data from the past few years of similar or the same equipment under various working conditions. This data will form the basis of comparison for anomaly detection.

  Manufacturing shop floor use computer numeric control (CNC) manufacturing mills, which are multipurpose and run with different tooling for milling, shaping, drilling, and more. Vibration and temperature values will thus fall in different ranges depending on the mode in which the machine is being operated. These parameters can be grouped under each mode of operation, and historical data for each mode can be collected for training the model.

- **Remaining useful life (RUL) prediction using Weibull algorithms**
  The Weibull algorithm calculates lifetime of the asset based on age and thereby predicts the remaining useful life of an asset. To train this model, you'll need data from machines of a similar model that have failed in the past and also similar machines that are still functioning. This algorithm calculates the probability of failure of an equipment based on time period.

- **Anomaly detection using multivariate autoregression (MAR)**
  MAR can read and detect data anomalies of up to 100 variables and provides an anomaly score. Based on the score, a suitable alert can be generated. The metals industry uses rotary furnaces with moving parts. The temperature will be different at various points in the furnace, and thus, monitoring vibration, pressure, and

10

rotation per minute at various points of the furnace is important. Typically, down-times can be scheduled periodically for preventive maintenance. By deploying this algorithm, your business can predict failures before they occur, and down-times can be avoided.

- **Failure prediction using tree ensemble classifier (TEC)**
  TEC works on tree model decision-making where the model is trained with multi-dimensional historical data. If a rare event occurs, the decision tree creates weights based on input data. TEC cannot use time-series data, but when the failure occurs, this algorithm can use the decision tree and assign weights to predict failure.

- **One class support vector machines (SVM) for anomaly detection**
  In a centrifugal pump, conditions are monitored using sensors that measure values like rotations per minute, temperature, and vibration at various modes of operation. The sensor values may be different during acceleration, idling, and deceleration modes of operation. The algorithm compares these values with the normal functioning data range to predicts failure, and anomaly scores are generated.

- **Logistic regression for failure prediction (LOR)**
  This algorithm uses logistic regression to perform a supervised binary classification of failure (0) or no failure (1). This algorithm is a decision tree performed in a regression and can detect the probability of failure occurrence to which the algorithm assigns a value 0 or 1. The slitting equipment in the paper packaging line usually fails due to slitting blade failure. This algorithm can help in detecting whether a failure was caused by the blade or by any other linked components.

Your organization need not restrict itself to the standard algorithms provided. SAP Predictive Maintenance and Service also provides the ability for you to create custom algorithms and integrate these algorithms with sensor data. Standard R integration APIs are available to integrate the R program with SAP Predictive Maintenance and Service. Some organizations also deploy SAP Predictive Analytics, which provides various statistical models and standard algorithms.

In summary, SAP Predictive Maintenance and Service can continuously monitor various health parameters of equipment and accurately predict failures before they occur. This solution also provides a platform for your organization to create machine learning models to help accurately predict failures. Organizations can unleash the potential of SAP Predictive Maintenance and Service by accurately measuring data and deploying well-trained models. The success of the prediction also depends on the organizational mindset regarding process change. The machine learning services

provided with SAP Predictive Maintenance and Service can help predict future failures and helps manufacturing organizations especially be proactive in taking corrective action.

10.5   Digital Twins

A digital twin is a digital representation of a physical asset, allowing the sharing and
updating of information from physical to digital formats, and vice versa. In a manufacturing process, an enterprise-wide network of digital twins can be especially powerful. Not only can digital twins serve as near real-time replicas of what is happening
on the factory floor, but also, through the collective knowledge of all your connected
digital twins, you can discover new patterns and optimize operational performance.
Knowledge about digital twins from the background of product and inventory was
covered in Chapter 9, Section 9.1.

Digital twins are based on the concept of integration between the physical and digital
world. In the manufacturing application, this integration helps in the collection of
data from the physical asset into the digital replica and implementing the insights
gained through analysis within the digital replica into the physical asset. And when
this can be done in an integrated, collaborative, and near real-time manner, then the
real value of digital twins can be realized. In addition of the manufacturing process
control and management, digital twins are highly useful for the asset maintenance
and reliability.

To use digital twins effectively, you'll need to understand its definition, its varieties,
and its integration with SAP Leonardo's portfolio for digital twins. These four topics
are covered in the next section in detail.

10.5.1   Digital Twins of a Physical Objects

Complex and critical physical objects form an ideal use case for digital representation, monitoring, and predictive maintenance. For example, the equipment at an oil
refinery, both crucial machines at a complex manufacturing plant and specific components of complex machines, are prone to failure and are appropriate for modeling
through digital twins.

For a digital twin model to be effective and efficient, you'll need to consider some
common characteristics such as the following:

- **Representation identity**

  A unique representation of a physical object through the digital object. For example, if the digital twin is oil refinery, the essential identified machinery that exists in the physical world must be easily identified and represented in the digital twin model.

- **Context and information**

  The main objective of a digital twin is to have information about the physical object easily available in an easy-to-understand format. For the oil refinery model, if the temperature and pressure of the physical machine is crucial, sensors on the physical equipment must provide this information to its digital counterpart in an easy-to-understand format.

- **Communication and control**

  Based on actual usage requirements, a digital twin can communicate in one directional or bidirectionally. In a single-direction digital twin, information from the physical object is available at the digital twin (say pressure and temperature); for any anomaly, a manual action is required to move back to optimum condition. In a bidirectional flow, the digital twin also provides the ability to control so that the physical object's parameter is controlled by the controlling the digital twin's parameter on the digital device.

- **Dashboard and analytics**

  Added analytics functionality in the form of a dashboard can greatly enhance the effectiveness of a digital twin. For example, the usage of a model to show anomalies that can lead to failure can greatly enhance the effectiveness of digital twins by making them crucial in your decision support system.

Digital twins can be used in multiple industrial and commercial applications, for example, the following:

- **Product lifecycle management**

  Following the product lifecycle of a critical and complex object through its digital twin can be an important efficiency multiplier and cost controller. In a wholly physical environment, working on failure mode effect analysis (FMEA) will require real testing on the actual part until failure occurs. In the digital world, supported by digital twin, you could conduct this analysis much more quickly and at exponentially less cost by not breaking the real object while still being able to finalize dimensions for product development.

- **Asset management**

  Operators use digital twins for running, maintaining, tracking, and optimizing their assets. Digital twins can also provide preventive maintenance alerts based on historical information and near real-time operating conditions.

- **Plant, store, or retail map**
  An integrated network of digital twins can be used to represent a store, a factory, or a shipping yard to identify and reduce inefficiencies and improve overall production or service levels.

- **Infrastructure management**
  Smart cities may use digital twin grids to manage the flow of traffic, balance power needs in a power grid, prevent water line breakage, and safeguard citizens.

10.5.2   Varieties of Digital Twins

In general, the four varieties of digital twins are as follows:

- **Product digital twin**
  A digital twin of a product has a 1:1 relationship with a physical object or product. It mirrors the physical object, and the digital profile evolves over the lifetime of the product. The digital twin may be created at the inception of the product itself, which helps develop a detailed digital profile of the product. As the product is put into productive use, the digital twin can then be used to process data from the product and provide insights like when to perform preventive maintenance and adjust the product as needed.

- **Asset digital twin**
  Digital twins can be used to represent an entire production process, interacting with every aspect of the production process in near real time and ingesting data at every step of the process. This data can then be compared with the baseline process steps, so deviations can be investigated and understood. By doing so, digital twins can help optimize the process and, in cases where the process is deviating from the baseline, bring the process back within boundaries of tolerance. A single asset digital twin can be comprised of multiple individual product digital twins. A digital twin of an asset enhances the asset's lifecycle as well as its operational efficiency. Instead of preventive time-based maintenance, the governance of the asset can be based on the actual usage and the lifecycle to get the highest possible lifetime while running at optimum efficiency and avoiding the probability of failure.

- **Plant digital twin**
  Digital twins can also be used to represent a manufacturing plant or factory to model all the vital installations of the assets within the plant and the real-life integration between them. Thousands of devices and assets are present in a factory,

and a digital twin can serve as a single holistic representation of the entire factory. The basic characteristics of digital twins are all retained in this model although at a much larger scale. The model helps you see the interactions between a multitude of devices and gain insights through a holistic view. The impact of failures or problems in one part of the plant ca be analyzed in the context of the overall impact on the plant, and appropriate action can be recommended. The digital twin of a plant enables a control tower for the full plant with the central view of the operations, product movements, and control parameter analysis. Integrating machine learning capabilities through the control parameter through real-time data can optimize the plant's performance at low operational cost.

- **Infrastructure digital twin**
  A digital twin for a connected infrastructure assumes a scale where a complete infrastructure has a connected twin. For example, water mains in a city form a vital infrastructure. The difficulty in monitoring this infrastructure has been highlighted in multiple studies. A digital twin for infrastructure can help solve and mitigate issues common in complex, costly, and vital infrastructures. By forming a grid structure, for example, a digital twin can represent all water mains in a city and can model and represent the flow and connections in the digital twin. The grid-like structure helps simulate and visualize the impact of problems and categorize according to impact (high, medium, low). As a result, you can prioritize problems and appropriately distribute scarce human resources to work on the biggest problems first.

  The biggest advantage of a connected digital twin is that it can monitor an evolving situation with near real-time interaction. So, the corrective actions taken are fed back into the virtual profile of the digital twin in near real time, and any actions suggested by the digital twin can be applied in the real world. Consider, for example, a digital twin of a public drinking water distribution system enabled with real-time data processing sensors. Any issues that arise during transmission (a pipe leak causing a quality issue in the water undetected by naked eye) immediately create notifications and recommend actions, thus preventing potential life-threatening illness.

10.5.3   Digital Twin Integration in SAP Leonardo

Digital twins can be integrated in different ways with SAP Leonardo. No specific rules must be followed, and based on your business requirements, identified value areas, and solution innovation, you can follow one of the following approaches:

- **Digital twin to device**

  Digital twin-to-device integration is the integration of a digital twin to a product, asset, machine, fleet, and/or device. The physical object is integrated securely to the digital object. Through the secure integration, the status of the object is communicated in near real time to the digital twin for analysis. Any alerts or exceptions from the digital twin are communicated back to the physical asset in terms of actuation or actions.

- **Digital twin to system of intelligence**

  Systems of intelligence are algorithms, routines, and rule-handling tools, all specialized tools focused on identifying anomalies, forecasting potential breakdowns, and calculating the remaining lifetime of an asset. The integration of a digital twin to this system of intelligence can be quite beneficial, enabling advanced analysis using the tools and systems best suited for the application on hand. These external systems can either query the digital twin for data, or the digital twin can push historical information to such systems.

- **Digital twin to system of record**

  A system of record is composed of ERP systems, manufacturing systems, ERP/CRM systems, and supplier networks for service contracts, which can all benefit from digital twin integration because the data available from digital twin can help you understand the current condition of your assets or physical objects without physically interacting with them. Financial valuation, insurance, and depreciation calculations are some important applications of such an integration.

- **Digital twin to digital twin**

  If the physical object is not managed by the provider of the digital twin, then a digital twin-to-digital twin integration is needed. The digital twin can thus be managed by a service provider specializing in the management of digital twins.

An example of a digital twin of a product is shown in Figure 10.31, which represents the digital twin of a power transformer. In the digital representation, live control parameters are available for review in real time along with information from alerts, analytics, or notifications.

The example shown in Figure 10.31 displays one individual part, the information and handling of which is managed through a digital twin. In a smart manufacturing setup, you can represent a group of machines, a part of the manufacturing process, or the entire manufacturing floor through a digital twin or a combination of many digital twins. As a result, you'll have the flexibility to monitor and control the shop floor with a level of ease and efficiency only dreamed of in the past. For example, consider the heat treatment process in steel manufacturing, where an operator can be comfortable in his or her office while monitoring a process running at more than 1,000°F, monitoring purity and process control parameters on a digital device. This option of monitoring and controlling complex processes as a singular unit and the ability to react in real time based on analytics and alerts have highly enhanced the use of digital twins in manufacturing environments.

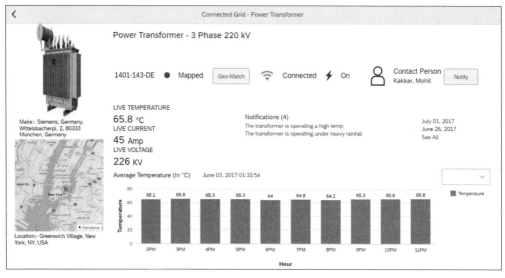

Figure 10.31 Digital Twin of a Power Transformer

10.5.4   SAP Leonardo Digital Twin Portfolio

The concept of digital twins is applied to various modules of SAP Leonardo. Digital twins help to monitor the physical equipment, vehicle, or asset, as follows:

- **SAP Predictive Maintenance and Service**

  SAP Predictive Maintenance and Service continuously monitors the health of your physical assets to predict failures. As discussed in the previous sections, SAP Predictive Maintenance and Service uses statistical methods and machine learning techniques to predict failures before they occur, which means you can can schedule maintenance activity in a cost-effective manner.

- **SAP Leonardo IoT**

  SAP Leonardo IoT connects moving assets, for example, cars, tractors, forklifts, and earthmovers, and helps in monitoring vehicle conditions remotely at a large scale.

This solution can enable your business to offer usage-based services and pay-as-you-drive contracts. This application enables these capabilities through the integration of telematics, enterprise and customer data, analysis of user behavior, and location-tracking services. With the advancement in telecommunications, near real-time data can be integrated at low cost.

- **SAP 3D Visual Enterprise**

  SAP 3D Visual Enterprise help faster decision-making and improves productivity by combining interactive visualization and factory and process information with business content and context. SAP 3D Visual Enterprise consists of visualization applications called *VE viewers* and supports content generation solutions. The VE viewers provide ways to navigate the SAP data. Users can interact with the VE viewers to perform actions on an object based on alerts. SAP 3D Visual Enterprise includes has the following features:

  - VE viewers: These user-friendly applications allow users to view and interact with the published content.

  - Animated procedures: SAP 3D Visual Enterprise Author is used to create animated procedures, 3D embedded documents, and high-definition images.

  - Visual restructuring of bills of materials (BOM): SAP 3D Visual Enterprise Manufacturing Planner helps users visually interact and change BOMs.

  - Hotspotting: SAP 3D Visual Enterprise Link allows images in multiple formats to be embedded with hotspots of data.

  - SAP 3D Visual Enterprise Generator: Integrated with external data sources, SAP 3D Visual Enterprise Generator combines graphical data with textual information. This information can then be stored in multiple formats, for example, graphics, videos, and documents.

- **Asset Manager**

  Remote asset management, th rough integrating the physical, operational, and external environment into a digital profile is a key business driver for the future. An operator of an asset can achieve high asset efficiency and usage to drive profits. Managing risk and safety are equally important when managing costly and complex assets. By gathering information from sensors embedded in critical components of an asset, a digital profile of the asset can be created. The analysis of this digital profile can help manage the asset, reduce downtime, and predict potential failures.

10.6   Summary

Smart manufacturing and smart operations provide a myriad of opportunities for a manufacturing organization. These benefits will be felt across the organization, specifically in functional areas immediately connected with manufacturing. Manufacturing operations can be benefit from technologies like additive manufacturing, digital twins, and detailed scheduling. Similarly, warehouse operations can use augmented reality and autonomous robots for material movements. Quality; maintenance; and the environment, health, and safety are other areas that can leverage the power of sensors to get greater benefits.

While looking into the benefits of a smart factory, manufacturers often ask the question, "How and where do I start?" No one answer is sufficient. The smart factory is an ongoing journey, and top management commitment is required to sustain the data needs, and business processes will need to be updated to build an intelligent enterprise. We recommend you first have in place a digital core that can provide end-to-end data access, which then can be followed by initial, limited, focused manufacturing automation projects, thus allowing you to harness value along the way while strategically building a roadmap to automation to address your business objectives. You'll need to focus in the areas of data management, technology selection, process governance, talent acquisition, and cybersecurity to successfully implement the smart factory and to reap its benefits.

Chapter 11
Transportation and Warehousing

Transportation and warehouse logistics play a fundamental role in an enterprise's digital transformation. With industries being redefined and new enterprises arising, transportation and warehouse logistics will be a major component in improving operational efficiencies and customer service experiences.

In the future, logistics services and network-based business will become more important and govern a larger market than selling assets in areas like the automotive industry. Some enterprises are already identifying and resolving various logistics challenges in the areas of transportation and warehouse storage. Technology to increase visibility into a fleet can improve fleet utilization by optimizing driver behavior to reduce fuel spend as part of fleet utilization reporting in SAP S/4HANA Finance. In asset management reporting, asset spend can be reduced, and fleet routes optimized, to improve supply chain operation efficiency. Efficiently using fleet assets reduces costs, reduces your carbon footprint, and can result in concrete improvements across the board for your business.

SAP Leonardo provides several features for responding to these challenges and improving transportation and warehouse operations, from connecting assets like road and warehouse fleets, to providing fleet insights, increasing fleet utilization, to optimizing planning processes to improve execution and to repurpose waste to do more with less. Asset insights can also be used to improve strategic decision-making, for example, for right-sizing a fleet and for brand cost-benefit comparisons.

SAP Leonardo enables you to reimagine your transportation and warehousing processes with new priorities in mind, such as harnessing multimodal logistics to meet the needs of omnichannel businesses, increasing the efficiency of your supply chain by optimizing spend, integrating networks more completely, and establishing transparent processes. As shown in Figure 11.1, SAP Leonardo can enhance SAP's digital logistics software portfolio, which includes functional and integrated solutions such as SAP Extended Warehouse Management, SAP Yard Logistics, SAP Transportation

Management, and SAP Global Track and Trace. SAP Leonardo also offers network-based solutions like the SAP Logistics Business Network and the SAP Leonardo Internet of Things (SAP Leonardo IoT) connected fleet solution.

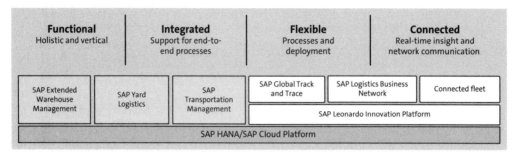

Figure 11.1 Digital Logistics and End-to-End Transformation

In this chapter, you'll learn how to leverage SAP Leonardo to digitally transform your transportation and warehousing processes. You'll learn how transportation and warehouse logistics processes are traditionally managed, how these processes can be digitized and transformed, and how SAP Leonardo, in conjunction with traditional SAP products, is changing transportation and warehousing processes.

Let's begin with transportation logistics.

11.1   Transportation Logistics

In this section, you'll learn how you can use SAP Leonardo to manage and optimize your transportation processes. We'll discuss the digitization of inbound and outbound processes, look at how SAP Transportation Management in SAP S/4HANA ties in with SAP Leonardo, and look at specific SAP Leonardo technologies that enable transformation.

> **Note**
>
> We'll refer to SAP Transportation Management in SAP S/4HANA (both the embedded and standalone versions) as SAP Transportation Management throughout this chapter.

However, before we dive into how SAP Leonardo can be incorporated into your system to transform your transportation processes, let's take a step back and discuss how transportation is managed traditionally and how processes must evolve to keep up in a digital world.

11.1.1   Digitalizing Transportation with Dynamic Planning

At a surface level, transportation is about the movement of goods and people, but this definition belies the complexity of transportation processes and the important role they play in logistics operations. Having the right assets in the right place at the right time is the basic economics of supply chain planning and execution. Good transportation management not just benefits the bottom line in terms of cost reduction or increased efficiency in the use of assets but also effects the customer experience. From an asset point of view, transportation planning can enhance total cost of ownership (TCO), smaller footprint and higher asset utilization, lower total miles, and reduce fuel costs. Reliable transportation and delivery form the bedrock of the supply chain. Any hitch in the process can result in business-damaging delays and significant costs.

Traditionally, supply chain planning and transportation planning relied on historic trends. How many orders are usually placed? How many moving assets are typically available at a certain distribution center? Master routes are created for frequent, repeatable orders, based on seasonal and periodic demand. These routes are known as *static route plans*. But this type of planning means that any change in order timing or fleet availability is unforeseen, unplanned for, and difficult to accommodate. This problem can be avoided by implementing *dynamic route planning*.

Dynamic route planning uses historical patterns to make planning decisions but also includes *replanning* during execution to assign new logistics orders to incoming fleet resources with open capacity. Empty truck loads or space that opens up as deliveries are completed is traditionally considered wasted space, but making use of this space can greatly increase efficiency. Pilot projects have achieved efficiency optimization improvements of up to 35% and operational cost reduction of up to 40%.

How does dynamic route planning work? Rather than just creating static route plans through traditional batch optimization techniques, you can connect the position of a *connected fleet* by training and optimizing the planning system. By including a *dynamic planning algorithm* to accommodate change up to the time the truck is loaded, even when in route, you'll be able to adjust to almost any variability, taking into consideration current conditions using last-minute planning changes. Adjustments can be made to find the best possible resource for execution by adding an or-

11

der or deleting an order from an existing plan. The routing plan can also evaluate the most cost-effective approach, either increasing customer experience or adhering to the service level agreement windows to deliver orders on-time by resequencing stops along the route. Further improvements can be achieved by incorporating customers' best time to receive orders, which is determined by a historical analysis of idle times, for example, waiting for access to the loading dock, or when implementing customer-specific delivery windows. A grade system may also be used to adjust delivery service, giving preference to premium deliveries and more flexible deliveries for discounted transport orders. External data such as weather data, incidents and temporary road closures, and traffic data can be used to improve the performance of dynamic routing further.

In addition, you can also change the way the way logistics billing is performed, such as adopting a *usage-based billing* model. Usage-based billing is used by logistics companies to charge customers for the exact distance traveled and time taken to deliver instead of a flat rate. Internally, cost center billing can also be used to account for exact usage of fleets within an organization.

Let's briefly consider what dynamic route planning looks like in action, in comparison to static route planning.

With static planning, the system determines a route plan based on normal travel times and demand data available on hand at the beginning of the day. The system may spend a substantial amount of time determining a route plan that takes into account all known factors—but it can only base planning on data that currently exists. Unforeseen events will deteriorate the effectiveness of these predefined and static routing decisions. Unforeseen events create a dynamically changing problem state and may include traffic conditions, vehicle-related incidents (like breakdowns), and market-triggered events (such as changing customer orders or delivery times).

On the other hand, with dynamic planning, dynamic data arrives throughout the day. This data includes information, such as changing traffic conditions captured by GPS, which results in changes in the travel time and thus the delivery times for new customer orders. The system will use this new information to update and reoptimize the route plan. When a new customer order arrives, the system will also attempt to update the route plan immediately to determine if the order should be accepted; if no feasible route plan can be identified, the order will be rejected. Once the new customer order is accepted, the system will reoptimize the route plan. This kind of reoptimization is performed quickly with minimal computational time—in about 30 seconds. Since, when a new customer order arrives, a "near real-time" response is particularly desirable, you should develop an efficient procedure for the reoptimization.

As you can see, transportation processes can be greatly improved using the overarching concept of dynamic planning. In reality, this concept is applied differently depending on the industry, conditions, or supply chain strategy, and research has been limited to laboratory conditions with small sample sizes. However, SAP provides a toolset for different techniques and algorithms in SAP Leonardo that help move this capability from a theoretical exercise into a practical, enterprise-ready solution. One way SAP Leonardo does apply dynamic planning in the real world is by enabling Logistics 4.0 and connected fleet functionality. Let's look at these concepts more closely in the next section.

11.1.2 Logistics 4.0 and the Connected Fleet

Logistics 4.0 encompasses all emerging logistics paradigms and is defined by the use of Internet of Things (IoT) technology to connect logistics systems. Logistics 4.0 emphasizes a value chain that showcases the enterprise use of IoT. SAP Leonardo enables Logistics 4.0 through the following functionalities:

- **Connected fleet**
  SAP Leonardo enables you to combine telematics data from several connectivity providers or vehicle original equipment manufacturers (OEMs). SAP Leonardo also includes the harmonization of data from different connectivity technologies such as radio frequency identification (RFID), ultra-wide band RFID, and Bluetooth Low Energy real-time locating service. In addition, you can extend supply chain visibility beyond our own fleet with third-party logistics (3PL) order tracking integration. Connected fleet functionality is the cornerstone of transportation digitization.

- **Informed insights**
  SAP Leonardo provides the ability to monitor and derive new insights such as utilization and efficiency across an entire fleet while extending end-to-end supply network track and trace capabilities.

- **Process automation**
  This functionality allows you to create new processes such as customer order and parcel tracking, utilized billing, predictive maintenance, or the repurposing of underutilized assets.

- **Optimized planning**
  This functionality is the ability to improve the way you perform planning, through the use of dynamic planning (as discussed in Section 11.1.1).

- **Alert and react**
  SAP Leonardo helps improve operations by intervening to improve or prevent bottleneck inefficiencies, a great example of how IoT can change outcomes, not just provide insights.

Let's discuss the connected fleet in more detail. Fleet management generates a wealth of data that you can use to improve and transform your transportation processes. SAP Leonardo collect, map, store, and analyze telematics and sensor data from vehicles and similar assets. This increased transparency results in better utilization of moving assets and can even reduce emissions by optimizing routes and processes. Over time, these enhancements can enhance customer satisfaction and create new opportunities. This application of IoT is what we'll refer to as the *connected fleet*.

A connected fleet is not a single product but rather the synergies achieved through the combination of IoT, supply chain processes, and enterprise resource management products. A connected fleet enables businesses and public service organizations that own fleets of moving assets like vehicles, robots, and forklifts to collect live telemetry and sensor data and integrate them with core business processes to improve services, planning, execution, and safety for operators. At the same time, a connected fleet provides visibility to the end-to-end logistics and improves customer service.

As a result, you can create new business models and opportunities to reduce costs, improve efficiency, and create opportunities. In addition, a connected fleet allows your organization to be more compliant and provide better working conditions with safety analysis of drivers and assets to reduce accidents and provide feedback to multiple stakeholders, such as facility management, human resources, warehouse planning, or research and development. End-to-end logistics visibility can be improved with electronic logging device (ELD) compliance, safety records, procurement analysis of vehicle conditions, environmental impacts, and "people safety" by monitoring driver's biophysical health and driving behavior.

Connected fleets have implications for many organizations. Moving assets are also part of manufacturing, and manufacturers can use connected fleets to gain new visibility into their supply chains, lowering transportation costs and improving their throughput and fleet efficiency. Distribution, especially last-mile distribution, uses the supply chain to compete by providing a better experience to customers therefore competing on customer service through on-time and dynamic delivery.

Logistics providers can also compete by providing better and more effective services to their customers (B2B), which in turn rely on their service providers to execute more effectively. Doing more with less by being more efficient increases profitability, reduces unused capacity, and improves the customer service experience. Even heavy-equipment operators such as in mining and cement companies can manage trucks, loaders, mixers, and other expensive equipment in remote locations better through better planning.

Figure 11.2 shows the capabilities that SAP Leonardo's connected fleet portfolio provides as an innovation platform. These building blocks include vehicle analytics, e-mobility, a shared-based economy, and platform technology.

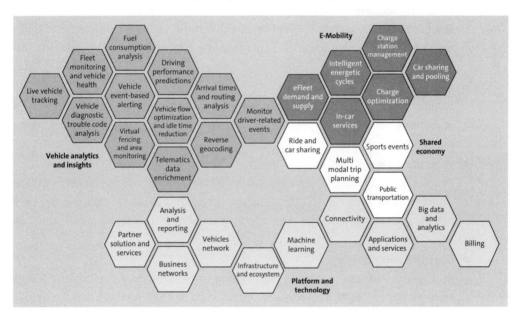

Figure 11.2 SAP Connected Fleet: Capabilities View

SAP Leonardo's connected fleet functionality enables the following:

- **Vehicle diagnostics**
  Provides the ability to analyze vehicle performance through live data and manages driver efficiency accordingly.

327

- **Fleet economics**
  Provides the ability to make vehicle economy decisions, such as fleet sizing based on utilization and efficiency metrics in SAP S/4HANA, and the integration of fleet planning with functionalities like asset management and finance.

- **Driver behavior**
  Provides valuable insights into reckless driving, braking, and speeding behaviors that may generate unnecessary wear and tear and result in higher fuel costs.

- **Vehicle maintenance**
  Enables the analysis and prioritization of fleet trouble code analysis among critical maintenance orders. Helps identify noncritical errors and integrate these errors into existing maintenance schedules. Includes vehicle event-based alerting and SAP S/4HANA line of business (LOB) integration.

- **Predictive analytics**
  Enables predictive capabilities to prevent downtime. Helps provide better maintenance for fleets with a lower TCO, maximizing vehicle uptime and reducing impact on profit and loss.

- **Logistics optimization**
  Enables the optimization of fleet usage to ensure higher uptime through improved scheduling and dynamic planning. Reduces waste by using resource-sharing opportunities.

- **Logistics safety**
  Enables organizations to improve safety of assets and goods in transit as well as improve workforce safety. Using historical trip and accident data can improve planning, operator behavior, and operator assistance in cases of predictable risk situations.

- **Logistics compliance**
  Provides the ability to comply with requirements for operator/driver ELDs or transportation logistics for sensitive goods such as food, medical, and dangerous goods.

- **Logistics networks**
  Allows organizations to optimize supply chain logistics from a planning, execution, and visibility perspective. In this case, insight into inbound logistics, intralogistics, and outbound logistics (as well as the extended supply chain) provides valuable insights to streamline operations and increase end-to-end supply chain network visibility.

- **Virtual fencing and location monitoring**
  Enables vehicle management to reduce inefficiencies from an execution point-of-view by reducing idle time and better predict estimated time of arrival (ETA). This capability also enables some housekeeping improvements such as reporting for compliance and tax credits.

- **Telematics data enrichment**
  Enables the monitoring of driver-related events. For example, insurance companies can determine areas with higher accident rates in certain conditions, such as foggy and rainy weather.

Later, we'll look at how SAP Leonardo and its connected fleet functionality can be used to optimize processes, coordinate, and manage your fleet to improve transportation logistics operations. First, we'll look at inbound and outbound transportation, as shown in Figure 11.3.

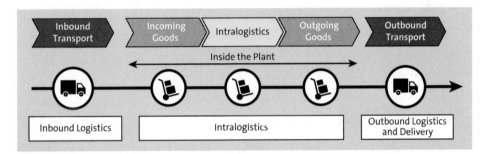

Figure 11.3 Inbound and Outbound Transportation

11.1.3   Inbound Transportation

Inbound transportation is the movement of goods and assets into a business. The SAP Leonardo IoT connected fleet can be used to detect incoming vehicles within a certain distance or time from loading dock. Using telematics and SAP Leonardo IoT geolocation services, ETAs can be calculated, which allows for several process improvements, including the following:

- Transparency about incoming trucks
- Real-time determination of deviations in the logistics chain
- Insights about the impact of certain delays and issues
- Transparency about the current situation in the yard

This type of monitoring increases the speed and efficiency of truck dispatch, increases the volume of truck traffic within a given infrastructure, and reduces failures and delays while also enabling faster replanning for dynamic route planning processes.

11.1.4   Outbound Transportation

Outbound transportation is the movement of goods and assets from a business and includes the execution of ordering, loading of goods, and delivery processes. Distribution can be optimized by combining live vehicle data (like speed or mileage) and machine data (like temperature or cooling) with business data (from SAP S/4HANA) and relevant external information (such as weather or traffic). The SAP Leonardo IoT connected fleet enables condition monitoring and enhances planning, routing, and scheduling of multidrop shipment deliveries. Other improvements include the following:

- Increase inventory accuracy and availability
- Reduce shipping and billing errors
- Raise customer service levels through high efficiency and accuracy
- Shorten order turnaround times
- Provide value-added services quickly
- Take advantage of cross-docking opportunities

With an SAP Leonardo IoT connected fleet, you can determine and track the status of your moving assets and obtain information about fleet health, asset location, and what the assets are carrying. You can track performance and get deeper insights into your moving assets such as utilization, driving behavior, and operational costs. Position-based capabilities include driven routes, location analytics and maps, and driver support. Capabilities to improve maintenance include issue detection, service prediction, and process automation.

11.1.5   SAP Leonardo Integration with SAP S/4HANA

An SAP Leonardo IoT connected fleet can also be integrated with SAP supply chain solutions like SAP Extended Warehouse Management and SAP Transportation Management to further optimize operations.

SAP Leonardo IoT connected fleet is integrated with SAP S/4HANA and includes multiple process optimization and automation opportunities, such as the following:

- **SAP S/4HANA Finance**
  Key performance indicators (KPIs) combining finance and telematics movement data to obtain transparency into operational costs, asset comparisons, and investment decision-making. For example, data can be used to deduce the total cost of ownership of two brands of tires.

- **SAP S/4HANA Supply Chain**
  Integration of real-time updates about fleet location and transport quality to detect execution challenges. For example, you can communicate a two-hour delay across the supply chain.

- **SAP S/4HANA Manufacturing**
  Optimize and automate intralogistics and manufacturing processes by tracking fleet. Benefits include the reduction of cycle times for production and the reduction of safety issues on the shop floor.

- **SAP S/4HANA Asset Management**
  Maintain the value of any moving asset by including real-time data about position, performance, and usage and asset health. Real-time data can reduce the time needed to detect and resolve a service and can improve asset value.

11.1.6   SAP Transportation Management

Managing the movement of goods can be a costly exercise, which is why innovation in the area of transportation management often focuses on cost-cutting measures that can improve service, efficiency, and sustainability. SAP Transportation Management supports the optimization of asset utilization, freight consolidation, and routing processes to decrease operational costs. This solution also enables transparency, data-driven decision-making, and streamlining to develop a holistic, multimode management setup. Integrating SAP Leonardo with SAP Transportation Management enables real-time fleet monitoring and improves logistics planning using asset tracking data. In addition, planning can move from static to dynamic planning based on current capacity and resource allocation. The Transportation Cockpit, shown in Figure 11.4, illustrates how static planning can be used as the starting point for dynamic planning.

Figure 11.4 SAP Transportation Management Cockpit

SAP Transportation Management is now integrated and embedded as part of SAP S/4HANA and powered by SAP Leonardo. Its components include the following:

- **Strategic freight management**
  Includes strategic freight procurement, strategic freight sales, contract negotiation, ocean and air scheduling and capacity management, carrier booking, and Descartes integration.

- **Order management**
  Includes integrated transportation demand, personal worklists, sales and stock transfer order scheduling, schedule management, order lifecycle management and visibility.

- **Transportation planning**
  Includes manual and automated planning and dispatching, selection of routing, resources, and carriers, order tendering, dangerous goods management, and parcel planning.

- **Transportation execution**
  Includes extended warehouse integration for execution, logistics execution, execution monitoring and event tracking, capacity monitoring, transportation print documents, and trade regulation compliance using SAP Global Trade Services.

- **Freight costing and settlement**
  Includes freight agreement management, charge and tariff management, and transportation charge calculation.
- **Analytics and reporting**
  Includes dashboards for SAP HANA, landed cost analysis, flexible business warehouse cost reporting, and a collaboration portal to enable collaborative business processes between logistics partners.

The digitization of supply chain operations for transportation includes processes such as freight management that provide the basis for innovation. Since our focus is on the transition from static planning to dynamic planning, let's take a deeper look at three SAP Transportation Management processes that employ static planning: freight management, package building, and load planning.

Freight Management

Freight management in SAP S/4HANA includes two areas as part of static planning operations:

- Strategic freight procurement consists of a group of shippers or logistics service providers (LSPs). This functionality is used by shippers to submit a freight agreement request for quotations (RFQ) to carriers or LSPs, in order to create or renew a freight agreement for a mode of transport or trade lane. The carriers or LSPs will reply to the RFQ, while a shipper decides with whom to create a new or renew a freight agreement.
- Strategic freight selling consist of carriers and LSPs. The shipper sends an RFQ, which links back to the shipper's strategic facility planning (SFP) process, or a carrier/LSP sends a quotation to a shipper in order to create/renew a forwarding agreement for a certain service offering. The shipper will respond to the quotation while a forwarding agreement is created.

Freight planning consist of transport tendering with the most optimal plan, resource scheduling, and utilization in mind. Often fleets consist of a combination of a mix of owned and contracted fleet vehicles.

Package Building

The aim of package building is to optimize the number of pallets that can fit onto a payload, which can increase fleet utilization and reduce the number of resources used, while cutting costs and carbon dioxide emissions. The same process is performed for mixed package building with multiple drops and customer orders. In addition to the traditional package building processes, a planner also must consider stackability, incompatibility, height, volume, weight constraints, and orientation constraints on the products. Figure 11.5 shows an example of package building functionality that forms part of the basis of static planning.

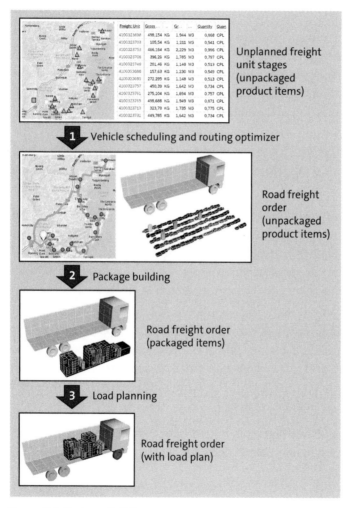

Figure 11.5 Package Building

Load Planning

Load planning consists of businesses processes that enable the optimal use of loading space and fleet resources. The optimizer locates the best position for each payload package or pallet on a resource. The optimizer considers multiple constraints such as fleet attributes, dimensions, stacking rules, loading sequence, and a flexible split deck (a trailer with two separate floors is referred to as a split deck). Load planning and consolidation use a visual interface, shown in Figure 11.6, which shows an example of load planning functionality, again a core component of static planning.

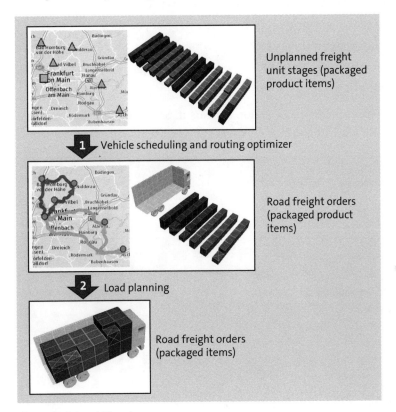

Figure 11.6 Load Planning

11.1.7 SAP Leonardo for Transportation

In the following sections, we'll discuss how SAP Leonardo can improve transportation operations, including load planning, local delivery, global delivery, and multi-drop delivery.

Load Planning

SAP Transportation Management can execute load planning using virtual reality by leveraging SAP Leonardo virtual reality (VR) technologies. The planning workbench allows you to simulate load optimization processes using VR visualization. SAP Leonardo VR technology can help you improve the quality of static planning practices by providing higher-quality visual simulations for load planning.

VR technology can provide the following benefits for load planning:

- 3D representation of main component of the functionality.
- Manual adjustment of optimizer results is currently not possible.
- Object manipulation is intuitive in VR
- Application extends an existing SAP Transportation Management process for load planning benefits from 3D environment in VR.

Figure 11.7 shows how the VR visualization appears in SAP Transportation Management's load planning functionality.

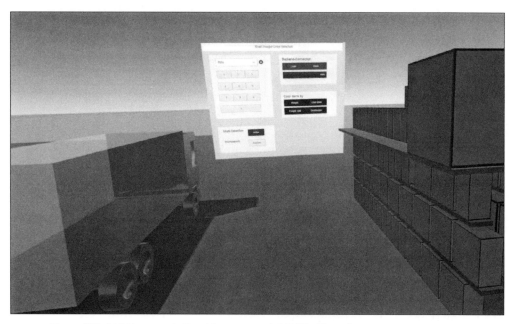

Figure 11.7 SAP Transportation Management: VR Workbench

Local Delivery

In terms of road logistics, you can now integrate tracking data such as arrival times, departure times, events, and position status to improve planning operations. By combining SAP Transportation Management with SAP Leonardo, you can improve planning operations by moving from static planning to dynamic planning. A generic dynamic planning algorithm can be customized to fit each unique use case. In the architecture shown in Figure 11.8, we'll focus more on local delivery using a single mode of transportation like truck deliveries. In this case, we'll start with static planning in SAP Transportation Management and optimize the original plan during execution using dynamic routing principles based on an algorithm that considers current conditions and prioritizes current orders an a connected fleet. For example, if capacity opens up during a trip and a return order or pickup is scheduled close to the vehicle's current location, a static plan can be updated through dynamic rerouting capabilities. The optimizer is continuously triggered based on certain activities like new orders or requests, current conditions, and environmental conditions.

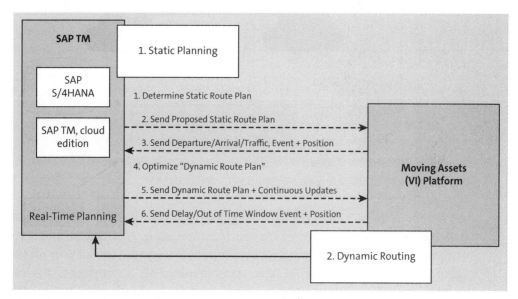

Figure 11.8 SAP Solution IoT for Road Logistics: Local Delivery

Global Delivery

In terms of global logistics, you can now integrate tracking data such as arrival times, departure times, events, and position status from your own fleet operations as well as your extended supply chain, such as 3PLs, to improve planning operations. By combining SAP Transportation Management with SAP Leonardo IoT and SAP Global Track and Trace, you can now improve planning operations from static planning to dynamic planning. In the architecture diagram shown in Figure 11.9, global delivery requires a more sophisticated supply chain network that might contain multiple modes of transportation across global borders. Often, documentation beyond driver job cards will be required, and you may need to track and trace shipments across multiple fleets, whether your own vehicles or as shared information from 3PL carrier systems. Also, customs and clearance documentation add additional complexity and risk, which are covered by the capabilities found in SAP Global Track and Trace.

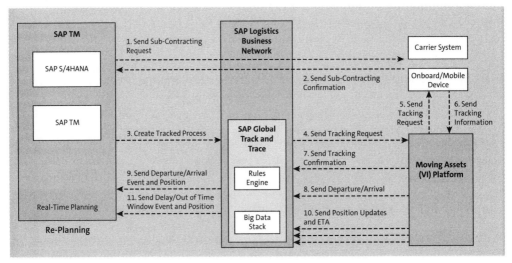

Figure 11.9 SAP Solution IoT for Road Logistics (Global Delivery)

An SAP Leonardo IoT connected fleet, integrated with SAP S/4HANA order data and SAP Transportation Management transportation planning, provides the ability to track orders using your own managed fleet. In addition, you can extend your supply chain visibility by integrating 3PL order tracking using SAP Global Track and Trace. Combining all this together allows you to track end-to-end logistics operations for multimode global deliveries across the entire supply network. As shown in Figure 11.10, combining and tracking the entire supply network provides you the ability of real-time (or near real-time) order tracking and insights into conditions along the way such as temperature. You can easily detect which step in a shipment is delayed and see the reason for the delay, which allows you to react appropriately.

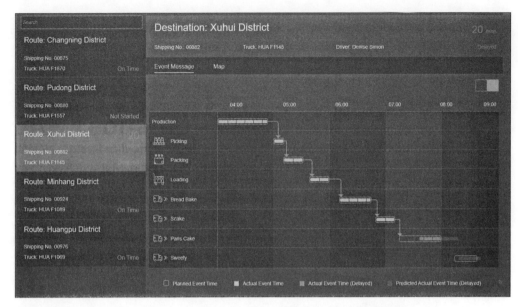

Figure 11.10 SAP IoT for Logistics: Dynamic Routing with Global Track and Trace

Multidrop Delivery

With dynamic routing, you can continuously optimize planning during execution and repurpose open capacity to meet real-time changes in demand. This concept is often referred to as "Uber for Logistics." As shown in Figure 11.11, fleet efficiency can be improved by more than 40% by adding new orders in close proximity as capacity or space opens up from completed deliveries.

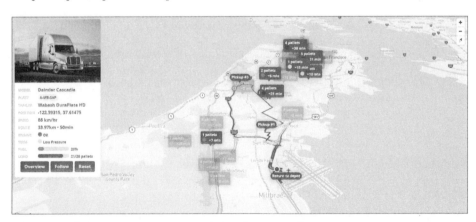

Figure 11.11 Fleet Management: Dynamic Routing Execution

Also, additional pickups such as returns can be scheduled, which often involved out-sourced operations previously. Therefore, both costs are reduced and efficiency increased while increasing customer service levels.

Figure 11.12 List Report for Fleet Tracking

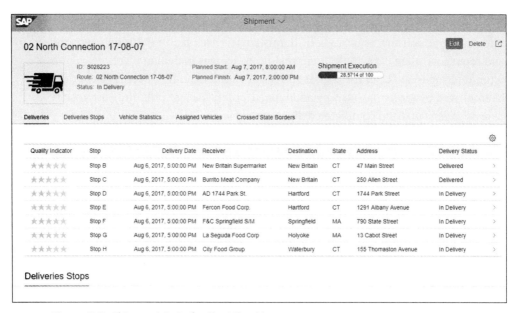

Figure 11.13 Shipment Data for Fleet Tracking

Figure 11.12 and Figure 11.13 show IoT fleet tracking data combined with enterprise order data either from an SAP S/4HANA (or SAP ERP) system or from order planning data from SAP Transportation Management, which enables real-time fleet operation monitoring and order tracking. For example, as shown in Figure 11.13, you can view the shipment monitor of a truck in real time and track orders in sequence by delivery status (delivered, currently in delivery, and planned).

Figure 11.14 shows route optimization capabilities, either to improve a continuous delivery run or a multidrop dynamic route, which are continuously updated with events such as traffic changes, customer preferences, or new orders within close proximity.

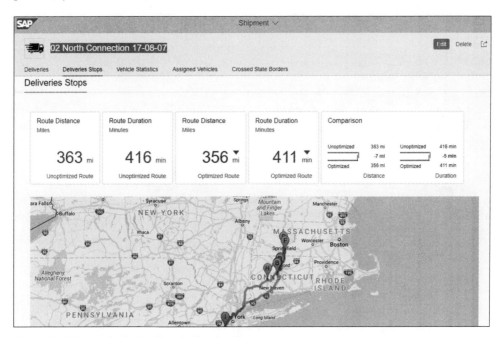

Figure 11.14 Route Optimization: Deliveries Stops

Figure 11.15, Figure 11.16, and Figure 11.17 show event management capabilities using trailer temperature sensors to track temperature for compliance and manage a cold supply chain. In this case, a threshold has been set by which you can track orders with a temperature log. The fleet manager and operations can also receive alerts when a certain lower or upper threshold is exceeded, which might be caused by a failing cooler unit or a cooler door not properly closed.

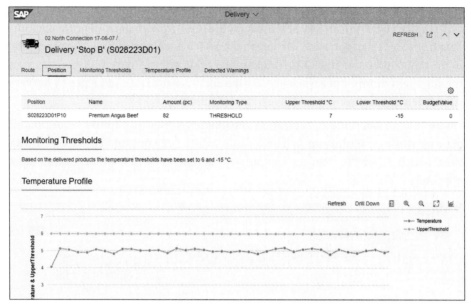

Figure 11.15 Temperature Monitoring for Deliveries

Figure 11.16 Vehicle Statistics for Shipment

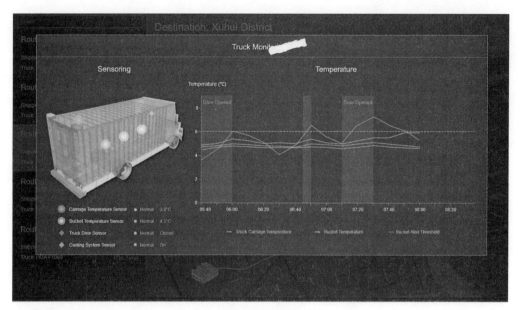

Figure 11.17 SAP IoT for Logistics: Fleet and Trailer Insights

11.2   Intralogistics

Intralogistics is the management of operations and material flows in a warehouse, including the interior of the warehouse and the exterior yard. Process improvements in this area are related to the seamless handover of goods from incoming trucks, the operation of moving assets like forklifts, and the flow of goods throughout the warehouse.

In this section. we'll discuss how SAP Leonardo can be used to manage and optimize warehouse and yard operations. We'll first explore how yard and warehouse processes are being digitized using dynamic planning. Then, we'll look at how SAP Leonardo solutions can be used to enable yard and warehouse logistics transformation.

11.2.1   Digitizing the Yard and Warehouse with Dynamic Planning

Dynamic planning within a warehouse or yard provides the ability to create dynamic routing algorithms to take advantage of just-in-time manufacturing concepts, while using moving asset data from inbound logistics, outbound logistics, and intralogistics as this data is dynamically revealed during operations.

Dynamic routing can be used for safety, rerouting, and flow within a warehouse or yard. The idea is to optimize and speed up supply chain operations while taking all current constraints and priorities into account for optimized paths and execution to both robotic or human-operated forklifts. When current conditions change or problems occur, the tasks priorities, routes, or execution plans are recalculated. Routing simulations can also be used to simulate and compare configuration to the algorithm and can continuously be refined against KPIs as part of system learning.

In this case, several reinforcement learning algorithms available for vehicle routing with stochastic demands within a warehouse or yard.

11.2.2   Inbound and Outbound Processing

Warehouses are core components in a supply chain, and coordinating labor, storage, and fulfillment involves the execution of a variety of complex processes. Digitization of warehouse management aims to ease this complexity, while still delivering value, through a combination of acceleration and automation.

Inbound processing and *outbound processing* are fundamental warehousing processes. During inbound processing, goods and materials are received by the warehouse. Deliveries will be accepted, checked, unloaded, and stored. During outbound processing, goods and materials are sent from the warehouse. Goods will be picked, packed, loaded, and processed. SAP Leonardo enables a number of process enhancements in these areas.

For example, tracking enables a warehouse to know the exact arrival time of each truck, which enables better orchestration of intralogistics operations, such as positioning forklifts at the right time and place on the loading dock. Outgoing goods picking, packaging, and provisioning should occur only when delivery trucks arrive in a given time slot. Other SAP Leonardo intralogistics capabilities include the following:

- **Automatic assignment**
  Orders will be assigned to the operator automatically based on the operator's current position and workload.

- **Failure detection**
  Real-time monitoring allows you to check whether a transport order has executed correctly.

- **Automatic confirmation**
  Based on the exact position and height of the transport bin, the storage location can be determined automatically, and the order confirmed.

Robotic automation using IoT-based robotics systems can be used to make warehouse operations more efficient, with robotic carts to pick products, place products in bins, and deliver bins to workers. Companies such as Amazon are now even using autonomous robots in their warehouses.

Other SAP Leonardo improvements for inbound and outbound processing include the following:

- Optimizing the use of manpower through integration with SAP SuccessFactors and SAP Fieldglass
- Facilitating cross-docking
- Streamlining receiving processes and dock management
- Optimizing inventory placement in the warehouse with flexible putaway strategies
- Improving visibility into inbound inventory

Integrating SAP Leonardo with SAP S/4HANA can also help optimize inbound and outbound processing to accelerate fulfillment. For example, embedded Extended Warehouse Management in SAP S/4HANA, can use data collection devices and material handling equipment to automate processes. SAP Leonardo can feed asset movement and tracking data into logistics warehouse operations. Real-time asset tracking data can be used for the following activities:

- Tracking current order execution in terms of completion, time, and status
- Improving planning operations towards optimized routing
- Improving the ability to generate and explore deeper insights and increasing visibility into bottlenecks, time-of-day traffic analysis, and incident analytics
- Switching from static planning to dynamic planning
- Real-time tracking of inbound and outbound logistics

SAP Leonardo can also be used for simpler tasks in the warehouse, such as building controls and systems monitoring to reduce energy consumption for everything from light fixtures to HVAC units.

> **SAP EWM Integration with SAP TM**
>
> SAP Transportation Management can be integrated with SAP Extended Warehouse Management to seamlessly integrate transportation and warehouse processes for overall process optimization using SAP Leonardo. Integration can involve either an embedded or a decentralized SAP EWM system. Real-time integration results a number of benefits, such as enabling the tight integration of master data and better communications.

11.2.3 SAP Warehouse Insights

In addition to general warehouse automation and process acceleration for SAP EWM, further benefits can be had from greater insights into processes. SAP Warehouse Insights is an advanced planning tool in the cloud for modern warehouses to optimize their operations. With algorithms, SAP Warehouse Insights visualizes warehouse layouts, analyzes operational warehouse KPIs, simulates optimization scenarios, monitors warehouse operations (even in real time), and integrates with SAP Leonardo IoT for dynamic routing as described earlier in Section 11.2.5. The standard processes related to SAP Warehouse Insights in this section still describe static planning optimization using historical warehouse planning operational data.

SAP Warehouse Insights is not a new warehouse management system, so you can't use it to execute warehouse tasks such as picking or putaway. Instead, SAP Warehouse Insights complements the functionality found in SAP Extended Warehouse Management by leveraging cloud computing and scalability.

SAP Warehouse Insights is built and delivered on SAP Cloud Platform (in the Cloud Foundry environment) and enables the following improvements:

- Better view into warehouse layout and travel network design
- Optimized task assignment
- Better usage of warehouse resources

SAP Warehouse Insights can be integrated with SAP Extended Warehouse Management, as shown in Figure 11.18.

In the following sections, we'll discuss SAP Warehouse Insights capabilities in greater detail.

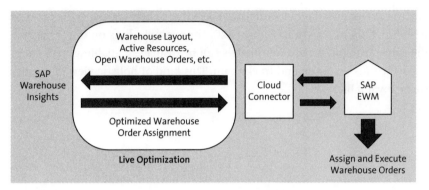

Figure 11.18 SAP Warehouse Insights and SAP Extended Warehouse Management Integration

Interactive Warehouse Layout

Interactive warehouse layout capabilities, shown in Figure 11.19, provide a visualized warehouse layout to check the completeness of warehouse data, like bins and edges, and to correct them in the SAP EWM system if needed. Furthermore, you can use this capability to check the distance between bins and recommend the best paths for traveling between bins.

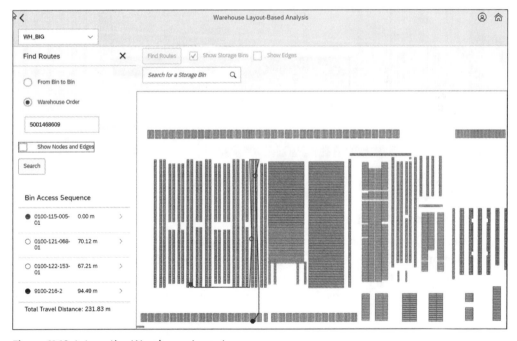

Figure 11.19 Interactive Warehouse Layout

The interactive warehouse layout can also be used to search for a specific bin and view the bin's details, as shown in Figure 11.20. For example, bins on the same rack and in the same aisle but on different levels can be displayed, enabling workers to identify specific bins instantly and track them. This kind of holistic view of a warehouse can be invaluable.

Figure 11.20 Interactive Warehouse Layout: Bin Details

Empty Travel Reduction

Empty travel is the distance that is traveled by a fleet without a load. Empty travel reduction is based on historical data and optimizes the assignment of historical warehouse orders to show how much empty travel can be reduced for resources. Empty travel reduction saves cost by doing more with less but also improving operational efficiency and freeing up capacity to handle more orders. The result of the optimization will meet the latest start date (LSD) of warehouse orders. Path visualizations are created for comparison before and after optimization.

As shown in Figure 11.21, you can track empty travel distance without an order assignment or payload. On the left, you'll see the unoptimized routing with a larger empty distance when compared to the optimized routing with a greater degree of loaded travel distance, therefore representing a higher degree of efficiency. This kind of optimization is only possible by feeding real-time moving asset tracking data through SAP Leonardo IoT. The optimization algorithm improves not just the on-time fulfillment of warehouse tasks, but also the customer service.

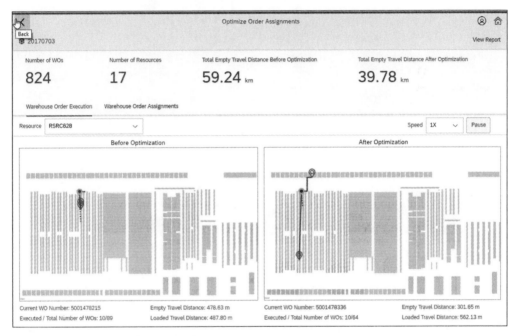

Figure 11.21 Empty Travel Optimization

The summary report shown in Figure 11.22 displays the optimization results, including the optimization gained by reducing by empty travel as a proportion of total travel distance. You'll also see KPIs for travel distance and on-time rates with the ability to drill down to each time interval for details about optimized warehouse orders and resources in that time frame.

Figure 11.22 Empty Travel: Summary Report

Resource Utilization Dashboard

Resource utilization calculates how much of the fleet is being used at any given time. Insight into how much fleet assets are being used can influence multiple process, such as lifecycle management, fleet maintenance, and fleet sizing. The **Daily Dashboard** shown in Figure 11.23 includes daily operational KPIs for resource utilization. The specific utilization KPIs include the following:

- Workload distribution by resource group
- Empty travel distance by resource type
- Total travel distance by resource

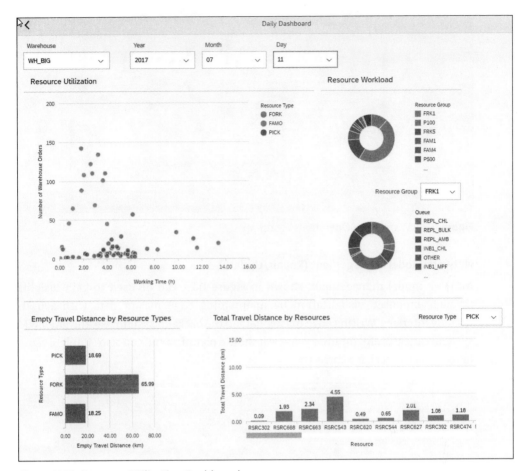

Figure 11.23 Resource Utilization Dashboard

Heat Map for Warehouse Operations

Heat maps can be used for multiple purposes in warehouses, such as mapping warehouse layouts for improved order execution or informing safety analytics, by showing where most incidents or picking failures occur. The heat map, as shown in Figure 11.24, for warehouse operations include the following:

- Activities (warehouse orders) in bins
- Activities (warehouse orders) in aisles/areas
- Basis for warehouse layout and product arrangement review

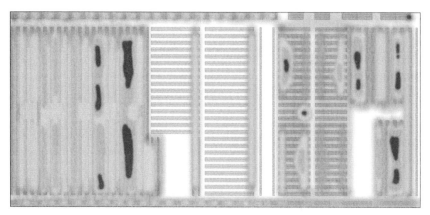

Figure 11.24 Warehouse Operations Heatmap

Network Model Management (Repair/Update)

Network model management, shown in Figure 11.25, can be used to gain insights through enhanced visualization by maintaining edge master data with a user-friendly interface. Writing edge master data to the backend system (e.g. the SAP EWM system) can be useful for improving warehouse planning and can also simulate warehouse data to check for correctness.

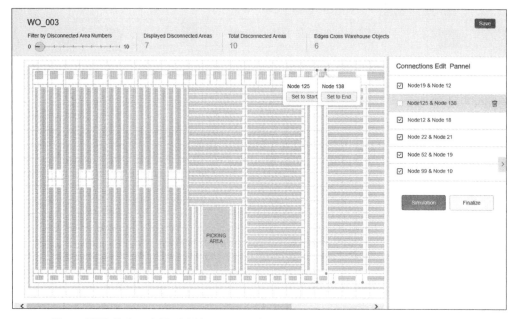

Figure 11.25 Network Model Management

Live Optimization

Live optimization, shown in Figure 11.26, includes the optimization of open ware-house orders. This capability allows you to monitor real-time results of the optimization, including working resources management, travel path visualization, status warning, and replay of historical warehouse operations.

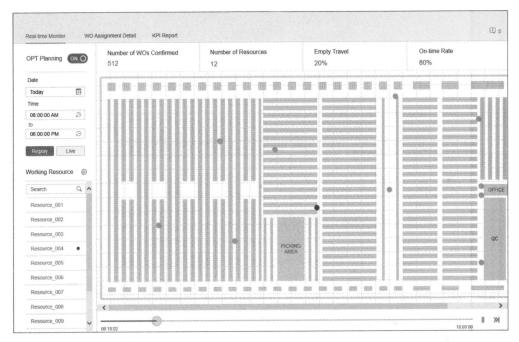

Figure 11.26 Live Optimization

11.2.4 Yard and Hub Logistics

Yard processes encompass all activities that must occur between goods leaving the warehouse and reaching the mode of transportation. The planning and execution of these processes ensures that goods reach the right place at the right time. SAP Yard Logistics helps transform traditional yard processes through backend SAP S/4HANA integration to abstract order data, enhanced data capture for routing and monitoring of transport units, and mobile support. Yard routing is optimized by synchronizing inbound/outbound transport and warehouse execution. Yard and hub logistics are improved by SAP Leonardo, which provides asset tracking and multimode visibility between inbound and outbound processes and intralogistics optimization within a yard. Figure 11.27 shows a yard task for transportation from one gate to another.

Figure 11.27 Yard Task List

11.2.5   SAP Leonardo for Intralogistics

Now that you've learned how intralogistics processes can be digitized with SAP Leonardo, in conjunction with SAP S/4HANA, let's see SAP Leonardo in action.

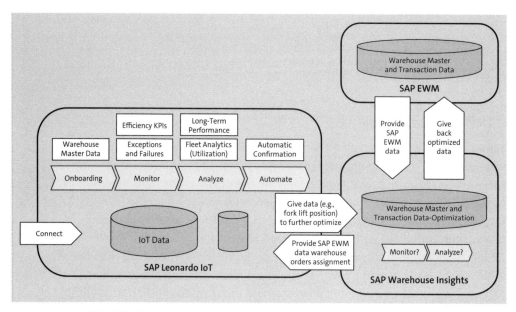

Figure 11.28 SAP Solution IoT for Intralogistics

Figure 11.28 shows how SAP Leonardo IoT, SAP Extended Warehouse Management, and SAP Warehouse Insights work together to enhance and optimize warehouse and yard processes.

In the following sections, we'll explore the improvements SAP Leonardo can make to warehouse and yard processes in three areas: moving assets, warehouses, and autonomous assets.

Moving Assets

Tracking moving assets within a warehouse or yard provides opportunities for increasing visibility, not just in terms of the physical flow of assets but also in terms of operational costs. Let's look at one example of monitoring moving assets. The Forklift Analytics application is created as an extension via SAPUI5 or by using SAP Analytics Cloud running on top of SAP Leonardo IoT. The application provides detailed information about each forklift's live location, battery performance, cost efficiency, and safety. As shown in Figure 11.29, the **Live Warehouse Monitor** tab of the application contains real-time operational KPIs such as operational costs (such as cost per hour/cost per distance) while efficiency KPIs monitor how long forklifts need to execute orders as well as the number of picking failures. In addition, this application also shows when assets are used efficiently (colored green) or not (colored red). Efficiency is calculated by monitoring asset batteries.

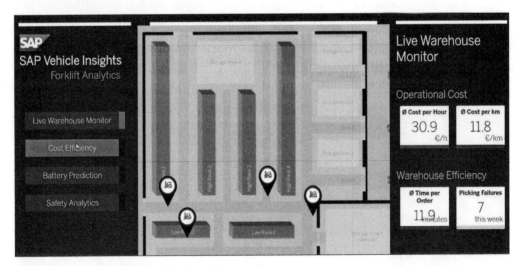

Figure 11.29 Live Warehouse Monitor: KPIs

Warehouse operational efficiency often depends not just on the assets in operation but also the planning and execution. As shown in Figure 11.30, cost efficiency is calculated based on utilization and orders completed and then compared to a cost breakdown structure, for example, capital investment versus running costs.

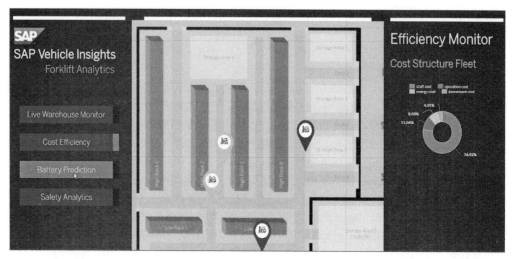

Figure 11.30 Efficiency Monitor: Cost Structure

Another efficiency KPI is battery prediction and charge management, thus ensuring the right assets, in terms of battery and energy efficiency, are used for the correct tasks.

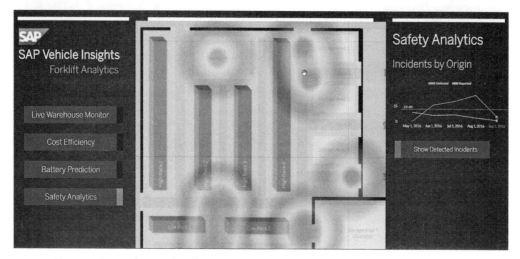

Figure 11.31 Incident and Collision Hotspots

Warehouse and manufacturing safety analytics should provide the ability to play back incidents and near misses to investigate cases but also, over time, reveal vulnerabilities in warehouse design with the help of sensors. An updated design can streamline the physical flow of assets with safety in mind. Through heat maps, like the one shown in Figure 11.31, you can view incident and collision hotspots, which can improve warehouse layout improvements or enforce restrictions such as maximum speeds.

Warehouse Optimizing

Warehouse asset tracking starts with visibility. Tracking moving assets beyond telematics is now an opportunity to further optimize supply chain planning. At a large retailer in Europe, forklifts and robotics were tracked in terms of distance driven with a load versus with empty loads, as shown in Figure 11.32.

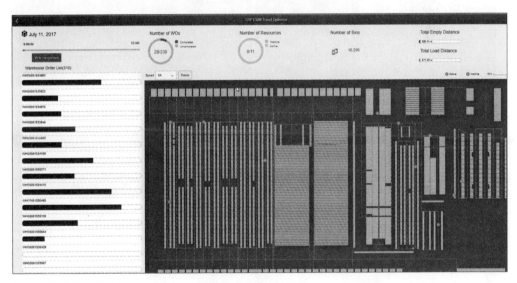

Figure 11.32 Load Distance versus Empty Distance

By tracking their fleet, they could track the performance of the execution plan and strategy and measure this performance against new KPIs, such as **Total Empty Distance** representing waste, as shown in Figure 11.33.

The optimizer could apply machine learning to detect patterns and use dynamic routing principles to improve from static to dynamic plans based on current conditions to optimize the routes within the warehouse. Think of this capability as Uber

Pool; as trucks approach, orders associated with these inbound fleets are prioritized based on estimated time of arrival, and picking routes are updated to execute these orders first. Figure 11.34 shows an **Order list (As-Is)** delivered via static planning (planning in SAP EWM) and an **Order List (Suggested)** after optimization.

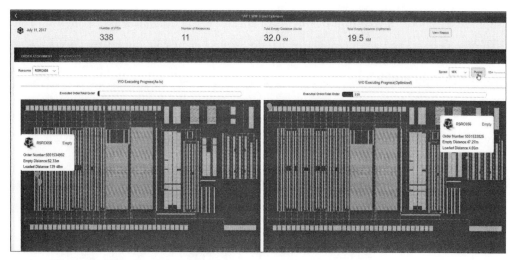

Figure 11.33 Total Empty Distance

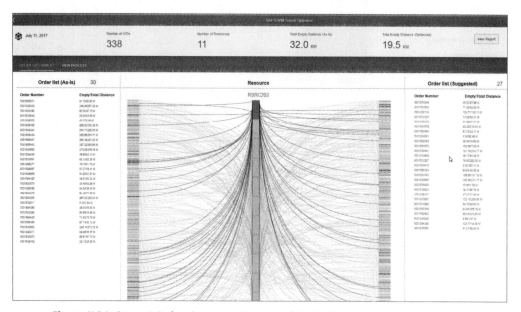

Figure 11.34 Current Order List versus Suggested Order List

As a result of these changes, as shown in Figure 11.35, the retailer warehouse operations saw improvements, specifically a reduction in execution time, empty travel time, and total delay time. The end-to-end supply chain handover time between intralogistics and outbound logistics was reduced, and improved route planning minimized the distance traveled with empty payloads.

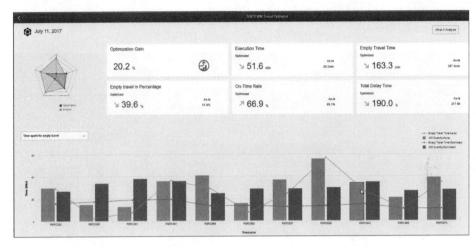

Figure 11.35 KPIs for Optimized Process

Finally, machine learning was applied to continuously look for opportunities for improvement. As shown in Figure 11.36 a simulator running on historical tracking data was used to simulate different supply chain plans and strategies.

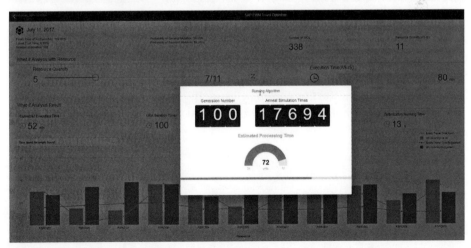

Figure 11.36 Simulating Supply Chain Strategies

Autonomous Assets

Autonomous vehicles will lead to significant operating cost reduction in transportation and product handling and at the same time benefit lead times and lower environmental costs. Self-guided vehicles are already being used in warehouse environments, and we can expect their use to increase. Figure 11.37 shows how SAP Analytics Cloud, as a part of SAP Leonardo, can be used to create a warehouse tracking monitor for autonomous fleets.

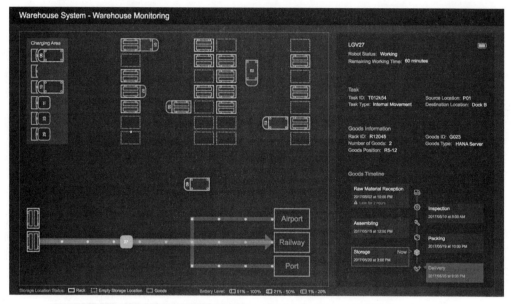

Figure 11.37 Warehouse Tracking Monitor

Charge management, condition monitoring, event tracking, and execution performance all come together in a single operational dashboard, as shown in Figure 11.38.

Key performance indicators, as shown in Figure 11.39, can be used to train the execution plan for autonomous assets acting as coherent fleet.

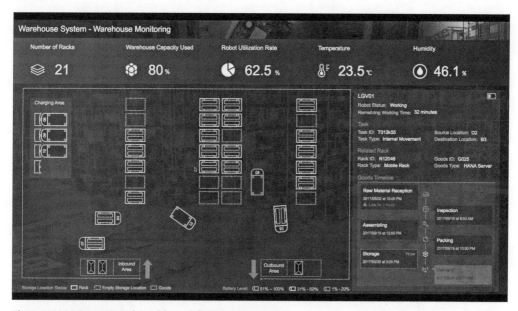

Figure 11.38 Operational Dashboard for Warehousing

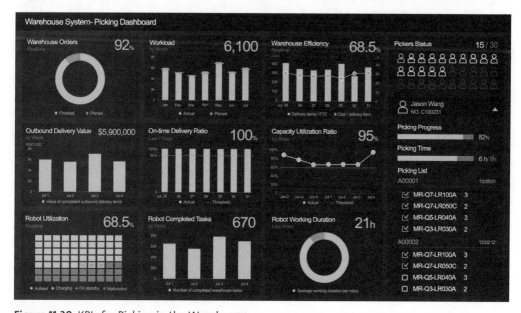

Figure 11.39 KPIs for Picking in the Warehouse

11.3   Logistics Network

SAP Leonardo allows organizations to optimize supply chain logistics and enhance regulatory compliance across their global networks, which can be especially useful for organizations like transportation hubs and port authorities. How can you continually increase throughput without increasing physical capacity? By running fleets more efficiently.

Track and trace capabilities help you understand how many orders will enter a port, for example. A network logistics hub allows you to orchestrate the right number of containers, cranes, trains, trucks, and other equipment at the right time. Further, because the data is in real time, you can quickly adjust to changing conditions, such as weather. Track and trace also improves regulatory compliance, for example, by helping you to avoid packing or storing incompatible hazardous materials together.

SAP Leonardo IoT provides track and trace capabilities with the ability to track connected fleets via telematics for your own fleet and/or a contracted fleet including tracking containers, pallets, and goods with sensors.

Logistics providers can increase revenue by offering unused capacity to a logistics business network. Matching capabilities could create a marketplace to match demand and supply for shippers and carriers. Airports can improve operations both inside and outside the airport, from parking to security, catering, fueling, cleaning, and fleet management such as real-time airplane tracking.

The resulting efficiencies of connected fleets often pay off in better customer experiences. The key is to go beyond the simple gathering of IoT data. You need to combine sensor data with contextual and business data and then analyze this data to gain insights and make predictions. At this informational intersection, connected fleets will truly deliver value.

11.3.1   Supply Chain Visibility

SAP Global Track and Trace provides real-time delivery transparency in your extended supply chain.

As companies move from a reactive to a proactive approach to maintenance, fixed asset insights provide an end-to-end solution for predictive maintenance and service from the identification of emerging issues to procuring spare parts, scheduling, and executing maintenance. These capabilities can service assets, whether owned and operated by your company or installed at your site by a vendor and covered by service contracts.

An SAP Leonardo IoT connected fleet provides visibility into the internal tracking orders and into the fleet. SAP Global Track and Trace provides visibility into the extended supply chain, while the SAP Logistics Business Network provides a full overview consisting of both internal and extended supply chain.

11.3.2   SAP Global Track and Trace

As you've learned from previous sections, having insight into logistics processes is useful across the board, whether you're managing transportation or yard activities. SAP Leonardo's track and trace functionality, the SAP Global Track and Trace service, can ensure that all relevant stakeholders have a real-time view into the business. IoT technology connects the business network and enables organizations to track all parts of the logistics puzzle: processes, materials, products, and assets. Figure 11.40 shows the details of an event message view for a PO item in a procurement process of SAP Global Track and Trace, and Figure 11.41 shows a geographic overview.

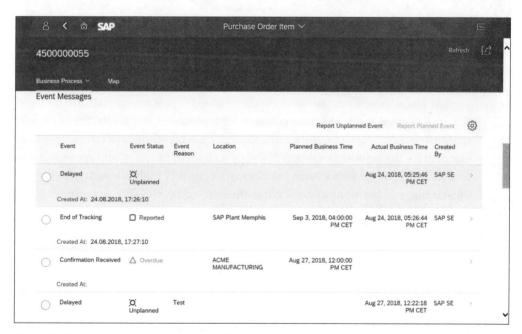

Figure 11.40 Purchase Order Item in SAP Global Track and Trace

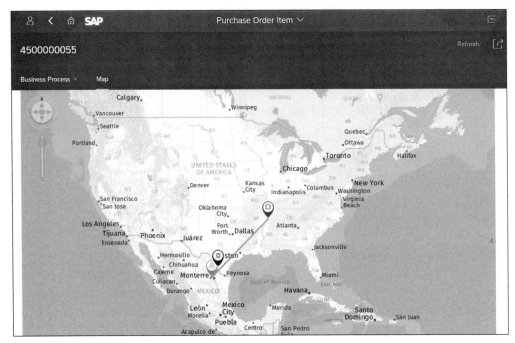

Figure 11.41 Purchase Order Item in SAP Global Track and Trace with Geographic Overview

11.3.3   SAP Logistics Business Network

The SAP Logistics Business Network is a cloud-based collaboration platform for logistics. If SAP Global Track and Trace connects your processes and assets, the SAP Logistics Business Network connects stakeholders. Collaboration between people is as essential for the smooth operation of a supply chain as in any other type of logistics process. The SAP Logistics Business Network connects logistics partners through onboarding and harmonization services thus providing visibility across both internal and extended supply chains by combining content and allowing data harmonization through various business processes.

The goal is to build a network where all parties (logistics providers) can collaborate and exchange information and documents on a single common platform. The extended logistics value chain is connected to overcome operational issues, IoT provides real-time visibility and responsive decision-making, collaborations are scalable and cost-efficient, and transparency is provided based on the needs of each stakeholder.

SAP Logistics Business Network's first release included freight tendering and subcontracting integrated with SAP Transportation Management. The freight execution processes include the following capabilities:

- Freight document management and sharing
- Real-time shipment visibility
- Event tracking and exception handling
- Dynamic estimated time of arrival (ETA)

Freight settlement processes include self-billing, carrier invoicing, and dispute management.

The freight request shown in Figure 11.42 showcases the SAP Logistics Business Network's ability to follow the same process for all partner freight requests.

Figure 11.42 Freight Request for Quotation

The SAP Logistics Business Network also provides capabilities to discover new LSP's and service providers, connect to internal and extended supply chains, and collaborate through digital communication and insights with alerting. Its core functionalities include the following capabilities:

- Discover new trading partners, communities, and business opportunities
- Connect to logistics partners anytime, anywhere, and to any device, backend system, and level of technical ability
- Collaborate using a comprehensive set of intercompany collaboration processes in a multimodal, global, and seamless environment
- Gain insights using analytics, benchmarking, real-time alerts, and notifications

Figure 11.43 shows a business process flow for end-to-end, collaborative logistics for truck shipments in a freight request for quotation. The SAP Logistics Business Network was used to source a quote from multiple 3PLs within the network.

Figure 11.43 SAP Logistics Business Network Process Example

11.4 Summary

Applying IoT to logistics provides several opportunities to improve asset and fleet insight and to increase asset utilization by repurposing waste and improving efficiency. Telematics data enables real-time route planning for outbound logistics, with the ability to respond to changing conditions such as traffic. You can also improve efficiency when accommodating priority orders or incoming orders for share-load logistics. Historical telematics data allows for operational improvements used for fleet management in warehouses and on the shop floor.

SAP Leonardo IoT for moving assets can help improve operational efficiencies by collecting, mapping, storing, and analyzing vehicle and sensor data in real time. The integration of telematics, enterprise data, and customer data enables you to improve services and execution of ordering processes, the collection of goods, and delivery processes.

Moreover, SAP Leonardo IoT creates opportunities to optimize processes and create value through new business opportunities. The integration of telematics data with enterprise and customer data enables you to provide new use cases that benefit drivers/operators, enhances safety, and achieves sustainability goals.

With SAP HANA, we now have the processing capability to handle the big data needed to run complex algorithms in real time. With SAP Leonardo, you now have a foundation to create templates of algorithms and combine them with system learning principles. For the first time, you can now test, improve, and create new models and algorithms by training models with historical planning and execution data from SAP Digital Supply Chain management systems in combination with real-time connected fleet movement data. Putting all this together in SAP Cloud Platform results in lower total cost of ownership, even as dynamic planning concepts become more financially and operationally feasible.

Chapter 12
Finance

Finance is one of the most stable processes within a given organization and, as such, is a good candidate for future automation. In this chapter, we'll provide a high-level overview of key topics within finance and describe how the SAP Leonardo suite of technologies can help you improve financial processes, thereby resulting in lower operational costs.

If business leaders around the world are going to compete in the digital world, they'll need to process more information more efficiently and turn this information into deeper insights faster than ever, especially given the rapid evolution of digital technology over the past few years. The SAP Leonardo suite of digital technologies offers varied tools for implementing smarter and intelligent business applications that will enable your organization to fast track your digital transformation. The aim of this chapter is to explore and understand how the SAP Leonardo suite of digital technologies can influence some core finance functions and what these new tools can mean to an organization's revenue growth and bottom line.

Prior to SAP Leonardo and SAP S/4HANA innovations, finance and accounting processes were among the most stable activities in any given enterprise. Accounting experts have been performing accounting and finance tasks the same way for many decades. Now is the time to change; to rethink how repetitive and predictable tasks can be automated with the help of new cutting-edge technologies. A significant step towards a more intelligent enterprise will require a paradigm shift in the way finance and accounting tasks are performed. SAP envisions that, with the help of SAP Leonardo capabilities coupled with a smarter business suite (SAP S/4HANA), the goal of reducing manually intensive financial and accounting processes may mean automating close to 70% of current repetitive tasks.

Clearly, the future will result in additional challenges created due to disruptive technologies. However, this disruption can be leveraged to build new revenue-generating business models. Traditional investing and budgeting methods, like financial month-end and year-end closing cycles, are things of the past for an accountant. The role of finance and accounting professionals will change dramatically from being recordkeepers and managers of day-to-day finance operations. Accountants will be boardroom strategists, advising CEOs and boards of directors about new market trends and opportunities while providing timely and accurate insights into the company's performance.

12.1   Financial Planning and Analysis

The financial planning and analysis (FP&A) team can play a crucial role in providing accurate and timely financial analysis and advice to the leaders of your organization. The great speed at which companies move today, the complexity of today's business environment, and the emergence of the digital economy has made FP&A critical for the central finance team. FP&A supports an organization's business plan and provides a framework to ensure the success of short-term and long-term financial goals.

Using SAP S/4HANA, FP&A can predict outcomes through real-time scenario analysis. SAP S/4HANA provides the ability to access accurate financial data and provide management with better and faster actionable insights that enable robust decision-making. In this age of digital transformation, time is money, and key business decisions must be made before the market opportunity disappears. The SAP Leonardo suite of technologies, based on business intelligence, machine learning, and analytics, can provide the additional capabilities required to perform FP&A and render valuable and timely insights to the business leaders. SAP Analytics Cloud and SAP Digital Boardroom can leverage SAP Leonardo's capabilities to deliver new features such as smart discovery, smart insights, smart grouping, what-if analysis, and automated dashboards that can deliver interactive visualizations and render key inputs for faster decision-making. SAP Analytics Cloud and SAP Digital Boardroom, coupled with SAP S/4HANA, can provide advanced analytics to help your business make strategic business decisions to improve top-line growth.

Some limitations and challenges that organizations commonly face in their financial planning and analysis functions can be addressed by SAP S/4HANA and SAP Analytics Cloud, which can help build a streamlined FP&A function.

The SAP Analytics Cloud platform provides new set of tools and techniques to help improve FP&A functions within any given organization. SAP Analytics Cloud is powered by SAP Leonardo and combines business intelligence, planning, and predictive analytics capabilities into a single smart solution. Analytics, an important ingredient of SAP Leonardo technologies, is a core foundation of SAP Analytics Cloud, which uses advanced tools and embedded machine learning capabilities to generate intelligent insights more quickly.

Key capabilities of SAP Analytics Cloud with respect to FP&A include the following:

- Real-time analytics
- Analytics based on SAP and non-SAP data
- Planning, business intelligence, and predictive capabilities

Let's review how SAP Analytics Cloud and SAP Digital Boardroom capabilities empower business users by providing the data required for decision-making in several key FP&A areas: budgeting and forecasting, planning and predictive finance, and dynamic reporting.

12.1.1   Budgeting and Forecasting

Budgeting and forecasting are important financial functions within an FP&A framework. Budgets must be planned and approved to ensure continuity in operating, investing, and financing activities. The ability of an organization to forecast key financial metrics based on historical data and other relevant business information can equip executive leadership for future business situations and for making informed decisions.

In this section, we'll review some key features within SAP Analytics Cloud that support budgeting and forecasting capabilities.

Budgeting

Budgeting processes can allow your entire organization to come together and focus on goals to achieve, draw action plan to achieve these goals, and describe your goals in financial terms. This process helps business leaders anticipate what the next year looks may look like and also facilities in summarizing how your organization is performing and its future growth path to various stakeholders, including investors, the board of directors, top management, employees, customers, and prospects. Defining and monitoring the financial budget across different financial objects, such as projects, internal orders, and cost centers, are critical to driving important budgeting decisions. SAP S/4HANA allows you to perform fine-grained analysis of actual and future expenses that will enable critical decisions regarding future expenses.

SAP Analytics Cloud provides new features that can enhance the budgeting experience for planners. To support budgeting processes within FP&A functions, version management within SAP Analytics Cloud provides options for you to define various categories for a given dataset and also save different versions of the same dataset. Version management provides the ability to simulate managerial decisions related to expenses and budget situations. It is possible to define different categories such as actuals, budgets, forecast, and rolling forecasts, thus enabling you to have all your budget, actual, and forecast data in a single system.

During model creation within SAP Analytics Cloud, you have the option of selecting a version, as shown in Figure 12.1, for an understanding of how the different versions are maintained within SAP Analytics Cloud. Once the model is defined, with the budget version selected, the FP&A team can create a private version of the model, which can be used for additional what-if analysis.

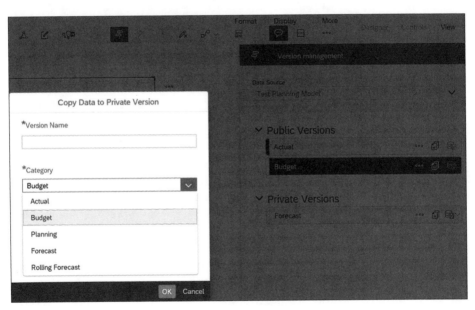

Figure 12.1 Version Management in SAP Analytics Cloud

SAP Analytics Cloud also provides the ability to spread, distribute, and assign budgets in an intuitive manner with just a click of a button. Figure 12.2 shows a quick overview of this feature within SAP Analytics Cloud.

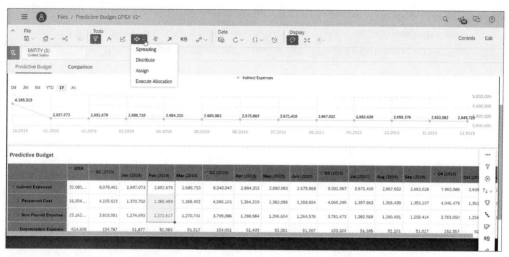

Figure 12.2 Spreading, Distributing, and Assigning Budgets within SAP Analytics Cloud

Budgeting models built within SAP Analytics Cloud platform can leverage business intelligence and SAP S/4HANA-based tools to provide your organization accurate and fast insights related to budgeting.

Forecasting

An organization needs to be dynamic and be able to adjust to changing markets and economic policies. For success, your organization must possess the ability to predict market opportunities, growth, and challenges for the upcoming financial year. Accuracy in making good forecasts can make your organization ready for both expected and unexpected economic conditions and help make rational budgeting decisions and allocate resources efficiently.

The FP&A team provides senior management with a forecast of a company's profit and loss (income) metrics and operating performance metrics for the upcoming quarter/year. These forecasts can inform management on the company's strategic plans and investments and can be communicated to external stakeholders as well. Increasingly, FP&A teams create a "rolling" forecast that enables an organization to continuously plan over a set time horizon, rather than a static annual forecast. Management may use ERP and other innovative technologies to help create forecasts of expected financial metrics/numbers to help make informed decisions.

The SAP Analytics Cloud platform can be leveraged for forecasting capabilities as well. You can forecast a particular measure within a model based on date parameters (using the **From** and **To** fields), as shown in detail in Figure 12.3.

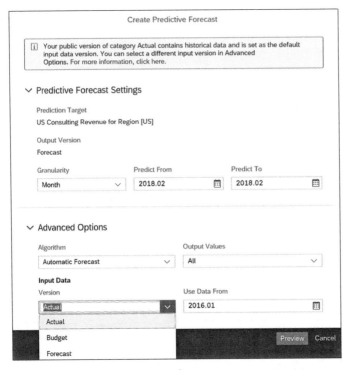

Figure 12.3 Setting Forecast Timelines

SAP Analytics Cloud offers two varieties of forecasting techniques:

- Quick forecasts depend purely on historical data and the length of past periods to forecast future values.
- Advanced forecasts provide additional flexibility to include other parameters that may have significant influence on financial outcomes, such as discounts or promotions planned for the future period for which the forecast is being generated.

The forecasts created by SAP Analytics Cloud use machine learning algorithms based on historical data and planning models as well as other functions such as distributions, allocations, and more.

Figure 12.4 shows a forecast generated in SAP Analytics Cloud with a click of a button.

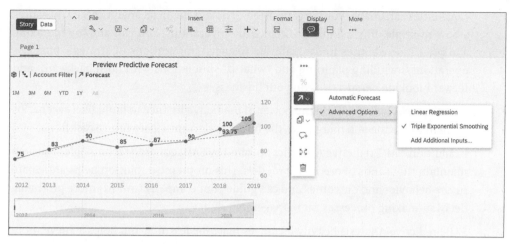

Figure 12.4 Forecasting on Time-Series Chart

As shown in Figure 12.5, the dataset behind the model is updated with forecast data against all financial measures.

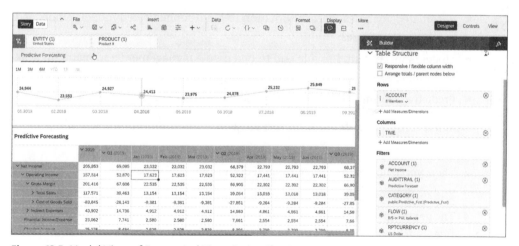

Figure 12.5 Model View of Forecasted Time-Series Chart

12.1.2   Planning and Predictive Finance

Predictive analytics can help chief financial officers (CFOs) use existing data to identify trends for more accurate planning, forecasting, and decision-making. By using predictive analytics, your organization can predict outcomes, identify untapped opportunities, expose hidden risks, anticipate the future, and act quickly. Predictive capabilities can enable your organization to obtain financial analytics/key measures across multiple dimensions for finance and operations. You can employ modeling and prediction abilities to evaluate the financial implications of strategic business operations, including planning and "what-if" simulations with both backward- and forward-looking perspectives on your business.

SAP S/4HANA helps you use the power of predictive finance to build likely scenarios for better revenue and margins in the future and to anticipate future cashflows.

In addition, SAP Predictive Analytics powered by SAP Leonardo technologies can help maintain thousands of predictive models. This on-premise solution helps anticipate future behavior and outcomes and can guide your company towards more profitable decision-making processes for management.

SAP Predictive Analysis heavily leverages machine learning and helps achieve more accurate business outcomes more quickly by providing predictive results for better insights incorporating predictive analytics to line of business (LOB) applications and core business processes.

Key capabilities provided by SAP Predictive Analytics include the following:

- Automated analytics: Uses automation to build sophisticated models embedded in business processes.
- Model management: Provide end-to-end model management and maintain peak performance.
- Predictive scoring: Create predictive models and provide real-time simulation.

A high-level overview of key steps to build a predictive model is as follows:

1. The first step is to make the historical dataset ready for upload.
2. Then, you'll define the target, weighted, and excluded variables.
3. The algorithms in the backend will run once you move ahead with the model.
4. The next step would be to check the model summary including the prediction confidence (closer to 1 means the model is robust) and the number of columns (variables that are retained for further analysis), as shown in detail in Figure 12.6.
5. Key attributes or variables that have an impact on the model can be seen. This model was run to review key variables that impacts marketing of a certain product. The purpose of this exercise was to identify which customer behavior influences their decision to buy a certain product. The software also provides options for simulating the model. As shown in Figure 12.7, the prior sale and the month in which the marketing effort was launched has a close relation with the actual sale.

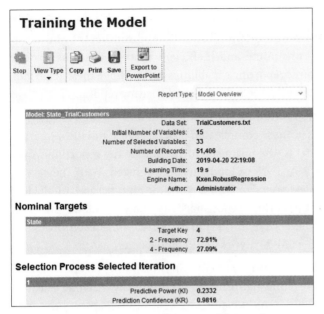

Figure 12.6 SAP Predictive Analytics: Model Overview

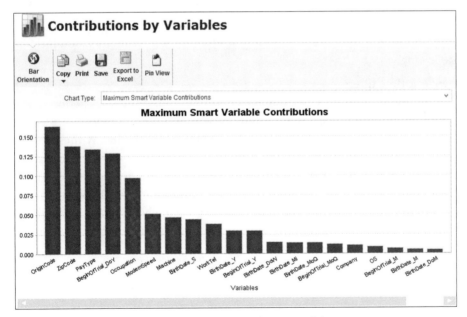

Figure 12.7 Key Variables That Influence the Predictive Model

12.1.3   Dynamic Reporting

The process of FP&A encompasses the analysis of multiple spreadsheets by business users, which is often a time-consuming and inefficient process. Business leaders could really benefit from dynamic reporting capabilities that will give them real-time insights with less time spent fetching the right data and creating reports.

Traditional reporting processes are often inconsistent, cumbersome, and lengthy, to say the very least. In some cases, these complicated processes result in lost opportunities and could be detrimental to the business. To streamline the reporting workflow and increase agility, SAP Analytics Cloud can be leveraged. With the recent evolution of technology, a huge demand exists for real-time reports based on the latest financial data. To achieve real-time reporting, SAP Analytics Cloud provides options to select various parameters dynamically to reflect real-time results from the most recent data every time the SAP Analytics Cloud model is run.

SAP Analytics Cloud is a unique offering that combines planning, business intelligence, and collaboration tools on one platform and is powered by machine learning and predictive analytics capabilities. As explained earlier in this chapter, SAP Leonardo technologies like machine learning, analytics, and data intelligence are deeply embedded within SAP Analytics Cloud to provide unparalleled transparency in financial performance.

Some parameters that can be dynamically selected for SAP Analytics Cloud include the following:

- **Dynamic time filters**
  SAP Analytics Cloud provides the ability to understand financial performance across different time frames that can be dynamically selected. SAP Analytics Cloud lets you define specific time filters relative to the current period. Within a time-series chart, you can select a fixed or a dynamic chart type. If you select a dynamic chart type, you can provide a reference point (usually the current period). Then, you can specify a time-period range in the past or in the future and select the granularity (year, quarter, or month) depending on the data; how this feature works is shown in Figure 12.8. Once you select your dynamic time filters, the timeline will be updated accordingly to reflect your selections.

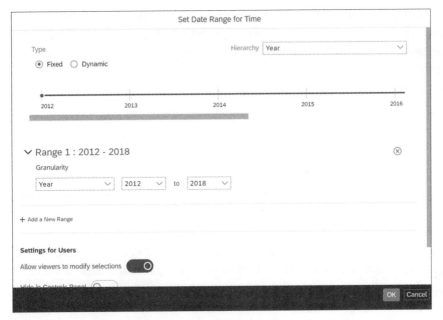

Figure 12.8 Dynamic Time Filters in SAP Analytics Cloud

- **Dynamic reference line**

   Another example where SAP Analytics provides dynamic reporting capabilities is its ability to add a dynamic reference line in a chart. As shown in Figure 12.9, for the given measure, you can choose a reference line that is an average value.

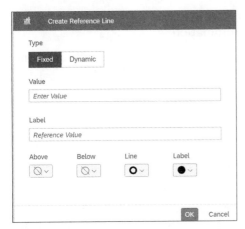

Figure 12.9 Dynamic Reference Line in SAP Analytics Cloud

The other options for a dynamic reference line are the minimum and maximum values. This reference line can help interpret the significance of the values in the chart with respect the dynamic value selected. The dynamic reference line will change based on the filters, rankings, and hierarchy chosen in the chart and can also change based on the chart view selected.

- **Other options**
  Other options include adding dynamic text and images to reflect the changes that happen when we interact with the chart and change filters, hierarchy, etc.

12.2   Financial Accounting

Businesses are responsible for documenting all monetary transactions in its books of accounts and for generating financial statements at the end of the reporting period. Statements of cash flow, statements of profit and loss, and statements of financial position (balance sheets) are the key components in financial accounting. Working capital is part of the balance sheet and is an important factor that depicts the liquidity health of an entity, with emphasis on its ability to meet short-term obligations and the availability of sufficient funds to operate the business. Managing accounts receivables (AR) and accounts payables (AP) appropriately is essential for the liquidity and profitability of a business. In this section, we'll review accounts receivables and accounts payables in the context of digital automation and learn how to improve working capital using the latest technologies provided by SAP Leonardo.

12.2.1   Accounts Receivable and Digital Automation

Given the cost of raising new capital, no business can afford to underutilize existing capital. Some businesses don't realize how much cash is trapped on its own balance sheets. Freeing up that cash—by optimizing working capital—delivers improved operational efficiency and also gives companies the added liquidity it needs to fund growth, reduce debt levels, lower costs, maximize shareholder returns, and even outperform their competitors. Numerous ways exist for freeing up working capital, and a core strategy that organizations should focus on is AR.

Organizations generally focus more on sales, and AR becomes an afterthought. Limited attention to accounts receivable could lead to issues for the business in general. Days sales outstanding (DSO) is a key indicator for measures the success of the accounts receivable team in any given organization. Higher DSO means a greater number of days (than average) are needed to collect payment from customers after the sale is made, which could result in higher costs to fund accounts receivables. A ripple effect could impact other functions within an organization. Some of these challenges can be overcome by maintaining accurate customer master data with defined payment terms and credit limits, having regular invoicing, and having regular reporting capabilities. Employing the latest cutting edge-technologies, such as adapting e-invoicing processes, to support cash application and collection processes can help reduce operational costs.

Including integration with SAP Leonardo capabilities, SAP Cash Application has additional innovative features embedded and available for managing working capital more effectively. SAP Cash Application integrates with SAP S/4HANA and uses machine learning to speed up the tedious process of payment matching. SAP also provides cloud-based solution for machine learning that integrates with SAP S/4HANA Cloud. Machine learning helps drastically reduce manual effort by automatically extracting additional information about payments from unstructured information, such as PDF documents, and uses this information to automate the clearing process.

Some features of machine learning that can help improve accounts receivables processes include the following:

- Machine learning can tie a payment to the correct invoice automatically based on historical data.
- Alternatively, machine learning can provide information to the responsible employee about relevant invoices to which the payment is most likely a match. The system then remembers the steps taken by employee to assign the payment correctly and then proposes similar corrective steps in similar future scenarios.

In a nutshell, SAP's machine learning capabilities help identify issues, make matches, and update the rules to improve the success rate when matching payments received against open invoices. Figure 12.10 shows the SAP Cash Application homepage, where you'll see various tiles related to incoming payments, AR jobs, and items that need reprocessing.

This application also stores historical data to show how the automated invoice matching process has improved over time, thereby resulting in fewer payments needing to be manually reprocessed. As shown in Figure 12.11, in the given data sample, the number of items that require reprocessing can be reduced considerably by the machine learning capabilities built into the SAP Cash Application.

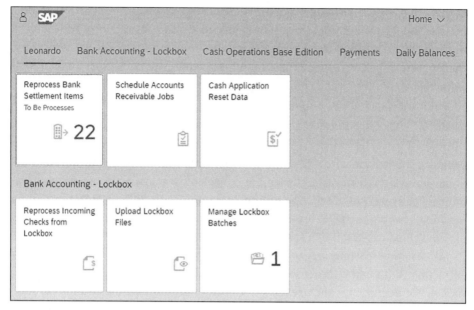

Figure 12.10 SAP Cash Application Homepage

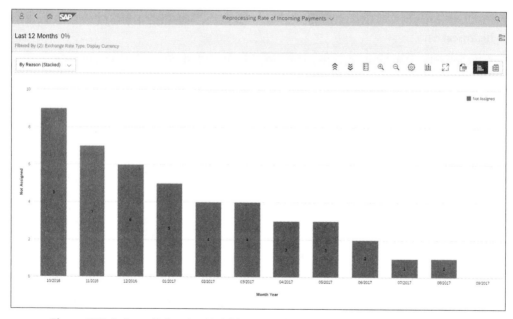

Figure 12.11 Automatic Invoice Matching over Time

Figure 12.12 shows a high-level overview of how machine learning features can be integrated into the traditional accounts receivable process.

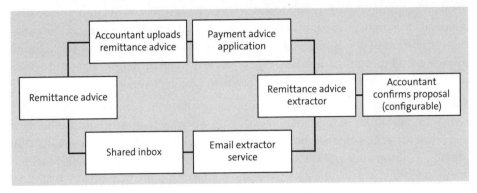

Figure 12.12 SAP Machine Learning and Accounts Receivables

Machine learning capabilities provided by SAP Leonardo can analyze your customers' subtle payment behaviors, analyze the aging of open items in real time, and can also automatically write off any differences based on predefined rules. These capabilities can help you record and manage dispute cases using historical interactions with a customer. All these features aim to reduce DSO and improve the operating cash flow of the organization.

Let's look at another use case where blockchain capabilities can improve the accounts receivable process using B2B invoicing. To avoid the hassle of sending invoices to your customers and then requesting payment, invoices can be shared directly with your customers via a request network or a smart contract. Once the payment is due, your company can send a request for payment via the same request network, and the payment itself can be completed by the customer, which is then recorded in the SAP S/4HANA system.

As your accounting system would be directly connected to payments, integrated functions can easily help detect delayed payments, and bad debts can be easily identified. The payment history will help you analyze risk factors and enable businesses to evaluate credit scores and credit ratings continuously. Thus, the integration of blockchain networks with SAP S/4HANA Finance will enable greater accuracy and efficiency in the AR process, thereby providing the opportunity to reduce DSO dramatically. Blockchain technology is explained in more detail in the next section related to AP.

12.2.2   Accounts Payable and Digital Automation

Procure-to-pay (P2P) processes are integral to the success of any business. The demand/requirement to buy goods and services, budgeting and obtaining necessary approvals to purchase goods and services, the actual receipt of goods and services, the verification of goods received, the receipt of invoices to the actual payment of invoice are all part of the procure-to-pay process. Payment terms dictate the time period during which payments must be made to suppliers/vendors.

SAP has taken the next step to streamline and automate processes by using SAP Leonardo capabilities in combination with SAP S/4HANA to bring in more efficiency and reliability across different business functions including AP process. SAP S/4HANA provides real-time integration with purchasing software; accounts payable postings are updated in the general ledger (G/L) and enables liquidity planning by updating cash management records on a real-time basis.

Machine learning technology provided by SAP aims to automate many of the repetitive tasks within the procure-to-pay process (P2P). Table 12.1 provides a view of key areas where machine learning can help with automation, including the following areas:

- **Image-based requisition**
  Machine learning technologies can assist the requisition of goods based on digital images and also can recommend material groups to classify products into correct product categories.

- **Receipt of goods and services**
  The goods receipt/invoice receipt (GR/IR) monitor provides a high-level overview showing the status of all purchase orders, open financial accoutning items, and any outstanding balances to be paid to vendors. Additional details related to the GR/IR monitor described later in this section.

- **Dashboard**
  The AP dashboard can assist the accounts payable manager who can have all the relevant numbers available at a glance.

- **Invoice processing**
  Machine learning helps record all incoming invoices and enables vendor matching based on historical data. With machine learning features, you can now match at the invoice line level and help correct invoices intelligently.

- **Reconciliation and closing**
  SAP now provides three-way invoice matching (GR/PO/IR) with the help of the SAP Leonardo suite of technologies, thereby reducing the manual intervention needed

to reconcile purchase orders with goods received and against payments made to vendors.

	Request Goods and Services	Order Goods and Services	Receive Goods and Services	Perform Invoice	Discount and Payment Term Opt.	Make Payments	Reconciliation and Closing
Manual Process	Create sources of supply Determine future demand	Create purchase orders Plan delivery timelines	Check received goods Post received material Goods quality control	Receive and manage customer payments Apply cash payment Identify and investigate bad debt	Check payment runs Check usage of discount options	Create payment runs Triggers execution of payments via banking	Reconcile account records
Machine Learning	Image based Requisition Material Group recommender	PR optimization RFQ approved Source of supply assignment Catalogue item proposal Contract update	GR/IR monitor status proposal Goods receipt to record Approver recommender	Invoice to record Vendor matching Invoice line item matching	Payment block recommender	Correctness of outgoing payments Payment request duplication check Remove payment block	GR/PO/IR matching (3-way matching) Approver recommender Account recommender

Table 12.1 SAP Leonardo Machine Learning and Procure-to-Pay Process

To master the real-time business, you must integrate processes across various financial functions and provide management with options for maintaining a healthy current ratio, which is feasible by maintaining optimal AR and AP balances. SAP Analytics Cloud can help simplify planning and help align to common goals for each function by providing the right tools for financial planning and analysis, collaborative budgeting, long-range strategic planning, workforce and capital planning, predictive forecasting, and scenario modeling. SAP Analytics Cloud complements the capabilities provided by SAP Leonardo Machine Learning to help make effective decisions related to accounts payable goals and understand deviations from the planned goal.

For organizations facing working capital problems, SAP Analytics Cloud has several options for dashboards you can use for a view of current performance and market trends. Analytics dashboards can provide instant details into the root cause of an issue in real time, enabling you to take necessary actions to resolve issues and also help monitor impacts over time. The dashboards contain a set of prebuilt visualizations that you can use for both accounts receivables and accounts payables. The dashboard provides granular insights into aging balances, where financial analysts can exactly pinpoint any cause for concern and resolve these problems and help optimize cash flows faster. Figure 12.13 shows a high-level overview of what the AR and AP dashboard looks like.

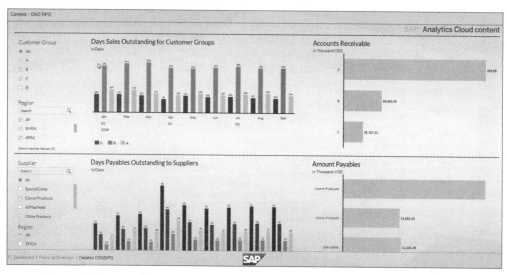

Figure 12.13 AR and AP Dashboard Created in SAP Analytics Cloud

Let's look at some cases within the accounts payables process where the SAP Leonardo suite of technologies can be valuable, for example, in GR/IR clearing. Identifying the reasons for differences between a purchase order and the goods received and what was actually invoiced by a vendor requires coordination across different teams including accounting, purchasing, logistics, and suppliers, which could mean lot of time and resources spent discrepancies. This complexity increases exponentially if numerous items are ordered on an invoice and a huge number of purchases are made in a given period.

To enable effective GR/IR clearing, a new intelligent GR/IR monitor, shown in Figure 12.15, has been released by SAP as part of SAP S/4HANA Cloud. This monitor (in the form of an app) provides real-time insights into all purchase orders, including the latest status associated with the purchase orders, quantity, amounts, and balances. The monitor also provides information on open financial accounting items, contacts, history, and notes. Embedded collaboration capabilities provide seamless integration across business processes.

To facilitate the clearing process via the GR/IR monitor, SAP has implemented machine learning technology to automatically provide recommendations to users on the next steps related to purchase orders if any problem is detected. The application learns from historical GR/IR account clearing data in the system, and the action taken by the user to resolve prior discrepancies, and then proposes the most accurate steps that should resolve the difference between the GR and the IR. The monitor enables end users make better decisions more quickly, thereby reducing time required by the accounts payable team to spend on reconciliation activities.

Figure 12.14 shows a flowchart of machine learning as part of the GR/IR process, while Figure 12.15 shows an overview of how the GR/IR monitor looks in SAP.

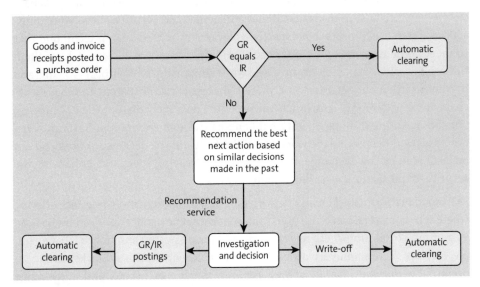

Figure 12.14 GR/IR and Machine Learning Flowchart

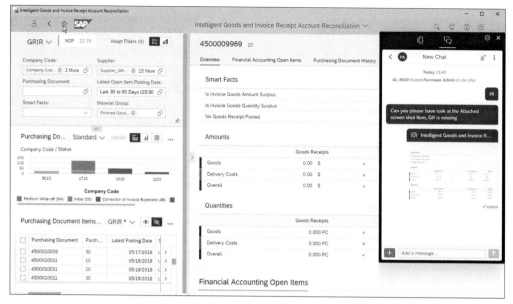

Figure 12.15 The GR/IR Monitor

Furthermore, you can integrate blockchain technology into the financial accounting process and benefit from latest blockchain innovations. The objective of blockchain technology is to ensure the transparency, efficiency, and security of everyday transactions. From a P2P process perspective, blockchain is a multistep technique that connects a client to one or more service providers. Blockchain allows for the authentication of various stakeholders involved while supporting budgeting, invoicing, and payment settlement activities in a more seamless and transparent fashion. Blockchain along with SAP S/4HANA has the potential positively disrupt the P2P process, possibly resulting in huge operational benefits through the standardization of key processes thus decreasing the workload of the AP team. The decrease in workload can be facilitated by the exchange of information, improving speed and enhancing the security of transactions over blockchain network.

SAP Cloud Platform Blockchain offers a cloud-based, blockchain-as-a-service offering where sellers, buyers, banks, insurers, and government organizations can interact on a common portal, and where relevant documents are posted and tracked. For example, let's say there's an overview page within SAP Cloud Platform Blockchain for an ocean shipping use case, where we can see the list of parties and agreements involved. These parties can update the status of a document as when workflow steps are updated.

Blockchain provides an efficient collaboration tool where documents can be securely shared and approved. In our example shown, the bill of lading can be securely transferred electronically for the various parties involved to view and use. These parties can also have visibility into the approvals workflow and can pinpoint exactly who needs to take the next action to ensure that the workflow is completed and the goods reach their destinations.

As a document flows through the approval process, an approver can digitally sign the document. This feature can drastically reduce the time needed for a document to be approved, uploaded, and communicated to the other parties involved. A sample document can be digitally approved from a smart phone, which would instantly update the document workflow.

Additional value provided by blockchain technology includes the following:

- **Enhanced validation and authentication**
  This feature helps prevent fraud and ensure security by distributing authentication rights across the P2P value chain.

- **Accelerated and efficient purchase order management**
  Purchase order data, goods received data, and invoice receipt data can all be exchanged on the blockchain network, which will in turn accelerate and improve communications and exchange of information among different parties.

  When a goods receipt is created, the purchase order can be validated for price and quantity using a smart contract. Using a smart contract requires a consensus between the parties involved before a smart contract can be leveraged. As your vendors are also on the same network, the closest vendors can be identified to reduce the delivery times for goods. The quality of the goods can also be verified as the quality management team will also be on the network. Vendors with the shortest lead times and the highest quality of goods can be continuously evaluated for effective P2P process management.

- **Strong audit trail**
  All the stakeholders and parties involved are in the same network. Blockchain ensures that a strong, tamper-proof audit trail is maintained. Audit trails also provide end-to-end visibility in the tracking of the physical goods.

- **Better invoice processing and accelerated payment settlements**
  Since your vendors are also on the same blockchain network, invoices need not be sent to vendors separately. Vendors can directly view invoices on the user interface designed for this purpose. Due to complete transparency and real-time access to data, reconciliations and payments can be accelerated. Banks can also be part of the blockchain network which in turn also accelerates the payment process.

Some key steps that your organization can take to start its blockchain journey include the following:

- Identify process areas within procure-to-pay process that could benefit from blockchain capabilities.
- Recognize the key stakeholders who need to be on board to venture into the blockchain space.
- Assess technological options the organization has available to implement blockchain capabilities along with the building network that is required to start the blockchain journey.
- Evaluate the cost-benefit of various options for implementing blockchain technologies.
- Present a proposal to obtain key sponsor buy-in to start the blockchain journey.

Now, let's look at how payments are made within a blockchain process. Once a buyer confirms the receipt of goods and service and is satisfied with the quality and quantity of goods and service received, a request can be created between the payer and the payee. Once the notification is received by the payer, the payer makes a payment to the payee. Standing instructions can also be processed via blockchain. A bank need not be involved in the payments since cryptocurrencies like Ripple and Stellar can be used for payments without any third party being involved.

The payer can be given the option to choose a mode of payment, and once the amount has been received, the payee can confirm payment. The entire process can be implemented without sharing any sensitive bank information by using a smart contract in a blockchain that can be integrated with the SAP S/4HANA system.

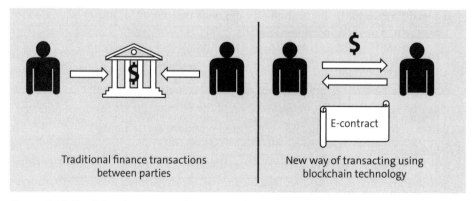

Traditional finance transactions between parties

New way of transacting using blockchain technology

Figure 12.16 Traditional versus Modern View of Transacting between Parties

The aim of blockchain for finance is to remove the dependencies on intermediaries for processing any financial transactions. Figure 12.16 shows an overview of how financial transactions were traditionally executed with the help of financial intermediaries versus how parties can directly interact without the need of intermediaries.

Overall, the latest capabilities in machine learning, analytics, and blockchain will improve process efficiencies and the effectiveness of the AP function. Additional challenges still need to be resolved before these technologies can be completely leveraged to improve the efficiency of financial accounting process.

12.3   Accounting and Financial Close

Companies that are publicly owned and traded must comply with financial disclosure rules and regulations enforced in the country in which the company is registered and traded. For example, companies such as Apple, Bank of America, and others that are registered in the United States and publicly traded in US financial markets are required by the US Securities and Exchange Commission (SEC) to disclose specific information on a regular basis. Annual reports (Form 10-K), quarterly reports (Form 10-Q), and current report of any major events that shareholders should be aware of (Form 8-K) will need to be disclosed according to the timelines stipulated by the SEC.

Annual reports typically comprise of the following information:

- General corporate information
- Financial statements
- Director's report and chairperson's statement
- Auditor's report and auditor's notes
- Corporate governance information

In this section, we'll understand the latest technologies available to support key accounting and financial close processes: reconciliation and year-end reporting and continuous soft close.

12.3.1   Reconciliation and Year-End Reporting

Why are financial statements important, and what is the urgency to disclose financial data in a timely manner?

Financial statements summarize the profitability of an organization at the end of the financial year and showcase how the company has performed financially for a given year, as well as when compared to previous year(s) and within the industry in general. This information is extremely critical for shareholders to make informed decisions related to the organization. Capital markets react immediately to any financial and corporate information that becomes known to the public. The timing of annual reports (and quarterly reports) is extremely important. According to the laws of the land, these reports must be filed with the regulatory agencies according to the relevant legal deadlines.

Another important aspect related to financial accounting is the need to adhere to and record financial transactions based on accounting principles as according to local laws. For example, International Accounting Standard (IASC) or US Generally Accepted Accounting Principles (US GAAP) are some accepted international accounting principles; most multinational organizations report in either IASC or US GAAP or both.

Numerous manual steps and reconciliations needs to be performed in order to close the books of accounts and generate annual financial statements. Several closing steps that can only be started once batch jobs related to costing allocations, intercompany postings, GR/IR postings, and depreciation runs are completed. These batch jobs can take anywhere from several hours to a few days to complete, depending on the complexity, type, and quantity of postings. In addition, for organizations that have a presence across multiple countries, the local books of accounts will need to be closed, and the relevant files/data transferred to another system where consolidated financial reports can be generated. In some organizations, the consolidation process can be manually intensive and can depend purely on Excel capabilities to come up with consolidation financial results to be filed with federal authorities. This approach is prone to manual and human errors that could lead to potential delays in filing the reports and may result in huge fines for noncompliance as well.

SAP has come up with new solution that transforms the way financial consolidation can be performed. The SAP S/4HANA Finance for group reporting solution is delivered as part of SAP S/4HANA 1809 and can be thought of as another module within SAP S/4HANA. SAP S/4HANA is powered by SAP Leonardo technologies to improve key processes such as record to report and order to cash.

SAP S/4HANA Finance for group reporting has tremendous potential to help organizations, especially multinational organizations, generate consolidated financial reports close to real time. SAP S/4HANA Finance for group reporting comes with embedded analytics that can help businesses to evolve into intelligent enterprises, as shown in Figure 12.17. Embedded analytics within SAP S/4HANA can support operational accounting and consolidation.

Figure 12.17 SAP S/4HANA Finance for Group Reporting with Embedded Analytics to Support Consolidation

Embedded analytics can assist your financial users slice and dice data to retrieve the relevant information required for completing consolidation tasks to generate the year-end financial reports. Embedded analytics within SAP S/4HANA provides a common environment where reporting and analytics activities for accounting can be accomplished.

Embedded analytics, along with SAP S/4HANA's Universal Journal, can be combined to support creation of integrated legal and management reports within SAP S/4HANA. Some benefits of SAP S/4HANA Finance for group reporting include the following:

- Improved quality of data as part of entity and group close
- Ability to continuously check posting data against central validation rules

- Accelerate entity and group close by completing local adjustments
- Ability to provide unparalleled transparency, with drilldown features from consolidated data into line-item data

SAP S/4HANA Finance for group reporting can be one-stop shop to support year-end legal reporting, by ensuring financial data is consolidated across multiple data sources (SAP and non-SAP systems) within SAP S/4HANA. Data from other cloud-based and on-premise systems can flow into SAP S/4HANA Finance for group reporting via standard APIs supported by the SAP S/4HANA system.

SAP S/4HANA Finance for group reporting provides your business with the ability to make quick decisions related to reconciliations and financial closing without having to switch between systems, or even between screens.

The global accounting hierarchy feature is supported by latest SAP S/4HANA version. This feature can be leveraged to define and maintain global hierarchies such as profit center hierarchies, cost center hierarchies, and financial statement versions by defining a sequence of attributes. This supports reporting on the fly by fetching hierarchies based on the sequence of attributes.

Group reporting capabilities within SAP S/4HANA, the ability to change and report on global accounting hierarchies, and machine learning capabilities to detect anomalies provide huge opportunities within the finance and accounting space to gain automated and actionable financial insights, as shown in Figure 12.18.

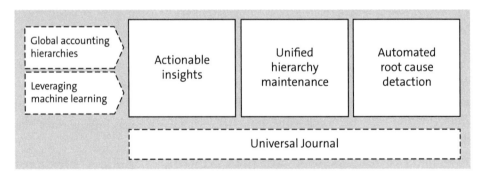

Figure 12.18 Latest Finance Innovations That Support Financial Reporting

In addition, other technologies in the SAP Leonardo suite can be leveraged along with SAP S/4HANA to further improve the financial closing process. Blockchain as a technology can be used to automate some auditing steps and ensure the no fraudulent transactions are part of the financial reports; we'll explain this process in much more detail later in Section 12.4.1.

Many repetitive financial and tax accounting tasks can be automated using machine learning capabilities to reconcile transactions and identify any discrepancies, which is a part of the future machine learning use cases currently being explored by SAP.

12.3.2   Continuous Soft Close

In recent years, a shift has occurred in how to approach to financial closings. We've seen corporations moving away from period-end closings to a more continuous soft close process. Continuous soft close is based on the relatively new concept of continuous accounting, coined by Ventana Research, where real-time financial information is available to management all the time.

To embrace the concept of continuous accounting, many period-end tasks must be performed on a regular (continuous) basis over the course of the month, quarter, or year. Tasks such as accruals/deferrals, bank reconciliations, and intercompany postings can be performed throughout the month, which will in turn alleviate the stress related to period-end closing activities.

A notable benefit of continuous accounting is its ability to generate information related to the financial health of a company instantaneously; at any given point in time, the finance team can provide a snapshot of the financial performance of the organization based on trial balances and other reports.

SAP S/4HANA Finance for group reporting enables businesses to unify local closing processes with group closing processes within a single system—SAP S/4HANA (see Figure 12.19). SAP S/4HANA Finance for group reporting offers a number of features to support the adoption of continuous accounting, such as the following:

- Shared master data and rules support local and group close activities.
- Any adjustments posted with local books of accounts are immediately available for group reporting.
- Provides the capability for real-time audits and supports drilldown views into operational line items.
- Support for early translation activities as part of local close.
- Ability to receive and store data from non-SAP ERP systems.

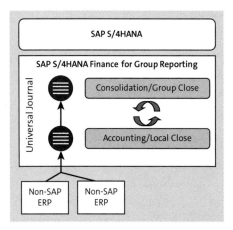

Figure 12.19 SAP S/4HANA Finance for Group Reporting and Continuous Accounting

SAP S/4HANA Finance for group reporting provides a set of consolidation features as SAP Fiori apps, as shown in Figure 12.20. These apps will enable your business to monitor all activities, from financial data collection to the generation of final consolidated financial statements. These features support the ability to generate local close and group close in real time.

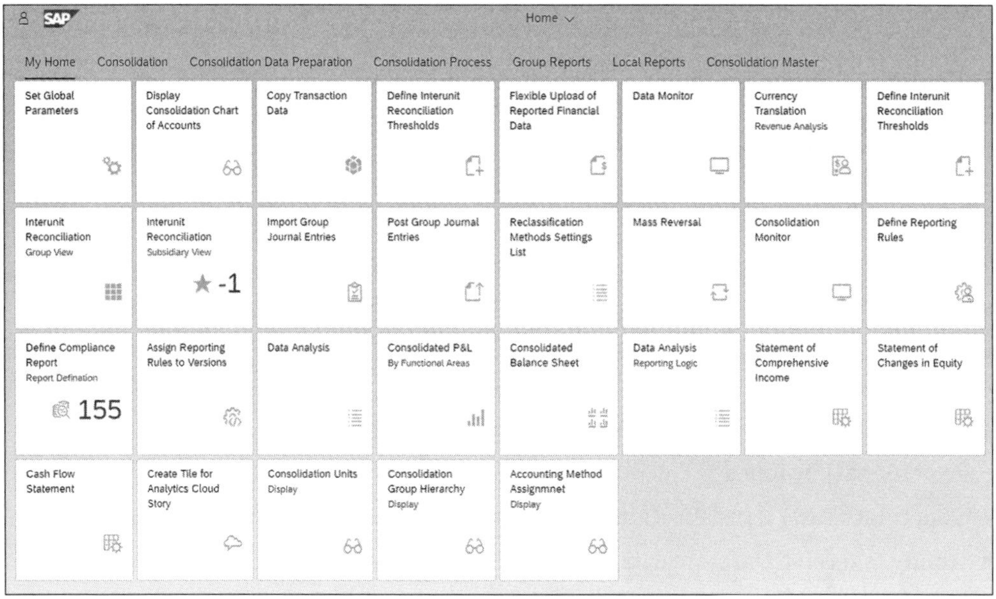

Figure 12.20 Consolidation Features Provided by SAP S/4HANA Finance for Group Reporting

12.4   Financial Controls

Financial controls are integral to any organization, whether a for-profit organization or a nonprofit. You must ensure that finances are in order and reported accurately for both internal and external purposes. While external reporting is essential to meet regulatory compliance requirements, internal reporting is indispensable to the success of the organization in meeting its long-term vision and short-term goals. In Section 12.3, we discussed regulatory compliance. In this section, we'll look at how financial controls are critical for any entity and what technological options are available to address some of the fraud-, risk-, and audit- and compliance-related tasks.

Financial controls are a combination of processes, rules, and procedures implemented to ensure the financial goals and obligations for any given entity are successfully met and to ensure that finances are accounted correctly. Some important steps can be taken to ensure accounts and finances represent the true state of affairs of your organization and no discrepancies of any nature exist. Some key steps in this direction include the following:

- Separation of roles and responsibilities to ensure separate persons are responsible for various tasks within the financial process.
- Regular budgeting and analysis to seek the causes of differences between forecasted budgets and actual spending can help identify the real reason for discrepancies.
- Review of bank statements will enable reconciliation with actual balances with payments/receipts.
- Solid inventory control systems will ensure goods and services can't be misused.

In the area of financial controls, SAP offers a wide range of solutions to support businesses. The solutions provided by SAP fall within the ambit of governance, risk, and compliance processes. Chief among these solutions are audit management, fraud management, and risk management solutions. In this section, we'll delve further into each of finance area and look at how the latest technological advancements can support your business by providing effective solutions in each of these process areas.

12.4.1   Audit and Compliance Management

In recent years, the role of an auditor has evolved beyond being responsible for internal controls; auditors are also required to closely monitor the ever-changing business environments. These auditors can then counsel the leadership team and share critical information related to enterprise risks, regulatory changes, and any other business risks that may impact an entity's goals and future growth.

Internal audits and external regulatory compliance are essential to the regular functioning of any business. By taking care of audit and compliance on a regular basis, the board of directors and your leadership team can stay focused on ever-changing socioeconomic and political environments that may affect day-to-day operations as well as an entity's long-term strategies and vision. It is vital that your company has a sound and stable process in place to identify and address any risks related to audit and compliance. SAP solutions leverage the latest technologies such as blockchain, big data, and analytics to help improve the efficiency of audit processes.

Now, let's look at how blockchain capabilities can be leveraged to improve audit processes. Blockchain features are also being explored as part of the SAP Leonardo suite of technologies to improve financial accounting activities. The traditional financial accounting practice is based on double-entry bookkeeping. To ensure trust among all stakeholders and clients, auditors must verify the company's financial information. Each audit is extremely costly and time consuming.

Blockchain can help address audit-related tasks for financial accounting. Some benefits available from blockchain technology for conducting audits include the following:

- Instead of writing individual transaction receipts, transactions can be directly stored on a distributed ledger that can be verified by all parties.
- The ledger will be encrypted cryptographically and misusing, falsifying, or destroying the recorded transactions will be impossible.
- The payer, the payee, and other third parties can verify the transactions are genuine and authentic.

The concept behind blockchain involves contracts/ledgers replicated across multiple databases linked via a network of blockchain systems. This technology aims to reduce, if not eliminate, misuse and/or fraudulent practices. The blockchain network also provides future opportunities to build new network-based, multiparty business models, thus opening up new revenue streams leveraging blockchain technologies.

In an extremely complex and costly transactional ecosystem, security and trust are basic requirements for doing business. Blockchain can be the backbone of your transactional infrastructure due to its ability to support distributed ledger technologies. Blockchain also supports peer-to-peer network technology, which uses advanced cryptographic techniques to enable trustworthy interactions among the involved parties. The ledger can be accessed and managed by multiple (even unknown or anonymous) parties and remain reliable, secure, and immutable, without the presence of a third-party intermediary (e.g. banks, brokers, or regulatory entities), which helps lower cost. With blockchain and SAP S/4HANA, you company can reliably execute and record transactions and share information, while still controlling what information is shared with whom.

Let's now look at a specific industry where blockchain solutions can be leveraged to support regulatory audits. In the United States, pharma companies must comply with lot serialization and traceability requirements that helps control the risk of counterfeit or stolen drugs on the market. Serialization requirements for the pharma industry is supported by SAP Advanced Track and Trace for Pharmaceuticals. Blockchain tools, and capabilities are integrated with this solution, thus providing accurate visibility into the end-to-end supply chain process for drugs. As part of this solution, pharma companies can capture and exchange serial numbers with its supply chain partners. As part of Good Manufacturing Practice (GMP) audit, which is necessary for pharma businesses, auditors check to ensure that products are produced according to the regulatory standards stipulated by health authorities, in this case, the Food and Drug Administration (FDA). Auditors must verify which serial numbers were part of shipments and to which retailers those shipments were sent. SAP Advanced Track and Trace for Pharmaceuticals, powered by blockchain capabilities, can track lot numbers, which is essential part of auditing as part of US serialization requirements. Figure 12.21 shows the cockpit view of this solution where each transaction, along with its corresponding lot number, can be tracked throughout the supply chain process.

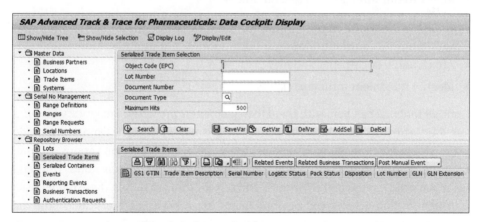

Figure 12.21 SAP Advanced Track and Trace for Pharmaceuticals Powered by Blockchain Tools

12.4.2   Fraud Management

The next topic under financial controls is to review and understand fraud management and how technology can help your business effectively manage fraud. With the evolution of digital technology, numerous channels exist through which businesses in today's world reach out to customers. Gone are the days where advertisements are targeted via newspapers or television. In the current era, so many channels exist to communicate, advertise, and engage with customers and to conduct business, which results in more opportunities for information and funds to be misused or misdirected. Identifying and preventing fraud, both internal and external, is critical for your business and must respond quickly to survive in an ever-challenging environment. Fraud management falls within the ambit of internal controls of the organization.

SAP offers solutions for identifying and effectively resolving fraud-related issues. The SAP fraud management solution is offered under SAP Business Integrity Screening. SAP Business Integrity Screening integrates with machine learning intelligence and can provide varied modeling options to help you identify and detect fraud by looking for patterns showing misuse of information, funds, and resources.

Some key features delivered as part of SAP Business Integrity Screening, integrated with machine learning, include the following:

- Ability to analyze from heterogeneous data
- Attention to abnormal behavior
- Simulation of multiple options
- Ability to run simulations based on time ranges
- Schedule and run alerts
- Generate cases for investigation
- Attach notes, documents, and files to cases
- Identify fraudulent insurance claims

Another tool that can help with fraud management is predictive analytics, which is a key SAP Leonardo capability. Predictive models use machine learning to provide users with predictions about future business performance based on various parameters. This feature comes with prebuilt models, algorithms, and schedules. Your end users can train models and algorithms and can continue to retrain these models easily, often without needing coding or modeling experience. End users can choose the object on which to run the prebuilt model and then choose the fields available under the object. If predictive confidence is close to 1, these models are quite good.

A user can create models as part of a fraud detection method and save these models as procedures. These procedures can be triggered by user interfaces and can be used to setup fraud alerts. Users can use standard objects to create and run models.

An additional feature is calibration. Calibration can help with different simulations, which in turn can create new alerts. These new alerts can be analyzed to detect valid exception scenarios related to fraud.

SAP Predictive Analytics identifies suspicious behavior by any person/entity doing business with the organization and provides models to predict fraudulent behavior, along with expected probabilities. Your historical data, along with an SAP HANA-based rules framework, can be used to derive what are likely to be fraudulent cases. The ability to identify and mitigate fraud-related activities at early stages can help you stay ahead of your competition.

Figure 12.22 shows an overview of the results of a fraud model and the key influencers that may have a significant impact on potential fraud claims.

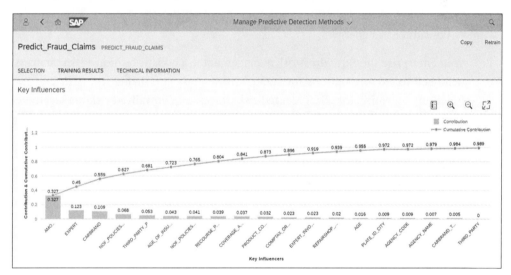

Figure 12.22 Fraud Management Model Using SAP Predictive Analytics

Some additional features provided by SAP Predictive Analytics include the following:

- Drilldown capability within the data
- Analyze and visualize data
- Forward-looking data
- Predictive analytic integrator integrated with the digital core

Predictive analysis provides additional ways of identifying new types of fraud and complements fraud management capabilities. Predictive analytics focuses on potentially new/alternate types of fraud, while SAP Business Integrity Screening focuses on historical data.

12.4.3   Risk Management

Another important topic under financial control is risk management. Risk management is the process of identifying, evaluating, and prioritizing risks to minimize impact of risk-related events/occurrences on the profitability of your organization. Risk management is critical for any enterprise in any industry. Some industries where risk management processes are essential to success include the following:

- Government organizations
- Financial sector
- Foreign exchange markets
- Consumer and energy
- Infrastructure
- Information technology
- Pharmaceuticals

Your enterprise should address risk management in a holistic fashion. Risk managers will need to explore options for standardizing and centralizing risk management functions by eliminating fragmented risk processes. Centralized risk management can avoid duplication of effort, resources, and costs and can support both top-down and bottom-up reporting capabilities.

Various activities involved in risk management include the following:

- Risk identification
- Rules and validations
- In-depth analysis
- Ongoing compliance
- Risk classification
- Remediation/mitigation

Implementing risk management processes will mean better alignment with the overall strategic vision of your organization. Automated risk assessment processes, including workflows, can provide the basis for more pervasive controls. Various kinds of risks that an organization faces at any given point in time include operational risks, enterprise risks, credit risks, market risks, sociopolitical risks, and compliance-related risks.

Now, let's look at how the latest technologies such as SAP Leonardo can help address risks such as credit and operational risks while also providing visibility into several risk factors that could potentially negatively impact your business. SAP Digital Boardroom leverages SAP Leonardo technologies to bring data together from multiple sources (both SAP and non-SAP) and present this data in a single, dynamic dashboard. This tool provides real-time business insights about business performance and key risk factors to executives and boards of directors.

SAP Digital Boardroom can explore risk analysis and drive insights based on SAP Governance, Risk, and Compliance data and other data points, which can help with of maximizing revenue growth in the coming financial years. SAP Digital Boardroom provides drilldown features to help you evaluate additional factors relevant to risk measurement and management. This tool provides the ability to further analyze the data, slice and dice different categories to understand the impact of risk, and explore options to mitigate the risk. Figure 12.23 shows a high-level overview of risk analysis produced by SAP Digital Boardroom.

Figure 12.23 Risk Analysis as Part of SAP Digital Boardroom

You can drill down and see further details, for example, as shown in Figure 12.24, to understand the top five factors that impact risk and to identify the key stakeholders responsible for mitigating the risk.

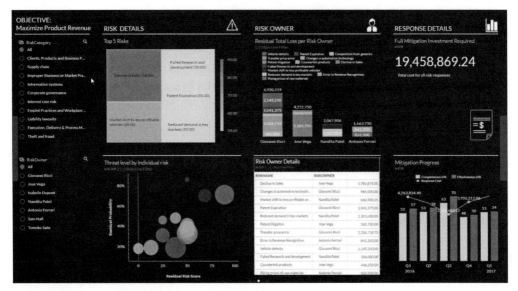

Figure 12.24 Risk Details Presented in SAP Digital Boardroom

12.5   Summary

In recent years, we've seen some significant technological changes that have changed the way day-to-day activities are performed. Gone are the days where doing the same repetitive accounting and finance tasks is acceptable; now is the time to embrace change and explore new options provided by technologies in the digital era. With heterogeneous data available from social media, new opportunities where organizations can harness the data to create new markets and revenue streams have emerged. In this chapter, we reviewed some key finance topics and discussed how SAP Leonardo along with SAP S/4HANA as the digital core can help improve efficiency in these processes. The need of the hour is for organizations to embark on a digital journey in order survive competition in today's market, which has resulted in numerous changes to the way finance and accounting activities are performed. Some of these tasks were unimaginable before but are now made possible due to digital technologies. Now is the time for your organization to embrace change, evolve, and stay tuned to technological updates, or face the fate of the dinosaurs.

Chapter 13

Assorted Business Processes

In this chapter, we'll focus on explaining the evolution of SAP architecture and provide insights into how advancements have optimized specific process functions such as human resources management, sourcing and procurement, and sales and marketing.

The connected world of SAP Leonardo and the Internet of Things (IoT) provides opportunities to change the way your business works as part of the digital core. SAP ERP and SAP S/4HANA processes can now help improve integration and help you accelerate innovation due to availability of new insights, decision-making, reporting and operational processes as part of the digital core. As your organization embarks on its digital transformation and SAP implementation journey, you'll need to understand the overall architecture and not mistakenly think that SAP ERP is simply being replaced with SAP S/4HANA.

In this chapter, we'll initially walk through some considerations around the need to reimagine architecture and then walk through some illustrative use cases and examples of the influence of SAP Leonardo on solution architecture and the business processes mentioned earlier.

13.1 Reimagined Solution Architecture

As we define the solution architecture, we must first look at its context. A solution architecture is a component of the enterprise architecture, which, as shown in Figure 13.1, broadly addresses people, process, and technology. This context is essential when you consider how different parts of the enterprise architecture impact each other. Once the context is set, you'll need to look at the advancements happening in one area and determine how to leverage those impacts into defining the architecture of other areas. As we take a closer look at the solution architecture, we'll investigate the impacts of people and technology on business processes.

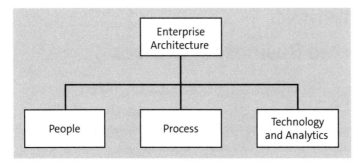

Figure 13.1 Enterprise Architecture Focus Areas

First, people (or user) considerations around enterprise architecture have changed, but not drastically, and enterprises have operated generally consistently over the years. User considerations have always utilized advancements in technology to enable workforces to enhance performance and increase productivity. The process architecture has been designed from a user perspective to enable a more flexible organization, which improves engagement and job satisfaction, which in turn allows for better yields from a business process and better overall effectiveness.

Next, the technology architecture is a deep topic covering a multitude of technology aspects, and many enterprise architects have been focused solely on utilizing advancements in technology to impact everything an organization does. Foundationally, technology has been the great enabler and has caused significant impact, both positive and negative, to both people and processes in any given organization.

Cloud computing has not just led to a revolution in infrastructure, but has also infused new life into technologies like machine learning (leading into artificial intelligence), big data, blockchain and IoT. These technologies, combined with cloud computing, are driving the new digital transformation at enterprises. The inception of a new solution architecture has now begun.

In the following sections, we'll dive more deeply into how the architecture has evolved, explore key architecture design considerations, and describe the capabilities unlocked by an architecture using software-as-a-service (SaaS) solutions and microservices.

13.1.1 Architecting the Digital Core

Reexamining your solution architecture is a point of reimagination. When the rules of the game have altered so much that the foundation on which the solution architecture has also changed, existing best practices and foundational principles may lose meaning. However, because of the newness of these technologies, a common set of best practices have not been tested. Yet, a clear view does exist into what digital technologies can do to business processes, as we've seen these technologies disrupt companies and industries. Before we dive more deeply into the new solution architecture, let's evaluate the foundation on which a solution architecture should be built. In the early days of these new technologies, these technologies are ripe for utilization in various processes that can add significant value to your enterprise.

A basic tenet to applying solution architecture principles rests on identifying those processes which are relevant and hugely impactful to the enterprise. Every business process within an enterprise belongs to one of the three categories: foundational processes, core processes, and strategic processes.

By categorizing business processes using a process segmentation approach, as shown in Figure 13.2, your organization can define an architecture strategy to effectively address specific segments with valid business cases. For example, processes that fall in the foundational segment would typically adopt an out of the box approach or a fit-to-standard approach, whereas for strategic processes you would invest in building niche solutions to drive market differentiators for these processes.

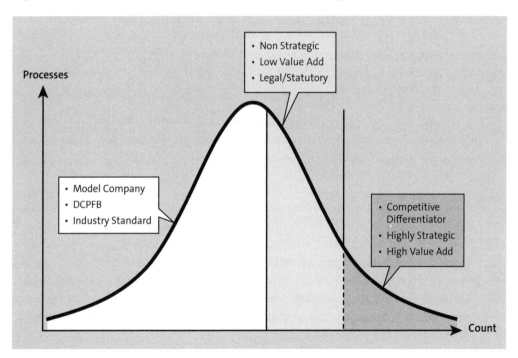

Figure 13.2 Process Segmentation

The new solution architecture calls for five golden principles that enable you to create a comprehensive solution architecture leveraging technological advancements by putting processes and frameworks in place to help you focus your company's time, effort, and money into high-value business processes that significantly develop differentiators. As we'll discuss in the following sections, these principles are as follows:

- Creating a clear and comprehensive solution map
- Pursuing a clean ERP strategy
- Using a platform-first approach
- Following a cloud-first approach
- Embedding innovative architecture into your solution

Solution Map

To reimagine your solution architecture, you can define a solution architecture by following these steps:

1. Define and group all business processes into logical groups, as shown in Figure 13.3, to develop a heat map:
    - Group 1: Low-value and standard practices
    - Group 2: Low-value and differentiating practices
    - Group 3: High-value and standard practices
    - Group 4: High-value and differentiating practices
2. Develop an enterprise-wide strategy around addressing (creating solutions for) these business processes based on the value they contribute to your organization.
3. Follow rigorous rules and principles when developing the solution for a business process.

Your solution map is critical because, when a solution is put together to address a low-value business process by putting a differentiated process into place, you'll need to ask why and how that impacts your overall enterprise strategy, and you'll need a differentiated business process, rather than adopting a standard process. This solution map will also provide your solution architects with a structured methodology and process to develop the solution and challenge your teams to design the business process so that the process stays within the boundaries of the heat map by putting up guard rails around this process.

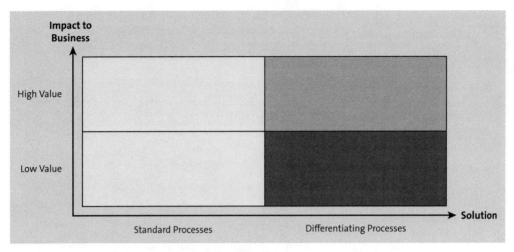

Figure 13.3 Business Process Categorization Heat Map

Once the solution map is in place, then a solution architect can evaluate and enmesh the business architecture on top of a cloud computing reference architecture to design the future state design in a way that impacts the enterprise in the most effective way.

Mapping the business architecture on the reference models will help solution architects find better ways to drive future-state business designs, which allows a sharp focus on the processes with the greatest impact to the enterprise, and you'll be able to utilize newer technologies now available to amplify your business processes.

Clean ERP

Clean ERP is an important principle to adhere to as part of the new solution architecture. The objective of adopting this principle is to keep the core clear of custom technical debt (dependencies) by leveraging SAP Cloud Platform or similar platform-as-a-service (PaaS) solutions as the default platforms for innovation. Coding in the core should be the exception. As shown in Figure 13.4, every SAP journey starts with great intentions. Solid rules and checks and balances are then put together to ensure all business processes are *fit-to-standard*. However, this discipline slowly erodes over time during and after implementation. As your business evolves, your investments in technical debt increase: Thousands of individual great intentions accumulate into massive technical burdens. A root cause of this increasing debt is that an ERP-centric approach to business transformation is not enough. You'll need to revisit the clean ERP paradigm periodically and should ensure you have a consistent process in place to continuously monitor your adherence to this principle.

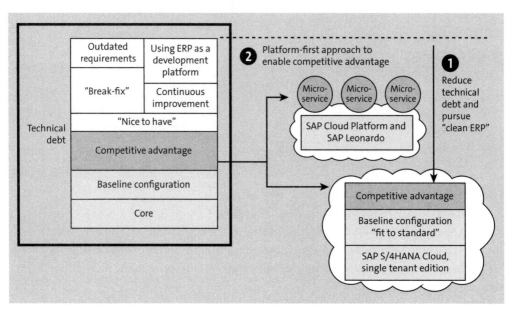

Figure 13.4 Clean ERP: Keeping the Core Light and Agile from Technical Debt

You should enforce a prerequisite, when developing a solution architecture, that clean ERP is followed as a first principle. Often, this strategy fails on multiple fronts due to the nature and complexity of how enterprises operate. Thus, you'll a need to stop using your ERP as a development platform and instead choose an ERP that prevents increases in technical debt.

Platform-First Approach

The next principle a solution architect needs to consider is the platform-first approach. The advent of cloud computing has led to the development of PaaS platforms. A platform-first approach is an essential principle that can move the needle of business process transformation and take innovation to the last mile. A platform-first approach cannot be successful if pursued in isolation; a clean ERP approach must be followed as well. This combination of clean ERP and innovation on platforms will allow you to simplify business process design and drive efficiencies.

With the architecture ecosystem available today, a better path forward can guide you. A modernized ERP enabled by SAP S/4HANA can greatly help reduce technical debt through simplified data structures and new functionalities like embedded analytics. With SAP Cloud Platform and SAP Leonardo, you can deploy a platform-first approach shown in Figure 13.5 to drive competitive advantage. SAP Cloud Platform and SAP Leonardo allow you to abstract new code and isolate code from your core system. Therefore, as your business evolves, you'll be able to pivot more quickly without worrying about impacting your ERP.

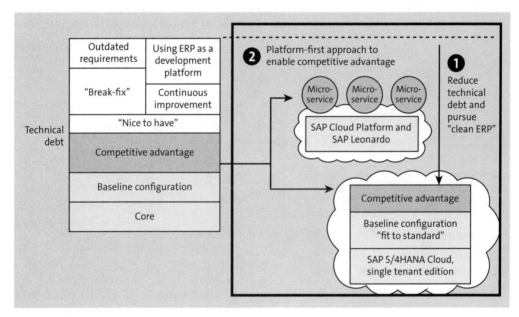

Figure 13.5 Clean ERP: Platform-First Approach

Furthermore, you can use the latest SAP S/4HANA innovations without worrying about how to retrofit newly discovered competitive advantages. Of course, not all scenarios can be addressed by SAP Cloud Platform and SAP Leonardo, and you'll need to adopt a controlled amount of competitive advantage in the core. But your new de facto approach should be a platform-first approach, which will open up choices for solution architects to make the best decisions. Figure 13.6 shows an example decision tree you can apply when deciding whether to deploy an enhancement in the core versus taking a platform-first approach.

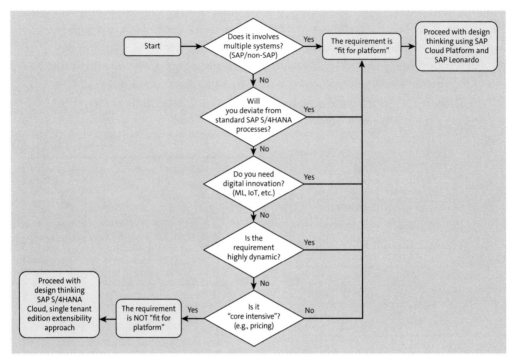

Figure 13.6 Decision Tree for a Platform-First Approach

Cloud-First Approach

The first two principles set the baseline for solution architects to approach business process design. The third principle keeps the first two principles honest and in check. To drive home a clean ERP approach, you'll need a systematic way of keeping technical debt down. The best option is to use an SaaS-based model, which systematically restricts the customizations that can be made within an ERP. At this same time, an SaaS model allows your enterprise take a platform-first approach by providing all the tools you'll need to reimagine traditional business process design using digital technologies.

If solution architects choose to take a clean ERP approach and a platform-first approach for all customizations, then why not keep the clean ERP in the cloud and reap the additional benefits that a cloud infrastructure provides? SAP has launched three digital core options available to an enterprise for an ERP: SAP S/4HANA (the traditional, on-premise model); SAP S/4HANA Cloud (a public cloud offering); and SAP S/4HANA Cloud, single-tenant edition. SAP S/4HANA Cloud is still maturing as an overall offering, but the focus in SAP S/4HANA Cloud has been to drive business processes in a completely redesigned way. In addition to standard SAP S/4HANA Cloud, a cloud-first SAP S/4HANA Cloud, single-tenant edition, is also available now with the full feature set of an on-premise SAP S/4HANA system while being delivered on the cloud via an SaaS model.

Solution architects can use the decision tree shown in Figure 13.7 to select the best options for your enterprise.

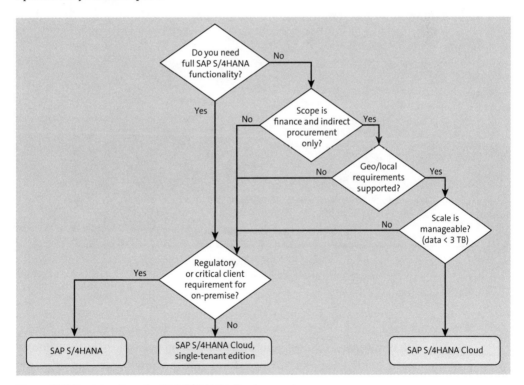

Figure 13.7 Decision Tree for SAP S/4HANA Deployment

Innovation Architecture

The last principle, which sums up the overall strategy for solution architectures, is having an innovation architecture embedded deep into the way a solution is designed. Innovation architecture is not a new paradigm to solution architects. Innovative technologies have always been utilized in delivering business process design. However, with cloud-based ERP and a platform-first approach, the paradigm has shifted to making digital technologies readily available to solution architects so they can transform businesses process in fundamentally new ways. Taking a step back, let's look at the digital technologies available to solution architects, as shown in Figure 13.8.

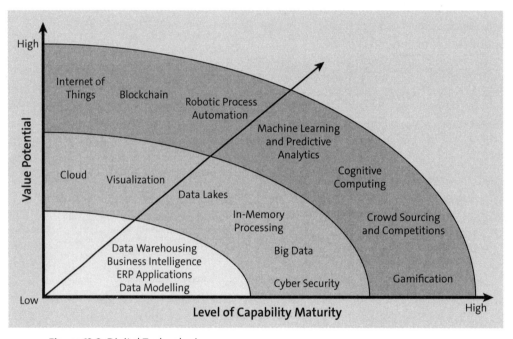

Figure 13.8 Digital Technologies

When you take a platform-first approach, business process design can use a fundamentally different toolset for designing and redesigning solutions. These technologies can enable your enterprise to transform into an *intelligent enterprise*. An intelligent enterprise delivers value from the system of record (SAP S/4HANA or SAP S/4HANA Cloud) to the surrounding technologies and systems (SAP Cloud Platform and other SaaS solutions). However, traditional technologies often fail to deliver on the overall promise of value. Thus, when creating solutions for business problems, utilizing these new technologies is extremely important. The only way a solution architect can ensure the flexibility to adopt new technologies is to follow a platform-first approach, as shown in Figure 13.9.

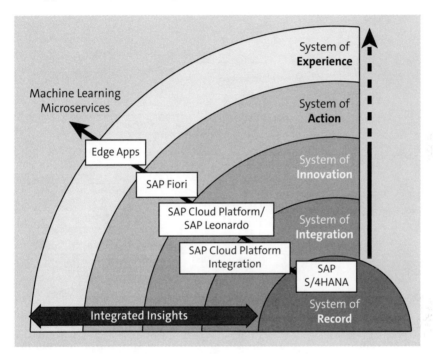

Figure 13.9 Platform First Approach Adopting Innovation

Innovation architecture is essentially the heart of the new solution architecture. Solution architects should now consider all these principles to drive the business process design utilizing new technologies, thereby increasing efficiency and even reimagining your business. To set up the foundation of the new solution architecture, the decision tree shown in Figure 13.10 will enable your solution architects to put in the right framework for the future of the enterprise.

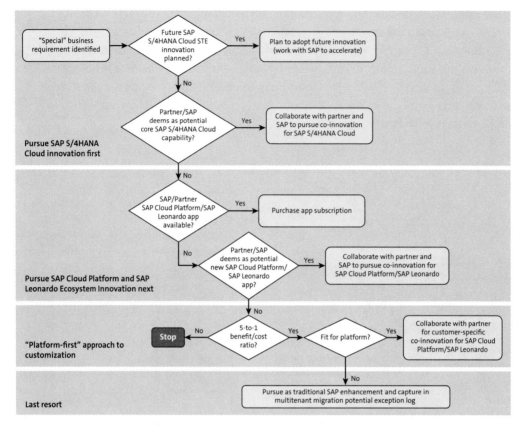

Figure 13.10 New Solution Architecture: Framework for the Future Enterprise

13.1.2   Microservices

Imagine a big suitcase with clothes, books, and accessories tightly packed in together, where moving a small piece could disturb the entire arrangement and there is no space for additional items. This arrangement is known as a monolithic arrangement, with the suitcase serving as one big container.

In software terms, a monolithic application describes a single-tiered software application in which the user interface, the application logic, and database access are combined into a single thread on a single platform, as shown in Figure 13.11. A monolithic application is self-contained and acts independently of other applications.

Traditional ERP suites like SAP ERP were based on a highly customized monolithic architecture of on-premise systems. SAP ERP is built in three main parts: a client-side user interface, a common relational database, and an ABAP-based application server. The application server handles UI requests, executes domain logic, retrieves and updates data from the database in a single logical executable unit. The domain logic includes multiple components that are tightly coupled. Although object-oriented ABAP always provided mechanisms to modularize application logic using classes, namespaces, and persistent objects, a change to a specific component invariably leads to extensive regression testing and codeployment to production environments. These limitations are common in monolithic software. The application can horizontally scale the monolith by running many instances behind a load balancer.

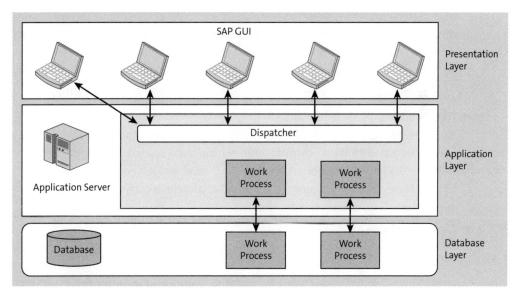

Figure 13.11 Representative Monolithic Architecture

The advent of cloud-based ERPs has led to a disruption in software and integration architecture. Focus has now shifted to faster time to value, lower total cost of ownership (TCO), flexibility, and an integrated but lean IT footprint.

SAP S/4HANA Cloud, along with line of business (LOB) cloud applications such as SAP SuccessFactors, SAP Ariba, SAP Concur, and SAP Integrated Business Planning (SAP IBP) has led the transformation of digital landscapes for SAP customers. Innovations built on top of these platforms provide for greater flexibility, providing improvements and upgrades without impacting the core, which has truly transformed SAP solution landscapes by following the clean ERP approach. Implementing SAP Cloud Platform enables an open architecture for connecting the core to other digital products using a modern integration layer, while optimizing and automating processes is enabled by SAP Leonardo and microservices. The traditional monolithic architecture is now being replaced with a microservices architecture.

In software terms, microservices are an architectural paradigm wherein a monolithic application is decomposed into small, discrete microapplications (microservices). Key characteristics of microservices are its segregation by line of business and its integration via contractual APIs.

Microservices are small, self-contained services that can be brought together to create a business or consumer application. Self-organizing and autonomous teams can easily build out needed application features by leveraging services produced by other teams. Updates can be rapidly pushed out at a granular level with little disruption to customers. Determining which services and features are being used across the enterprise, versus those that should be retired, is also a simpler task.

Key benefits derived from a microservices architecture include the following:

- **Clean core**
  SAP S/4HANA Cloud works on the principle of clean core or zero-code core, which means that traditional customizations, which often caused incompatibilities or upgrade challenges, are not allowed. Instead side-by-side extensions using whitelisted APIs are the only customizations allowed. A clean core ultimately results in benefitting more quickly from newer innovations.

- **Line of business apps**
  SAP S/4HANA Cloud now provides applications segregated line of business (e.g. SAP SuccessFactors for employee management, SAP Ariba for vendor management, SAP C/4HANA for customer management, SAP Fieldglass for contractor management, etc.). This segregation drives application isolation, which means that specific applications can be individually upgraded or scaled without impacting the entire ecosystem.

- **Contractual APIs**
  Powered via SAP Cloud Platform services, SAP's public cloud applications now provision whitelisted APIs. These APIs have a defined and contractual signature, abstracting complex implementation details from the consumer of the method. APIs typically support open protocols such as REST, thus enabling seamless integrations.

- **SAP Cloud Platform API Management**
  SAP Cloud Platform API Management is a one-stop shop for managing both SAP- and non-SAP-provided APIs. SAP Cloud Platform API Management supports the

orchestration of cross-system APIs while following the key principles of isolation, reusability, and scalability. This solution also serves as the backbone of the flexible, lean, and loosely coupled integration between the various isolated components of SAP's public cloud offerings.

- **Cloud Foundry**
  SAP Cloud Platform offers Cloud Foundry services, which allow your customers, partners, and developers to build compelling applications powered by SAP Leonardo technologies. SAP is a key member and contributor of the Cloud Foundry community-based platform, one of the most dynamic open source projects on the market today. Cloud Foundry provides flexibility to developers, who had been restricted to building applications using runtimes like Java and XSJS. Now, developers can build microservices using business services from Cloud Foundry such as Node.js, ABAP, Python, Ruby, or any BYOL (bring your own language) model, which enables the development of platform-agnostic microservices, which then can more easily be orchestrated to build consumer-grade applications.

13.2   Human Resource Management

The personnel in any given organization will have different expectations about the work environment, culture, and technology enablement. The nature of work itself is changing, requiring different skills and greater collaboration, which will be needed by personnel in order to develop and execute strategies to perform work-related tasks. We've seen new, tech-savvy workers replace old-fashioned, experienced managers. In today's environment, your employees will need to invest time and build new capabilities to support your organization's mission and goals.

Your organization must be able to quickly respond to market changes, including product development and merger and acquisition activities. Future acquisitions will bring and engage creative talent and exploit new market opportunities. To meet these changes, you may need to revisit how human resources (HR) are managed within your organization. Moving to cloud-based solutions is one way that can change the way human resources work gets done.

Recently, technological innovations have caused marketplace disruptions in how human resources are managed. These market disruptions are forcing paradigm shifts in how workforces are defined, measured, and supported.

The HR function is in the middle of unprecedented workforce and business disruptions. This presents new challenges as well as new opportunities for HR managers.

For the first time, technology capabilities have outpaced HR's ability to adopt new tools, solutions, and approaches, presenting a major opportunity for HR to help transform the organization. To seize the opportunity ahead and set the stage for continuous improvement, organizations need more than technology; continued success requires a new organizational structure and mindset. Some key opportunities to improve HR functions include the following:

- Increasing employee productivity
- Expanding and improving employee self-service experiences
- Attracting and retaining the best talent in the business and building your brand as a talent leader in communications, media, entertainment, and digital technology
- Managing your workforce efficiently, investing in quality over quantity
- Driving improvements in engagement, collaboration, and the execution of complex strategic initiatives

In the following sections, we'll dive more deeply into how edge technologies are driving the transformation of processes in the HR domain and show how evolving technologies, such as digital assistants and robotic process automation (RPA), are driving new opportunities and solutions in HR management.

13.2.1   Intelligent HR Solutions

Improving HR technology remains a central focus for any HR transformation project. Across industries, many organizations face the ongoing need to build smarter, more effective, more efficient systems that automate and streamline daily administrative work. In the following sections, we'll dive more deeply into how SAP SuccessFactors intelligent services can drive change around HR.

HR Intelligent Services

SAP SuccessFactors intelligent services, an advanced approach to self-services, enables you to deploy and manage new end-to-end human resources events based on workforce changes. By deploying intelligent services for HR, your organization can deliver benefits for your third parties, for your employees, and for the HR department by helping reduce the overall time for completing any HR transaction. In addition, intelligent services for HR can generate notifications to keep all relevant stakeholders informed and engaged in critical decision-making. An intelligent system providing proactive alerts can serve as a huge timesaver, relieving HR business partners or managers from having to manually analyze information—and helping to avoid the delays that can come from waiting for specific team members to pass along information or escalate issues. Figure 13.12 shows an example where an employee leave application can trigger other dependent events/tasks automatically.

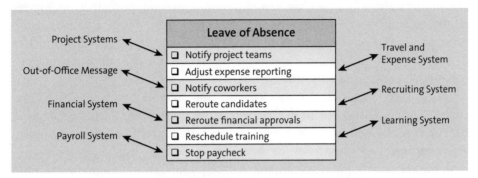

Figure 13.12 Example of an HR Application Providing Automated Alerts

Intelligent services are redefining end-to-end process with the total workforce experience in mind. Intelligent services essentially permit a more sophisticated integration than simply data flows between applications. Now user experiences, process maps, and data flows across the business can be integrated. Given HR technology does not operate in a vacuum, SAP is also extending these integrations to downstream systems to optimize the total workforce experience. An example of a deeper level of integration made possible by intelligent services (transactions associated with employee leaves of absence) is shown in Figure 13.13.

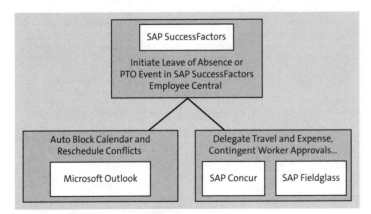

Figure 13.13 Example of Intelligent Integration with Downstream Applications

Robotic Process Automation

As the HR world moves rapidly toward digital platforms, robotic process automation (RPA) can be leveraged for routine, repetitive tasks, which results in a number of benefits. For example, RPA can eliminate the need for humans to perform routine, time-consuming activities. In turn, your employees can increase productivity and spend more time making more strategic decisions that lead to improved customer satisfaction and other business-critical results. By leveraging a disruptive technology such as RPA for HR transformation, your organization can take a massive leap toward tangible benefits. While RPA is a good candidate for HR processes that involve high volume and repetitive tasks, cognitive/AI technology is better suited for judgment-based processes. Figure 13.14 shows a list of tasks within the scope of HR functions that could benefit RPA or cognitive technologies to automate manual and time-consuming activities, organized by the following color scheme:

- Boxes in red represent current candidates for cognitive/AI enablement.
- Boxes in green represent current candidates for RPA enablement.
- Boxes in yellow represent future candidates for possible cognitive/AI enablement.

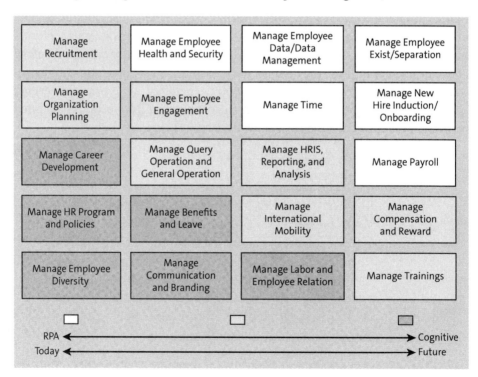

Figure 13.14 Candidate HR Tasks That Can Leverage RPA and Cognitive Technologies

Digital Assistant

SAP CoPilot is a digital assistant and bot integration hub for enterprise users to get things done more easily and more quickly, in a more user-friendly manner.

SAP SuccessFactors continues to invest in the development of SAP CoPilot's digital assistant capabilities to support HR functions, turning complex, multidimensional processes into intelligent digital interactions. For example, SAP SuccessFactors plans to leverage digital assistant capabilities to deliver great employee onboarding experiences and help set new hires up for success, with guidance tailored to their specific roles on day 1.

Figure 13.15 shows a simple use case demonstrating digital assistant capabilities as a mechanism to provide alerts, capture feedback, and trigger other user actions or HR bots to complete employee actions.

Figure 13.15 Example to Demonstrate Digital Assistant Conversation Capabilities and Abilities to Conduct Surveys

The goal of making employee experiences personalized has always been elusive but important, and now with machine learning-based digital assistants, personalized experiences are finally possible. Whether better matching of employees to the right roles or making training recommendations relevant so employees can move further along on their career paths, SAP SuccessFactors aims to continually create better experiences by building intelligent and intuitive interactions using SAP Leonardo machine learning capabilities. Using these latest technologies, users will have a single intuitive interface through which they'll engage with HR solutions. SAP SuccessFactors is partnering with work apps people use every day, like Slack, Microsoft Teams, and Google Hangouts, which means the SAP SuccessFactors digital assistant can be accessed from those apps to complete HR tasks with ease and immediacy without interrupting workflow.

13.2.2   Examples and Use Cases

Use of AI and machine learning capabilities to handle repeatable tasks that humans have traditionally performed is already changing the delivery of HR services. The SAP Leonardo portfolio, which includes machine learning, will become a critical part of building ecosystems that can support sustainable HR in the digital age. The following sections discuss some scenarios and use cases in this area.

Recruitment: AI-Enabled Talent Search

Resume reading and data processing/correlating can be automated, allowing human talent to be better used in more strategic aspects of the HR role. The SAP Leonardo-powered Resume Matching service for SAP SuccessFactors solutions is based on machine learning and offers intelligent candidate screening and matching features so you can find the best applicants more quickly.

Machine learning algorithms automatically match the most qualified candidates to open positions by following these steps:

1. Extracting key information from a resume and presenting this information in a more readable format
2. Visualizing key selection criteria such as education, skills, and experience
3. Identifying the best talent based on a relevance scores to create a candidate short list with bias correction

An AI-powered deep learning platform could enables your recruiters to make better, faster hiring decisions without bias. Machine learning matches top talent to open job positions, which allows for the following activities:

- Fast-tracking the screening process to save time and effort
- Identifying the best candidates and reducing false positives
- Reducing the possibility of missing potential candidates
- Mitigating a recruiter's personal bias in screening candidates

An AI-based solution speeds up the candidate screening process. In a traditional approach, on average, filling an open position take 52 days. Recruiters spend up to 60% of their time on administrative tasks, candidate screening, and sourcing. As shown in Figure 13.16, SAP's resume scanner solution can use machine learning to scan through resumes and provides a prioritized list of prospective candidates for recruiters.

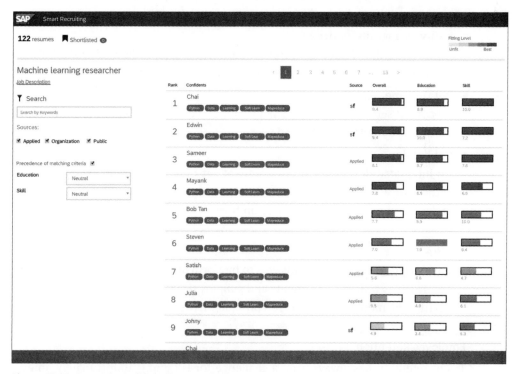

Figure 13.16 Smart Recruiting: Resume Scanner

HR Bot to Automate Repetitive HR Tasks

Cognitive agents transform the interaction between HR and employees. Always-on chat agents can answer questions instantaneously and be available on employee phones, a rather different service experience than calling an HR hotline. AI- and machine learning-powered bots encourage ongoing and continuous use of HR systems and processes with voice recognition, messenger apps, and chat bots. AI-powered bots can engage with candidates over messaging platforms, asking contextual questions relating to job requirements, offering personalized updates and feedback, and suggesting next steps. SAP Conversational AI (formerly SAP Leonardo Conversational AI Foundation) includes the following essential components for building intelligent and intuitive interactions:

- **Intent matching service**
  A deep learning-based service that helps you understand what users want to do by processing user utterances using SAP Conversational AI for natural language processing.

- **Entity extraction service**
  Allows the SAP CoPilot digital assistant and other apps to determine attributes in a sentence, including all the different ways a user might express an idea.

- **Bot runtime**
  A backend service that allows SAP CoPilot and chatbots to communicate consistently and dynamically with end users.

- **Bot builder**
  An integrated development environment for building chatbots by chaining together processes using SAP Fiori user experience design principles and SAP backend services to establish conversation flow, system logic, personality, and more, without the need for hard coding. These chatbots have the ability to self-improve.

- **Q&A service**
  Enables chatbots to retrieve answers to freeform questions based on unstructured text (such as training documents and support tickets). These chatbots, which get smarter the more information you provide, answer users in a natural way.

Employee Retention

Talent retention has always been a challenge for HR and is unfortunately an ever more pressing issue. Cognitive technologies can provide key insights into what employees are really looking for within their roles and will allow you to start predicting behavior patterns. The technology spots patterns in your historical data to predict future behavior, identify risks, and uncover opportunities while intelligently listening and responding to feedback. AI technologies embedded in employee feedback tools can automatically channel concerns to the HR team member with the right emotional background, expertise, and leadership role needed to resolve these issues quickly. Equipped with every employee's history and recommendations on how to best engage them, HR can provide real-time counseling that is relevant and matches the perceived gravity of the situation in tone, word use, and urgency.

13.3   Sourcing and Procurement

Procurement organizations are evolving from supporting functions to a more strategic advisory role. Procurement has typically not had a strategic role because, previously, gathering data and generating insights to build business cases in procurement was almost impossible. New technologies and market dynamics have set the stage for digitally transformed procurement. Next-generation technologies such as machine learning, analytics, and better data visualizations will help make the procurement process more intelligent and data driven. Digital procurement is the application of disruptive technologies that enable the following activities:

- Strategic sourcing can now be predictive, with supply bases, prices, and costs all visible, empowering professionals to reach transparent agreements with high-value suppliers through the following capabilities:
    - Categorizing and managing spend in real time, leveraging machine learning
    - Predicting demand with artificial intelligence
    - Knowing the landed cost for any commodity for all alternate countries of origin
    - Predicting future sources of supply
    - Acting on timely alerts from all negotiated agreements (e.g. indexed pricing, penalties, and renewals) through smart contracts
- Procure-to-pay (P2P) processes are automated in the digital world. Transactions (processing purchase orders, requisitioning goods and services, validating the receipt of materials, paying invoices, etc.) are not routinized and require minimal human intervention, as in the following capabilities:
    - Automatically sensing material demand and requisition replenishment deliveries from suppliers
    - Eliminating repetitive processing through robotic process automation
    - Triggering payments utilizing real-time signals of material delivery
    - Executing automated secure payments
    - Exchanging goods through validated and trusted decentralized ledgers
- Supplier risk management (SRM) can now be proactive, with risk mitigation strategies now preemptive, allowing professionals to focus on continuously optimizing operations, as opposed to conducting damage control, as in the following capabilities:
    - Monitoring potential supplier risks in real time through the aggregation and visualization of third-party data feeds

– Conducting supplier visits remotely utilizing augmented reality

– Enhancing supplier audits through crowdsourcing and external data feeds

Leveraging better data from source-to-cash (S2C), P2P, and SRM processes; advanced analytics; increased computing power; and improved visualization technologies, digital procurement ultimately provides better evidence-based options for decision-making and improve the accuracy of strategic decisions.

In the following sections, we'll dive more deeply into how SAP Ariba enables cognitive procurement and specific areas where AI and machine learning are making an impact.

13.3.1   Cognitive Procurement

Pairing SAP Ariba with SAP Leonardo capabilities, procurement services have started a cognitive transformation journey. Capabilities such as data mining, pattern recognition, and natural language processing enable you to build self-learning sourcing and procurement applications. SAP cognitive procurement comprises of procurement services such as purchase requisitioning, order processing, invoice processing, order confirmation, and operational contract management. Core SAP S/4HANA procurement processes can be enhanced with the SAP Ariba solutions, which extend these core processes with guided buying; collaborative sourcing and contracting; and networked-based, end-to-end supplier collaboration. SAP Leonardo's AI-driven data insights can empower your procurement professionals to make smarter decisions more quickly.

Figure 13.17 shows the **Procurement Overview** page in SAP S/4HANA, which provides end users with an insight-driven overview from which they can drill down into specific areas that require additional action. The same capabilities are further enhanced by SAP Leonardo technologies, such as machine learning and other automation technologies like RPA, to take the additional step of executing business processes on trained AI models or automating tasks based on specific business rules.

Some important areas with AI and machine learning capabilities include the following:

- **Contract intelligence**
  Provides customers with the knowledge and insights to create, negotiate, structure, and execute a comprehensive contract by analyzing supplier information, commodity insights, and similar contract/negotiation. The application makes the contract negotiation process smarter and more comprehensive. It automatically identifies the relevant terms and conditions from contracts and matched to a legal

library and taxonomy and finds insights from similar contracts for a specific commodity or region. The AI capability allows mapping contracts to company policies and government regulations and suggests optimal target prices for prices. A natural language processing-driven conversational interface recommends templates; contract-specific clauses, terms, and conditions; and the most suitable suppliers.

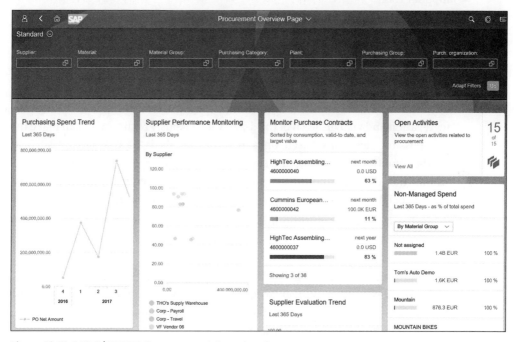

Figure 13.17 SAP S/4HANA Procurement Overview Page

- **Sourcing intelligence**
  Provides buyers with the knowledge and insights to structure and execute the right sourcing event at the right time with the right suppliers, for the right duration. The application monitors commodity-relevant trends to find better information and insights faster from online news and media and access richer and broader sets of data to uncover hidden patterns and discover new insights. These insights will help sourcing managers identify pricing trends by category and develop optimized sourcing strategies and speed up the decision-making process. The solution can also aid in recommending ideal numbers and types of suppliers based on market dynamics, best practices, and company policies. Cognitive processes uncover insights, automate tasks, drive efficiencies, and increase savings. Cognitive capabilities can help you perform the following activities:

- Prepare requests for proposals (RFPs)
- Prepare a list of preferred suppliers to participate based on product category, industry, or location
- Delivering intelligence on market trends and pricing points

- **Supplier risk**
Machine learning capabilities help expand existing solutions to include additional knowledge sources and natural disaster events and establish resolution rooms to find alternatives to resolve risk. Anticipated and unforeseen risks associated with suppliers can affect manufacturing, on-time product delivery, company brand, and more. SAP Leonardo cognitive technologies help procurement professionals stay ahead of the curve and mitigate potential supplier risk situations through the aggregation and visualization of third-party data feeds. Procurement can make the best possible decisions based on a real-time analysis of risk factors such as weather, politics, geography, and similar considerations. Furthermore, other factors, such as natural calamities or traffic data, can be used for logistics optimization, or social media monitoring can be used for supplier brand-related events.

  Analyzing events in real time improves decision-making and business performance. Using cognitive technologies, procurement solutions enable professionals to get early alerts into risk situations, assess potential risk levels, and look at resolutions/alternatives to mitigate risks. Analyzing external or crowdsourcing data feeds provides greater supplier insight and improves supplier audit. Figure 13.18 shows the standard SAP Ariba Supplier Risk capability that can be further enhanced by RPA and cognitive capabilities.

- **Spend analysis (invoice classification)**
The solution improves the quality and coverage of invoice classification and enhance delivery time for quarterly refreshes. Invoice classification is a complex process due to the large volumes of invoices that can exist across thousands of product categories. Machine learning algorithms such as convolutional neural networks help analyze visual imagery, for example, enriching spend data to provide enhanced features like company information and vendor details in a fraction of the time than the traditional approach. AI models can tailor themselves to your specific needs by learning the spending categories through the aggregation and classification of spend data across the enterprise, which provides 360-degree visibility into spending, suppliers, and related market information, which greatly improves the accuracy of spend classification.

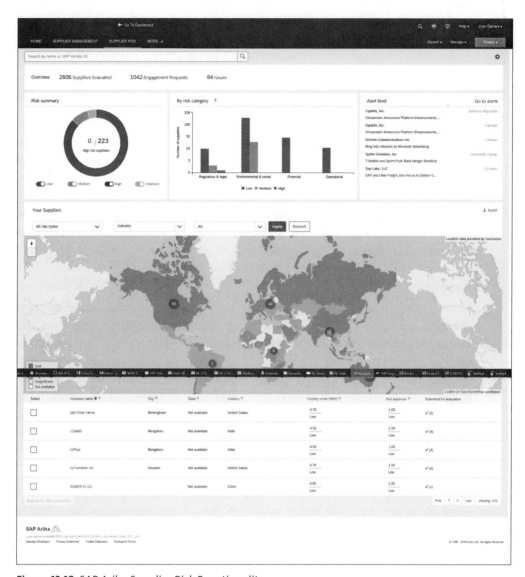

Figure 13.18 SAP Ariba Supplier Risk Functionality

- **Catalogs**

   Provides content/attribute normalization for better search results and richer content. Natural language processing APIs support intelligent content parsing and autopopulates the catalog with relevant supplier information. Thus, enabling supplier catalogs, from creation through cleaning and onboarding, is fast and easy. Guided buying utilizes smart catalog to navigates users through proper buying channels to leverage preferred suppliers, negotiated pricing, and in-context policies.

13.3.2   Examples and Use Cases

Advances in software and artificial intelligence have vastly expanded both the number of activities that can be automated and the degree of automation that is possible. SAP Leonardo enables data insights to empower procurement professionals to make smarter, faster decisions across their supply chains. These new applications can impact the entire procurement process, from improving spend visibility to assisting buyers and enriching content management. Let's look next at some representative use cases that drive the last mile of value using edge technologies such as IoT and cognitive technologies.

Supplier Selection and Supplier Relationship Management

Supplier selection and sourcing from the right suppliers are increasingly important concerns and essential in highly regulated industries, including aerospace and defense, food and beverages, and medical products. SAP Leonardo provides the capability to analyze previously unavailable data or to bring order to massive unstructured datasets. Datasets, generated from SRM actions such as supplier assessments, audits, and credit scoring, provide an important basis for further decisions regarding a supplier. With the help of machine learning and intelligible algorithms, supplier selection is more predictive and intelligible, creating a platform for success from the very first collaboration. AI algorithms are providing multiple best supplier scenarios based on identified parameters.

An intelligent content extraction solution enabled by machine learning will convert static documents into data points for review and action. Information that is buried under thousands of files (e.g. contracts) in hard copy or PDF form prevents rapid access to detailed specs, negotiated terms and conditions, indexed pricing, penalties, etc.

Contracts become intelligent and more comprehensive with applications that can perform the following tasks:

- Uncover similar contract terms for a specific commodity by industry or region based on benchmarking data.
- Suggest optimal prices to target based on expected volume and contractual discounts.

- Automatically identify relevant terms and conditions matched to legal library and taxonomy.
- With the SAP Leonardo's natural language processing capability, contracts written in complex legal language, often several hundred pages long, can be processed in a fraction of the time it would take a team of human experts.

A cognitive computing and artificial intelligence solution must be able to read, interpret, and recognize the information procurement professionals require and must serve as a single, constantly refreshed source of supplier spend data. Predictive analytics models could calculate total landed cost differences across products, country viability, country risk, and future-state forecasts by category and country. Applying new technologies, new forms of contract execution could become available, for example, to address volatile pricing issues using an AI that continually scans current market conditions.

Automated Quality Inspection and Maintenance of Goods/Assets

Machine learning excels at recognizing and identifying visual pattern, opening up many applications in physical inspection and maintenance of physical assets across an entire supply chain network. Designed using algorithms that quickly seek out comparable patterns in multiple datasets, machine learning has proven to be effective at automating inbound quality inspection throughout logistics hubs, isolating product shipments with damage and wear. Machine learning algorithms can determine if a shipping container or product was damaged, classify and record the damage by time, and recommend the best corrective action to repair the assets in real time. Combining machine learning with advanced analytics, IoT sensors, and real-time monitoring can provide end-to-end visibility across many supply chains in the following ways:

- IoT and sensor devices can collect goods movement conditions including location, weather, and temperature as well as collect images of packages or containers.
- The SAP Leonardo Image Classification API can analyze raw images to detect anomalies.
- AI can identify different damage types and classify damage into categories (stress fracture, oiled surface, corrosion, missing parts, etc.).
- Anomalies are displayed, and teams are notified to take action.

Figure 13.19 and Figure 13.20 show how SAP Predictive Maintenance and Service can trigger a proactive maintenance alert, which could in turn lead to an RPA action or proactively trigger the execution of a business process. Both figures show how IoT data captured can be further optimized by automating the next steps using RPA or cognitive technologies.

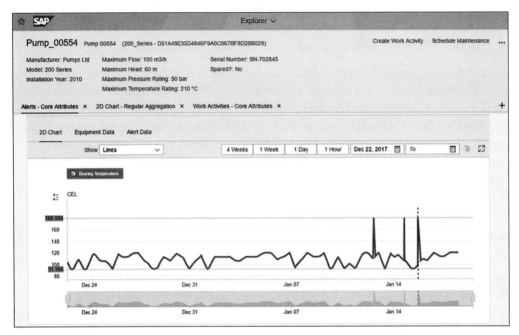

Figure 13.19 IoT-Driven SAP Predictive Maintenance and Service Enabling Proactive Machine Inspection Schedules

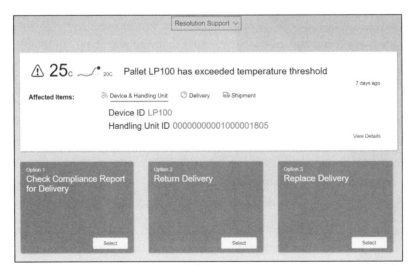

Figure 13.20 IoT-Enabled Business Processes That Can Be Further Automated Using RPA

Procurement Bot

Bots can automate repetitive, routine tasks to reduce costs, improve efficiency and accuracy, and accelerate execution. In the process, human resources are freed up for other higher-value activities that require judgment and intuition. Bots can assume responsibility for any procurement activity or process that involves a high degree of both structured information (such as a supplier name, category, commodity code, discrete item description, or SKU number) and rules-based processing ("if X, then do Y"). Bots can create a purchase order based on requisition data when all required fields are complete and accurate. Bots paired with analytics and artificial intelligence can be critical to future procurement organizations that rely more on data than processes to make better business decisions, potentially reduce operating costs, and improve overall efficiency.

Bots are effectively helping procurement professionals in activities such as the following:

- In supplier record management, bots can help in the registration/onboarding of vendors, prepare scenario-based approved vendor lists, enhance supplier performance, and provide risk-based alerts.

- During invoice payment processes, bots can scan and OCR hard-copy invoices, conduct AI-based invoice verification and approval routing, and payment issue resolution and query processes.

- In procurement audits, bots can perform noninvasive audits of transactions/records including OCR of documents/emails to identify areas for further investigation.

Note

Other emerging technologies that will also have an impact on innovation in the procurement and sourcing space, such as the following:

- **Blockchain**
  This cryptologic data structure uses a trusted peer-to-peer network to create digital transaction ledgers that can verify and validate transactions in the P2P process (or any other supply chain process) and then be used to trigger automated payments.

- **Cybertracking**
  Real-time tracking of online or physical activity can provide proactive monitoring of supplier behavior and performance. When combined with third-party data,

this technology can deliver trends and predictions on supplier (or supply chain) risks.

- **Crowdsourcing**
  Through the capture of large and diverse inputs (e.g. data, sentiment) and usually leveraging mobile technology, your organization can monitor trends and events impacting supply chains and supplier performance.
- **Virtual reality and spatial analytics**
  Detecting events or changes of status using video, location data, or pattern analysis and conducting supplier visits or audits can empower procurement professionals to do more with less.

13.4   Sales and Marketing

Artificial intelligence and machine learning improvements are poised to unleash the next wave of digital disruption, and companies must prepare for this wave. The SAP Leonardo suite of technologies provides various options to help support and improve sales and marketing processes.

Sales, service, marketing, and commerce teams can all benefit from automation, intelligent data, and more informed decision-making in conducting their day-to-day tasks. Chatbots are a quintessential example. Most of us have already heard of or interacted personally with a chatbot, which can serve as a smart assistant that puts the customer first and helps eliminate back-and-forth wait times.

Artificial intelligence/machine learning is a magic bullet that takes the guesswork out of boundless sales and marketing activities. Once initial processes are built by an organization to manage marketing and sales activities, the next step(s) would be to start using edge technologies that can leverage different data models, revenue streams, and other IT processes for increased sales once enough data is put through algorithms for use. Of course, companies will need to spend some time on fine-tuning and maintenance and will probably want to add more features down the line. Depending on the industry, market, and products, revenue could grow if new technologies are put to the right use, especially by focusing on new avenues to attract and retain customers.

SAP Leonardo technologies use sophisticated algorithms to help software learn from the massive volumes of data available across different platforms. This data is turn can help with product suggestions as part of the sales process through the display of similar products bought by other customers. These real-world examples are everywhere in today's smart phone era—think of personalized product recommendations on Amazon, facial recognition on Facebook, or the fastest routes in Google Maps.

The digital economy is changing customers' buying behavior. Living in a world where sensors, artificial intelligence, and social media data (structured and unstructured) flows are just one click away, customers expect individualized products and a unified buying experience on any device delivered quickly. To support sales, marketing, and other key business processes, SAP has embedded SAP Leonardo capabilities within SAP S/4HANA.

In the next section, we'll review some key areas in sales and marketing where remarkable technological changes have occurred in recent years.

13.4.1 Sales and E-Commerce

The emergence of vast volumes of data from multiple sources and platforms generating new information every minute has gifted companies with data related to consumer interests and buying behaviors. SAP Leonardo capabilities, along with best-in-class front-office applications across sales, services, marketing, and commerce functions using SAP C/4HANA, can deliver on the promise of creating unique and personalized experiences for your front-office team.

Edge technologies supported by SAP provide additional tools that can enable machine learning and artificial intelligence to help optimize processes, assist workforce, and make customers happy. SAP C/4HANA with embedded machine learning capabilities can help your enterprise better leverage customer information, analyze customer sentiment and buying patterns, improve upon customer interactions, and leverage structured and unstructured data that you can transform into truly intelligent and smart experiences for your customers.

A paradigm shift has occurred in sales processes, from being reactive to being proactive, from being instinct-driven to being data-driven. Artificial intelligence can guide your sales team or your go-to-market (GTM) team on the sales journey starting from identifying potential customers to steps to retaining customers. Sales applications based on SAP S/4HANA can identify customer actions/signals that can help close deals, while the other hand machine learning capabilities can help you continuously improve actions, offers, and processes that your sales team/GTM team can use to achieve their revenue targets.

Machine learning capabilities embedded into sales processes can offer your organization the ability to compare its historical sales data with current prospect data (company size, stakeholders, turnaround, etc.). This information can in turn help predict which solutions would be most effective to influence and close the sale, what activities could increase the likelihood of closing the deal, how long will closing the deal will take, and whether any potential exists for upselling/cross-selling other products to a prospect.

Two relevant features available in SAP S/4HANA include the following:

- **Sales forecast**
  The sales forecast solution leverages new mathematical techniques and near real-time information, along with machine learning, to create an accurate forecast of demand based on the current realities. The solution creates a forecast based on prior sales history and draws on several years of data and close to real-time information to provide insights into predictable seasonal patterns.

- **Selling recommender**
  This solution creates a recommendation model (recommender) and uses this model to generate a list of items (recommendations) to suggest to a specific user, all using machine learning.

13.4.2   Smart Campaigns

Machine learning across the sales pipeline provides tremendous value whether related to opportunities to close deals or to simply identify prospects for future sales. Your marketing team is often faced with the crucial challenge of identifying the right target groups to focus on to enhance the probability of a prospect being converted into a business partner, which can only happen when the sale deal is closed. A huge amount of effort, time, and resources is spent identifying customers to be potential targets for marketing campaigns.

SAP C/4HANA supports smart campaigns through the use of SAP Marketing Cloud's geolocation segmentation, which provides capabilities for supporting campaign management, multichannel campaign automation, and other marketing features. This solution can bring in multiple data sources and analyze huge datasets to identify buying patterns, customer behaviors that can help you narrow down target audiences for particular marketing campaigns. SAP C/4HANA provides users with the ability to slice and dice data from multiple sources/systems and to use geolocation to help model and target marketing campaigns for specific geographical areas.

SAP Marketing Cloud is a single platform, an end-to-end marketing solution that includes the following capabilities:

- Geolocation segmentation, which can be used to target a particular region for marketing a particular strategy or campaign
- Product recommendations
- Intelligent scoring that you can leverage to target the right prospects
- Campaign analytics (available out of the box) to track the success of your campaigns without requiring additional business intelligence capabilities

Figure 13.21 shows an example of a customer segmentation model for targeted marketing solutions, thus leading to improved customer experience.

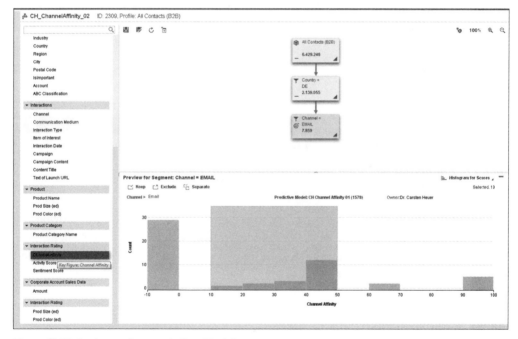

Figure 13.21 Customer Segmentation Model

Figure 13.22 shows a standard SAP dashboard for providing a spend analysis view of marketing plans.

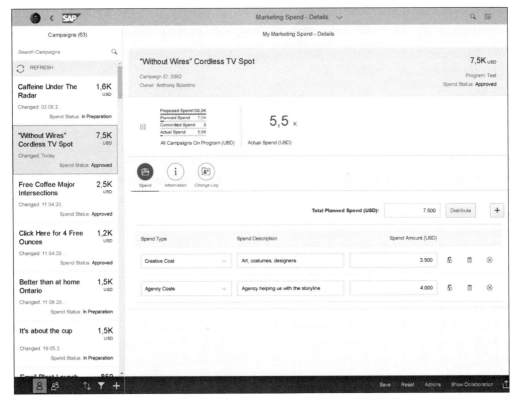

Figure 13.22 Spend Management for Marketing Plans

13.4.3   Examples and Use Cases

In this section, we'll look at two of the use cases where edge technologies provided by SAP helps monitor sales deals, thereby improving conversion rate (of sales quotations to sales orders) while media sentiment analysis can be tracked to understand market campaign effectiveness.

Increasing Sales Conversions

Some of the toughest work for a sales manager is predicting the probability of a sales quotation being converted into a sales order, which represents a sealed deal and eventually turns into sales revenue. Currently, a great deal of manual work is involved in entering the sales order probability, after conducting some estimations and calculations. With embedded predictive analytics capabilities, you can use the Quotation Conversion Rates app in SAP S/4HANA 1809, shown in Figure 13.23, to calculate the probability of the sales quotation being converted into a sales order. This app utilizes core classification and regression modeling techniques embedded into the sales quotation process, thus predicting the probability of a sales order, which is expressed as a percentage or the net value of the sales quotation. Using this app, your sales managers can greatly to improve their sales forecasting and boost revenues based on achievable sales volumes.

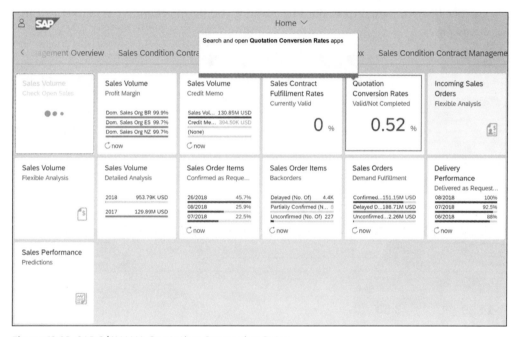

Figure 13.23 SAP S/4HANA Quotation Conversion Rates

This app can be leveraged to compare sales volume actually achieved versus predicted and planned sales volumes. This analysis can be performed according to different dimensions (for example, sales organizations, customers, products, etc.), and the app also provides visuals for comparison. The sales and marketing team can gain predictive insights into current sales performance and impact of simplifying sales planning process. They can further predict the probability that a quotation will be converted into a sales order and also take action on open quotations that have the most potential to generate sales.

Sentiment Media Analysis

Given the growing impact of social media on an organization's fortunes, tracking demographic-specific customer sentiment (both positive and negative) and correlating sentiment to the social media data generated are imperative. SAP Marketing Cloud provides standard dashboards, as shown in Figure 13.24, to track demographic-specific sentiment, interactions by channel, and the effectiveness of marketing campaigns.

Figure 13.24 Customer Demographics, Behaviors, and Sentiments

These capabilities can be further extended by building dashboards that mash up data from SAP Marketing Cloud with other popular social medial channels to track user sentiment. Figure 13.25 shows an example dashboard that illustrates how social media generated can be further analyzed to understand the impact of specific social media channels.

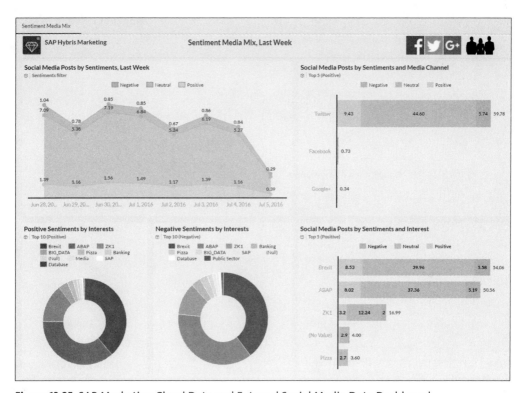

Figure 13.25 SAP Marketing Cloud Data and External Social Media Data Dashboard

13.5 Summary

Still in its formative years, SAP Leonardo represents the next generation of digital disruption technologies and is synonymous with the vanguard of innovation in the SAP digital space, and the near future will define how these technologies are applied and how niche solutions are developed.

As mentioned in Section 13.1, current and future generations of architects must understand current market trends, predict the future of business, and apply these insights and the latest technologies to enable their organizations to take advantage of the rapidly changing IT ecosystem.

Chapter 14
Digitization of Industries

A focus on business value and outcomes should be a key consideration in achieving IT effectiveness. Regardless of the industry, businesses strive for strategic and quantitative business benefits with rapid time to value. SAP Leonardo can provide the underpinnings of a robust solution architecture ready to scale with needs of your business.

In all industries, business as usual is no longer the norm. Rapid process innovations, both within an organization as well as across business networks are in play. A digital revolution powered by intelligent technologies has changed the game. By applying intelligent technologies from SAP Leonardo, you can transform your company into an event-driven business by automating repetitive tasks, enabling your employees to focus on higher value-add tasks and invent new business models and revenue streams by monetizing data-driven capabilities that build upon your core competencies in new ways.

Digitization is a journey anchored on foundational elements like customer-centricity, delivering personalized outcomes, serving the segment of "one," competing in an ecosystem, and enabling and monetizing new business models. As described in earlier chapters, these activities require building operational and channel flexibility with digital smart products, digital supply chains and logistics, smart factories, service digitization, and the ability to compete as an ecosystem.

In this chapter, we'll cover current trends, digitization opportunities, and examples of digitization in various industries to illustrate the innovative practices that can be put in place leveraging SAP Leonardo and the intelligent suite of solutions from SAP. We'll cover several use cases in various industry segments that can leverage SAP's intelligent suite, intelligent technologies, and digital platform in detail. You can implement these use cases via a service engagement from SAP or from SAP's vast ecosystem of partners.

These use cases are examples pointing to where you can improve the way you run your current business as well as innovate for tomorrow while focusing on specific

14

business outcomes. These examples can help you gain the agility to disrupt and out-maneuver your competition by building flexibility and insights into your business processes to rapidly respond to changes, pivot towards the right outcomes, and guard against disruptive competitors. Also covered in this chapter are customer success stories that demonstrate the business value that can be achieved via the use of intelligent technologies.

14.1   Discrete Manufacturing Industry

The meaning of customer-centricity in the discrete manufacturing industry has evolved to where customers decide how they want to purchase, use, and pay for products and services. Satisfying customer needs now is more about being able to personalize the products and services. With digital smart products, software and sensors are technically enabled, thus providing digital capabilities and value-added services bundled with the physical products via these digital smart products.

The use of digital technologies on the shop floor and in the supply chain is not new, but what is new is the way products and logistics are intelligently connected to the rest of the business and able to deal with external signals like short-term fluctuations in supply and demand or changes in the configuration of customer orders, which require necessary adjustments while ensuring services levels are not compromised.

Time to volume is of essence as companies face volatile customer demand and heightened expectations for responsiveness while supply chains grow more complex and become more vulnerable to disruption. With new service-based business models, companies are shifting from selling products to selling complete business solutions and charging for outcomes, in some cases, even monetizing asset data to create new revenue streams. Services are becoming a new source of revenue for manufacturers to achieve higher profit margins while simultaneously increasing customer intimacy.

In the following sections, we'll first look at sample use cases enabling the digitization of discrete manufacturing. Then, we'll look at some example customer success stories in the discrete manufacturing industry.

14.1.1   Digital Innovation Use Cases

Intelligent technologies can help leverage information out of your data, which you can use in conjunction with capabilities enabled by the intelligent suite of applications to automate insights to action. The data not only can originate from within your enterprise but also come from across the ecosystem. Some uses cases in the discrete manufacturing industry that can be implemented via service engagements with SAP or SAP partners include the following:

- **Delivering value-added services and managing assets based on live data**
  Manufacturers of complex assets need to provide excellent service to their customers to ensure that these assets provide the best performance and availability to meet the high customer expectations. You'll need to collaborate closely with your customers and other stakeholders on asset performance information. Manufacturers who own and operate complex equipment need the most optimal performance and uptimes from these assets. Service costs can jeopardize your overall profitability as your production processes may rely on these assets. Thus, sharing asset-related information with your service providers is in your best interests. By leveraging sensor information and asset condition data, maintenance service strategies can be optimized. Sharing asset-related information on a central platform is beneficial to all parties involved. With higher reliability, lower maintenance costs, and real-time visibility of the asset performance data, your company can explore offering innovative service-based business models. SAP Predictive Maintenance and Service, along with SAP Asset Intelligence Network and SAP Analytics Cloud, can help you achieve these goals.

- **Establishing pay-for-outcome business model**
  A pay-for-outcome business model can help you switch from a capital expenditure (CapEx) to an operational expenditure (OpEx) approach. The advantage of an OpEx model is that the equipment provider installs the equipment and maintains it for a small up-front cost, and the customer pays a fixed amount per use. Pay-for-outcome provides significant benefits to both the manufacturer as well as the customer. Equipment operators enjoy lower risk and reliable equipment performance, while equipment providers can broaden their customer base, generate sustainable income, and develop closer relationships with their customers.

  SAP Predictive Maintenance and Service, SAP Asset Intelligence Network, SAP Analytics Cloud, SAP Leonardo Internet of Things (SAP Leonardo IoT), and SAP Leonardo Machine Learning Foundation can together help proactively monitor asset maintenance to reduce or avoid repair expenses, optimize maintenance agreements, analyze the risk of offering pay-for-outcome contracts based on customer information, use every new contract in future predictions, and automate pricing in a way that is fair to the operator and profitable for the provider.

14

- **Managing spare parts**

  Manufacturers producing complex assets need to efficiently provide spare parts and service parts for their customers, service partners, and dealers. For meeting service levels and differentiating themselves from the competition, these companies need to optimize spare parts inventories as well as reduce delivery costs and lead times. 3D printing or additive manufacturing is an emerging technology that is fast becoming important for spare parts but needs efficient integration of additive manufacturing processes into the supply and delivery chains of spare parts. This integration includes sending orders for additive manufacturing to internal and external 3D print shops and sharing the required construction drawings for spare parts management processes.

  SAP Leonardo IoT for SAP Distributed Manufacturing along with SAP Asset Intelligence Network can help integrate these processes. SAP Cloud Platform Blockchain services can be used to ensure that the intellectual property of the print files is protected, and smart contracts on the blockchain can be used to monitor and automate billing based on customer usage.

In addition to these capabilities, another use case is optimizing delivery logistics and fleet insights (described in Section 14.4), which is relevant to the discrete manufacturing industry, while fleet insights would be relevant to the automotive industry.

14.1.2   Business Examples

In this section, we'll look at a number of business examples of digitization in the discrete manufacturing industry that make use of SAP Leonardo's intelligent technologies.

Customer Service

This business case involves an industrial machine supplier with manufacturing facilities in the US, Europe, the Asia Pacific region, and Japan, with customers across the globe. This organization supplies machines to perform manufacturing operations and automated robots for assembly lines.

The problem this organization faces is that the dependence on manual processes in customer service reduced efficiency and increased the total time to repair. For any issue customers identified on the shop floor, analysis was performed by the customer, and the identified broken part or system was reported to the organization. The organization would then log the issue as a service ticket, assign a technician to identify and perform the fix, and the customer would be charged accordingly. This heavy dependence on manual activities and the reactive nature of the process were time consuming and inefficient.

To solve this problem, SAP Leonardo technologies can use machine learning algorithms to automate the process. During the service ticket log process, data was collected through the form as well as audio information through the phone. Ticket data can be analyzed with historical information using classification and clustering algorithms to identify potential issues from similar cases in the past. Issue identification, spare part identification, technician assignment, and work scheduling were automated through the algorithm while optimizing service requirements and expanding support availability.

For future value attainment, the organization also piloted a solution to connect the critical parts at one of its strategic customers through a family of IoT devices to monitor solutions in real time. Any deviation from optimal performance detected will be monitored, controlled, and acted upon in real time in collaboration with the customer. This pilot was based on creating a business solution partnership for support-as-a-service, delivering value to both the organization and its customers.

The inclusion of the advanced technologies through SAP Leonardo has enhanced service ticket management process efficiency by more than 15%. Higher value was attained at the organization with a smaller number of breakdown hours through better issue prediction and faster resolution by automating long, manual processes and removing some of the guesswork through advanced predictive models. Further value-creating areas were identified for enhancing the automation of the process.

Real-time monitoring of machines at a customer's site adds both strategic and operational value for the organization. By guaranteeing a long-term relationship based on collaborative success, a stable revenue stream is created through support service and higher machine lifetimes, saving money for both the organization and its customers. For customers, this proposition adds a great deal of value because maintenance is controlled by the experts, and the mode of operation can change from reactive to predictive. The net result for the customer will be lower operational costs as well as higher revenue based on higher machine availability and utilization.

Smart Plants

This business case involves a global leader in industrial machines and power transmission equipment. This company has more than twelve manufacturing plants, each specializing in the design and manufacturing of a specific power transmission component. With presence in more than seventy-five countries, this organization serves the global market, working in close collaboration with its customers.

The company had been seeking efficiency improvements through better energy management, parts availability, and higher overall equipment effectiveness (OEE) goals. Furthermore, this company had been dealing with lost information, missing data due to an inability to collect and process different data types from multiple sources.

The solution that was implemented was a completely integrated manufacturing unit with the integration of machine lines through IoT devices. Data acquisition from different types of machinery could be performed, including power consumption data, with data standardization performed in the cloud. User dashboards were created with the use of digital twins and real-time analytics data. An automated work order solution was implemented with scanning devices working in collaboration with manufacturing execution systems and SAP ERP.

Data is now captured in the integrated manufacturing plant through all machine lines and processes, enabling efficiency improvements by running the machines at peak performance by controlling parameters based on the information gathered and analyzed on real-time dashboards. Improvements in OEE and the automatic calculation of real-time OEE and quality parameters were achieved. The automation of work order processes was realized through the usage of bar codes and time monitoring with IoT devices.

Automated Receiving and Replenishment

This case study involves an automobile components supplier involved in the manufacturing and supplying of engine parts. This company procures raw and semi-finished materials from its suppliers, and components are planned through an advanced planning application based on the finished goods forecast. The procurement process was long and inefficient due to the manual checking of the order match, quantity, dates, and specifications. Storage in the warehouse and the material issued to the production floor against a production order also involved multiple manual steps. The automation of the receipt process and the automatic issuing of the relevant materials to the shop floor were seen as opportunities to enhance efficiency.

The implemented solution involves the integration of the company's procurement system with their planning and manufacturing systems for real-time data updates with the use of IoT devices, bar codes, and serial number tracking. The solution now automatically checks received material, matching purchase orders with shipping notifications and the actual material received. Lean inventory optimization is achieved by the IoT device, which suggests the automatic movement of the right components to the production floor against a production order.

Efficiency was gained in the procurement process through automation of the material receipt and account settlement. Cost savings were achieved through the elimination of redundant movements and of manual checking. Efficiency was also gained through better working capital management, leaner inventory, and the automatic assignment of the components directly from supplier to the production floor.

Digital Twins

This business cases involves one of the largest providers of compressed-air systems and a provider of consulting services worldwide, with operations in more than a hundred countries. With distributed sales and services teams, this company needed a single source for product, component, spare parts, and service information to achieve transparency across the install base and the ability to offer differentiating services to its customers. A business opportunity was identified in the capture and analysis of IoT streaming data and the conversion of insights into actions with analytical applications.

This company established digital twins using SAP Leonardo intelligent technologies along with SAP Asset Intelligence Network and SAP Predictive Maintenance and Service to gain greater transparency on asset health and usage with predictive analytics. By leveraging design thinking, this company gained insights and ideas for the most effective solution to address business needs.

Globally distributed sales and service teams now are supported with intelligence captured from real-world data to meet the customer needs more effectively with greater transparency across the company's install base. In this way, the company built a competitive differentiation with increased machine availability and cost-efficient maintenance and service offerings for their customers. Using up-to-date replicas of digital twins, they can achieve higher customer and dealer satisfaction and improved supplier collaboration. This approach also enabled the creation of a new business model; instead of selling compressors, now they also sell compressed air and offer additional digital services to their customers.

Consumables On-Demand with IoT

This organization is a manufacturer of innovative packaging solutions, systems, and materials, serving customers like online retailers who ship products to consumers from the retailers' distribution centers. Their goal was to leverage IoT data from sensor-equipped packaging machines that are maintained at customer distribution centers to monitor the consumption of packaging materials, replenish them on time, and immediately address any mechanical issues before they become problems.

To meet these objectives, the packaging company used SAP Leonardo IoT, SAP Edge Services, and the SAP SMS 365 mobile service in conjunction with SAP Analytics Cloud to operationalize site-specific data in their service, sales, and purchasing operations. The company also leveraged design thinking to gain insights and ideas focused on the user experience and the use of role-based analytics dashboards. Finally, integration with the SAP ERP, SAP S/4HANA, and SAP C/4HANA solutions allowed the company to improve their overall service management.

As a result, fewer manual processes were involved in servicing the packaging machines and in the replenishment of consumables. Machine uptime was improved with more timely inventory control. With data-driven scheduling of preventive maintenance and support for remote machine configuration, machine uptime was improved. Increased demand visibility across the network, helped improve customer satisfaction, reduce costs, and improve margins.

Precision Farming with IoT

This organization is a manufacturer of farm equipment dedicated to using IoT technology to anticipate the needs of farmers and help them achieve higher productivity and profits with precision farming solutions. Their goal was to use smart machinery to apply seeds and fertilizers at variable rates based on characteristics measured in the soil like nitrogen levels, organic matter content, and moisture at different points in the field to help farmers get the most out of their land, seeds, and other assets.

To achieve their goals, the farm equipment company integrated data from sensors placed on agricultural machinery and transferred data about planting, soil preparation, fertilizing, soil correction, spraying, and harvesting to SAP ERP to enable real-time analysis using SAP HANA's in-memory computing and cloud-based analytics capabilities.

Through IoT, the farms are carefully mapped, so that farm equipment like seed spreaders could measure the quality, size, and shape of seeds and adjust the quantity of seeds sown in real time. These capabilities helped them recover their investment in implementing the solution and significantly increased productivity in two years.

14.2   Process Industry

Companies in the process industry are faced with volatile energy and raw material prices, mass customization, supply chain complexity, and geopolitical risks. Companies need to transform from purely selling products to delivering new, differentiating, customer-centric services and business outcomes while combating margin pressures by striving for touchless operations as a first step to creating an autonomous enterprise. Increasing regulations and legislation are influencing the industry more than ever. Companies need to demonstrate strong environmental and product stewardship and safe operations while minimizing the use of resources and energy, as well as managing environmental impacts, along the entire value chain to protect their brand and reputation. Success is largely determined by three variables: safety, cost, and agility. Companies are pushing the boundaries of augmented reality and the use of robotics in operations to improve safety and productivity and seamlessly share data, calling upon ecosystem partners to work together to ensure that production, profitability, and safety targets are met.

Digital innovations can improve customer-centric research and development to increase productivity, create new services, and decrease time to market. One area of innovation is integrated operations management, which allows companies to capture process data along with business context to improve overall operational visibility and control. Applying digital technologies in operations helps with analyzing production process variables in real-time including simulating their impact on product quality, costs, and yield. You can anticipate downstream supply chain disruptions and take corrective actions in real time, enabling you optimize production processes, improve the reliability of assets, and increase overall customer satisfaction.

Enabling a digital twin and IoT connectivity of assets allows for the continuous monitoring of asset health, process quality, throughput, waste, and emissions. By combining asset information with predictive analytics, companies can predict the likelihood of asset failures and plan and adjust maintenance and production plans accordingly to avoid costly asset downtimes as well as avoid safety risks and compliance incidents.

IoT and blockchain can be leveraged to help optimize trading and shipping as well as product authentication and integrity management to ensure that that the product is secured and its location is always known. Any incursions and exceptions along the route can be flagged with mobile alerts, giving you the opportunity to intervene to

14

save valuable shipments and data, even after wholesale transactions, which helps with regulatory compliance and performing recalls with surgical precision.

Thus, digital technologies like blockchain, IoT, and machine learning provide opportunities for optimizing, extending, and even disrupting supply chain processes and models in the process industry.

In the following sections, we'll first look at some sample uses cases that can enable digitization in the process industry. Then, we'll look at some example customer success stories.

14.2.1   Digital Innovation Use Cases

Companies in the process industry have global supply networks, high degree of automation, and often country-specific regulations to follow. The following digital innovation uses cases in the process industry can be implemented via service engagements through SAP or SAP partners:

- **Optimization and automation of cold chain logistics**
  Life science companies that produce drugs, medications, and blood products are subject to compliance and regulations and must maintain "cold chain" operations throughout their logistics and manufacturing processes. Ingredients and products must be kept within tight temperature limits at every stage, from raw material receipt, to storage, manufacturing, warehousing, and packaging, to shipment. During inbound logistics, data must be collected on shipments from suppliers, and quality checks must be performed during material receipt. The material must always be stored under temperature-controlled conditions and fully monitored.

  During manufacturing, shop floor automation must include integration to sensor data to monitor time-out-of-refrigeration (TOR) as well as monitor variances and failures at each stage of the manufacturing process. Visibility into storage conditions must be maintained through the process of delivery to the cold storage freezer in the warehouse. Similarly, during outbound logistics of finished goods to distributors, any out of bound tolerances must be monitored and controlled. You would need data collection on shipments and shipping lanes from logistics providers. With SAP Leonardo IoT, SAP Analytics Cloud, SAP Advanced Track and Trace for Pharmaceuticals, and SAP Global Batch Traceability, real-time insights into tolerance limits to ensure the required quality of each batch produced and delivered can be achieved. In addition, SAP Cloud Platform Blockchain services can provide transparency into cold chain integrity across your business partners.

- **Verification of saleable returns of pharmaceuticals in the US**

  In the US, around 3% of total sales of pharmaceutical drugs are saleable returns, drugs returned from hospitals and pharmacies to wholesalers, amounting to millions of units in volume. Since counterfeit drugs are a major issue, under the US Drug Supply Chain Security Act, in 2017, Food and Drug Administration (FDA) started requiring manufacturers to implement serialization for each individual package and homogeneous case of product. The next phase is verification of saleable returned product at the package level by November 2019, followed by full track and trace at the individual package level at a later stage.

  SAP Information Collaboration Hub for Life Sciences, option for the US supply chain, uses blockchains to enable pharmaceutical product verification and authentication to prevent counterfeit products from entering the supply chain. Manufacturers write product package data on the blockchain using standard EPCIS (Electronic Product Code Information Services) messages from SAP Advanced Track and Trace for Pharmaceuticals. Since this information is on the blockchain, the data is immutable and cannot be changed or tampered with. Wholesale distributors can then execute verification requests against the blockchain-based repository. The multichain blockchain protocol is used in this solution. You can perform statistics and analysis on the data stored in the blockchain as well create your own analytics and use alerting capabilities.

In addition, the digital innovation use case for optimizing delivery logistics described in Section 14.4 is also relevant to the process industry, just as fleet operations are relevant to the mill and mining industry as mining companies often operate several hundred vehicles as part of their mining operations. The digital innovation use case, delivering value-added services and managing assets based on live data described under discrete industries is relevant to the chemical industry as well as to oil and gas companies (along with SAP HANA IoT Integrator by OSIsoft). A further digital innovation use case includes field asset monitoring, relevant to life science companies that produce complex medical assets and need to meet high asset service, performance, and availability requirements.

14.2.2   Business Examples

In this section, we'll look at a number of business examples of digitization in the process industry that make use of SAP Leonardo intelligent technologies.

Quality Enhancement Using IoT

This organization is a large European metal producer with the majority of its products used in building and construction. This organization produces a variety of product groups through its own manufacturing plants. Their goal was to identify and control the parameters that impact the quality of the finish goods as well as identify potential quality issues in advance through analyzing current working parameters.

To reach this goal, this company used IoT to gather data on manufacturing parameters in real time. They applied machine learning algorithms to control the parameters of product quality as well as to predict quality factors that could then be checked, monitored, and controlled in a real-time environment. SAP Leonardo IoT Edge, SAP Cloud Platform, and R for enhancing the predictive model's capability helped them achieve their goals.

A real-time predictive quality dashboard was created that showed recommended control parameters like temperature, pressure, and additives, based on the millions of records of past data. Machine learning was used for causal analysis involving parameters and output quality. The planned parameter value was then compared against actual parameters and then fed into the algorithm in real time to predict potential quality issues that could be checked, monitored, and controlled in real time.

Agile Product Development

This organization is a manufacturer of paints and coatings with applications in various industries, such as building materials, automobile manufacturing, home appliances, and furniture.

Their goal was to strengthen brand perception in a highly competitive and commoditized market by using customer input and behaviors to help forecast demand. They applied technological innovations to make compelling offerings to customers by using cross-system analytics on structured information from SAP applications stored in SAP HANA along with semi-structured and unstructured data from their website logs, such as visitor browsing histories at regional locations stored in a Hadoop big data store.

This company then extended and optimized real-time reporting and analytics through the integration of its business warehouse system to SAP HANA, and unified analysis was made possible by linking Apache Hadoop with SAP application data. Use of the SAP HANA platform helped fully leverage the advanced vector extensions offered by Intel Xeon processors as a base for new analytics solutions that consume customer and product details in SAP applications, along with customer website log information held in a Hadoop Distributed File System (HDFS).

Going forward, this organization plans to build upon this foundation and apply predictive analytics to other areas of the business while continuing to incorporate information from big data sources such as Hadoop to gain a much better and more comprehensive understanding of its customers, partners, competitors, and markets.

Now, this company can have unprecedented access to the voices of its customers through the collection of real-time analysis calculations and user-friendly dashboards that depict crucial details, such as website visits, retention rates, advertisement effectiveness, referrals, and client design preferences to help product designers confidently develop solutions that are in tune with customer requests and market momentum. With a much better understanding of upcoming demand patterns, the marketing team can respond quickly with accurate messaging and targeted campaigns so that customers are presented with better and more personalized recommendations.

Real-Time Analytics

This company is a manufacturer of additives for coatings, paints, and printing inks, with customers including some of the largest paint producers in the world. Rapid business growth resulted in questionable data quality given the company had diverse information sources, which created an opportunity to integrate various data sources and establish a trusted, single source of data for better decision-making.

By deploying SAP Analytics Cloud on SAP Cloud Platform, this company now has real-time access to data consolidated from diverse operational units via a next-generation reporting tool. Their solution footprint also included SAP Business Suite and SAP Business Planning and Consolidation (SAP BPC) to form a single business intelligence platform.

This company now enjoys improved data quality with simplified, instant access to a single source of information on operations, opportunities, profitability, and product requirements, allowing users to trust the data for decision-making and generate enhanced insights into customer profitability.

Energy Costs and Combating Energy Fraud

This organization is an international, vertically integrated steel and steel-related mining company. By focusing on cost discipline and efficiency enhancements, this company wanted to reduce energy costs through the accurate monitoring of power consumption; by addressing imbalances by quickly detecting, minimizing, and eliminating fraud and the unauthorized use of electricity; and by addressing incorrect energy forecasting and fraud that resulted in extra costs and fines.

This organization developed a prototype using IoT to harness meter data, as well as machine learning and advanced analytics solutions from SAP Leonardo. Design thinking was used to help create a system to monitor real-time energy usage and analyze energy consumption disparities. SAP Leonardo machine learning algorithms were used to train the system to recognize patterns in electricity use to help detect and flag deviations. SAP Analytics Cloud was used to provide security officers with transparency into areas where aberrations exist and highlight problem zones.

As a next step, this company plans to productize the solution and expand its scope beyond energy management to address changes resulting from imbalances. Using this solution, various users, such as planners, security staff, and plant electricians, can immediately detect and act upon imbalances. The electricity management system prototype also enables more accurate forecasts for energy consumption, which will result in substantial savings.

14.3   Consumer Products and Retail Industries

Increasingly, well-informed consumers with Gen X and Gen Y needs and preferences expect timely, tailored, relevant, and increasingly local ways to buy products. Consumers are prepared to share their data and expect new types of shopping experiences in return. No longer loyal to a retail brand, these customers can and will switch for better service and faster delivery, which requires a company to employ transformative consumer engagement strategies that focus on consumer experiences and outcomes as well as extend and expand consumer lifecycles. Meanwhile, smaller, more nimble, and more agile competitors are entering the market, challenging the old order and becoming the new engines of category growth and innovation.

Channel proliferation and increasing cost pressures across product categories are driving new, nontraditional growth models. Engaging customers through the entire consumer journey means going beyond purchase and use, to inclusion of content and services. New digital leaders are creating value by delivering health, joy, comfort, control, security, and confidence in their product offerings to consumers. By embracing unique partnerships, these innovators seek to deliver new value as information, offers, products, and services. Today's innovative companies are capitalizing on economies of speed by sensing opportunities "in-the-moment" and analyzing data from various sources to provide options to optimize the best consumer response. The goal is shopper engagement that creates compelling, immersive experiences via smart stores, thus creating lifelong loyalty and growing the share of customer spend. These smart stores make use of digital technologies like virtual reality (VR) and augmented reality (AR) to let consumers interact with digital content that is overlaid on real-world content.

Intelligent technologies can help the consumer product and retail industry optimize current business processes and achieve business outcomes more efficiently and reliably. In addition, processes can be automated using machine learning and made aware of the real world via IoT to get the right products to the right places at the right time in the right conditions. Advanced analytical tools can help make sense of the vast volumes of data being generated from production to when the product is stocked at the retail shelf or made available on an e-commerce store front. Source-to-consumer traceability, connected agriculture, and fleet management optimizations are some example areas where digitization can greatly improve processes.

In the following sections, we'll first look at some use cases in the consumer products and retail industries. Then, we'll look at some example customer success stories.

14.3.1   Digital Innovation Uses Cases

In this section, we'll describe some use cases that can help companies in the consumer product and retail industries to leverage intelligent technologies to improve efficiencies, provide personalized offerings, and delight their consumers. The following use cases can be implemented through service engagements with SAP or SAP partners:

- **Monitoring refrigeration units, freezers, and coolers**
  For retailers selling beverages, refrigerated foods, and frozen foods, cooling units represent a significant investment. The return on investment on these assets can be a key financial indicator for the business. Retailers need to ensure these units are working within the required temperature tolerances in order to maintain product quality and maintain sufficient stock to meet consumer demand, all while avoiding any product spoilage and expiration. The placement of these assets will

need to be monitored so that units are not vandalized, damaged, or stolen. For companies with large global operations, the procurement and maintenance of these units can be significant investments. By using SAP Leonardo IoT, retailers can monitor ambient temperatures, operating temperatures, and temperature variations resulting from the door opening and closing to help manage losses from spoilage or asset malfunctions. By centrally monitoring the units, retailers can reduce losses due to theft or damage, maximize equipment uptime and ensure required storage, optimize sales while reducing spoilage of product, and use predictive maintenance with SAP Machine Learning Foundation to replace and maintain assets in advance of failure.

- **Minimizing waste at stores**
  Retailers often make educated guesses about foot traffic and consumer demand to make replenishment decisions about stocking shelves. For freshly prepared and labor-intensive products, given their thin margins, these guesses can be risky because you would want to avoid any expired or wasted food. With daily demand forecasting using the power of machine learning from SAP Leonardo Machine Learning Foundation, while taking inputs like marketing campaigns, external events, etc., you can more accurately predict the units that will be sold, which allows you to sell what you shelve and avoiding empty shelves. You can seamlessly integrate with your current store opening routine and assist store associates by showing them upcoming demand. By automating daily instructions on what to prepare or stock, you can optimally meet your customer demand and maximize sales. You can automate instructions to prepare for future shifts and order new materials and ingredients as needed. Using SAP Analytics Cloud, you can create easy-to-consume visualizations on product demand and potential wastage to inform stakeholders quickly with suggested actions.

In addition to these use cases, optimizing delivery logistics is a use case described in Section 14.4 that is also relevant in the consumer products and retail industries. Furthermore, the optimizing and automation of cold chain logistics is a use case described in Section 14.2, which is also relevant for industry segments that produce and sell fresh and frozen foods.

14.3.2   Business Examples

In this section, we'll look at some examples of digitization in the consumer products and retail industries that make use of SAP Leonardo.

Food Movement

This organization is a food manufacturer supplying perishable food products to the US and South America. The organization manufactures and procures multiple food products in different segments, and many of its product categories like meat and freshly cooked food have short shelf lives.

The company suffered from huge wastage due to supply chain inefficiencies. Their products required storage and transportation within a temperature range, and any deviations would reduce product shelf life and perhaps even make products unusable. The company wanted to build an efficient supply network with transparent flows that can maximize shelf life, control the waste, enhance revenue, and increase end-customer satisfaction.

To address these business needs, the organization used SAP Leonardo's intelligent technologies connected with SAP ERP and SAP Cloud Platform to create a connected, predictable, and transparent supply chain network. Through better demand sensing and supply algorithms, the product flows and holdings were optimized to retain the maximum freshness for the customer. SAP Integrated Business Planning (SAP IBP) for demand and SAP IBP for response and supply, supported by the demand sensing and supply optimization capabilities, were used for flow optimization. IoT devices such as temperature sensors were used during the transportation of the product. The information was centrally monitored in real time in a dashboard as products moved from one location to another. Any unwanted temperature conditions generated alerts to the supply chain personnel who in turn alerted the transport service provider for immediate corrective action.

The organization has started enjoying benefits in terms of costs, revenues, and profits, supported through better demand-supply match, lower wastage, higher revenue, longer shelf lives, and more satisfied customers. Addressing the unpredictive part of the supply chain flow has made their processes efficient, automated, and transparent.

Shopping Experience with Machine Learning

This organization is a shoe company providing online web-based shopping to its customers. Given that, in the footwear industry, only 5% of design proposals reach the production stage, significant overstock and wastage occurs often. With the fierce competition and the difficulty of catching fashion trends in a timely manner, this company wanted to adopt digital innovations to gain agility and precision in design and production to reduce inventories.

This company used SAP S/4HANA Cloud for intelligent product design on SAP Cloud Platform with product lifecycle management and virtual reality (VR) technologies in the SAP Leonardo IoT Bridge digital operations center to collect and analyze customer requirements to design products that fit market needs. The company could initiate the design process by using trending elements based on different algorithms and shoe models created by machine learning engines.

Using machine learning allowed their customers to design personalized pairs, select the desired color and fit, virtually test the end product, and place an order. With integrated R&D, production, sales, and service to quickly react to upcoming business opportunities, this company is now able to provide its customers the opportunity to purchase customized shoes at an affordable price.

Predicting Demand

This organization is one of the largest retailers with in-store bakery sections. Previously, although excess unsold fresh goods were donated to homeless shelters, spending time and resources in making these products in the first place itself was a waste. Through better predictions about which products are needed, when, and where, this company saw opportunities for reducing waste, saving money, and optimizing the productivity of its employees.

This company started a pilot program at a store where seven years of sales data, along with external data like weather, which can affect foot traffic and sales, were processed using machine learning in SAP Leonardo to improve forecasting for the in-store production of bakery items. This pilot program resulted in a significant reduction in waste while achieving cost savings through optimized production schedules and reduced labor hours. Given its success, the company plans to roll out this solution to 500 of their bakeries as well as its service delis and food courts.

Supply Chain Transparency for Sustainability

This organization is a seafood company dedicated to promoting healthy lifestyles and preserving precious natural resources. To maintain the highest quality of food and food safety, this company wanted to use technology to prove the sources of their fish and to share the food safety data generated in their laboratories with restaurants and retailers efficiently. In the process, this company is also dedicated to promoting fair trade practices and helping Indonesian fishermen and their families.

This company used SAP Leonardo Blockchain to track fish from the time it is brought to shore and sold by the fishermen, through the processing and finished goods plant, and all the way to the retail stores. Consumers can scan QR codes on retail packages with their smartphones to see various information, like where the tuna was caught, the fishing method used, the species of tuna, and whether the fish is fair-trade certified and caught in a sustainable way. The consumer app also depicts stories depicting the benefits of fair trade to the fishermen and their livelihoods and benefits to their local fishing communities as well as recipes.

This company uses SAP Analytics Cloud for a supplier dashboard to analyze fish buying trends and perform catch data analysis to help improve catches in fishing villages, in partnership with nongovernmental organizations.

Future plans include continuing to onboard new fish suppliers, evaluating the incorporation of IoT, and implementing blockchain into their other brands.

14.4 Other Industries and Sectors

Companies in the utilities industry own and operate complex equipment, especially companies that own energy generation and distribution assets. These companies rely on high-performing assets and need to leverage sensors and condition data from connected assets to optimize maintenance strategies to reduce power outages and improve overall equipment effectiveness. In this process, the aim is to keep maintenance costs and effort low by improving asset replacement and investment strategies.

In this section, we'll first look at some example use cases of digital innovation. Then, we'll look at some example customer success stories.

14.4.1 Digital Innovation Use Cases

Some use cases can help companies leverage intelligent technologies to improve business efficiencies and achieve desired outcomes. The following use cases can be implemented through service engagements with SAP or with SAP partners:

- **Optimizing delivery logistics and fleet insights**
  Logistics companies need to have real-time control and exception management capabilities for their entire logistics chain because their customers rely on constant on-time delivery. Their production operations must have all the material required to fulfill production orders, and their distribution operations must have products delivered at the planned and promised delivery schedules. SAP Leonardo

intelligent technologies can provide real-time geospatial data, predictive analytics capabilities, and the ability to integrate sensor data into logistics business processes to enable real-time, exception-driven visibility into order deliveries.

Transportation equipment, such as trucks, planes, ships, and railcars, can be constantly monitored, providing a real-time overview of their current location, expected arrival, expected delays, and more, so you can quickly react to exceptions and deviations from the planned arrival or pickup times to ensure that the supply and delivery networks of customers are not disrupted. The company could now utilize their equipment and resources most efficiently. SAP Leonardo IoT, combined with SAP Global Track and Trace and SAP Analytics Cloud, can help companies achieve these goals.

- **Leveraging big data for creating new business models**
  Companies in the telecommunication industry have been facing increasing pressure on profitability while their operational and investments costs remain high. Facing regulations, commoditization, and market saturation in traditional services, these companies need to diversify into areas of IoT, content, and B2B services. This use case can help transform the business into a business driven by real-time margins by identifying margin leakage and switching from average revenue per unit (ARPU) to new average margin per unit (AMPU) business models.

- **Efficient operation of sports and entertainment venues**
  In the sports and entertainment industry, stadium, venue, and entertainment park operators manage complex and heterogeneous landscapes of many outdated systems with no real-time dashboards and predictive maintenance systems in place. Switching from routine operations to peak times, such as game days or concerts, in a short period of time can be a real challenge. Critical infrastructure components, such as turnstiles and refreshment refrigeration units, must be working, parking operations must be optimized, the optimal temporary workforce must be available at the venue, and resource consumption, like water and electricity, must be managed. Collecting real-time information about the current state of the facilities in the venue through sensors can help reduce energy costs, proactively manage queues, and maximize equipment uptime with predictive maintenance on the day of the event. Using SAP Leonardo IoT, SAP Analytics Cloud, SAP Leonardo Machine Learning Foundation, SAP Connected Parking (a future innovation), and SAP Predictive Maintenance and Service can help address these needs.

In addition to these use cases, delivering value-added services and managing assets based on live data is a use case for the discrete manufacturing industry, described earlier in Section 14.1, that is relevant to the utilities industries as well.

14.4.2   Business Examples

In this section, we'll look at some examples of digitization that make use of SAP Leonardo in a number of industries and sectors.

Measuring Delivery Performance

This organization is a distributor of paper and pulp products in the forest products, furniture, and textiles industry. Their supply chain group manages multiple trucks (both internally owned and contracted trucks) for delivering goods to customer locations. These trucks transport the goods to multiple locations (500+) all over Indonesia. The trucks are operated by multiple transportation providers. The distributor measures the performance of its contracted transportation providers based on key performance indicators (KPIs) like on-time delivery, unloading times, number of trips, and other utilization-related KPIs.

Because the trucks are fitted with different GPS devices, users had to log in to multiple GPS provider portals to consolidate the information and manually generate KPI reports.

The distributor decided to use SAP Leonardo IoT and IoT services to integrate the data from several GPS providers onto a single platform to enable a holistic view into their transport business. The calculation of the key KPIs and stakeholder reporting could be performed via SAP Analytics Cloud, which enables the monitoring of trucks fitted with sensors from various GPS providers on a single platform and get real-time visibility into delivery-related KPIs.

The project was delivered in just 6 weeks. The distributors' customers experienced higher on-time deliveries. A single platform provided a holistic view into the distributor's transport business with real-time visibility into the location of trucks to accurately measure arrival times and unloading times at customer locations while providing the ability to rank various transporters based on their on-time delivery performance.

Digitization of Transportation Processes

This organization is a provider of fleet vehicles and a supplier of trailer equipment, for example, commercial vehicles, agricultural equipment, trucks and buses, and trailers.

This company wanted to digitize their transport processes to accelerate and optimize end-to-end transport processes using trailer telematics.

To achieve this goal, this company used SAP Leonardo IoT for real time-sensor data analysis integrating automotive telematics data like acceleration, speed, current position, braking events, and error codes, from all kinds of vehicles equipped with telematics sensors. This company also connected logistics-relevant information (e.g. transportation orders, traffic information) with business data.

This advancement resulted in improved transparency, efficiency, and security in managing the end-to-end transport processes provided by the fleet as well as created opportunities for new service business models for the automotive industry.

Usage Based Insurance

This organization is an automobile insurance provider that wanted to offer personalized automobile insurance packages on the global market and serve the high demand for pay-as-you-drive individual insurance offerings.

SAP Leonardo IoT enabled dedicated partners with special domain expertise in the areas of usage-based insurance (UBI) to build scoring models as a cloud solution. The telematics data was used for mile- and driving behavior-based vehicle insurance. Insurance prices were modeled based on type of vehicle measured against time, distance, driving behavior, and location.

This company can now connect to various types of sensors in various types of vehicles and store the collected data for complete transparency. They use a flexible data model which can easily be enhanced based on specific needs of a use case. This company can now apply advanced analytics and use case-specific logic to enable new business opportunities as well as trip recognition and trip map visualization, geocoding analytics, and car-specific analytics out of the box.

Inter-Bank Payment Processing

This organization is a large financial institution with more than 750,000 customers and more than $50 billion in assets, providing financial and investment advice and products and services to its customers.

This company wanted to leverage blockchain technology to transform cross-country payments by making them almost instantaneous and reducing potential errors, thereby enhancing their global network and increasing competitiveness.

To achieve this goal, the financial institution used SAP Cloud Platform Blockchain services in a proof of concept, along with Ripple Lab Inc.'s network and the SAP Payment Engine, for centralizing payment processing with a mobile user interface to execute interbank payments.

This company was able to demonstrate that they could now execute a blockchain-based international payment in just 20 seconds. Such a transaction typically takes between 2 to 6 business days to process given requirements such as settling with the counter-party bank and reconciling accounts. Blockchain's distributed ledger allows a network of computers to settle transactions almost instantly with built-in security, which speeds up cross-border payments. In addition, by running business processes on a digital core, the company can react quickly to emerging technological innovations and avoid the threat of disruption. Streamlined business processes thus can provide analytical insights to deliver innovative products and services through a variety of distribution channels and meet customer demands.

The next stage of the project is to design a frontend user experience that will enhance the customer experience and meet their needs.

Boosting Investments in Renewable Energies

This organization is a service provider for renewable energy asset and portfolio management across solar parks, wind farms, biomass facilities, and hydroelectric power plants. In an industry with opaque markets and investments, integrating technical and financial data into a single solution can help catalyze investments in renewable energies and meet the ambitious energy targets inscribed in the Paris Climate Agreement. This integration will help minimize investment risk by creating transparency to maximize asset performance in the energy portfolio and increase return on investment.

Using SAP Leonardo capabilities, this company transformed their client engagement by combining IoT and big data to aggregate technical, meteorological, and financial data to facilitate capital investments in renewable assets. As a result, this company could develop a customer-as-a-partner model to allow customers to build their own solutions with go-to-market (GTM) sales and marketing support by using SAP Leonardo's IoT and predictive analytics capability. In the future, the plan is to expand scope by leveraging machine learning and blockchain technologies.

Now, this company supports executive-level dashboards with automated KPI calculations by automating the aggregation of technical and financial data for each type of energy-generating asset while considering climate factors by using big data mining and smart data analytics.

Simplifying Citizen Engagement with Blockchain

This case study involves a provincial government in a European country. This government wanted to digitize citizen data and provide secure, authorized access for government employees to provide better and faster services to citizens while reducing operational costs and saving taxpayer money. To achieve this goal, they built digital government services using SAP Leonardo Blockchain on the scalable architecture of SAP Cloud Platform.

This development helped them streamline the delivery of government services to its citizens, who only needed to enter their information once before authorized government employees could access the individual's information across multiple government agencies. In this way, operational costs were lowered by eliminating layers of redundant bureaucracy and inefficient legacy systems. The government also now has a foundation for ongoing experimentation with new technologies to achieve the government's vision and to create a model for data sharing that could scale across the country.

14.5   Summary

Given the fast pace of innovation, digitization is imperative in all industries. While all the usual pressures of a business continue, like reducing costs, increasing profitability, meeting rising customer expectations, and outflanking the competition, every industry can unlock new business value by using intelligent technologies in combination with SAP's intelligent suite and industry-specific solutions. With innovative ways to use the enormous volumes of data being generated (e.g. from IoT sensors and smart products) via advanced analytics and predictive techniques of machine learning, as well as sharing secure and immutable information across the business network with blockchain, digitization initiatives can not only let industries optimize existing processes but can extend current processes to capture new sources of value. Entities in all industries and sectors can entirely transform their operations by creating new business models and revenue streams like pay-as-you-go and usage-based models, opening up infinite new opportunities.

Chapter 15
Roadmap and Outlook

The digital world and SAP Leonardo technologies are evolving at such a fast pace that many new transformative developments are occurring. Considering this pace of change, in this chapter, we'll detail the current roadmap ahead for SAP Leonardo.

With the ongoing success and increasing adoption of SAP Leonardo solutions, SAP has planned multiple innovations in the technology and business process areas. In this chapter, we'll summarize the technological and process innovations enabled by SAP Leonardo in supply chain, finance, production development, etc. A significant innovation push is occurring in the Internet of Things (IoT), which we'll cover as a separate section in this chapter. As these features are still under development and subject to change, we'll only summarize this information because the vision of the solution can always be aligned with an organization's vision even if the solutions themselves diverge from the roadmap.

The planned developments on the roadmap can be categorized as either technological innovations or process innovations, and we'll cover these two areas in Sections Section 15.1 and Section 15.2. In addition, SAP Leonardo IoT will also see further upgrades, which we included in Section 15.3.

15.1   SAP Leonardo Technological Innovation Roadmap

The developments planned in this area will allow machines to converse with users, enhance the usage of the technology, and upgrade the various solutions we discussed throughout this book to make them more robust and useful. To achieve these goals, the following developments are expected on the technological innovation roadmap:

- **SAP Leonardo Machine Learning Foundation with added flexibility**
  SAP Leonardo Machine Learning Foundation will provide further flexibility in the machine learning capabilities by allowing you to bring your own model (BYOL) as well as to scale and train your models through unique training algorithms, data,

and key considerations particularly relevant to a business case. Considering the current interest in building in-house data analytics and machine learning capabilities in organizations of all sizes, this flexibility will integrate SAP Leonardo's capabilities with your in-house innovations.

- **SAP Conversational AI**
  With developments in machine learning and AI capabilities, the most wished-for feature across industries is the ability to offload manual, labor-intensive, and repetitive tasks, as well as cognitive tasks, to the machine. To achieve this goal, conversational capabilities of the system can be quite important. Consumers and employees are now used to talking to Siri (Apple) and Alexa (Amazon), and expectations are growing for the same interactivity in the workplace. SAP Leonardo team is working to make conversational AI achievable and usable. However, completely seamless usage will require some time before this vision can realized.

- **SAP Intelligent Robotic Process Automation**
  With SAP Leonardo and associated technologies, repetitive processes and tasks are already getting automated through robotic process automation (RPA). Further work in this innovation area is happening to improve the robotic capabilities in cognitive and intelligent areas as well, with research on the overall vision, on natural language processing, and on cognitive capability building for bots to be used across processes and places, from office work to warehouses and factories, to logistics, and all the way directly to customer during service engagements.

- **SAP Predictive Analytics and SAP Analytics Cloud**
  Further improvements in predictive analytics are on the roadmap that will enhance the decision-making capabilities of the system as well as facilitate the migration of predictive models to SAP Analytics Cloud. Moving your models to SAP Analytics Cloud will expand their use and development by your organization as well as by your partners. Another anticipated development is embedding SAP S/4HANA Cloud into SAP Cloud Platform.

- **SAP Digital Boardroom**
  Enhanced connectivity is planned with cross-process technologies and solutions involving CRM sources, Asset Intelligence Network (AIN), and smart manufacturing capabilities. Support geolocation worldwide will enhance the strength of global tracking and tracing of assets and products. Continued enhancement is planned for live data and data import connections.

- **Large-scale blockchain**
  Further enhancements in the blockchain capabilities of SAP Leonardo solution is planned to support large-scale operations, especially in the pharmaceutical and food

manufacturing industries. The future solution is expected to support blockchain-based business models and new blockchain markets.

- **SAP SuccessFactors integration**
  Enhancing SAP Leonardo with SAP SuccessFactors integration is planned to enable advanced job matching, job analysis, and searches like "people like me" or "people like Melissa"!

15.2   SAP Leonardo Process Innovation Roadmap

Planned solution, technology, and process improvements in SAP Leonardo will touch end-to-end business processes like finance, supply chains, customer service, commerce, sales and marketing, and master data. Most of these developments are in the final design and build stages with more detail expected in the next few quarters.

The innovations planned will further enhance and intelligently automate business processes, especially in the following business areas:

- **Finance**
  On the SAP Leonardo product innovation roadmap, more finance processes will be identified for end-to-end management and automation. A current innovation focus is centered on enhancing containing customer account identification, posting rule determination, and payment classification in SAP Cash Application. Cash and liquidity forecasting and intercompany reconciliation are two processes identified for automation through SAP Leonardo. As discussed in Section 15.1, with further developments in robotic process automation (RPA), many finance processes will be positively influenced in terms of accuracy and efficiency.

- **Supply chains**
  For innovation in supply chain management, a major focus area is related to inventory management, including predictive physical inventory counting, defect code management, detection of and recommendations on slow-moving stock, and dangerous goods detection and classification processes.

  The intelligent use of variant materials and even the smart management of variant configurations are planned for enhancing SAP Leonardo technologies. In the future, SAP Leonardo will further integrate variant configurations to address specific quality issues in production.

  Automatic approval workflows for the procured materials, along with picture-based product requisition processes leveraging enhanced machine learning, are

15

planned on the solution roadmap. In addition, source of supply assignments will be automated for efficient and cost-optimized procurement planning without manual intervention. Blockchain solution enhancements will also result in further improvements, automation, and the realization of smart contracting goals with suppliers.

- **Sales, marketing, and commerce**
  The enhanced usage of the unstructured data to create and manage sales orders, product recommendation, and predictive ordering is on the solution roadmap for SAP Leonardo. Sales assistance using cognitive robotics processes will further transform the sales organization.

  For commerce functions, real-time microsegmentation for understanding and acting on customer and promotional activities is planned on the SAP Leonardo product roadmap. Cognitive and natural language processing capabilities will be used for conversational commerce activities. For smart marketing, the solution roadmap includes further enhancement and automation of lead conversion, customer retention, and smart campaign activities.

- **Master data**
  Data-driven and completely automated big data enterprise applications will be further improved as SAP Leonardo is further connected with SAP Data Hub. Self-learning metadata management with the machine learning models will multiply the usage potential of SAP Leonardo solutions.

15.3 SAP Leonardo IoT Roadmap

SAP Leonardo IoT's focus is now on changing the way standard operations are run. Standard SAP business processes will include optional IoT data in intelligent suite and supply chain planning systems. SAP Leonardo IoT will enhance standard SAP solutions while also providing an environment for creating intelligent enterprises directly through customer development and SAP partners. SAP Leonardo IoT will consume an asset core shared with existing SAP solutions such as SAP Supply Chain Management, SAP Asset Intelligence Network, and the SAP S/4HANA digital core.

In this section, we'll discuss the SAP Leonardo IoT roadmap. Value-added capabilities emphasize consuming IoT data for business systems, therefore bringing intelligence to enterprises by embedding IoT into business contexts to empower business process automation and enable innovation for all lines of business (LOBs). Improvements can be expected in the following areas:

- **SAP Leonardo Edge**
  In many use cases, you'll need to extend the intelligent enterprise to the edge, which includes deployment and lifecycle management through edge services. Essential business function services will make business contexts (data and processes) available at the edge, which will enable you to deploy, execute, and update predictive analytical models at the edge as well.

- **Data integration**
  SAP Leonardo will have a core common asset data model that shares master data with other SAP solutions. IoT master data is a new object that can also be derived from data, such as material numbers from the ERP suite, which can then be mapped to IoT data. Integrated services intertwined with the intelligent suite will provide content and support for embedded processes.

- **Use case templates**
  SAP Leonardo IoT will be designed as a scalable platform that allows you and your partners to build solutions that consume services. SAP Leonardo IoT includes SAP Web IDE controls and libraries that allow you to create use case templates efficiently.

- **Time series management**
  Data sharing capabilities will be added that allow data transformation with big data as a service while getting access to raw data and data exports via APIs. The following capabilities will be included:
  - Access to both raw and aggregate data for large data volumes
  - Intelligent data processing with time series transformations and derivations
  - Lifecycle management and semantics
  - Lifecycle management for enriched semantic business context across things, master data, and locations
  - Semantic context based on models, time series, and master data
  - Convenient and integrated onboarding experience for large volumes of things

- **Analytics**
  Analytic services and query model capabilities will be available with direct access to IoT data while powerful queries from SAP Analytics Cloud will allow you to combine IoT and business data views. Dedicated calculation views using live data connections in SAP Analytics Cloud (via adapters) will be part of the solution.

- **Geoservices and floor plans**
  Floor plan service allow you to model geolocation data and relate this data to the

15

thing model, which will allow you to create geofences as polygons and define floor plans.

- **Rules**
Streaming rules and rules on persisted data will be available. Based on these rules, you can create events, and sub mechanism for events, and events can be stored and picked up by other services and integration services and ultimately trigger other events and integrated services. Streaming rules in the ingestion pipeline for thing properties and geofencing capabilities will require fast processing, while rules processing will include rule scheduling capabilities.

- **Bringing IoT intelligence to business systems**
Bringing intelligence into the enterprise by embedding IoT into business contexts empowers business process automation and enables innovation in all lines of business. Business Integration will be included to keep track of time series-related event history, severity, and status with publish and subscribe capabilities on the rule processing results. IoT line of business integration include:
  - Enrich backend systems with IoT data
  - Integration of IoT data into existing backend system applications (e.g. the Service Ticket App in SAP C/4HANA)
  - Delivery of configurable and predelivered SAP Cloud Platform Integration templates, such as the following:
    - Purchase requisitions
    - Sales orders
    - Service tickets
    - Time-series matching with master data and transactional data
    - Association of time-series data and sensor events with locations

15.4   Summary

As SAP Leonardo matures, further enhancements in multiple areas like technology, business processes, data management and model management will enhance SAP Leonardo's capabilities and make adopting SAP Leonardo technologies key to realizing the dream of a totally connected and intelligently operated business, bringing together business processes, people, industries, and even societies. SAP Leonardo, which is already harnessing value through revenue increases and efficiency gains, will continue to totally transform the way we work and operate.

Appendix A
Future Cities

The first decade of the millennium defined the availability of information on demand. The current decade is defining how information can be used to analyze the behaviors of people, determine the needs of the common man, and predict general responses from the population. As we head into the next decade, we'll see an increased rate of digitization with embedded intelligence, which will enable entities provide customized services. For example, this digitization will enable governments to more actively gather feedback, not only about the services they provide, but also to automate services. As society, in the microcosm of a city, requires additional services and information, a mature community with advanced technical capabilities will need to answer the following questions:

- How can an urban society sustain and improve on good quality of life with increasing urbanization and population density in cities?
- What can an advanced society use technology to stay secure from destabilizing internal and external influences?
- How will the microeconomics of smart buildings and smart communities contribute to form a larger smart city?
- How should decision rights be transferred from the elected representatives of the people to the people themselves as technology and information are made readily available? How much of the decision-making in a democracy can be decentralized?

In addition of transforming organizations, SAP Leonardo's bigger goals involve better communities and a better planet. In this chapter, we'll explore the application of the technology to achieve smart cities with better communities and more efficient buildings.

Throughout this discussion about enabling the smart city, the smart community, or the smart building, we'll also discuss a specific example of a building fire to describe how a smart building, the people in the building, the smart community they live in, and the smart city can all come together to extinguish the fire and resettle the affected inhabitants. This example will also explore the technical components and infrastructure needed to support emergency response systems as well to manage post-emergency response and stabilization. The initial response of the community to support people affected by fire is also something we'll discuss. Some components that we'll describe in the use cases may not exist today and may seem futuristic, but through the knowledge you gained throughout this book, you can visualize a world with SAP Leonardo that anticipates how cities, communities, and buildings may exist not too far in the future.

A.1   Smart Cities

Let's take a minute and define smart cities, smart communities, and smart buildings to understand what each term means individually:

- **Smart city**
  A city is considered "smart" when it uses technology to provide high-quality services and improves the quality of living in the city by improving operations across every aspect of the city. The city not only collects data and processes data for its own functions for governance but also provides this data to entities such as hospitals, businesses, communities, etc., thus building a network that can collectively provide better services to residents.

- **Smart community**
  A smart community is a group of people and organizations that come together and digitize the services that a community needs. These services may include booking community halls, finding parking spaces, temporary and permanent housing, event planning and management, and volunteer activities.

- **Smart building**
  A smart building is one that provides personalized services to its occupants. Some examples of services rendered are parking spot availability and reservations, printing services, identity management, security services, intelligent emergency response systems, and rental space management. In the case of office buildings, in addition to all of the above services, other services will be included such as rental space check-in and checkout, alerts for colleagues in the office, cafeteria menus, and gym schedules and management.

Table A.1 provides a quick reference to keywords, solution ownership, and solution types across smart cities, connected communities, and smart buildings.

	Keywords	Solution Ownership	Solution Type
Smart city	Water, air, gas, electricity, parks, roads, public service alerts, parking management, smart waste management	City government and public service providers	SAP S/4HANA Cloud and public clouds for add-on solutions such as SAP Ariba, SAP Concur, SAP C/4HANA, SAP Cloud Platform
Connected community	Community halls, parking management, temporary housing, event planning and management, volunteer activities	City government, with community-level admins, private entities sending data feeds into the community center	
Smart building	Concierge services, gym schedules, office alerts, office and rental space management, personnel management	Building management	SAP S/4HANA (private cloud or public cloud) with SAP Cloud Platform for third-party application integration

Table A.1 Defining Smart Cities, Communities, and Buildings

The focus areas for the smart cities is as follows:

- Intelligent assets and infrastructure
- Smart telecom
- Smart energy
- Smart government
- Intelligent travel, transportation, and mobility
- Smart population health
- Intelligence buildings
- Smart city planning and construction
- Sustainable economy
- Sustainable environment and resources

The following sections detail the objectives of smart cities, their key functions, and the SAP solutions that can enable these functions.

A.1.1   Smart City Objectives

In today's world, many smart city projects require collaboration between public sector entities and perhaps multiple private entities that provide services to the city's population. Today's leading technology adopters are using cutting-edge technologies such as the Internet of Things (IoT), machine learning, advanced analytics, and predictive analytics to become key partners in machine learning initiatives.

A.1.2   Smart City Functions

In the following sections, we'll discuss ten major functions that smart cities may fulfill.

Public Sector

Government organizations are the driving force behind the smart city initiative, bringing together different organizations that operate within a city such as utilities, information technology, education, services, etc. Along the way, public-private partnerships may be involved, such as utilities companies, nongovernmental organizations (NGOs), and more.

Public sector organizations generate revenue through grants and taxation and have a responsibility to the general public to provide transparency. These organizations fulfill a variety of business functions:

- Public sector financials
  The main objective for optimizing public sector financials is to ensure transparency and compliance. Public sector financials provided by SAP S/4HANA allows public sector organizations to plan and execute against budgets and to create and execute a financial shared services organization across functions. SAP Concur allows for travel and expense management, while SAP Analytics for Microsoft Office and SAP Analytics Cloud provide a reporting layer.

- Program planning and management
  Program planning and management aims to leverage predictive insights to uncover trends, opportunities, and potential competitive edges. SAP Business Planning and Consolidation (SAP BPC) supports businesses by maximizing the time

spent on growth opportunities and minimizing the time spent on closing books by streamlining planning and enabling a faster, more accurate closing process.

- **Accounting and financial close**
  Enhancing better financial insight and control through a faster, compliant financial close with reduced costs and efforts. SAP S/4HANA helps build a foundational core across business processes to facilitate the digitization of end-to-end processes and the unification of the user experience.

- **Treasury and financial risk management**
  Providing greater insights and control over convoluted business processes for managing cash, liquidity, and risk. SAP S/4HANA enables multiple treasury and financial risk management functions. SAP Business Integrity Screening can go through large volumes of real-time data with high accuracy to determine errors and potential fraud threats.

- **Governance risk and compliance**
  Enhancing effective enterprise capability, minimizing risk, and ensuring efficient compliance management with the least effort and expense. SAP Risk Management helps gain detailed insights into how risk drivers can impact business. Better decisions are made by efficiently identifying risk, assessment, analysis, and monitoring.

- **Operational procurement, sourcing, and contract management**
  Sourcing and contract management are some of the most important functions of a government office. These departments are typically responsible for managing contracts, services, and direct and indirect material procurement. While SAP S/4HANA is the main ERP, SAP Ariba Sourcing can help streamline high-value sourcing tasks and improve bottom lines. Effectively negotiating the best agreements can achieve sustainable savings.

- **City analytics**
  To get a holistic and detailed view of the city pulse across all city domains. SAP BusinessObjects Enterprise provides a framework to empower businesses with intelligent information and insights for better and more informed decision-making.

Utilities

Technology is reshaping the utilities industry in many ways. With a significant focus on reducing our dependence on fossil fuels, companies are not only providing alternative power sources but also finding ways to help consumers be more efficient in power consumption. IoT devices can help monitor power consumption through analytics can help consumers and providers provide better services.

One of the biggest changes is in the area of power generation. The old paradigm of suppliers and consumers doesn't always hold true anymore. With the explosion of micropower generation capabilities in solar cells, consumers can generate power in their own homes and share their surplus power with the power grid.

As the market matures, the utilities industry can bring together experts, cities, and citizens together for design thinking workshops to build initiatives to meet the sustainability goals of cities.

SAP for Utilities provides utilities management and SAP Energy Portfolio Management brings together energy procurement and customer operations and forecasting to streamline procurement and to reduce operational costs.

Waste and Recycling

In a traditional sense, waste and recycling companies focus on maximizing the volume of services in the post-disposal economy. Today's communities are environmentally more aware and are looking at sustainable approaches. Organizations supporting waste management and recycling must look for ways to create a circular economy that generates zero waste. By recycling everything from water to consumer goods to construction materials, companies can improve the experience of a city by enhancing it environmentally while also opening up new business opportunities.

Smart trash bins on city streets help keep a city clean and lessen the human intervention needed to check garbage cans. Existing planning and scheduling tools, routing software, and geographical information systems, in combination with smart sensors, can be deployed to monitor trash cans. Monitors can measure fill levels, rate of usage, time/days of maximum usage, and more. This generated data can be fed into SAP HANA via the SAP Cloud Platform with SAP Leonardo. SAP Analytics Cloud can be used to build analytics functions, and SAP Data Hub or SAP Predictive Analytics along with machine learning can build and execute algorithms to develop efficient routes for trash collection. Cities may be able to reduce the number of trucks, thus reducing pollution and noise while keeping the city streets clean.

Telecommunications

Telecommunication companies (telcos) play a vital role in digitizing the city. These companies create a fundamental platform for every device to communicate with hubs to support data processing. As such, some providers have used their platforms to deliver individual smart city services. Telcos can help reduce the time to generate benefit from smart city initiatives. Services provided by telcos shift costs from being capital expenditures (CapEx) to being operational expenditures (OpEx), which in turn can free up funds for additional smart city initiatives.

SAP S/4HANA provides revenue management solutions that can be tailored by a telco to support a smart city initiative.

Automotive and Transportation

With increasing population density, most cities in the world either have or are planning to build multimodal transport services. A city like Philadelphia operates regional train services, rapid transit services, light rail services, electric and motor trolley buses operated by several companies like SEPTA, Amtrak, PATCO, and NJ Transit. Although smart cities must have public mass transit systems, solutions for personal transportation are also important. Traditional fossil fuel-based vehicles create more pollution, congestion, and noise than public transportation. Incentives to encourage car pooling and a variety of options for mass transit will provide consumers options that can be chosen based on season, time, or traffic.

In the near future, the electrification of personal vehicle systems can help with pollution. At the same time, digitization can lead to analytics that can predict traffic patterns and provide solutions that can optimize routing. Moving goods in cities will also become easier and less time consuming and will have better predictability. Enforcing speed limits will be easier. Emergency responders can get vehicle data from a crash to better serve the victims of accidents. Collecting data from the vehicles in real time and providing that information to the right party is key to making the right decisions. SAP Data Hub provides a data orchestration layer that can collect, parse, transform, and distribute data. The serverless architecture will enable on-demand data processing capacity that will be key in handling large-scale incidents and peak traffic management.

The same technology can also help clear traffic for emergency vehicles and first responders by rerouting the traffic in the area between the service provider's location and emergency location.

Travel and transportation services improve the quality of life in a city. Residents expect that travel transitions between intermodal and cost-effective travel options are smooth and congestion free. A single place to book end-to-end travel services can go a long way in improving the quality of travel. Smart phone-based travel services to book travel, receive notifications, and support services is already commonplace.

Today's transportation hubs are massive buildings with multiple terminals, levels, and navigations. Personalized navigational support systems to help users go from one point to another in a building will soon become a norm. A handicapped user's profile may automatically route the user through an elevator rather than an escalator. Kid-friendly food spots can be made prominent when traveling with kids of certain ages. Senior citizens may be able to use autonomous vehicles and location-based navigation services to get them to care appointments without the assistance of relatives or caregivers.

The growing prevalence of e-commerce in the current world has changed the landscape around last-mile delivery. The speed of last-mile delivery services have increased drastically, which raises the challenge of congestion in the city. Using advanced technologies to improve efficiencies in transportation services is an open opportunity for logistics providers to exploit.

Healthcare

Health and wellness are not only a concern of individuals and their families but also have an impact on the economic and social health of a community. Thus, the healthcare sector is one of the most valuable partners in smart city initiatives.

Healthcare leaders are recognizing the challenges facing communities and addressing these challenges using connected digital technologies. Apps such as Fitbit and Apple Health are helping in the collection and sharing of healthcare data with loved ones, caregivers, and medical service providers. This data can be used to actively monitor elderly or chronically ill people while allowing them to live independently.

As the technical foundation for these services (bandwidth, wiring, handicap access) still develops, momentum is building. These technologies will come together to mitigate challenges in providing care in an environment of relative scarcity in providers. These applications will generate huge volumes of data, and thus, the technology must have features that will process signals quickly, create alerts, detect anomalies, and pinpoint data that requires further review. Once the tools identify the right circumstances, healthcare professionals can reach out to the patients to learn more and initiate treatment or activate emergency response measures.

The data generated by these devices and hospitals will also allow for better management of inventory. SAP Cloud Platform can be used to collect data from multiple sources and distribute this data for further processing. For example, once a surgery kit (such as a single use kit for wrist fractures) is removed, the vendor must be invoiced. Location information and item information must be passed to the vendor so that replenishment can occur at the right spot with the right material. With these capabilities, hospitals and emergency medical device/drug suppliers can run advanced analytics to better estimate the levels of inventory to be stocked at storage units. Smart locker systems not only provide better inventory management solutions but also visibility into the inventory of emergency drugs/devices that may be distributed to different parts of the hospital or even located in a hospital nearby. This visibility will enable better services during emergencies.

Higher Education

Higher education institutions and administrators can play important roles in smart city initiatives. These hubs of education provide knowledge resources and can partner with urban governments and nongovernmental organizations in areas of research and development. With established laboratories, leading-edge technologies, and intellectual capital, universities are well placed to serve as ideal R&D leaders in solving critical problems and, in some cases, also act as test beds.

Public universities and other higher education institutions are under high pressure to serve students and use public funds responsibly. Universities need to produce workers and who are educated and have a variety of skills to contribute to the digital economy while at the same time ensuring lower costs for education. Lowering the cost of education will enable students to graduate with lower levels of debt, thereby helping them live more independently. Meeting the goal of reducing costs will require universities to adopt technology to boost efficiency in operations. Technology can assist in the end-to-end processes involved in running a higher education organization, from admissions, to operating schedules, to department budgets, etc. New operating models such as shared services can be enabled, and greater use of analytics can help in real-time decision-making.

Engineering Construction and Operations

Smart cities must keep pace with expanding urban populations and changes to the infrastructure requirements of the citizens. For cities to get greener, ease congestion, and become safer, extensive collaboration between the city and construction firms will be needed.

For example, as technology changes, as the number of connected devices grow, and as transportation systems move away from fossil fuels, demand for electricity will continue to grow. This new demand for electricity and the amount of consumption will require building codes to be updated for urban, suburban, and rural buildings.

Changes in technology and the growing number of devices in a connected home will change building codes, especially in the areas of power consumption and internal wiring.

Digital technologies can help companies build future cities. Visualization and augmented reality tools can help designers better understand population shifts, demographic changes, and traffic patterns so that they can plan and develop an infrastructure that best addresses a city's goals.

Engineering, construction, and operations (ECO) companies also have large procurement needs and machine maintenance needs. Intelligent fraud detection and resolution applications at both the city's application landscape and the ECO companies' application landscape will increase financial transparency and accountability. SAP S/4HANA integrated with SAP Ariba can provide an intelligent technology backend for ECO companies. A city also needs predictability around equipment availability. Intelligent asset management planning using machine data, rather than maintenance on a fixed schedule, enables predictive maintenance, which can ensure that the city and the ECO companies have the right equipment available at the right time, which will reduce equipment downtimes and provide faster resolution during unplanned outages.

High-Tech Industry

As technological advancements outpace the usage and rate of return of an investment in an asset, technology companies are offering products as services. These services enable cities to focus on choosing the best technology platform for their citizens while not being stuck with a specific product. Services enable traditionally product-based companies to bring new technologies out relatively quickly and at the same time maximize revenue.

To enable a service-based transactional relationship between cities and companies, enterprise software must have the capability to track, quantify, validate, bill, and pay for services. Intelligent analytics can help both cities and high-tech companies maximize benefits from a service-based relationship model.

Nonprofit Community Organizations

Nonprofit organizations have historically complemented and collaborated with city services in areas such as social care, homelessness, healthcare, education, training, culture, and entertainment. As budget constraints put pressure on municipal leaders, innovation in alternative service delivery models is needed. Digital technologies such as social media, analytics, and mobile are offering nonprofits avenues to integrate their processes more closely with local governments.

As technology enables decentralization in democratic processes, citizens will have a more direct say in decisions about public services. Nonprofits have a larger role, becoming the connective tissue between city mandates and neighborhood realities. SAP S/4HANA Cloud can provide a cost-effective alternative for small NGOs to manage their finances and provide financial transparency.

A.1.3 Solution Approach

Public sector organizations are leading the way in digitizing their systems to meet policy goals and improve lives by:

- Establishing a coherent digital vision with a clearly articulated roadmap for their digital transformation
- Creating an IT architecture that provides long-term stability for core processes and agility where needed

Four key initiatives require new capabilities along the value chain:

- Digital management of governance and operations
- Data driven decision-making
- Smart cities
- Focus on citizens

SAP supports these initiatives across a cross-section of public sector functions, many of which we've described already. Let's look briefly at some individual SAP solutions and the functions they bring:

- SAP S/4HANA digital core
  - Accounting, financial close, treasury management
  - Financial planning and analysis
  - Budget maintenance and execution
  - Master data management (suppliers, tax entities, payers, etc.)
  - Receivables, payables, credit, and collection management
  - Payroll
  - Human resources and time and attendance management
  - Operational procurement, sourcing, and contract management

- – Infrastructure maintenance and repair
- – Portfolio and lease management
- – Space and facility management
- ■ SAP C/4HANA
  - – Taxpayer online services
  - – Collection online services
  - – Debt enforcement
  - – Constituent experience and self-service
  - – Inbound and outbound contact center
  - – Case management
- ■ SAP Fieldglass
  - – External workforce management
  - – Resume matching
  - – Job matching
- ■ SAP SuccessFactors
  - – Core HR and payroll
  - – Talent management
  - – Human capital analytics
- ■ SAP Concur
  - – Time and attendance management
  - – Expense management
- ■ SAP Ariba
  - – Procurement for public sector
  - – Supplier collaboration
  - – Business network
  - – Guided end-user buying
- ■ SAP Leonardo
  - – Use of distributed ledger technology such as blockchain to reduce middlemen and simplify complex multiparty processes
  - – Integration of sensors and smart devices
  - – Artificial intelligence by using existing machine learning algorithms or building new ones
  - – Managing digital twins for expensive and high-maintenance machinery

- Analytics:
  - Automate what-if analysis
  - Analyze patterns to avoid fraud, waste, and abuse
  - Data driven policy decisions
  - Set goals and measure performance
  - Improve transparency of information across constituents and agencies
  - Analyze resource strategies to impact budgets
  - Predictive models to optimize investments in infrastructure, maintenance, and portfolio analysis
  - Integrate to data lakes and document management systems for big data analytics

A.1.4   Example

Let's say a fire alarm has sounded within city limits, and the city's emergency rapid information delivery system, called GRID, has received a notification of that alarm. GRID then notifies the city's Predictive Emergency Tracking System (PETS), which calculates which station has the highest probability of getting to the location most quickly and then activates the alarm at the right fire station.

Once the alarm sounds, the fire chief can speak to his or her voice-enabled watch to enable emergency mode. This smart watch, encased in a heat-resistant coating, turns into an emergency response management subsystem (ERMS) when the emergency mode is enabled and can also act as a backup personal alert safety system (PASS) device when working with the firefighter's suit. The watch provides a lot of key information, such as the address, needed for immediate view.

The firefighters' suits have sensors built in that can monitor the health of the firefighter and can gather key statistics about the surrounding environment. Additionally, these suits can act as an energy store, with advanced bionics that provide additional power to the firefighter when needed. By tapping the gloves while suiting up, the firefighters' gloves are instructed to take over the controls of the smart watch. The suit also has a preinstalled wireless device that connects straight to the helmet. When the team is assembled, the helmet creates a secure communication channel among team members and PETS. The suit also has built-in oxygen tanks and air filters, since it is a personal breathing apparatus (PBA)-integrated PASS device.

By the time the team has suited up, the firetruck is already communicating with PETS. The firetruck can download detailed plans of the building, including exit routes, occupants' details, location of the fire, and the response plan filed for the building. An active link to the building is established both to the firetruck and the city grid. The active link to the building provides the team with the location of active fires, the number of residents closest to the fire, and their ages. Based on real-time data on the number of fires and people, the firetruck's SAP HANA analytics engine can play out multiple response simulations and provide the best course of action with minimal loss of life. The firetruck will also call out to other fire stations in the city if additional assistance is needed.

Before the firetruck has even left the station, PETS has rerouted the traffic around the fire station. When the firetruck leaves the fire station, green lights are activated along a GPS-calculated route that maps the best way to get to the fire. As the firetruck goes through the city, PETS can continue to reroute some of the traffic. Some gridlock couldn't be resolved in time, so PETS can reroute the firetruck to an alternative route. All non-local, pass-through traffic could be rerouted away from the impacted areas. An emergency rerouting signal could be sent to all GPS-based routing providers such as Google, Garmin, etc. to reroute the traffic. All online smart cars could also receive an emergency signal to reroute. PETS can determine traffic patterns for not just this one fire incident but other emergency responses where ambulances or cops are needed; the system can intelligently managed over a hundred city emergency responses in parallel. In this example, PETS can also dispatch dozens of police cars to create a safe zone around the building, to help with evacuations, and to manage law and order.

At this point, GRID had already notified multiple public utilities and emergency services and established active links. The electric company, through its active established link to the building, can isolate the transfer switches that provide electricity to the area around the fire. The emergency response team at the public utility could use real-time data from the fire location in predictive fire progress algorithms to monitor the switches at risk to ensure that the following activities were completed:

- Emergency services had the power needed to bring the fire under control.
- Any active electric sources close to fire, not related to the emergency response, were turned off.

The water company's active link can monitor the water pressure in the fire hydrants if needed. The company can also monitor the water levels in the building's emergency response tanks to ensure proper functioning.

The city grid's active link could track the number of people closest to the fire. The grid can also use a predictive fire progress algorithm, along with real-time data, to estimate the number of people that may require emergency support and thus can dispatch enough ambulances while also alerting the hospitals in the surrounding area.

Prior to the firetruck arriving, the active link reported another parallel fire was picked up on the opposite side of the building and three floors above the original fire. PETS could decide that this fire needed another firetruck, and the one with the highest probability of get to the fire the fastest was alerted. All involved parties were alerted of the second fire, and PETS informed the original firetruck that the second one was coming.

PETS assigned the alpha designation to the firetruck that was likely to arrive on the scene first. The alpha designation is important: The alpha firetruck runs analytics and provides instructions to all the other firetrucks and all other emergency vehicles assigned to this case. Since firetrucks have more space for hardware, they have the largest onboard analytics infrastructure embedded. The alpha firetruck also takes over the hardware of the other firetrucks to perform faster analytics, which gives the alpha firetruck the ability to act as an onsite authority independently of any decision-making from PETS. PETS could then focus on all the other emergency sites. PETS would take back the alpha designation once emergency services were completed, and all the vehicles were dispatched back to station or assigned another case.

Upon arrival, the alpha firetruck evaluates the situation and creates an action plan. The firefighters themselves then review and approve the action plan. Once approved, the alpha firetruck can send the plan to all the firefighters, including those in the second firetruck, and other emergency responders, including police and ambulance crew assigned to this case. Once the firetruck is set into response mode, smart watches worn by firefighters tell each firefighter what needs to be done.

After an hour of firefighting and bringing the fire under control, the fire is out with no loss of life and minimal property damage. When the firetruck returns to the station, an automated physical inventory of fire-retardant materials in tanks could be conducted, which could result in instructions sent to SAP Ariba to procure inventory.

A.2   Connected Communities

A connected community is a microcosm of a larger smart city. A connected community focuses on bringing together people, information, and services provided by public and private entities to a localized geographic area. The following sections describe some key objectives of a connected community, including their functions, and also builds on our earlier example of how a community reacts to help people affected by a fire.

A.2.1   Connected Communities Objectives

The most important objective of a connected community must be to bring people, government, and businesses together. As cities focus on providing services, infrastructure, and better quality of living standards to its citizens based on real-time data collection and analytics across the city, smart communities are providing services, data, and most importantly collaboration platforms in a localized geographic area. In a typical smart city, the providers are public sector entities or industries that are focused on providing services to the general population. However, in the case of a connected community, the picture is more vibrant. Providers can also come from the general population or from small business that serve in that area.

A connected community thrives in an area where consumers and providers are connected digitally. For a connected community to work, the city must provide infrastructure and a digital collaboration platform. Entities that are privately or publicly owned, such as healthcare providers, libraries, community halls, parking, temporary housing, volunteering organizations, event management, and public safety, can use this platform to collaborate with local populations or businesses in an area. For example, a city may have the ownership of maintaining and running parks, but some of the services that parks provide, such as toddler days or petting zoo, may be directly related to the residents in a smaller geographic area while the service itself is provided by members of the community or a small business that operates in that area.

One important result of digitizing the larger population by providing access to technology and information is that doing so allows a larger proportion of the population to make decisions in a community, a key component to ensuring that political power can be transferred from the elected representatives of the people to the people themselves.

A.2.2   Connected Communities Functions

In the following sections, we'll discuss some of the most important functions that a connected community provides its residents.

Automotive and Transportation

With a renewed push for the electrification of transport systems, and a growing focus on conserving energy, the community will need to provide solutions for electric vehicle charging at available parking and charging points. A few ideas in this area include the following:

■ **Intelligent parking systems**

One of the most visible markers for an intelligent community is in ease of finding parking spots, which can be achieved in one of the following ways:

– **On-demand check-in and checkout**

A central tenet to an on-demand application is to have a mobile device-enabled app. For on-demand parking systems, a driver would use the parking app to find an open parking spot. Once the driver is at the parking spot, the driver can scan the URL on the parking meter, which can check the car into the spot. The scanner on the parking meter ensures that a vehicle is parked in that location and will remove the space from the pool of available parking spaces. Once the driver leaves the spot, the scanner will recognize the checkout and open the parking spot. Parking time limits and parking fee tiering can be enforced automatically using smart parking meters.

These capabilities will enable city resources (parking enforcers) to become customer service personnel resolving issues rather than enforcing rules.

– **Parking reservations**

Once available, the parking app can be used in certain places to reserve a spot. These parking meters will display a visual indicator that says that a spot is reserved. Any loitering in an unreserved spot can be avoided by having the sensors pick up vehicle identification information and, when integrated with vehicle and driver database, issue appropriate parking tickets. Once a reservation is successful and a driver comes to the reserved spot, the app and the sensor on the parking meter will follow the same process to confirm that the right car is in the spot.

The reservation approach can generate additional revenue in areas such as meeting venues and sport stadiums by setting up a proximity-based, event-specific parking metering system. Having reserved spots will also ensure that traffic flow is controlled, and having knowledge of an exact spot will mean that drivers won't have to search for spots but instead will go straight to the right spot every time. This function can in turn reduce the number of active vehicles on the road at any point in time, thus saving energy and controlling pollution. Spot reservation systems at large events will also encourage carpooling, additionally saving spots and time.

Overall, intelligent parking systems will offer communities incremental revenue and avoid wasted time for people and wasted energy for vehicles, thus reducing pollution on the road. For billing purposes, the parking app requires a valid credit card. The smart meter can send the data to the city's billing system, which will consolidate and bill the registered credit card.

- **Gasoline and charging stations**
  Over the next few years, we'll see a sea change in drivetrain design for the personal automobiles on the road. Energy needed to run these automobiles will come from both electricity and gasoline. Over time, gas stations will reinvent their services to accommodate electric charging capabilities as new technology will allow for faster charging. Cars already can plan routes and suggest the next location to fill up or charge up. Cars can also tap into a variety of sources for charging. Intelligent parking locations with superchargers can provide not just parking services but also charging services. Gas stations and highway rest areas can publish open charging spaces that can be subscribed to by cars and reserved based on routing.

  As multiple homes start owning electric cars and have solar power, they can host charging services that can generate revenue for homeowners, while surplus power can go back into the grid, thus reducing dependence on nonrenewable sources of electricity.

- **Smart analytics on ride sharing**
  Many residents in a community share rides to work. With knowledge about the typical start locations and destinations of daily commutes, services can be created to provide predictive ride sharing and other services. These services not only reduce the overall cost of commuting but also reduce the number of vehicles on the road, thus reducing congestion and pollution.

Event Management

A vibrant community has events going on throughout the year, perhaps even daily. These events are generally not just for specific age groups or cultural groups. In today's world, a person may need to go to multiple locations to find these events. For example, the local library, the public swimming pool, and the zoo all have events for children, but a parent must go to all these places separately to track events. A connected community will offer one place where all these events can be published, perhaps the town/community website or a Facebook page or a Twitter feed that can be subscribed to. Some key areas that hold events including the following:

- **Libraries**
  Today's libraries are not just a place for adults to read and borrow books; open to all age groups, libraries often have activities specific to age group. In many communities, a network of libraries may support a group of communities. As libraries

go online, they can better manage the demand and supply of books in stock and also have ability to share books across the network as they support a community. Providing visibility into the library's catalog and events not just helps subscribers of the library, but also the inclusion of other libraries will help the network attract more subscribers and increase revenue.

- **Parks and events**

  Similar to libraries, a network of parks support a community. Each park may have one or more events going on at the same time, perhaps targeted at multiple age groups. For members of the community, having a single place to see information filtered by age group or preference can have a significant impact on advertising the event and consequently the event's revenue generation. For example, Fourth of July fireworks is an event common in the US where many families gather and take kids. Actively providing information about the best viewing areas, parking zones, and timing will help more members of the community gather to celebrate together.

  Publishing the same feed to other communities that are nearby or through websites or other channels associated with tourism can bring in additional tourism and help generate revenue in the local community. For example, many grocery or convenience stores have bulletin boards. Digitizing these bulletin boards and providing information on local events will help generate additional footfalls.

- **Food scene**

  Good food is a vital part of a vibrant community. Many communities have a great variety of food choices. Food trucks are embracing a digital economy by actively publishing their schedules. Community boards where food truck schedules and food events can be published will bring additional footfalls, leading to revenue generation.

In summary, actively managing events in a community and providing great food options can generate additional footfalls and generate revenue in taxes for the city and actively help the community in its other local initiatives.

Opportunities

Job and volunteering opportunities are leading indicators of the activities that occur in a community. Improving the visibility of available opportunities can go a long way to attracting talent to a community in the following ways:

- **Volunteering opportunities**
  Most community- and city-run public establishments, such as parks, libraries, hospitals, and events, need a lot of volunteers. Each establishment today manages its own opportunities. Even for community members, volunteers must go to each site to find opportunities for volunteering. When such public entities are incorporated into a single shared platform, they can manage opportunities separately, but these opportunities are published in a single location. Community members can review opportunities in a single place and can also subscribe to the feed, perhaps with appropriate filters.

- **Local job openings**
  Understanding the jobs and skills required is an important part of community building. As businesses publish local jobs to multiple sites, they could also publish the same data to the city's infrastructure, which would help derive a better count of the number of jobs open in the city and help with a better understanding of the local labor market. Over time, the same data could help the city and its education systems to better predict the kind of jobs common in the city and offer community education programs and higher education programs relevant to the jobs available in the community. This capability will also help the community better understand the local housing market and provide the data needed to make decisions about zoning for residential areas.

  Providing jobs locally and having a good view of the housing market will employ locals and also attract new members to the community, essentially helping maintain tax revenue and keeping money in circulation within the community.

Care

Proving age-appropriate care facilities in a community can help balance the population in an area from skewing too far in any one direction. This balance is important for ensuring that enough wage earners per capita exist in the community to support economic activity.

Care facilities include hospitals, senior care facilities, and childcare facilities. In many cases, hospitals may be private, nonprofit, state-run, or university-run while adult housing, adult care, and childcare are mostly private services. The census data of a town and knowledge about the age distribution of the population can help these institutions plan for capacity, emergency response systems, and also the type of care facilities most needed. Knowledge of these facilities can assist medical device companies that have smart lockers at these sites to keep the lockers filled with medicines and equipment at appropriate levels.

Temporary Housing

Temporary housing such as hostels, lodges, and hotels allow visitors to come and stay for a period of time. Apps such as Airbnb also help in identifying and providing temporary stay services.

Temporary housing has become a critical part of a community's emergency response plan. Temporary housing facilities must be built to a code and must withstand most weather-related damage. As weather plays havoc and people must leave their homes, temporary housing built to higher code standards can help alleviate the housing situation.

During emergencies, the city can take over the excess capacity found in temporary housing and provide this housing to local community members in need. To enable this capability, housing companies and entities must publish their capacity and occupancy to the city. When disaster strikes, the city can provide this information to affected community members so that they can move to temporary housing. For example, if a house is damaged in a fire and deemed unlivable, the fire department can provide the temporary housing information to the impacted family.

Decision Management

An important question that technology has helped solved is getting information to the masses so that they can make appropriate decisions about government. As seen throughout this decade, the availability and speed of information has enhanced people's ability to make decisions.

Many community activities are conducted by locally elected representatives. With new technologies, the information needed by community members to make decisions can be readily available. That said, local community voting on issues and elections can be simplified with technology, which can enable a process where some decisions previously made by elected representatives can now made directly by the people.

This method will call for additional dialogue within the community and the active engagement of community members in the administration of the community. Decentralization of decisions that impact a community will generate traction for prioritizing issues critical to the community and improve transparency in decision-making. The same concept can also be applied on a larger scale with stronger security setups and appropriate user and location identification process.

SAP's solutions such as SAP Digital Documents by Open Text, integrated with SAP Cloud Platform with a web-based frontend, can go a long way to keeping documents organized while providing transparency to the community. Imagine a community using something like SAP Support Portal, a wonderful example of knowledgebase search functions for relevant articles, dependencies, and version management.

City Functions

A variety of city functions can be made available online and integrated directly with the entities operating them. Communities around a smart city can use existing IT infrastructure and application platforms for a variety of applications. These functions can be implemented using existing SAP functionalities, while SAP Cloud Platform can used as the innovation layer for other applications. City functions that are necessary for a smooth operation of a city/community include the following:

- Payment of taxes
- Local laws
- Trash routes/traveling collection routes
- City/school/emergency alerts
- Security/neighborhood watch

A.2.3   Example

Let's say a community had 4 buildings—one on each side of a common square. Each building had 11 levels, with the ground level dedicated for shopping and restaurants. Each level has 16 apartments with 8 on each side. The community park on the inside has a secure entry open only for occupants or their guests.

When the community started up, one of the biggest challenges it faced was the lack of participation in voting. Usually only 10% to 15% of residents voted, and widespread resentment existed among residents. To overcome this barrier, an app was built using the same security measures as the rest of the building. This ability accelerated the ability of the community to make decisions.

With the help of the new app, about five years ago, the community decided to commercialize its exterior parking lots by enabling reserved paid parking along with superchargers. This decision also helped the stores and restaurants in the area by increasing footfalls. In addition to paying for parking and supercharger services, visitors were incentivized to buy products or services in the commercial properties. The increased footfalls from the adopted measure improved the overall financial position of the commercial entities in the community and generated revenue for the community. The community invested the additional revenue in events for residents.

As the community became active, technologically advanced, secure, and well maintained, the building generally enjoyed full occupancy and almost always ranked high among the best communities for living in the city. An SAP S/4HANA backend was used for predictive maintenance of all the equipment necessary for managing building assets.

Residents were actively involved in the community, and many were fire marshals. The community had a fire marshal on each floor, and the fire marshals trained along with the fire department on each fire drill. The community's security systems segregated the residential and commercial sections. Residents had to check in and out each time they entered or left the community. Residents were trained on emergency processes, and each resident had a safety spot where they would go to in case of an emergency.

The system's autonotification system alerts the fire marshals of emergencies. The first notification was a carbon monoxide alarm in an apartment in the north complex's fifth floor. A few seconds later, a fire extinguisher turned on, which triggered an alert to the city's GRID. In parallel, the building's emergency response kicked in.

In the next five minutes, more notifications of tripped alarms are sent to the fire marshal's phone. The fire had spread to three more floors, but this time on the opposite side of the building.

The fire marshal receives another alert on his phone to assist in evacuating the common area. This alert is sent via the public alert system of the community as well as her phone. The residents are asked to go to their assigned safety points, while visitors are told to proceed to the visitor safety point.

In the next few minutes, both firetrucks report that firefighters had spent the next hour bringing the fire under control. As soon as the fire was extinguished, PETS was notified, and the emergency vehicles were released. Local road restrictions were also lifted, and alerts were sent to all the GPS navigation service providers.

Based on city's guidelines, about three floors of apartments had to be evacuated, and the residents couldn't return to their homes until city investigations and inspections were completed. Based on known occupancy, data about the floors impacted, and actual observations, the firetruck notified the city GRID that about 20 families would need temporary housing. The city GRID could make emergency reservations for these 20 families in nearby hotels. The city had negotiated rates with hotels and home insurance providers for emergency housing needs precisely for these situations, which takes the burden away from families to negotiate rates and housing since they know that their insurance will cover the cost of temporary housing.

During emergencies, the city GRID could issue an alert to the main grocery and convenience stores in the neighborhood to build emergency kits. These kits could include toiletries, warm jackets, socks, and coupons for meals at restaurants nearby. They should provide families at least a week's worth of food and toiletries, enough to get by while affected residents wait to gather their belongings and make long-term plans.

Once the firetrucks leave, the fire chief stays back to assist the affected families with temporary housing and to provide emergency kits. Any unused hotel reservations are automatically released to house victims.

Once the fire chief returns at the station, he goes to the suit station and releases the emergency switch on his watch, which enables him to remove the suit and participate in debriefing and follow-up sessions. The team can analyze some of the data captured and provide the grid with feedback that would then translate to better analytics for next emergency.

A.3   Smart Buildings

Smart and connected buildings have processes and technology built into them to enable automated operations. Traditionally, building operations, such as ventilation, air conditioning, heating, security, and lighting, were automated. With new smart and connected technology, a building has the ability to do more than simply automate processes. In this section, we'll describe some key objectives of a smart building and its key functions and also illustrate an example of how a smart building can react to help residents evacuate and help firefighters decide the best course of action.

A.3.1   Smart Buildings Objectives

Today's objectives for buildings and building management are directed towards maximizing the collection of data from building subsystems to perform analytics and use these insights to improve the experience of resident or users of the building's services.

Technology has enabled the automation of many more building operations than were traditionally the case. Some opportunities that new technology enables include the following:

- **Building operations**
  Procurement of goods and services needed for operations like cleaning common areas or predictive maintenance of equipment.

- **Conservation**
  Use of advanced predictive analytics to efficiently use energy, conserve water, reduce pollution, and recycle.

- **Emergency response systems**
  For guiding people out of a building during an emergency. Intelligent devices can deduce the direction of the fire and the composition of the flames to proactively raise alarms and evacuate people.

- **Communicate**
  Communication in real time with city operational grids by providing information for taxation, emergency response, and occupancy information.

- **Security**
  Facial recognition to identify and segregate occupants from registered visitors in order to restrict visitors to approved areas.

- **Spaces**
  Reserve spaces in buildings, especially offices, meeting rooms, etc.

- **Services**
  Reserve and order services such as time slots for specific activities, personal trainers, elevators for moving in and moving out. Personalize building services such as food/catering to suit specific health goals.

- **Car recharge spots**
  Reserve and recharge using superchargers.

A.3.2   Smart Buildings functions

SAP offers solutions such as SAP S/4HANA or SAP Ariba that can work at the backend to enable operational functionalities, while SAP Cloud Platform can be used to build apps on SAP Fiori and act as the innovation layer. SAP Predictive Analytics can enable analytics, which is key to providing automated and intelligent services across functions. Let's look at some key functions of a smart building next.

Financials

Building financials must ensure that all aspects of building revenues and expenditures are captured correctly. As new service-based models come into play, cash flow and treasury management become more important. Building financials must account for cash flow and must enable analytics for predicting cash flows and adjusting payment schedules.

Through robotic process automation (RPA), bots and intelligent applications with machine learning can shift staff focus onto analytics and problem-solving rather than managing day-to-day activities. Manual activities such as goods receipt/invoice receipt (GR/IR) clearing and accounting document creation can be expedited using apps and bots.

Just like companies, buildings can now report financial statements more quickly and more accurately.

Both SAP S/4HANA and SAP S/4HANA Cloud offer key functionalities that can be used to finance operations through an integrated solution.

Asset Management

As digital technologies help better visualize and build efficiency while providing a great user experience. Predictive maintenance of building equipment is key to ensuring that the user experience continues to be good. SAP's predictive analytics, coupled with asset management in SAP S/4HANA, can provide buildings with the capabilities and information needed for the best use its assets.

For every building, some assets and equipment are so integral to operations that traditional service delivery models may not work. Data analytics can help understand usage patterns for assets and equipment while predictive maintenance can help ensure that the assets are ready for use and will not break down.

For example, every college town has peak seasons when students are moving in/moving out. During this time, demand is higher on certain building assets, such as the following:

- Elevators
- Luggage carts
- Parking spots with smart metering
- Trash collection
- Utilities such as water, ventilation systems, heat, and air conditioning

Predictive maintenance can reduce the probability of elevators and other operational systems breaking down and can improve user experience.

Procurement

Operational procurement, sourcing, and contract management are among the most important functions of a building. Innovation in the procurement space is creating novel service delivery models. These innovative service delivery models allow operations to be conducted using an operating cost model (OpEx) instead of investing in people and expensive assets, which would be a capital expense (CapEx).

New service models are emerging to assist buildings and building managers to contract key services. An innovation in this space is hygiene-as-a-service. Cleaning companies could offer periodic services to maintain the hygiene of all areas of building, including cleaning of kitchens, bathrooms, and common areas like gyms, and maintaining records as required by code. This capability will ensure that the building is paying directly for services and the refilling of consumables such as soaps and sanitizers in a single bill.

Another innovation in the cleanliness space is using robots to vacuum clean common areas. The building doesn't need to invest in buying the devices. Instead, a service provider could bill for the device to service fixed areas on a fixed schedule. The service provider will ensure that the bots are operating to established service level agreements (SLAs).

With these innovations, the building can now focus on ensuring that service providers are providing the right service rather than focus on providing the service itself.

SAP Ariba, integrated with SAP S/4HANA, provides solutions for direct and indirect procurement, contract management, and financial integration.

Building Services

An intelligent building will have many features that are automated and controlled by devices and processes. Some key areas were introduced earlier, but here is a quick summary:

- **Security**
  Facial recognition can identify occupants and registered visitors, which can be used to restrict visitors to approved areas. Unregistered visitors can be directed towards a registration desk for further processing.

■ **Spaces and services**

Residents other approved stakeholders can reserve spaces and services using building apps. Spaces such as offices and meeting rooms can be registered. Building services as supercharger spaces, gym slots, personal trainers, spa facilities, and elevators for moving in/moving out can also be automated.

Utility Management

A greater recognition around utilizing resources efficiently through technology is inspiring the analysis of usage patterns to improve the mechanisms that manage utilities.

Smart buildings can use a variety of connected devices to manage the consumption of utilities. Key items that must be managed include the following:

■ **Electricity**

As the number of devices that are connected and constantly communicating increases, electricity consumption also has increased. Effort must be made not only to ensure that spikes in consumption or emergency situations do not bring the electrical grid of the entire building down, but also to turn off electricity in impacted areas. Home- and switch-level consumption data can allow building managers to pinpoint potential wiring and device issues and provide maintenance opportunities to avoid shutdowns. Monitoring systems can remotely turn on/off electricity during emergencies.

Subsystems for micropower generation through solar or wind energy can be installed to supplement the building's power demands on the grid.

■ **Gas**

Similar to electricity, gas usage can be monitored and remotely billed. Intelligent devices can detect gas leaks and provide alerts to prevent fires.

■ **Water**

Water conservation is a key area for most buildings. Multiple water conservation approaches are used today. Onsite rain water conservation systems integrated with predictive weather monitoring can help divert water to maintain common green areas. Connected water tanks can be used to intelligently manage rain water, perhaps slowly releasing water to the storm drain system over a period of time to reduce local flooding. Intelligent metering systems can ensure that consumption data is remotely shared with water supply companies.

- **Trash collection**

  Trash collection can be managed by having pickups scheduled on-demand rather than on a fixed schedule for the whole building. Devices can measure how much bins have filled up and send alerts to waste management companies for pickup. Capacity management systems by waste management companies can be used to schedule trash pickups.

- **Lighting**

  Motion sensors can be used to turn on/off lights in common areas. These devices can measure the burn rate of lighting systems so that lightbulbs can be replaced when their shelf lives approach expiration. This information will mean that more frequently used lights will be replaced more often and that less frequently used lights will last longer.

- **Temperature**

  Managing the temperature inside a building can be a challenge. Depending on the location of the vents, hot areas and cold areas almost always exist. Smart thermometers inside rooms, apartments, and common areas can open/close vents to help normalize airflow and conserve energy compared to traditional time-based heating and cooling systems.

  Analyzing the data from smart thermometers, along with data from predictive weather systems, can provide insight on energy needs during heat waves and cold snaps. Building managers working with utility companies can better prepare for the weather events and provide a better experience for their residents.

Emergency Response

Futuristic emergency response systems don't just provide visual cues to the people around the systems but also feed information to central city grids. Smart devices that detect not just heat and sound patterns but also the chemical composition of the area around them can better assist in fighting fires and providing the right healthcare resources. Data from devices can be used to detect the spread of the emergency and alert potentially affected groups to evacuate.

Knowledge about occupants can be combined with sensor data and help in tailoring evacuation plans, for example, by ensuring that children and the elderly get attention and priority over others. These systems can also create evacuation plans so that choke points and stampedes can be avoided. Intelligent emergency response systems are the need of the hour, not just for closed buildings, but also open-area events, so that the maximum number lives can be saved from tragedy.

Communication

Communication systems within a building are key to ensuring that, with all the devices, users can communicate. Three primary communication systems modes exist in this context, as follows:

- **Devices communicating with building central system**
  All the systems that we've referenced so far must be able to communicate, not just with centralized building systems, but also with backup systems. This feature is especially important in emergency scenarios when the city's grid requires information from the devices to handle emergencies. Secure communication networks with backup modes are important so that responders can communicate with the building's central system.

- **Devices communicating with users**
  A variety of devices may communicate with users in a building. Many buildings now have apps that show directions within a building; a shopping mall or stadium, for example, may have an app that determines a person's longitude and latitude using GPS and altitude using an altimeter to pinpoint the person's location in three dimensions and provide guidance on routing data. This technology can be used to direct occupants or visitors to the right areas for business services or emergency exits.

- **Devices communicating with other devices**
  Device-to-device communication is important in a scenario where localized decision-making is relevant. An example is closing off an emergency exit if the exit is no longer safe. The device tracking the safety of the exit could also communicate with devices that open/lock exits and with the signs that direct occupants to certain emergency exits.

A.3.3   Example

Let's say our example building is technically advanced. For a new resident, an interactive virtual reality (VR) system could conduct intelligent conversations around the person's budget and apartment preferences. The system could also book appointments and act as a concierge service for residents. New residents could tour apartments with a VR device and only physically inspect the units that they shortlisted.

Emergency response systems were present in multiple areas of the building. Every room and open space in the entire building had smart sensors that could detect fire, flooding, and chemical leaks. These sensors communicated directly with the building's systems, which then took information from the surrounding sensors to validate and generate alerts. Evacuation procedures were dependent on where the emergency occurred and who the occupants were. Apartments with kids and the elderly were given the evacuation instructions first to give them time. Fire marshals and backup marshals on each floor knew the occupants that needed assistance and were immediately dispatched to assist them. These occupants were diverted to stairwells with the highest probability of safe evacuation.

Sensors can also track how a fire or leak spreads and send evacuation alerts so that no bottlenecks occur at the emergency exits. Every fire marshal was assigned to group of residents for whom the marshal was responsible for ensuring that all were accounted for. Any missing residents could then be tracked down using the registered devices they carried.

Residents were actively trained on emergency protocols, which consisted of visual aids and a building app that would also give instructions. Once an alarm rang, residents would have about three minutes to pack emergency items. After three minutes, power to the apartment would turn off, and the emergency fire lighting would turn on. Residents would receive instructions to evacuate the floor. As they walk out of their apartments, they'll see their neighbors also walking out with them. Perhaps they also noticed the fire down the hallway and fire-retardant system engaged. Residents knew the drill, though, and trusted the system to give them the right instructions. They make their way to the emergency side exits of the building, away from the elevators.

Sensors in the building can send the chemical composition of what was burning to the grid, which can then be fed to the firetrucks. The firetruck's onboard analytics can deduce the composition of the premixes that firefighters will need and have them available on standby.

Firefighters required about an hour to bring the fire under control. Paramedics assisted a few residents that had scars or burns. Residents with higher-degree burns were taken to the nearby hospital with ambulances that were already present. Fire marshals required about 45 minutes to count and cross-verify that everyone was safe and accounted for using the emergency mode of the building app.

Initial investigations found that a gas leak started the fire. The fire-retardant system had kicked in and turned off the gas to the affected section of the building, which saved lives but also required other improvements to prevent the spread of fire in the future. Firefighters would be debriefed to gather these observations once back at the fire station, and recommendations could be sent to the city to update building codes.

A.4   Summary

In a world with rapid urbanization and resource shortages, technology can help bring together customized services and efficiencies to help make life better. In this endeavor, public sector, private sector, and nongovernmental organizations and citizens alike can play a role, from ideation to realization.

SAP is making rapid strides by bringing in an enterprise operation and process integration layers such as SAP Cloud Platform Integration and machine integration tools such as SAP Leonardo to making smart living a reality.

Appendix B
The Authors

Pierre Erasmus is a specialist in the Internet of Things. He is an expert in SAP Leonardo supply chain and logistics technologies like network logistics, vehicle insights, and moving assets. He has led organizations in IoT go-to-market and SAP solution strategy.

Vivek Vinayak Rao is a consulting managing director and SAP digital transformation leader at Deloitte Consulting, LLP. He has extensive experience in developing IT optimization strategies, providing both advisory and implementation services. He is passionate about architecting innovating solutions for traditional and edge technologies to address client business needs. Vivek has more than 18 years of global technology consulting experience and is a frequent speaker at nationally-recognized SAP forums and has presented on topics ranging from traditional SAP technologies to the latest trends such as SAP S/4HANA, cloud, and SAP Leonardo.

Amit Sinha is a leader for the enterprise operations practice at Deloitte Consulting LLP. He is an expert in digital transformation, digital supply networks, and value achievement through innovative business and technology transformation activities. Amit has led multiple business transformation projects for leading global organizations from different sectors. He has authored multiple books and research papers in his expertise areas. He is passionate about creating more efficient industries, collaborative workplaces, and a better society through innovative applications of resources, processes, and technologies.

Ganesh Wadawadigi is a chief demand insight expert for IoT and digital supply chain solutions at SAP, responsible for the global roll-out of solutions that help companies derive actionable insight from demand signals. He has more than two decades of experience in the areas of supply chain management and manufacturing. During his 14-year tenure at SAP, Ganesh has worked on various strategic and board-level initiatives and represented SAP as the vice chair of the International Board of Directors of Manufacturing Enterprise Solution Association (MESA) and as the chair of MESA's lean manufacturing strategic initiative.

Index

- Learn what SAP S/4HANA offers your company

- Explore key business processes and system architecture

- Consider your deployment options and implementation paths

Bardhan, Baumgartl, Choi, Dudgeon, Lahiri, Maijerink, Worsley-Tonks

SAP S/4HANA

An Introduction

Whether you're already en route to SAP S/4HANA or taking your first look, this book is your go-to introduction to the new suite. See what SAP S/4HANA offers for your core business processes: finance, manufacturing, sales, and more. Learn about your reporting, extension, and adoption options, and consult customer case studies to learn from current customers. From the cloud to SAP Leonardo, get on the cutting edge of SAP!

647 pages, 3rd edition, pub. 12/2018
E-Book: $69.99 | **Print:** $79.95 | **Bundle:** $89.99

www.sap-press.com/4782

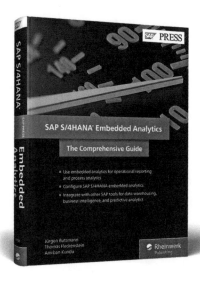

- Use embedded analytics for operational reporting and process analytics

- Configure SAP S/4HANA embedded analytics

- Integrate with other SAP tools for data warehousing, business intelligence, and predictive analytics

Butsmann, Fleckenstein, Kundu

SAP S/4HANA Embedded Analytics

The Comprehensive Guide

See how SAP S/4HANA will change your BI processes! Explore the embedded analytics architecture and data model to learn how to perform analytics on live transactional data. Business user? Walk step-by-step through SAP Smart Business KPIs and multidimensional reporting. Analytics specialist? Master the virtual data model and creating KPIs. Jack of all trades? Create CDS views, apply custom fields and logic, or see what's coming up with machine learning. This is your complete guide to SAP S/4HANA embedded analytics!

430 pages, pub. 09/2018
E-Book: $69.99 | **Print:** $79.95 | **Bundle:** $89.99

www.sap-press.com/4690

Interested in reading more?

Please visit our website for all new book
and e-book releases from SAP PRESS.

www.sap-press.com